KU-632-770

The Growth of the British Economy

1700–1850

P.F. Speed, M.A.

Wheaton
A Division of Pergamon Press

A. Wheaton & Company Limited
A Division of Pergamon Press
Hennock Road, Exeter EX2 8RP

Pergamon Press Ltd
Headington Hill Hall,
Oxford OX3 0BW

Pergamon Press Inc.
Maxwell House,
Fairview Park, Elmsford, New York 10523

Pergamon of Canada Ltd
Suite 104, 150 Consumers Road,
Willowdale, Ontario M2J 1P9

Pergamon Press (Australia) Pty Ltd
P.O. Box 544, Potts Point, N.S.W. 2011

Pergamon Press GmbH
6242 Kronberg/Taunus
Pferdstrasse 1, Frankfurt-am-Main,
Federal Republic of Germany

HERTFORDSHIRE
COUNTY LIBRARY
330. 941
1141346

27 SEP 1982

Copyright © 1980 P. F. Speed

All rights reserved. No part of this publication
may be reproduced, stored in a retrieval system,
or transmitted, in any form or by any means,
electronic, electrostatic, magnetic tape,
mechanical, photocopying, recording or
otherwise, without permission in writing from
the publishers.

First published 1980

Printed in Great Britain by A. Wheaton & Co. Ltd, Exeter (TS)

ISBN 0 08 024158 1

Contents

Introduction

There have been two major events in history. The first was the development of farming which began, probably, in the Middle East, about 8000 B.C. The other was the Industrial Revolution, which started in Britain during the eighteenth century.

With the passage of time, historians have realised how significant the Industrial Revolution was, so works on it have proliferated. There are generalised accounts of all lengths, from T.S. Ashton's excellent little book of barely 130 pages, to J.H. Clapham's monument of superb scholarship in three volumes. There are also numerous monographs on, for example, industries, regions, private firms, business men and inventors. In spite of all these, fundamental questions remain. What was the Industrial Revolution? Precisely when did it begin? What caused it? What machinery ensured that, once started, it gained momentum? Almost certainly there is not sufficient information to answer these, and many other equally important questions, while even if there were, or if it could be discovered, no one could comprehend it all: economic science has not advanced far enough. Moreover, should these two seemingly impossible conditions ever be fulfilled, we should still not have finished, since, like every great historical event, the Industrial Revolution must be reinterpreted by each new generation, in the light of its own experience.

As no final answers are possible, it cannot be the purpose of this book to attempt them. Its aim is rather to give an introduction to a complex subject by stating in outline the main facts and theories which are to hand at the moment, and to indicate some of the problems which it seems worthwhile to consider.

The titles of works cited in the text will be found either in the *Further reading* list at the end of the relevant section or in the *General bibliography* at the end of the book.

Acknowledgements

The author and publisher wish to thank the following organisations who kindly loaned photographs for use in this book: the British Museum; the Radio Times Hulton Picture Library; the Science Museum.

Agriculture

1 Farming in the seventeenth century

We can gain a good idea of seventeenth-century farming by looking at Laxton in Nottinghamshire. In 1635 the total area of this village was 3853 acres, which was large, in fact about twice the normal size for the Midland Plain. Laxton was also rather unusual in that it did not lie in the middle of its fields, but was close to their northern boundary. It was, however, quite typical in that it was tightly nucleated. There was just one house on the common, while all the others were grouped together. The farmhouses lay side by side, each with its buildings, yard, paddock and garden.

Even in the seventeenth century, and certainly in Saxon and medieval times, every village had to be self-sufficient. An ideal site was at the foot of a chalk or limestone escarpment, for then they had well-drained grazing on the hill, well-watered meadows deep in the vale, and intermediate land for growing crops. To the west of Wantage, for example, there are several parishes that look, on the map, like irregular chipolata sausages lying side by side, their long, thin shape allowing as many settlements as possible to have land running from the top of the Lambourn Downs far into the Vale of the White Horse. At Laxton the site is more level and the soil fairly uniform, but its people still divided their land into arable, meadow and pasture.

Most of the arable lay in three huge open fields, each being about 430 acres. The diagram on p. 2 shows the Mill Field. Most of it was divided into a multitude of strips, and not only were they small, but each farmer had his holding scattered throughout the three fields. There were perfectly good historical reasons for this arrangement but it was inconvenient.* Consequently, whenever they could, villagers acquired strips next to their own, or exchanged with each other, so that over the centuries families built up blocks of land. This explains why the strips on Laxton Mill Field are so different in width.

The next stage was to enclose. If a man had enough land in one piece he might put a fence round it, and his neighbours would not object,

Laxton village. Many of the homesteads keep the traditional pattern. The houses have their gable-ends facing the street to allow as many as possible a frontage on it. The farm buildings are in single rows, because of the narrow plots, and small paddocks lie behind them.

C.S. and C.S. Orwin, *The Open Fields* (1938).

1

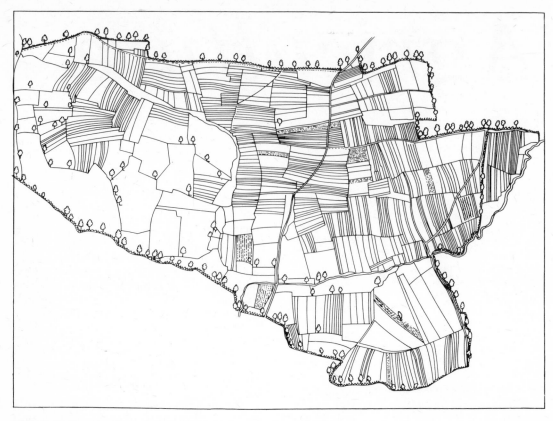

Mill Field, Laxton (from C.S. and C.S. Orwin, *The Open Fields*)

as long as he left the gate open after the harvest, to allow common grazing. Moreover, as the population of the village grew, the inhabitants ceased, after a time, to add new furlongs to the open fields, but made closes instead; they can be seen to the west and south-west of the Mill Field.

As we have seen, the arable land was divided into three, and each year one field lay fallow so that it recovered its fertility. It was grazed in the autumn, and the following summer the farmers ploughed it once or twice to kill weeds and break the soil. They then sowed it with wheat. As the villagers ate little but bread, the wheat crop gave them most of their food. When the harvest was over, the field was grazed again until mid-October, after which it was ploughed, ready for sowing with fodder crops in the spring. In many villages they grew only barley for fodder, but at Laxton they also had clover, beans and peas.

The livestock not only took one half the crops from the arable, they needed grass as well. For hay, there was the meadow land. At Laxton it was in four blocks, making in all 136 acres, or about one-tenth the size of the arable.

It lay alongside a stream where the soil was too wet to cultivate, but where the moisture helped the grass to grow. It was divided into doles; each had once been so small that a man could mow it in a day but, as with the arable, many farmers had managed to consolidate some of their tiny plots. None the less Long Meadow, which was 67 acres, still contained 256 parcels.

The animals also needed summer grazing. In a village bordering, say, Exmoor, there was no problem, for they went on the hills in the spring and returned in the autumn, but at Laxton in the seventeenth century the land was too scarce and valuable for any of it to lie waste. There were indeed Westwood and Towne Moor Commons, but they were only 110 acres and, moreover, it is likely that they were kept for villagers who had no land in the open fields. The other farmers had to use the arable and meadow as and when they could.

The best grazing was the aftermath that grew on the meadow. The farmers had to carry away their hay by Lammas Day, 1 August, and anyone who owned doles could then turn stock on the meadow until 1 November. Next,

2

there was the stubble of the crops on the open fields, the weeds that grew among it, the grass paths and, most important, the sikes. They lay in the dips, where the furrows between the strips drained. In all they amounted to 82 acres. Grazing began on the open fields when the church bells rang to announce that the harvest was gathered. In the field that had grown wheat, grazing went on unstinted until 15 October, when the animals left so that the farmers could cultivate for the spring sowing. The fodder field was looking forward to a year of fallow, so stock grazed it, again unstinted, until 23 November. Then the heavier animals and the pigs had to leave because of the damage they might do. Each farmer was allowed a stint of twenty sheep, however, until the following October. They helped by trampling the soil gently, as well as manuring it. The heavier animals had their turn in the spring, for, unlike sheep, they could be tethered, so they went on the sikes in the two fields that were growing crops. There was one sike for mares and foals, one for stallions, one for cows, and one for oxen. They all had to leave on 6 July, Old Midsummer Day.

Finally, some of the more fortunate farmers had closes, which they could use for grazing. The map of 1635 shows ploughing in some of these, and livestock in others. Probably the farmers were using 'convertible' husbandry, which meant they tilled the land for a few years, and then converted it to grass for a while. They called it 'up and down' husbandry, because the field was sometimes ploughed up, and sometimes laid down to grass.

It used to be reckoned that a family needed a virgate of land, which is about 30 acres, to make a living, and, possibly, that is what each one had in Saxon times. However, there was no equality left by the seventeenth century.

Clearly, some families had made themselves richer at the expense of their neighbours. They had so much land that they grew far more food than they could eat themselves, and sold the surplus for cash.

A survey of 1635 shows that there were then 3333 parcels of land in Laxton and, what is more, we know that nearly all the farmers had common rights over most of them. Administering the village would have been a nightmare but for the fact that nearly all the

Cultivating the open fields. The illustration shows ploughing, broadcast sowing and harrowing.

rules were embedded in customs centuries old. However, there were still problems enough, and it was the duty of the manor court to solve them.

Once, the manor court had belonged to the lord, but his authority had ended with the abolition of feudal dues. It met twice a year, when it selected a jury and appointed officers – a bailiff, a constable, two deputy constables, a pinder and a number of burlymen. Everyone had to do duty in turn. The pinder saw that the villagers kept their cattle from straying, while the burlymen, or by-law men, looked after the open fields. The jury, or any of the officers, could present offenders to the court, and, if found guilty, they were fined. The court also visited every field once in three years checking that the boundary stakes were present and correct, that no one had ploughed into the sikes, that the ditches were cleared and that

Size of Laxton Holdings 1635							
Size in acres	Under 5	5–9	9–20	20–40	40–70	70–200	Over 200	Total
Number	33	16	20	13	12	9	3	106

the fences were repaired. There were presentments on account of all of these things from time to time and we hear of others as, for example, failing to mend a chimney, blocking the street with timber, driving away a neighbour's heifer, depriving the tanner of work by killing calves too young, and harbouring vagrants.

Here then we have a village democracy. However, the manor court was to agriculture what the guild was to industry, and though they both had their good points, they regulated their members' lives in minute, irritating detail. They hampered freedom and progress, and as the Industrial Revolution destroyed the guild, so the agricultural revolution destroyed the manor court.

The lord of the manor of Laxton was a London merchant, Sir William Courten. He bought it in 1625, and then purchased any more land that was for sale, so that by 1635 he owned 2181 acres, about 500 of them commons and woodland, 350 of them demesne, while the remainder were let to Laxton farmers. Courten not only wanted to increase the size of his estate, but to have the highest possible rents. The common was no use to him at all, for the villagers grazed their stock free of charge and he could not take away their rights. On the other hand the demesne was valuable. It had been the farm which the lord of the manor kept for himself, but as Courten did not live permanently in Laxton, he let it. Some of it fetched 30 shillings an acre, and, on average, it was worth 7 shillings an acre. There remained the tenements. They had once been farmed by villeins who gave the lord labour and produce, but they had long ago commuted those services for money rents. At between 1 shilling and 2 shillings an acre such rents were reasonable for the Middle Ages, but they did not change, so by the seventeenth century they were far too low. Consequently, as tenements fell vacant, Courten relet them at a much higher figure. By raising rents, he did even the tenants a good turn, for a man who pays next to nothing for his land has little incentive to farm properly.

In conclusion, these are the main characteristics, and disadvantages, of the open-field village.

In the first place it was not designed for commercial agriculture. The people who had developed it in earlier times thought only of keeping alive. They ate almost all that they grew and, if there was not enough, they starved. It is true that they had to buy a few things, such as salt, and they sold a little of their produce, especially wool, but generally the peasant handled very little cash. His was a subsistence and not a money economy. For subsistence a man needs to keep the right proportions of arable, grazing and meadow, regardless of his soil. We have seen that an ideal site stretched from the top of chalk downs, deep into a clay vale, for this gave variety, but there were plenty of villages where the soil was fairly uniform – Wigston Magna is an example. Here the clay was better for grass, but the villagers still needed their arable for bread, so they were not using their land to the best advantage.

However, since the towns were growing, farmers had more and more incentive to produce food for sale. So that they could have a surplus, ambitious men acquired extra land from their neighbours. At the same time landowners who saw such tenants prosper, began to fidget at their miserable customary rents. They let their demesnes well enough, and thought longingly of the day when all their farms might give the same returns.

In the seventeenth century, then, a money economy was advancing, and the old subsistence economy was in retreat before it; but, for the victory to be complete, there would have to be an end to the open fields.

A second characteristic was that the farming was communal. Again that came from the need to survive. The small peasants could not afford expensive items, so they shared many things, from their ploughs to the village bull. They shared their fields as well, so they all had to work together in the same way.

A progressive man could indeed make improvements, but the system put severe limits to them.

Thirdly, in the open-field village, both arable and grassland tended to be permanent. Perhaps this is the most serious criticism of all, because it is bad farming. Unwanted plants spread insidiously in grassland, and the only cure is to plough it, crop it for two or three years and then sow it again to grass: however good the rotation, land in tillage cannot give the best of crops indefinitely but needs to be laid down to grass from time to time so that it can recover. By the sixteenth century many farmers had realised this. If they were lucky enough to have closes, they could practise 'up and down' husbandry and even on the open fields they could put strips in ley. However, in any open-field village, most of the land was permanently either in tillage or under grass.

The open-field organisation, then, was rather like an eggshell. There was enough room inside for the new creature to develop, but it was none the less a rigid structure. Sooner or later its inmate would smash it in order to emerge and grow.

2 Crops, manures and soil improvement

In the open-field village a farmer kept his soil fertile by fallowing it one year in three. This was acceptable when there was land to spare, in Saxon and early medieval times. However, as the population grew, the arable land bit deeper into the common pasture so that feeding the livestock became a problem. Farmers must have looked longingly at the fallow field, wondering how they could use it without destroying its fertility. Eventually they were able to do so because they found new crops. As the great need was to feed animals, most of them were grown for fodder; they were of two kinds, root crops and leaf crops.

The most famous of the new root crops was the turnip, which came from Holland some time in the sixteenth century. Dutch immigrants at Norwich had them in their gardens in 1565, and, by the mid-seventeenth century, the farmers of High Suffolk were growing them for their sheep. Turnips then spread over the country, though farmers accepted them with varying degrees of enthusiasm.

One way of giving turnips to sheep was to 'feed' them, which meant folding the animals in the turnip field. They did not particularly enjoy gnawing at the roots, especially if they were embedded in frozen soil. It was better if the turnips were first lifted, cleaned and sliced.

Turnips have their limitations. In the first place they do not do well on heavy, 'poaching' soils. 'Poaching' is what happens when wet clay is trampled, and since turnips need regular hoeing, there has to be a lot of trampling. Lifting the roots from clay is also a problem and, when they can be induced to come away, they leave hollows that fill with rain. Also, turnips cannot stand very cold weather, which meant that in the depths of winter there was a 'hungry gap'. By the early nineteenth century farmers found they could fill it by growing Swedish turnips, or swedes.

We turn now to the leaf crops, most of them leguminous plants like trefoil, lucerne and sainfoin. They all came to England from Holland at about the same time as turnips.

Sainfoin was invaluable where farmers had cultivated land for too long. Grass will not grow on exhausted soil, but sainfoin does, and helps it recover. Like all leguminous plants it takes nitrogen from the air and stores it in nodules in its roots. When the legume itself dies, or is killed by ploughing, the nitrogen remains in the soil for the next crop.

Rape was useful, for, not only did it make fodder, but its seeds gave oil. The plant also has a long tap-root which will penetrate the subsoil, deeper than the plough will go.

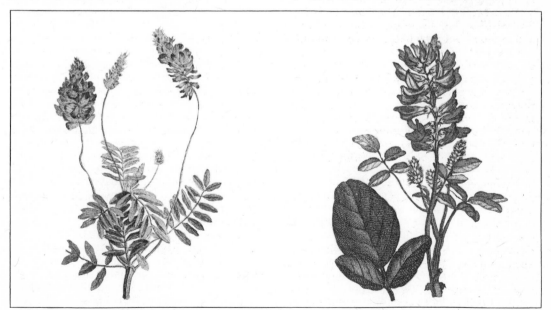

Sainfoin (Common and Giant)

However, the best known of the new leaf crops was clover, though to call it new is hardly accurate, because common white clover is a native of the British Isles. What was new was the selection of seed, the use of fresh varieties from Holland, and the systematic cultivation of the crop instead of just allowing it to flourish where Nature decreed. Farmers began growing it in the early 1600s, and by the end of the century 'to be in clover' was a common saying. It is valuable because it is a legume and also because it makes the best quality fodder and hay. Usually, farmers sowed it along with barley, which they called 'undersowing'. When they mowed the barley the clover remained, and the following year they could make it into hay, or feed their sheep on it.

Growing clover, though, brought problems. Jethro Tull described it as 'foul feed for horses, and injurious to cattle'. To call it 'foul feed' is unfair; it is just that, on its own, it is too rich. Tull was right about the horses, though, for it gives them wind and they then make life unpleasant for all who have dealings with them. More seriously, clover will not grow indefinitely on the same land. Farmers in south Norfolk told Arthur Young that their soil was 'clover sick' and that they could no longer sow the crop every fourth or fifth year, as they had once done.

The best way was to mix clover with other seeds. It went very well with its fellow legumes, like sainfoin and lucerne, or with grasses such as cocksfoot and meadow fescue. The most popular mixture, though, was clover and rye-grass, for it gave particularly heavy crops.

Grass has an advantage over other fodder crops in that it need not be resown every year. However, it cannot be left indefinitely, since plants like sedge, which are useless to the farmer, gradually spread in the turf. The land must then be ploughed and bear crops for two or three years before being sown again with grass seed.

The way to have the best crops of grass was to float water-meadows. This was an Italian idea which came to England in the sixteenth century, and it was quite common here by 1700. The easiest system was to dam a stream, so that the water flooded the grassland on either side. However, the catchwork method was better: a channel was dug along the top edge of a field, and the water spilled over to flow evenly down the slope at a depth of about one inch. Grass detests waterlogged soil, but it does like an abundance of moisture; much as a man who, though objecting to sitting in his beer, thoroughly enjoys drinking it. Also, if the stream ran through a farmyard or, what was much the same, a seventeenth-century town, it was enriched with all sorts of valuable plant foods. If it ran through chalk it was calcareous, and, indeed, it was in chalk country that floating water-meadows was most common.

In Dorset, farmers not only took massive crops of hay from their water-meadows, but grazed them heavily during spring and autumn as well.

New crops meant new crop rotations, the best known of which is the Norfolk four course – wheat, turnips, barley and clover. However, it is only possible on favoured land and was, moreover, not at all common before the early nineteenth century. If the agricultural revolution had waited on the Norfolk four-course system, it would have been an insignificant affair, and would have come very late. Something far more important had begun way back in the middle of the sixteenth century, and that was convertible, or 'up and down' husbandry.

All land was arable – that is, destined to be ploughed at some time or other – but only some of it was tillage, actually under the plough, while the rest was grass leys. Land was either ploughed up, or was down in grass.

Converting grassland to tillage was not a problem, though on good soil it was not wise to sow wheat as the first crop. The soil was too 'rank', so that the corn grew 6 feet high and then lodged – that is, was flattened by the rain. A farmer could skim off the cream, as it were, by planting woad. Conversion back to grass was more difficult. In the first place it was important not to wait too long, until all traces of grass had vanished, but even then the turf took a while to grow. Sometimes a farmer might leave Nature to take her course; sometimes he might scatter seeds which, all too often, were just sweepings from his hay-loft. In later years thorough men sowed mixtures of seeds, carefully selected and blended. With the old methods, the grass was in reasonable condition in a couple of years, but was not at its peak until three, so that once the leys were established it was best to leave them for some time. Normally they remained for up to twelve years and, as land was not in tillage for more than three years, it followed that three-quarters of the farm was in grass.

Ploughed land, particularly clay, was now much better than before. The rotting grass released plant food, and the soil was much easier to work. Raw clay, as Chambers and Mingay say (see *Further reading,* p. 32), falls behind the plough like putty and sets like concrete, but the roots and rotting blades of grass made it crumbly and fibrous. Probably the effects on grassland were even better. The ploughing improved drainage, it discouraged those industrious but inconvenient creatures, the moles and the ants, and it replaced old grass with new, which not only grows more quickly but is more nutritious.

We do not know how much more food the new method produced, but it was a lot. On the open fields the cereal yield was usually ten-fold, but on an 'up and down' farm it could be as high as twentyfold. As there was more grassland, there must also have been more livestock. For example, the same amount of land supported four times as many sheep, and each sheep produced twice as much wool. This was, moreover, long stapled, and fetched a better price than the short stapled wool from the hardy creatures that had subsisted on the fallow fields. A seventeenth-century author, Blith, summed it up admirably when he wrote, 'One acre beareth the fruit of three, and two acres are preserved to graze'. (Kerridge, p. 208)

Later, there were many complicated crop rotations, but most of them were only refinements of 'up and down' husbandry.

We will start with the classical Norfolk four-course system, which was wheat, turnips, barley and clover, or the two original open-field crops, along with two of the new fallow crops. Arthur Young explained that the main idea behind it was to avoid taking two corn crops in succession.

The striking difference with 'up and down' husbandry was that the leys only remained for a year, so the proportions of tillage and grass were completely reversed. Farmers made the change because they wanted to grow more wheat, and they were able to do so because the leys, which had once taken three years to establish, could now come and go in one. As we have seen, they undersowed their barley, which meant that the grass had germinated before the third year of the rotation was over. Moreover, they selected and graded their seed carefully: Stevenson spoke of 'mixed seeds, containing eight pounds of broad clover, four pounds of Dutch, half a bushel of Devonshire ray-grass, and sometimes a little hop clover'. (op. cit., p. 193)

However, the Norfolk four-course system was rather like the theme in an overture. In its pure form we hear it hardly ever, it has several variations and there is an abundance of music that resembles it not at all.

For one thing, the uncomplicated four-course was only possible on good soil, and provided the farmer sold neither fodder nor manure. Where the soil was less than perfect,

farmers often kept their leys for two years or more, so that the rotation was wheat, turnips, barley, grasses, grasses. However, there were many alternatives.

These are some rotations Brown of Markle advised:

Rotation for loams and clays: 1 Fallow, with dung; 2 Wheat; 3 Beans; 4 Barley; 5 Clover and rye-grass; 6 Oats or Wheat; 7 Beans, drilled and horse-hoed; 8 Wheat.

Dry soils of upland districts: 1 Turnips; 2 Barley with red clover and rye-grass; 3 Grass to be used for hay; 4 Wheat; 5 Peas; 6 Barley with seeds; 7 Pasture; 8 Pasture; 9 Pasture; 10 Oats. (op. cit., pp. 464, 474)

The four-course theme is barely audible.

Finally, we can look at an East Norfolk system which Kerridge describes. The course was: 1 Wheat; 2 Barley; 3 Turnips; 4 Barley, undersown with clover and perennial rye-grass; 5 Rye-grass and clover hay; 6 Rye-grass and clover ley. The farms were of twenty or so fields, divided into six shifts, each of three or four fields, but the crops did not follow one another on every field in each of these shifts. Let us liken the fields in one of the shifts to four people sitting down to a meal, and the farmer to the chef. He has a set menu of six courses, and he does indeed serve each in turn — but not to all the customers. At any given time one or more has some alternative, or perhaps even nothing at all. Here, then, the farmer had a general pattern to follow, but there was so much flexibility within it, that he could change his crops at will to suit the market or the weather. Many writers have been at pains to show that there was far more to the open-field system than a rigid rotation of wheat, barley and fallow. However, no open-field farmer ever had anything like the freedom that these men of East Anglia enjoyed.

We turn now to ways of feeding the soil. If anything, it is more important to manure land properly than it is to follow a good course of cropping.

Arthur Young found Norfolk farmers using, between them, nineteen different manures — 'marl, lime, gypsum, oyster shells, sea ouze, seaweed, pond weeds, burnt earth, sticklebacks, oil cakes, ashes, soot, malt dust, buckwheat (grown and then ploughed in as green manure), yard dung, leaves, burned stubble, river mud, town manure'. There were many others used in various parts of the country, anything from scrap leather to old thatch. Special mention must be made of town manure, if only because of the nuisance 'muck majors' caused by piling it in heaps in crowded areas. However, carting town manure was expensive, so only farmers living near towns used it, and even they were not enthusiastic. It was a mixture of all the garbage that the citizens wanted out of the way, so that any load could contain a most unpleasant surprise.

Generally, farmers used dung and then, towards the middle of the nineteenth century, artificial fertilisers as well.

Dung not only contains plant food, but also makes humus, which breaks the soil into fine particles, holds moisture and, at the same time, allows excess water to escape. Spreading yard dung by hand was hard work, but there was another way to manure land, which was by folding sheep. The animals fed on grass during the day, and were then penned in hurdles on the arable for the night. The hurdles were moved daily, systematically across the field, until the sheep had manured every part of it.

Excellent though animal manures are, they do have a drawback in that the farmer cannot vary the diet of his crops. As the foolish mother spoils her family by preparing separate meals for everyone, so the wise farmer suits his fertilisers to his plants. This, however, was not easy to do until scientists had discovered a little about the chemistry of the soil, and had made artificial fertilisers.

In 1803 Sir Humphry Davy became Professor of Agricultural Chemistry to the Board of Agriculture, but agricultural science was still in its infancy and Davy achieved little. John Lawes was more successful. He made both laboratory and field experiments and, along with Joseph Gilbert, discovered superphosphates. Lawes patented a process for their manufacture in 1842. Probably the most influential of the early scientists was a German, Justin von Liebig, who, in 1840, published his *Chemistry in Its Application to Agriculture and Physiology*. By the middle of the century farmers had, as well as superphosphates, nitrate of soda, sulphate of ammonia, and potash. There was also Peruvian guano which, though it was natural, being the droppings of sea-birds, was so rich that it was spread as sparingly as any chemical. Bone-meal was also popular. Smashing bones was a common occupation in workhouses.

The obvious result of using artificial fertilisers was more output. Farmers were able not only to follow the Norfolk four-course system, but to take catch crops too, as James Caird found in Oxfordshire (Caird, pp. 20–21). Secondly, it was no longer as important to follow rotations carefully. A farmer could sow what he wanted, within reason, and not worry that he was exhausting his land. That meant he could suit his crops to the market, and not to his soil.

However, feeding poor soil with manures and fertilisers is like giving a Christmas dinner to someone who has stomach-ache. Many soils needed drainage, which is important for a number of reasons. First of all, too much water discourages the plants which farmers wish to grow, while others, like reeds, appear in their place. Secondly, wet land is difficult to plough and cultivate. Finally, wet land is cold, for the wind changes the water to water vapour so that latent heat is taken from the soil. Seeds germinate slowly and the growing season is short.

In medieval times they managed as well as they could with surface drainage. Under draining began in the seventeenth century, but it was none too common until the early nineteenth century. It was then that James Smith of Deanston in Perthshire made himself famous, as Lord Ernle said, 'by converting a rush-grown marsh into a garden'. In 1831 he published his *Remarks on Thorough Draining and Deep Ploughing*.

Early drains were filled with stones, or even brushwood or straw, but when drainage became popular, manufacturers made draining tiles. They were laid in pairs, flat ones first and then others, like railway arches, on top of them. Finally, in 1843, John Reade developed the clay pipe, which is still used today, and in 1845 Thomas Scragg patented a machine to make it.

Drainage was costly, but some land-owners who wished to play the great improver went ahead with schemes that cost £12 or more an acre. Most of them saw little or no return on their capital. It was typical of Lord Shaftesbury to embark on a fancy project, mainly to give work to the unemployed. He plunged his ill-managed estate even further into debt and, in the long run, benefited no one.

Apart from drainage, another way to improve soil is to change its texture. Clays are easier to cultivate if dressed with sharp sand. Lime and chalk are also valuable, because they not only improve the texture of the clay, but make it less acid.

Sandy soils, unlike clay, drain too easily, and dry too quickly. They can be improved with dressings of marl. Marl is a name given to many different clays, the best coming from parts of the Weald where it is 'earthy, fatty and slippery as soap' (Kerridge, p. 246). Marl gives sandy soils more body, helping them to hold moisture and plant food. Probably it was most successful on the 'good sands' of West Norfolk.

8

Improvements by the different methods lasted varying lengths of time. They used to say in Pembrokeshire, 'A man doth sande for himself, lyme for his sonne and marle for his grandechild'. This is hardly correct. Once sand is mixed with clay it is there for good, lime lasts for about three years and marl anything from ten to a hundred. Generally, though, soil improvement was a long-term investment which a tenant would only make if he had a long lease or a lot of faith in his landlord.

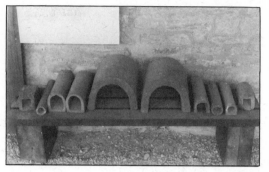

Drainage. First the plough took out a wide furrow. Next, this was deepened with the spade, to a total of about 18 inches or more, depending on conditions. The lower portion was filled with stones. These were covered with turf, and the top was refilled with soil. The lower picture shows drainage tiles, which were later used in place of stones.

3 *Livestock*

At the same time that farmers improved their systems of cropping, they also improved the management of their livestock. Indeed they could not have done the one without the other.

We have seen at Laxton that during the summer the animals shifted from one patch of grass to the next, while during the winter they ate all that could be grown on one of the open fields and on the meadow. Even so, they were likely to go hungry. Historians once thought there was a mass slaughter of animals every autumn, and that farmers kept only the best for breeding. Possibly, in a bad year, this might have happened, but it was not usual. Farm inventories from the Weald, for example, show that there were as many sheep there in the winter, as in the summer. However, it was usually impossible to fatten animals through the winter: their owners had done well merely keeping them alive. The new fodder crops, though, meant that stock could prosper all the year round; and not only that, the same acres fed far more of them. The animals, for their part, showed their gratitude

to the soil by manuring it. The proverb was, 'A full bullock-yard and a full fold make a full granary'.

E. L. Jones describes how it happened in the chalk areas of Hampshire (op. cit., Chap. 1). This was sheep and corn country at the beginning of the eighteenth century and it was sheep and corn country at the end, but with important differences. At first there was the usual division of the land into downland grazing, waterside meadows and arable between the two. The sheep lived on the hills in the summer, and managed as best they could on the open fields during the winter. Gaunt, hardy creatures they were. Later the farmers cultivated the chalk downs to grow fodder crops and were then able to keep sheep that had been bred for their mutton and their wool, rather than for their powers of survival. Moreover, they had far more of them. The extra sheep meant extra dung, which was as essential for the successful cultivation of the downs as were the new crop rotations.

There was a bewildering variety of sheep, every natural region in the country having its own breed. There were Norfolks, for example, and Berkshire 'heath croppers', while Stevenson found some remarkable creatures thriving on barren soil in the Isle of Portland; they were only one-third of the size of their neighbours, the Dorset sheep. However, all these

9

'unimproved' breeds had much the same characteristics. Their wool was short and there was little of it; they were slow to fatten and, even when fully grown, did not give much meat. On the other hand, the wool was fine, and the mutton was lean and well flavoured, while, even more important, these sheep were hardy creatures, able to live on very little, and active enough to make the daily pilgrimage from the pasture to the fold. Indeed, farmers kept them chiefly for their dung, since this was the only commodity they produced in reasonable amounts.

In the late seventeenth and eighteenth centuries these primitive breeds were much improved.

The most famous of the sheep breeders was Robert Bakewell, of Dishley Grange in Leicestershire. However, men like Joseph Allen, Major Hartopp and Captain Tate had already done a lot of work with Midland pasture sheep. Even more important, farmers had learnt to cultivate crops for the new breeds – cabbages, turnips, swedes and abundant grass from water-meadows. Here again we see the close link between improved systems of cropping and improved livestock.

Better feeding was not enough on its own, however, for there are animals, like the more fortunate members of the human race, that can eat as much as they want without putting on weight. Bakewell's contribution was to produce sheep that not only fattened well but did so quickly. His method, copied from racehorse breeders, was to mate parents and offspring; they called it 'breeding in-and-in'. In this way he quickly developed the New Leicesters, which had the qualities he sought. He became famous, so that everyone wanted his stock. In 1789 he made 6200 guineas from the sale of sheep, and he also raised a lot of money by letting his tups. One ram earned 1000 guineas in just a season. Many visitors came to Dishley Grange where Bakewell kept open house, entertaining so lavishly that he ruined himself.

Breeding in-and-in is strictly forbidden in the human race, because children inherit all their parents' bad qualities and in greater abundance. Also, they are often mentally deficient. In fact, stupidity is a good quality in sheep, but Bakewell's animals did have problems that mattered. In the first place, though their fleece was heavy and the wool long, it was decidedly coarse, which was to give trouble to manufacturers. Secondly, the mutton was fat and watery, while its

LEICESTER SHEEP.

Leicester sheep

10

flavour was not remarkable. Thirdly, as Kerridge says, 'While the old pasture sheep could be folded as stores, the new could only waddle about and their constitutions were too delicate to permit folding'. (op. cit., p. 324)

What then was the value of the New Leicesters? Bakewell concentrated on mutton, and whereas the older breeds made light carcasses in three or even four years, his own, much heavier animals, were ready for the market in just over two. Quality made way for quantity. Also, the New Leicester was useful to breeders all over the country. It was like an extra musical instrument in their orchestra: though not usually a success when played solo, it mingled beautifully with the others. In Herefordshire, for example, farmers improved their Ryelands enormously by crossing them with New Leicesters.

On poorer soils, in parts of Dorset, for example, New Leicesters were a disaster. A far more successful breed here was the Southdown, which had been developed by John Ellman of Glynde in Sussex. It gave less mutton than the New Leicester, and barely half as much wool. On the other hand its mutton and wool were of much better quality,

and it folded well. Here, then, was another useful breed, this time for farmers on thinner, poorer soils. They could either keep Southdowns, or they could cross them with their native breeds.

The decline in the quality of English wool caused a lot of heart-searching, for manufacturers had to import if they were to make the best cloth. Not surprisingly, many breeders, including George III, thought of the Spanish merino. A pound of merino wool made 4600 yards of yarn, and a pair of stockings knitted with it could be drawn through a lady's ring. Accordingly, merinos were brought from Spain. They gave fine wool, as long as they lived the same hard life they had suffered at home, but of course they produced no mutton worth having. As soon as their owners allowed them luxurious English foods to fatten them, their wool deteriorated at once. Manufacturers remarked sadly that, as long as Englishmen wanted fat mutton, they must manage without fine wool. Since the price of mutton doubled between 1780 and 1800, while that of wool remained much the same, there was no doubt which the farmers preferred.

The story of cattle is like that of sheep. There were, at first, many unimproved breeds,

Southdowns

11

each area having its own. They were classified according to their horns – Shorthorns, Middlehorns and Longhorns, the last rightly named because the tips were 3 feet apart. The length of horn might seem irrelevant, but the three types of cattle did have their own characteristics. Longhorns, for example, made the best draught animals. However, all cattle had to provide meat, milk and labour, and of these, the meat was the least important. A peasant, growing food just for himself, is not interested in a dead animal; he wants it alive to give milk

Longhorn bull

Shorthorns

Hereford bull

and help in the fields. As Lord Ernle said, 'The pail and the plough set the standard: the butcher was ignored'. (Ernle, p. 179)

As with sheep, improvements began on the Midland Plain, and were helped by the floating of water-meadows and the new fodder crops. Webster, a farmer living near Coventry, did some pioneer work with Longhorns, and Bakewell followed him. The result was much the same as with the New Leicesters – beasts which matured quickly but which made coarse, fatty meat. Bakewell's experiments failed, in that he lost money with them, but they succeeded in that they encouraged two brothers, Charles and Robert Colling of Ketton, near Darlington, to try their luck with Shorthorns. This time careful feeding, along with breeding in-and-in, had good results. It is not size which matters in beef animals. What they do need is to have small bones, and to put meat on the parts that supply the steaks. It was these qualities that the Colling brothers developed in their animals, and they enjoyed the same reputation as Bakewell's. Their bull, 'Comet', sold for 1000 guineas.

At the same time that the Durham Shorthorns were being improved, so too were Herefords. Formerly the Hereford had been expected to work for six years under the yoke before being fattened for the butcher. In the early nineteenth century he was excused the six years of toil, but was, instead, fattened in as little as two years. Herefords spread over the country, but their advance stopped when they encountered the improved Shorthorns, which were good milkers, as well as being good beef cattle. However, the Shorthorn did like a comfortable life, so farmers who had to keep stock on poor grass, in exposed places, were glad to have Herefords. Like New Leicesters and Southdowns, both breeds of cattle prospered in the areas that suited them best.

Dairy cattle were improved, like other livestock, by a combination of careful breeding and feeding. In the early eighteenth century breeders began to see the value of Dutch cattle, and imported increasing numbers. They also recognised the importance of choosing the right bull, which is not easy when trying to produce good milkers. At first they preferred Longhorns, but Bakewell and his kind, by trying to improve them for beef, had ruined them for milk. Once again it was the Shorthorn that triumphed, the improved breed spreading south from its native Durham. There was another invasion from the south, of Channel Islands cattle, but they could hardly compete. Their milk was rich and creamy compared with the pale liquid the Shorthorns gave, but there was not enough of it, and people only kept Jerseys, Guernseys and Alderneys if they drank the milk themselves. Gentlemen had small herds, while humble villagers who could only keep a solitary cow, often preferred one from the Channel Islands.

An open-field village was no place for milch cows. If they did not have enough to eat, they went dry, and many of them ended the winter in a sorry state. If their owner had closes, he moved them from one to the other systematically, so that they always had fresh young grass. This was far better than uncontrolled grazing on the common, but even closes did not solve the problem of winter feed. To give milk through the winter, a cow must calve in the autumn, but it is a disaster to make her do so and then starve her. The new fodder crops, therefore, were a godsend to the dairyman.

Most milk was made into butter and cheese. Claridge, in his description of Dorset, said:

The dairies in general are managed by making all the cream into butter: and from the skimmed milk an inferior sort of cheese, which sells from 25/- to 30/- a hundredweight in the county; and the butter, which is worth 8d or 10d a pound, is in general salted down in tubs and supplies the Portsmouth and London markets.

The waggons which carry butter and other articles are four days in their passage from Bridport to London. (Claridge, op. cit.)

Generally, dairy farmers were not as efficient as their colleagues who kept beef cattle. The reason was that most dairy farms were small, few being larger than 100 acres, and few herds more than twenty cows. Many cows, indeed, were owned singly, it being the ambition of every villager to have one, so that his family could enjoy fresh milk for ten months of the year.

There were no attempts to produce specialised breeds of working cattle; instead, farmers gave them up in favour of horses.

Cows will work, but oxen are stronger. The ox, or bullock, is a male that has been castrated when a young calf. The object of this operation is to help him fatten, and make sure he grows into a docile adult that will not start an argument whenever he goes under the yoke. Oxen have advantages in that they are powerful and, moreover, can be eaten shortly after their retirement, which is not true of horses, at least in England. The ox was ideal for subsistence farmers, but commercial farmers wanted specialist animals, so they bred some cattle for beef, others for milk and, as draught animals, they had horses. The great disadvantage of the ox is that no one can hurry

him. Give him a plough or a heavy cart to pull, and he will do as well as any horse; but hitch him to an empty wagon, and he still insists on plodding at a methodical 2 miles an hour. Our farmer, carting the last of his hay while a thunder-cloud is rolling up, will be frustrated if he cannot drive his empty wagon back to the field at a smart trot. His horse will oblige him, while his ox will not.

Working horses were of three main breeds, the Old English Black Horse, the Clydesdale, and the Suffolk Punch. The best of the three was the Suffolk Punch, so breeders concentrated on him. He would work for two shifts a day, of close on five hours each, provided he could have a good long break between the two and provided, of course, that he had enough of the right food, preferably carrots, corn and the aftermath of summer meadows. Kerridge says of the breed: 'Their peculiar characteristics were strength and compactness, arched, thickset necks, chestnut colour, featherless fetlocks, iron constitution and courageous, never-say-die attitude to the heaviest work.' (op. cit., p. 320)

The story of the pig is much the same. Formerly these animals had to fend for themselves on the common and in the woodland, so it is not surprising that they had trim figures. There was also a great variety of local breeds, such as the Gloucester Old Spot and the Wessex Saddleback. The Gloucester Old Spot was developed from the large, gaunt, Midlands pig in the late eighteenth century. Some quick-fattening Chinese pigs came to England at about the same time. In the nineteenth century Joseph Tuley, a weaver of Keighley, improved the Yorkshire pig, and Sanders Spencer of Huntingdon went on with his work, producing the ancestors of the famous Landrace breed to which the Danes owe so much.

Feeding was important as well. On Sir John Conroy's farm Caird found the pigs eating barley-meal to their hearts' content. During the few months that they were fattening, each one consumed about ten bushels. Shelter is also important for pigs, so they lived in luxury. Not for them the long hours of back-breaking labour, or even the daily walk from pasture to fold. The pigs remained in their sty.

Towards the end of our period there was a good network of railways, and they were a boon to livestock farmers. A Norfolk farmer told James Caird that when they walked to London his sheep lost 7 pounds each, his bullocks lost 28 pounds, and, over the year he lost £600. When the railway came he saved all that meat and money. Dairy farmers were slower to take advantage. Caird complained of a lack of enterprise among those of the Midlands, and he said of Essex, 'Intersected as the county is by railways, there is nothing in the distance to prevent daily supplies being sent to London'. (op. cit., p. 124) This failure, though, was not the fault of the farmers but of the London milkmen. Whether the livestock walked or travelled by train, there was always a reception for them; the markets were open and the butchers' knives were sharp. The city's milk, however, depended on the cow-keepers, who did nothing to welcome competition.

The livestock farmer's main problem was disease among his animals, for in those days people had little understanding of disease, and veterinary science hardly existed. There were times when farmers over wide areas lost nearly all their flocks and herds.

The stock farmer did have compensations, though. While the prices of cereals fluctuated considerably, those of meat and dairy produce remained fairly steady.

4 Machinery

During most of our period, on most farms, people and animals did their work with the simplest of equipment. Progress with machinery was slower than in any other branch of farming. In the sixteenth century there were only ploughs, harrows, and hand tools like scythes and flails. No one made any important invention until the eighteenth century, when all manner of new appliances were developed, like the drill, the horse hoe, rollers, improved ploughs and harrows and, finally, threshing machines and steam-engines. None the less, it was not until after 1850 that they were at all common, for they were expensive until there was plenty of cheap iron, mass production, and railways to carry the heavier goods. When we go through the list of inventions we must bear in mind, therefore, that it makes progress look far more rapid than it really was.

The best-known inventor of farm machines was Jethro Tull. This remarkable man was born at Basildon in 1674, and he trained to be a lawyer. When he was forty-five years old he acquired, by some chance, Mount Prosperous Farm at Shelbourn in Berkshire. He did not want it, but could not sell it, so he became a farmer by necessity. Almost at once he had trouble with his labourers, for it was, he said, 'about the time when Plough Servants first began to exalt their Dominion over their masters, so that a Gentleman Farmer was allowed to make but little profit from his Arable Lands' (Tull, p. xi). Tull decided to abandon tillage and sow his land with sainfoin, whereupon he met another difficulty. Sainfoin seed was so

scarce that he could not find enough to sow at the normal rate of seven bushels to the acre. Wondering if he could save seed, he had a look at some fields already growing sainfoin. They had been sown broadcast, so that in some places the plants were close together, and elsewhere far apart. Where the plants were thickest, he found the crop was poorest, the best yield being where they grew one to a square foot. He then calculated that if he sowed 7 bushels to the acre, he was scattering 140 seeds to the square foot. Another thing he discovered was that if the seeds were to germinate they had to be at just the right depth. Accordingly, he told his labourers to make shallow furrows, sow the seed thinly, and then cover it with the right amount of soil — just as a gardener would sow lettuce. He said, 'This way succeeded to my desire, and was in seed and labour but a fourth part of the expense of the common way, and yet the ground was better planted.' (op. cit., p. xiii)

The first year he sowed 10 acres, but the following year his labourers struck, afraid that when all the farm was converted to grass they would lose their jobs. Accordingly, he decided to make a machine. He was no mechanic, but he had studied music as a young man, so he copied the working parts of a church organ. He called his invention a 'drill', because sowing seeds in shallow furrows is known as 'drilling'.

Tull then went on to develop a theory of cultivation. He considered whether the food of plants was nitre, water, air, fire or earth, and decided that it was earth. It followed, therefore, that the farmer should increase the surface area of his soil by breaking it into as fine a powder as possible. It was then more available to the plants. From this followed even more curious ideas. In the first place Tull felt there

14

was no point in letting land lie fallow, and secondly it was little use spreading manure. Manure, he said had only one function and that was to break up the soil by 'fermentation'. Not only did tillage pulverise the soil more efficiently, but manure was positively harmful, since it harboured the seeds of unwanted plants. He also thought manure was poisonous because, wherever there was manure, there were toads, and it was obvious these were poisonous, since people died from eating them. This happened if a careless housewife flung a cabbage containing one into her cooking pot!

To prove his theory, Tull invented a horse hoe, which cultivated the soil more quickly and more deeply than the hand hoe. It fitted in well with his drill, which laid the seed in straight lines, for horse hoeing is impossible in a field sown broadcast. Hoeing is indeed good for crops: it destroys weeds; it allows air and moisture into the soil; it prevents ground drying, for it makes a dust mulch and widens the spaces between the particles of soil so that there is less capillary action. Although for the wrong reasons, Tull was doing the right thing. He was delighted with the results, for not only did he have heavier yields, but he saved so much seed and labour that he cropped an acre of wheat for 10 shillings instead of £4.10s. He also freed himself from the tyranny of his work people; his labour relations were never good. In the end he was growing wheat in double rows, on ridges, at the enormous distance of 6 feet apart.

No one else copied Tull's methods entirely, because farmers refused to believe it was possible to grow good crops without plenty of manure, and of course they were right. After about twelve years Tull's own yields dropped,

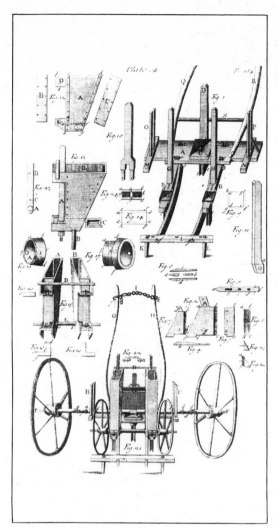

Tull's seed drill

Tull's horse hoe

although he said it was because he was ill and could not supervise his labourers. However, there remained the drill and the horse hoe. Tull had invented them before farmers, generally, felt the need for them, but by the end of the eighteenth century they were popular enough. They were also improved. The Suffolk drill, for example, sowed fifteen rows at a time, whereas Tull's had sown three.

A machine which farmers were happy to adopt was the thresher. During the Napoleonic Wars there was a shortage of labour in some parts of the country. In Hampshire, for example, many men joined the services, while others found work in the naval dockyard at Portsmouth. Those that were still on the farms began to give themselves airs and be difficult, so farmers bought threshing-machines.

Since prehistoric times, threshing had been done with the flail, which is like a rolling pin joined to a broom handle by some short lengths of leather. The thresher does not swing the flail over his head, as pictures usually show him, but stoops and turns the handshaft through a tight circle, so that the beater strikes rapidly. Even so, threshing was a long tedious task that took the men all through the winter. They had ways of enlivening it, though. One game was for a man to hold a straw in his mouth while his friend, if that is what he was, belaboured the end with a flail. He drew the straw slowly into his mouth until he lost his nerve. In their more sensible moods they practised their ringing, striking with their flails in the same order that they rang the church bells.

It was not easy to invent a thresher, but after others had failed, Andrew Meikle succeeded. With his machine, rollers fed in the wheat, head first, whereupon it was at once assailed by beaters which, moving at 2500 feet a minute, knocked the grain from the ear. Inside, large, revolving rakes took away the straw, a fan blew chaff from another opening, and the grain fell out at the bottom. There had to be six or eight attendants, but several could be women or boys.

Some of the early machines were turned by hand, but the only advantage was that unskilled women could do the job; it was no quicker than by the flail. Oxen were too slow to drive the machine efficiently, so the best animal to use was the horse. It was murderous work for him, eternally going round and round, with the weight on his shoulders never

Suffolk drill

16

Primitive ploughs

relaxing. That might not have bothered his owner, but the lack of power did, so that anyone who could afford it had a water-wheel or, later, a steam-engine.

A threshing-machine might cost £750, which was a labourer's wages for close on twenty-five years.

The flail still survived for a while. For a few years after the Swing Riots of 1830 farmers were cautious about using machines. Also, it was often better to give labourers work, even almost useless work, rather than turn them on the parish. Another advantage was that brewers preferred their barley threshed by the flail because it was less damaged.

The story of the plough is much like that of the livestock. At first, every area had its own plough, which suited its own soil. Then came better models, and they were crossed with the old ones, so that although there was still as much or even more variety at the end, the improvements everywhere had been considerable.

For all their differences, the early ploughs had two things in common. First of all they were not designed scientifically. By trial and error over centuries village craftsmen had evolved an implement that suited their customers, but they were satisfied if it worked tolerably well, and they did not try and develop, test, or compare new models. The

mould-board, for example, was often a straight piece of wood set on the skew, which simply lifted the turf on edge, so that it fell under its own weight. Secondly, ploughs had little iron in them, probably no more than the coulter, the share, and a few of the harness fittings: everything else was of wood, so that the plough was heavy and cumbersome. The exception was, perhaps, the Norfolk plough.

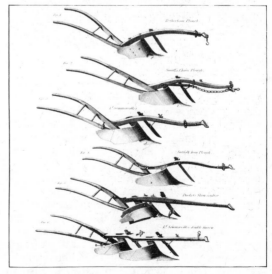

Improved iron ploughs

17

Strangers to the county were amazed to see a man and two horses plough 2 acres in a day, since, in most places, an acre was more than enough. They were less impressed when they saw the soil was light and sandy, and that at times the plough stirred it no more deeply than 2 inches.

Men began to study the plough properly in the seventeenth century, but made little progress until 1730 when Foljambe took out a patent for his Rotherham plough. He copied it, probably, from the Dutch. It was James Small, however, who did the most valuable work. In the first place he made his share so that it sliced easily through the soil instead of tearing it. Secondly, he studied the curve that the turf formed as it fell behind the plough, and he shaped his mould-board to match it exactly. His aim was to turn the conflict between the plough and the soil into something more like an agreement. John Bond made yet another improvement when, in 1770, he developed his Suffolk iron plough. Since it was entirely of iron, it was stronger and lighter than any made of wood. Writing in 1811, Robert Brown of Markle said that two horses could do as much work with the new plough as four had done with the old, which meant a farmer saved £80 a year.

There were machines for the barn and the yard as well as for the field. The most important was the threshing-machine which has already been described, but there were others as well, such as chaff cutters, turnip slicers and corn and cake bruisers. A few farmers even had steam-engines to drive their machinery, the first being perhaps Colonel Buller of Haydon, Norfolk, in 1813.

However, we must end this account of farm machinery on the same note of caution with which we began it. On the average farm there was little progress. In Gloucester Museum there is a plough which is dated 1850 and which, apart from the share and coulter, is almost entirely of timber. The mould-board is no more than a piece of wood, hacked roughly so that it has something of a twist. It would have made James Small blench.

5 Enclosures

An enclosure is a hedge, a fence, a wall, or any obstacle which a farmer puts around his land to prevent animals from straying: it also means the land within such a boundary. As we have seen, there was a time when much land was open, but today any that is worth farming is enclosed. The change came about in two ways. In the first place people divided their commons and wastes, and secondly they consolidated the strips which they held scattered throughout the open fields and meadows.

The reason for making enclosures was to make money. If a man had an enclosed farm, he could use the new farming techniques, so that he made more profit and could pay more rent. If we ask why the open-field farmers did not use the new techniques, the answer is that they could and they did, far more than was once imagined. There was no need to cover an open field with one crop: the fodder field, especially, could be quite a patchwork. Also, if a man wanted more grass, he could grow it on his strips of arable. Moreover, a village, as a body, could alter its system of farming if it wished, and there was an Act of Parliament in 1773 to make it easier for them to do so. Formerly everyone had had to agree to a change, but afterwards a majority of three-quarters was enough. Several villages in Nottinghamshire took advantage of the Act, including Oxted, which, among other things, converted its three fields to four, and, in consequence, was not enclosed until 1852.

However, in any open-field village there was a limit to the freedom individuals could have, and freedom was what the progressive man wanted. It was impossible for him to grow crops that had to be sown or harvested at different times from the rest. When the church bells rang to announce that the harvest was over, everyone's cattle appeared in the field, and it would have been useless for him to protest that he had undersown his barley with clover, which needed another season to establish itself. The contrast is striking between, say, the farmers of Laxton and those of East Norfolk. The former had their open fields and their court baron ruling every detail of their lives; the latter had their little enclosures and their six shifts, giving them complete freedom to adjust at will to the weather or the market.

People were anxious to enclose if they had land that they could improve a great deal. In Norfolk, for example, the 'good sands' gave but little if they remained in their natural state and were treated to two straw crops and a fallow. However, with marling, and rotations that included roots and grasses, they produced as much as any land in England. High prices also encouraged enclosure. The profits from wheat were enormous during the Napoleonic Wars and it was frustrating to see a common which was potentially good land being grazed by indifferent livestock.

Enclosure could take centuries, as we have seen at Laxton. Here, by the seventeenth century, most of the lord's demesne had been enclosed, while, as the area under cultivation spread, the villagers made closes for themselves. On the open fields progress was slower, but a family might lay strip to strip, either by exchange or purchase, until they had a compact block of land which they might then enclose. At first they had to leave the gate open after harvest to allow common grazing, but if they had common rights elsewhere which they were willing to give up, then they could have their close all to themselves. Much the same happened on the meadow land, but on the common pasture it was almost impossible.

Sometimes the lord of the manor, or a good number of the villagers, were not happy with this sluggish progress and wanted to hurry it. They might make private, informal agreements after persuasion of various kinds. More officially, the lord might order enclosure in the court baron, but he needed a lot of authority to do that. It was better to have a decree from a royal court, either Chancery or Exchequer, but even then the legal title was uncertain. However, the customs of the open-field village were like so many that survived from the Middle Ages, in that it was perfectly possible to give them a quiet burial, and ignore the letter of the law, as long as everyone who mattered was in agreement. Occasionally, though, there was strong opposition, and then those who wanted enclosure had to have an Act of Parliament. Obtaining one was complicated and expensive.

In the first place there had to be a petition, which, if it was to have any hope of success, needed the support of owners holding about two-thirds or three-quarters of the land to be enclosed. This did not mean a majority of the land-owners, for one of them could well have more than all his neighbours put together. Next, a Bill was ordered – that is, prepared for Parliament to consider – whereupon it was presented and read twice, these matters being little more than formalities. The serious work began when the Bill was committed. Usually the committee was made up of M.P.s of the county in which the village lay, with some from neighbouring counties as well. They examined the Bill in detail, heard objections and made any amendments they thought proper. They could recommend to the House of Commons that the Bill should be thrown out, but almost always they approved it, and it passed its third reading without much difficulty. It went next to the House of Lords, where it was most unlikely to meet trouble, though their lordships did keep a careful eye on the interests of the Church. Finally, His Majesty gave his assent, graciously, no doubt, but in execrable French – 'Soit faite comme il es désirer'.

Probably there was now more tension in the village than ever before. There had to be an Award. The Act had nominated Commissioners to divide the land, and only two things were certain, the first being that they would take a long time, and the other that they would make a lot of money for themselves.

There could be any number of Commissioners up to twelve, but usually there were three, one for the lord of the manor, one for the tithe owner, and one for the other freeholders. Most of them were amateurs, especially clergy, who had little else to do, but there were some professionals as well – lawyers, land agents and surveyors. Indeed, being an Enclosure Commissioner became almost a profession in itself, the same men helping to prepare numerous Awards, not only one after the other, but even at the same time. In the early nineteenth century their fees were about 5 or 6 guineas a day, besides which they put in bills for expenses containing all manner of interesting items.

Commissioners did do something for their money, for as Tate says, an average Award contained 'thirty or forty skins of parchment, each perhaps, three feet by two' (op. cit., p. 117). To begin, they took their oaths, appointed a surveyor and a clerk, and then invited claims. They published the claims in the church, usually provoking a flurry of counter-claims, so that they withdrew for a few weeks until the dust settled. They then returned to hear all the arguments and allot the land. Meanwhile the surveyor was busy, for preparing a plan of an open-field village was a long job, and he then had to measure out the allotments as the Commissioners made them, mark any new roads, tracks, footpaths or drains, and decide who was to make and maintain the boundary hedges. When they had finished, the Commissioners signed, sealed and delivered their Award, which the incumbent stored in the parish church. Finally, everyone who was lucky enough to have been given a piece of land, took possession of it.

Parliamentary enclosure was not cheap. There was of course the cost of making the ditches, banks and hedges, but that was by no means all. One advantage of the open fields was that everyone had a share of land close to the village, as well as land at a distance, but now that farms were in compact blocks, some were well over a mile away. Land-owners had usually to supply new buildings and roads. Finally, there were the fees charged by Members of Parliament, Enclosure Commissioners and any lawyers who might have been hired.

The three charges varied, but we can have an idea of what they were from these figures for 3000 acres of the Fitzwilliam estates in Northamptonshire:

Fences and hedges	£12000
New buildings and roads	4000
Parliamentary and legal expenses	8000
	£24000

This was £8 an acre, which was about average.

It is impossible to trace the progress of enclosure. In the first place most of it was by private agreements, all of which have been long forgotten, though Kerridge thinks that so much had been done that way by 1700, that only a quarter of the country was still unenclosed. We have the Enclosure Acts passed by Parliament, and they tell us precisely which places they affected, but give no idea of area. Some make no mention of the amount of land; others state it, and do so wrongly. Between them they use a confusing medley of measurements – acres, yardlands, oxgangs, toftsteads, beastgates and so on. Enclosure Awards on the other hand are accurate – they had to be – but few of them have survived. We have, then, a vast number of private agreements about which we know nothing, the Enclosure Acts, which are complete but unreliable, and the Enclosure Awards, which are reliable but incomplete. We can only hope to discover general trends.

In the first place some parts of the country had never had open fields. In the Weald there were some open meadows, as, for example, along the River Medway at Tonbridge, but mostly the farms had been made by clearing small areas of woodland, so that by the seventeenth century this part of Kent was a patchwork of small fields surrounded by copses. W. G. Hoskins describes East Devon as a country of 'dispersed farmsteads and hamlets, enclosed fields, winding lanes and large hedge banks' (*Making of the English Landscape*, pp. 46–7). It was of course possible to have open fields in a Welsh valley.

Few people objected to the enclosure of wastes, so it went forward rapidly. Industry took its toll. In 1629 a Durham man claimed he had felled 30000 oaks during his working life, and in the late seventeenth century the ironmasters of the Forest of Dean were turning 5000 trees into charcoal every year. New towns were built on waste land – for example, Poole, Liverpool and, in more recent times, Bournemouth. Mostly, though, the wastes vanished as the populations of the villages and little townships grew.

There was more opposition to enclosing common pasture, but it was happening as early as the thirteenth century. The proof is in the Statute of Merton of 1236, which said that a lord who enclosed, must leave enough common for his free tenants. The Black Death brought a check, but afterwards enclosure went on faster than ever, and not only by lords of the manor; squatters moved on to the commons and ordinary farmers converted them to arable. Villages were very different, though. As late as 1760, Chesterton in Oxfordshire still had 700 acres of common out of a total of 2300 acres, while at Mudford in Somerset there were no commons left by 1554.

Enclosing the meadows and open fields was the most difficult, but it happened, and again quite early. During the mid-sixteenth century particularly land-owners enclosed enough arable to cause a lot of upset. We have the impression that they converted numberless open fields to sheep pastures, depopulating villages and flooding the roads with vagabonds. Probably, though, the problem was confined to some of the areas especially suitable for sheep.

During the eighteenth and early nineteenth centuries the attack on the wastes, commons and open fields became more and more determined. Again, we have no idea how many private agreements there were, but the sheer number of Acts shows how much enthusiasm there was. Before 1760 there were only 259 Acts, but afterwards the numbers were:

1761–1801: 2700 – one quarter for commons, wastes and pastures only.
1801–1844: 1900 – one half for commons, wastes and pastures only.
After 1845: 670 – three-quarters for commons, wastes and pastures only.

In the first half of the nineteenth century there were also a number of General Enclosure Acts which simplified procedures, making it possible to tackle small parcels of land, none of which was worth an Act of its own. Tate thinks 5000 parishes were affected by these Acts.

At one time historians thought that most enclosures were made by Act, and that little had happened before, save perhaps in the sixteenth century. Now, parliamentary enclosure looks more like the last stage in a long operation. Down to the middle of the eighteenth century, land-owners only found enclosure worth their while where there was little opposition. The movement advanced, like the encroaching sea, wearing away the soft rocks, but leaving the hard ones standing. Everything changed, though, in the boom years at the end of the eighteenth century, and during the Napoleonic Wars. All agricultural goods mounted in price, while, at times, wheat was more expensive than it was ever to be again before the Second World War. What Chambers and Mingay call 'the truncated open fields and commons' had to be hurried out of the way. However, even if parliamentary enclosure was only a rounding-off operation, it was still important. The fact that so many people were willing to go to the trouble and expense of obtaining Acts, must be significant.

We turn now to the effects of enclosures. Most of the debate has been about their social consequences but, though the problems are interesting, we are more concerned here with the results for farming rather than for people.

We have already compared the open-field village to an eggshell. This is essential at first, but in the end it has to be smashed, and cast aside as useless, otherwise the creature that it has protected will never develop fully. The breaking of the shell does not create new growth, but it does make it possible. Similarly, while enclosure did not guarantee better farming, it did give freedom to progressive men. Landlords put covenants in their leases, insisting on improved methods; if a tenant found they did not suit him, he had only to convince one man, who had every incentive to help him prosper, instead of several dozen lethargic and indifferent neighbours.

Arthur Young said of Norfolk: 'In several parliamentary enclosures the effect has been, at least the doubling of produce. In respect to the rest, the first leases were at a low rate, from the allotted lands being in a most impoverished condition: but on being let a second time, the rise has been considerable.' (*Agriculture of Norfolk*, p. 184) Chambers and Mingay say that while some rents rose but little after enclosure, others were quadrupled and most, probably, doubled. The average rent of unenclosed land was 7 shillings an acre, whereas for enclosed land it was 15 shillings an acre.

Enclosures, then, gave greater freedom to landlords and tenants. This in turn meant better farming, higher output, higher profits and higher rents.

Apart from enclosing what was already farmed, men also brought new land into cultivation.

From prehistoric times they had nibbled away at the forests. Land cleared of timber needs care, or its best crop is moss, but it is usually fit for something worthwhile. However, marginal land, such as the Mendip Hills, that would not, naturally, have supported broad-leaved trees, was also cultivated.

Land was also reclaimed from the sea, for example, on parts of the Norfolk coast, Romney Marsh, and the estuaries of rivers such as the Trent, the Don and the Great Ouse. One method was 'warping'. They enclosed some salt-marsh with a sea-wall and allowed in the tide waters. They then closed their sluices until the silt had settled, whereupon they exchanged the clear water for another flooding of murky tide water. That way they slowly built the level of the land.

Inland marshes were drained as well, especially the Fens. Here the most famous engineer was a Dutchman, Cornelius Vermuyden. He did his work in the early seventeenth century, but others like the Duke of Bedford had been busy a hundred years before him. Men who lived by catching fish, eels and wildfowl, fought, often quite literally, for their rights, but they lost in the end and the country gained thousands of acres of fertile land. It was particularly good for rape, and its giant cousin, cole. As green crops they made excellent fodder, while their seeds gave oil for soap-making, lighting and lubrication. Two problems with the Fenland were that the outfalls of the ditches silted and, more seriously, that the peat shrank as it dried, so the land subsided and the pumps could never be idle.

6 The course of agricultural change

If we are to trace the progress of the agricultural revolution we have first to decide what it was and when it happened. In the past, writers have agreed that it consisted of the parliamentary enclosures and the improvements that went with them, and that it took place between about 1760 and 1815. They recognised that there were important developments after 1815, especially in the third quarter of the nineteenth century, which Lord Ernle called 'the Golden Age'. That, though, was more like a second agricultural revolution, separated from the first by long years of depression. They recognised, too, that there was progress before 1760 – as, for example, the spread of turnip husbandry and Tull's inventions. Such work, though, was seen as no more than preparation for the changes that mattered.

However, it is now clear that there were many outstanding improvements well before 1760, some of them as early as the sixteenth century. They included the floating of water-meadows, the introduction of new crops, marsh drainage, stock-breeding and, above all, the development of 'up and down' husbandry.

As for the period after 1815, recent research has shown that it was not a time of unrelieved gloom, and that there were in fact only five or six years of serious general depression. On the contrary, there was a good deal of progress. For example, E.L. Jones gives this graph of corn yields, taken from the records of some Liverpool merchants.

The question we are bound to ask, then, is whether there was an agricultural revolution at all. There is no doubt that farming altered completely, but it did so over the centuries, and though there were bursts of activity on occasion, it is quite possible that at no one time were there changes so drastic that they could be called revolutionary.

We will look now at three periods, the early and middle years of the eighteenth century, the time from 1760 to 1815, and the so-called post-war depression and recovery from 1815 to 1850. We shall do so, however, with little hope of locating an agricultural revolution on the way.

In the early eighteenth century the economy of the country was sometimes stagnating, and at best growing slowly. Prices were low, which gave little encouragement, save in a limited way. Farmers who found they were making less and less on, for instance, each bushel of wheat, grew more of it so as to maintain a reasonable income. However, the only ones who could do that successfully were those who could hold down their costs. They were the men who farmed the light soils of such areas as the chalk and limestone escarpments. Here the land drained itself, it was easy to cultivate and the working season was long. It grew little when treated to two straw crops and a fallow, but was well suited to the new rotations and the sheep-fold.

However, there is a limit to the amount people can eat, so there was a surplus of grain, and this had important results for industry and trade. In the first place food was cheap, to the delight of the labouring poor, and of their employers who were able to pay low wages. Secondly, farmers in the clay vales who could not grow wheat cheaply, put much of their land down to grass: they then needed less labour, so people had to look for work in industry. Thirdly, farmers grew industrial

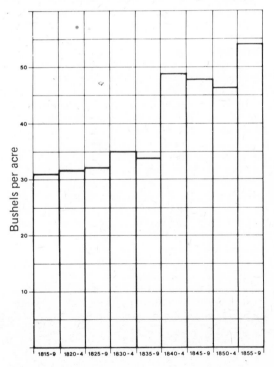

Wheat yields 1815–1859 – five-yearly averages (adapted from E.L. Jones, *Agriculture and the Industrial Revolution*)

Prosperous Farmer *c.*1800 (J.C. Loudun of Great Tew, Oxfordshire.) He watches his men at work in his magnificent farm buildings, from the comfort of his veranda – well away from the smells and noise. When he wishes to give instructions, he first attracts attention with the trumpet, then shouts down the megaphone.

crops as alternatives to wheat – malting barley and hops, hemp, flax and jute, rape seed for oil, and madder, woad and weld for dyes. Finally, much grain was exported. Kerridge says it amounted to 300000 quarters each year in the 1670s, or enough to feed 150000 people, while from 1732 to 1766 it was, on average, 675000 quarters, or enough to feed 340000 people. These exports paid for valuable imports, especially from Mediterranean countries.

After 1760 the economic climate changed. Instead of slow growth or stagnation, there was steady expansion followed by a boom during the Napoleonic Wars, the like of which had never happened before. Farmers prospered as the rest. They cultivated more land, they grew more wheat, and, along with their landlords, they invested more capital. Deane and Cole (op. cit., p. 65) give the net output of corn as follows:

Date	Net output ('000 quarters)
1760	15 265
1770	15 617
1780	16 706
1790	17 884
1800	18 991
1810	21 988
1820	25 086

Until 1813, the reason for the greater output was a rise in prices. They varied a lot from year to year, but the general trend was clear. Taking wheat prices as 100 in 1700, they were 117 in the 1760s, 142 in the 1780s and 250 in about 1800 (ibid., p. 91). Prices rose mainly because there were more people to feed. The population of Great Britain was, perhaps, 6.4 million in 1751, 10.7 million in 1801 and 14.2 million in 1821. Prices were especially high during the war because there was, by coincidence, a run of bad harvests at the same time. During the twenty-two years from 1793 to 1815, seven crops almost failed, seven were poor, six were average and only those of 1796 and 1813 were good. Here, then, was a splendid time for farmers, since they do not like good harvests. People want just so much wheat, and neither less nor more. Only a slight surplus sends prices tumbling, added to which a heavy crop is expensive to harvest. On the other hand a small shortage will quickly push up prices, while a poor crop is cheap to harvest.

The rise in prices encouraged farmers to grow wheat on all manner of soils. They grew it in the clay vales between the chalk escarpments, on the equally sticky boulder clays of the Midland Plain, and on dubious marginal land like the Mendips. During the war they were almost bound to make money, if they could produce any crop at all. Unhappily they were sowing not only wheat but trouble for themselves in the future.

For all their efforts, farmers barely kept pace with the growing population. There were no more exports of wheat in any quantity after 1764, but instead the country had to import. This happened most during the war. In 1805 Britain bought 560000 quarters from Prussia, and in 1806 a further 52000. In 1809 and 1810 there was virtually a famine here, while the French had a glut, so they sold us 252000 quarters. Agriculture no longer earned foreign currency. At the same time land that had grown industrial crops or grass now produced wheat.

New land was brought into cultivation. How much we do not know, but it must have been a great deal. Much of the reclamation was of marginal land, so that farmers who carried it out, only made profits while prices were high.

Our third period runs from the end of the war until 1850, which historians once thought was a time of general depression, save perhaps towards the end.

Prices began to fall with the excellent harvest of 1813, and two years later the Board of Agriculture published a report telling of distress and ruin in all parts of the kingdom. How real was the depression? Certainly the fall in the price of wheat was real enough. To give two extremes, it had been 155 shillings a quarter in 1812, and was 43s. 3d. in 1822. Very rarely was it as high as the 80 shillings which farmers said they needed to make a reasonable profit. Moreover, there was an acute depression affecting all farmers from 1821 to 1823, and another, less widespread, from 1833 to 1836. After that, though, came recovery, with the Poor Law Amendment Act of 1834 reducing rates, while the Tithe Redemption Act also gave some help. The railway network was spreading, but above all, thanks to the growth of industry, demand was good, so that prices began to creep upwards again. Between 1813 and 1850, then, there was not unrelieved gloom. In the last fourteen years there was increasing prosperity, in seventeen there were difficulties, but only in six at the most was their genuine hardship.

Nor did all farmers suffer equally. The graph shows how differently the prices of wheat and meat were moving:

Graziers had little reason to complain. We could reasonably expect tales of woe from the corn-growing counties, but although East Anglian farmers were far from happy about the fall in wheat prices, they could fight it by increasing production. They made more and more use of the Norfolk four-course system, which meant half their arable was under cereals, and this was possible because they were generous with every sort of fertiliser, natural and artificial.

The farmers with problems were those who were growing wheat on unsuitable soils – as, for example, the strong clays of Essex.

In the early nineteenth century, then, the situation was much the same as it had been a hundred years before. Farmers with light soils increased production to combat falling prices, so making difficulties for those who had clay. In the later period, clay farmers agitated so much that they convinced the Government that British agriculture was in ruins. They then persuaded it to give them protection against foreign competition, which hardly existed, with the Corn Laws.

None the less there had to be changes. Marginal land went out of cultivation. On the heavy clays, the more adaptable farmers gave up tillage in favour of grass, though many of their neighbours, convinced the good times must return, persisted with their wheat, grumbling all the while about foreigners and the weather.

Landlords and tenants had to make adjustments. If, for example, a man had taken a long lease in 1812, he was soon in trouble, since he could not pay 1812 rents in 1822. Cobbett describes how one of them sold everything he

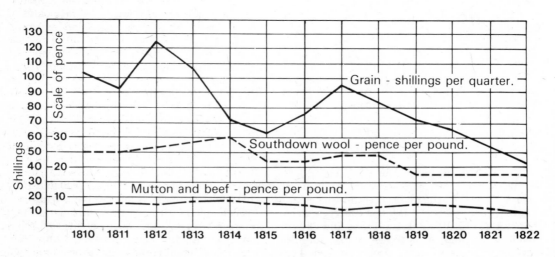

Comparative fluctuations in grain, wool and meat prices 1810–1822

could and absconded (op. cit., p. 136). However, it was more usual for the farmer to throw himself on the mercy of his landlord, for most landlords would help good tenants who were in genuine difficulties.

When farms fell vacant, it was hard to find new occupiers. A landlord could offer a low rent, but this he was reluctant to do. It gave the farm a stigma, so that it was difficult to raise the rent afterwards. It was better to draft a lease that was more generous in other ways, such as undertaking repairs to buildings. He could also make his farm more attractive – by land drainage, for instance. This he could afford quite easily, because the end of the war meant the end of wartime taxes, so there was money to spare for estates. Land-owners knew more enjoyable ways of spending it, but they could at least make all the drains they wanted, and be no worse off than before. There was, as Thompson says, 'a transfer of resources from the central government to tenant farmers by way of landowners' (op. cit., p. 236). The central government, of course, had never intended any such thing.

7 Agriculture and the economy

For nearly all of our period agriculture was the most important sector of the economy. Towards the end of the Napoleonic Wars, for example, it employed one-third of the working population, it produced one-third of the national income, while land and farm capital accounted for two-thirds of the national stock. Some time in the early nineteenth century, industry took first place, but by then agriculture had made no small contribution to the economy (see table p. 88).

Agriculture's most important service was to feed the growing population. London was particularly greedy. Between 1650 and 1750 it grew from 400 000 to 675 000, an increase of 70 per cent. By then 11 per cent of the population lived there. In Britain as a whole, the population increased from 6.8 million in 1700 to 10.6 million in 1801, and leapt to 20.8 million by 1850. However, the only substantial imports of grain were during a few bad years at the time of the Napoleonic Wars. As for imports of meat and dairy produce, they were insignificant throughout, unless we count Ireland as a foreign country, which contemporaries did not.

Admittedly tea, coffee, citrus fruits, dried fruits, sugar, rum and wines were all imported, but these luxuries can only have accounted for a small portion of the nation's food bill.

One result of the improvements in British agriculture, then, was that there was no need to spend foreign exchange on essential foods. Consequently it was easier to find the money for raw materials like cotton, and later wool. Industry was able to grow unchecked. This is in contrast with numbers of poorer states in the world today; they have been unable to develop their economies because, as soon as their populations have started to grow, they have had to spend scarce and precious foreign exchange on food, rather than industrial raw materials. It is in contrast, too, with Holland. Her economy was as advanced as Britain's in 1700, but she came to depend on imports of grain, and so by the end of the century was left behind.

British farmers not only saved foreign exchange but earned it as well. There were substantial exports of grain down to 1760, after which the growth of population meant it was all needed at home.

Farmers also supplied industry with raw materials. The most important of these was wool, but there were also flax, barley for breweries and distilleries, and woad and madder to make dyes. However, the pressure of population told here, as with exports of grain. Increasingly land was needed for food, so coffee and tea replaced beer, exotic products like sumac replaced native dyes, and, though cotton did not oust linen and wool, it left them far behind. The production of raw wool did indeed increase, but it could not keep pace with the growth of the woollen industry, while quality declined as farmers bred their sheep for mutton.

Agriculture also released certain factors of production for industrial development – capital, business talent and, to some extent, labour.

G.B.E.—C

The capital came, mainly, from land-owners. They developed industries connected with their estates, such as timber, or, if they had minerals, coal-mining and iron-smelting. However, these activities were only once removed from agriculture; land-owners withdrew even from these as they became more complicated to administer. It was easier to lease the mineral rights than to exploit the coal or iron directly. Certainly advanced ironworks were more the preserves of Quakers, very different people from landed aristocrats.

Farmers contributed business talent as aristocrats contributed capital – that is, in limited quantities and early in our period. They had to place their younger sons but, having a little money, were able to pay their apprenticeship premiums and, perhaps, help them later to start their own firms. Farmers themselves might become part-time manufacturers and then full-time when they, or more likely their sons or grandsons, saw how lucrative the work could be. The classic example was the first Robert Peel, who sold his land so that he could concentrate on the manufacture of cotton, so founding one of the most successful firms in that profitable industry. However, as time went on, industry recruited its leaders from its own ranks.

It would seem, then, that as long as industry was in its early stages of development, land-owners were prepared to finance at least those activities connected with their estates, and farmers were prepared to turn themselves or their sons into business men. However, when the units of production grew in size, and when processes became more complicated, both were happy to bow out. None the less, we must not, for that reason, underrate their contribution. In the later years, industry itself was able to generate the capital and managerial skills that it needed, but in the earlier years that was not so, and agriculture filled the gaps. English land-owners in general wished to exploit their estates in every possible way, even if it meant unaristocratic activities like building charcoal blast-furnaces or digging drift mines, while, at the same time, English farmers were not narrow-minded, unambitious peasants. Thanks to their help, industry made a quicker and surer start than it would otherwise have done.

Moreover, there were two kinds of indirect help which went on for much longer. In the first place rents and profits were often deposited in country banks, while the banks in turn made loans to business men. However, it was mainly small land-owners who saved, such as widows or clergymen of advanced years. Also, farmers and manufacturers were likely to need short-term loans of working capital at the same time – that is, in the late summer. Farmers were bringing in the harvest, while manufacturers were trying to accumulate stocks for the spending which followed it.

Secondly, there was investment in transport, and this was more important than bank deposits. Farmers and land-owners probably invested as much money in turnpike roads and canals, in proportion to their wealth, as any other class. An example from Berkshire shows how they could benefit. Dealers in Wantage bought barley from the farms on the downs, and then sent it to Wallingford for dispatch down the Thames to London. In the early 1750s the annual average was about 50000 bushels. Then the road from Wantage to Wallingford was turnpiked, and by the 1770s the annual average was 113000 bushels. Generally agriculturalists were only interested in projects like this, that were of direct value to themselves, but once a canal or a turnpike had been built, people in industry could use it as well.

The pattern with labour is broadly similar. In the first part of the eighteenth century there were changes that encouraged an outflow of labour from agriculture to industry. We have seen that this was a time when population was static, grain production was increasing, and prices, in consequence, were falling. The only arable farmers who could prosper at all were those on the light soils of, for example, the chalk and limestone escarpments. Clay farmers had to concentrate on livestock, which meant they employed less labour. As a result, the workers turned to domestic industry. There were, for instance, lace-making in Devon, Bedfordshire and Buckinghamshire, hosiery in Nottinghamshire, Derbyshire and Leicestershire, and nail-making in the West Midlands.

Later the supply dwindled. At one time it was thought that the enclosure movement drove numerous unemployed labourers and dispossessed smallholders to the towns, but, in fact, many of the new farming methods needed extra workers, so that the numbers engaged in agriculture increased from 1.7 million in 1801 to 2.1 million in 1851. It is true that many people did migrate to the towns, but that was because of an increase in the rural population and not of changes in farming.

So far we have been dealing with supply – food, raw materials, foreign currency, capital, business talent and labour. However, since so many people were connected with farming, demand was also important. One problem is to decide whether the people who bought most goods were the wealthy, but comparatively few, land-owners and large tenant farmers, or the poor, but comparatively numerous, small-holders and labourers. If it was the former, then the agricultural sector was the best market at times when food prices were high. If it was the latter, then it was better for food prices to be low, since real wages rose, and labourers could spend more on manufactured goods. Low food prices would of course increase the purchasing power of industrial workers as well.

Such statistics as there are seem to show that industrial output rose most rapidly when food prices were high:

Index Numbers of Output of Home Industries and Wheat Prices (1700 = 100)

Home industries			Wheat prices
1700	100	–1700	100
1710	98	1700–1710	105
1720	108	1710–1720	109
1730	105	1720–1730	99
1740	105	1730–1740	84
1750	107	1740–1750	84
1760	114	1750–1760	101
1770	114	1760–1770	117
1780	123	1770–1780	136
1790	137	1780–1790	142
1800	152	1790–1800	196

SOURCE: Dean and Cole, pp. 78, 91.

This is confirmed by what we know of social habits. Land-owners certainly did not stint themselves but plunged into debt as a matter of course, and not only the pleasure seekers among them. The seventh Earl of Shaftesbury was incapable of living within his means, complaining, 'Our Blessed Saviour knew every affliction, save that of being in debt'. As for the average English farmer, he was no gold-hoarding peasant, but a man with a taste for good living and, even more important, the will to improve his farm. Labourers, on the other hand, clung to the old values. If wage rates rose, they worked less, contenting themselves with the same wages and welcoming the extra leisure. We know, too, from numerous budgets collected by men like F.M. Eden, that after he had bought his food and paid his rent, the ordinary working man had little money left to spend on industrial goods.

If we can assume, then, that it was farmers and land-owners who bought most manufactured goods, we can link the changing value of the farming community as a market to the vicissitudes in their fortunes. As we have seen, they were most prosperous from 1780 until the end of the Napoleonic Wars. Rents and farm profits rose, so land-owners indulged in high living, while farmers disgusted William Cobbett by buying luxuries like carpets, curtains and pianos. After the war, prices fell. Rents tended to fall too, so land-owners had to divert money to investment in their estates; land drainage, for example, did little to stimulate industry. Also, farmers were none too prosperous and traders in the market towns complained that they did not spend as lavishly as before. However, by the nineteenth century the large towns were good markets for their own products. The farmers and land-owners had done their heavy buying when industry needed their money far more.

However, this question of food prices is by no means simple. So far we have shown how high prices helped industry, but if they were low it meant that employers could pay lower wages, an important consideration for them. Industry, indeed, stood to gain, whether food prices were high or low, but, on balance, it looks as if it gained more when they were high.

Finally, on the credit side, we must note that it was agriculture that found most of the money to pay for the Napoleonic Wars. From 1803 to 1814 taxes levied on incomes from trade and industry rose 10 per cent while taxes on land and agricultural incomes rose 60 per cent. Had industry paid its full share, it must have suffered a check.

There is, however, a debit side, since in one way, though quite unintentionally, the aristocrats did a great deal to hamper industry. They were the select few, the magic circle into which every social climber wished to break. It was indeed possible to enter it, but the cost was enormous. As Jane Austen said, a man with £10000 a year was as good as a lord. She did not add that he must have the income from land, since that was something she would have taken for granted. Consequently any merchant or manufacturer who made his fortune, bought an estate. Arkwright, who prospered more than any other man of his day, was worth £2½ million when he died, and £2 million of that was in land. As a cotton manufacturer, he made a success of spinning coarse yarn by machinery, but when his factories had earned enough to pay his entrance fee into the aristocracy, he did not develop them further. In the next century Sir Josiah John Guest, of the Dowlais Iron Works, paid £335000 for the manor of Canford in Dorset, without knowing whether it would make him a penny. Largely that was to please his wife, Lady Charlotte, who came from the aristocracy but had demeaned herself by marrying into trade.

It is clear that agriculture played a vital part in the Industrial Revolution. It is also clear that its comparative importance declined with the passing years. This is what one would expect, for Engel's Law states that, as incomes rise, so the proportion spent on food declines. We can distinguish three periods. The first runs to the 1760s when agriculture led the economy to the threshold of the Industrial Revolution. Farmers were supplying the towns with cheap food: they were earning foreign currency with exports: the farming community was supplying industry with capital and business men: agriculture still produced a high proportion of industry's raw materials: the success of the light soil farmers in growing wheat caused domestic crafts to spawn in the clay vales. In the next phase, to the end of the Napoleonic Wars, population pressure ended most of these advantages, but there were important compensations. Farmers

and land-owners prospered, so that they were good customers for industrial goods. They were also able to shoulder most of the burden of wartime taxation. That high prosperity declined somewhat in the third phase from 1815 to 1850; but even during these years, agriculture still underpinned the economy by producing all the basic foods for a population which was by then growing more rapidly than it has done at any other period.

However, to say that agriculture was an indispensable part of the Industrial Revolution does not necessarily mean that it was the prime cause. We have seen how its importance declined, while it takes far more than changes in agriculture to explain, for example, the growth of the iron industry, the meteoric rise of cotton, and the building of the railway network.

8 Case history: Coke of Norfolk and the Holkham Estates 1776–1842

Thomas William Coke

In the history of the agricultural revolution few men have been more revered than Thomas William Coke, otherwise known as Coke of Norfolk. He is said to have adopted the best farming practices of his day, and to have encouraged his tenants and neighbours to follow his example, so transforming West Norfolk from near-desert to one of the most productive areas in Britain. More than that, it is claimed that, by his annual sheep shearings, he spread the gospel of good farming throughout the country.

Such is the picture given to us by Lord Ernle and others. However, they drew it largely from two of Coke's contemporaries, Edward Rigby and Lord Spencer, and both these men had no other source than Coke himself. This great man, though, was a pageant-maker, given to boasting and exaggeration, so it is not surprising that he has seemed larger than life. However, in 1973 R.A.C. Parker produced his admirable book *Coke of Norfolk*, based on the records of the Holkham estate, so we now have a more objective account.

For one thing Coke did not inherit an estate of sandy wastes. There had been striking progress in Norfolk agriculture since the seventeenth century, so that all Coke had to do was to follow trends already well established, for example by his great uncle and predecessor, the first Earl of Leicester. However, Coke did so with success.

In the first place, he consolidated his estates, selling detached portions in various parts of England, and buying land in Norfolk.

Secondly he combed out the tangled mess of the open-field villages by engrossing and enclosing. For example, between 1780 and 1816 he spent £50000 buying land which lay intermingled with his own. Where it was needed in any village, he rounded everything off with an enclosure act.

Thirdly, he encouraged his tenants to farm well. He tried to stop them taking two straw crops in succession, and encouraged them to adopt the seed drill. While he did not introduce Southdowns to Norfolk, it was he who proved that they were better for that county than either New Leicesters or merinos. He also introduced Devon cattle. He vilified the native breeds of livestock, telling his tenants that if they could afford to keep them they could afford to pay him higher rents. Unfortunately some of the leases had clauses which contradicted each other: Francis Blaikie, who later became Coke's steward, called them 'the incomprehensibles'. Parker thinks that, on the whole, tenants farmed as they pleased.

Finally, Coke indulged in a marvellous piece of showmanship. He ran Park Farm at Holkham as a model farm and held sheep-shearings each year. They were magnificent, so it was irreverent of people to call them 'Coke's Clippings'. Almost anyone was sure of a warm welcome with free hospitality for the three or four days that the proceedings lasted. There were several important activities and the shearing of the sheep was not one of them. Coke gave silver cups for good work like breeding improved livestock, making water-meadows, measuring the progress of horses fed on swedes, and conducting experiments to show that drilling was better than broadcasting. There was a display of farm machinery. The guests toured Park Farm, and other show-farms on the estate. There was much eating and drinking, the afternoon dinner being the climax of the day. During it there were toasts to the King, to visiting notables and to such things as 'Breeding in all its branches' or 'A fine fleece and a fat carcase'. Sometimes a favourite tenant had his turn, as in 1808 when it was 'Mr Reeve, and may his example of good husbandry be followed throughout the United Kingdom'. Finally, there was a sale of livestock. Visitors paid fancy prices so that the takings more than met the expense of the shearing: in 1806, for example, Coke collected £2234.19s.

The most striking improvements to the estates came after 1816, when Coke appointed Francis Blaikie as his steward. Blaikie was a dour, humourless man, but hard-working and

Coke inspecting his Southdown sheep

29

dedicated. Moreover, he expected others to mind their duty as he did his own. He spoke for all of us when he told Stocks, a local solicitor, 'I assure you nothing gives me greater pleasure than when I hear the word "finished" pronounced, as applied to Legal and Official business'. (Parker, p. 136) The tenants felt his presence, too. He gave them pamphlets he had written, along with plenty of advice, and he wrote reports on them. John Overman, he said, 'was a very deserving, industrious and persevering good Tenant', while Charles Hill on the other hand had reduced his farm to 'a disgusting spectacle' (ibid., p. 137).

The three main developments in Blaikie's time were the enforcement of leases, an increase in the size of farms and the spread of the Norfolk four-course system.

Blaikie was not the man for convenants that contradicted each other, or for tenants who pleased themselves. He scrapped the 'incomprehensibles', drew up a blank form for leases and set out a variety of courses, each suitable for a particular soil. There was a penalty of £50 an acre for having two white straw crops following each other, and Blaikie would not allow anyone to sow more than half his land with cereals. His aim, he said, was 'to convince a Farmer that it is not to his advantage to take *quite* as many corn crops from the land he occupies as it will bear' (ibid., p. 141).

Farms had been increasing in size long before Blaikie's time, but he helped them to grow still further. Between 1780 and 1851 the number of farms of less than 500 acres remained about the same, but those of over 500 acres increased from eighteen to thirty-four.

The spread of the Norfolk four-course rotation meant an increase in the output of cereals. This was how the East Anglian farmers first of all took advantage of the high wartime prices, and then made up for the fall that came afterwards. Blaikie did not altogether approve, and his contribution was to prevent farmers from ruining their land with too many cereals. However, the spread of the Norfolk four-course rotation became possible on soil that would not have tolerated it before, because farmers bought fertilisers. At first they used powdered oilcake and bonemeal, and later, nitrate of soda, superphosphates and guano.

So far we have only modified the traditional picture of Coke of Norfolk by giving a fair share of credit to his predecessors and to his steward. However, we will now look at the finances of the estate.

Lord Leicester left debts of £90000, an unfinished mansion and, ironically, a will that required good housekeeping from his heirs.

The Norfolk estates were settled, which meant no one could sell them: £2000 a year was to be spent on Holkham Hall until it was finished; £3000 a year was to be paid into a sinking fund until all debts were extinguished.

Thomas William Coke outshone his illustrious great uncle. His income rose from £17000 nett in 1776 to £29000 in 1815, but his expenses rose even faster. In the first place he had a family to support. The wife of Lord Leicester's son, Lady Mary, was so inconsiderate as to live until 1811, spending £2000 every year; Coke's mother had £3000 a year; three daughters were married at £30000 each. Next, there was a charge of £4000 a year interest on Lord Leicester's debts. Local politics took perhaps £40000, for Coke was determined to play the great man. Household expenses mounted, so that in 1822 they were £12000, while Thomas William's 'personal spending' was £4000 a year. There was, though, one piece of expenditure from which he shrank, and that was the £3000 a year that Lord Leicester's will required him to pay into the sinking fund: that was quietly forgotten. By 1882 Coke owed £230000, and in the same year, aged sixty-eight, he acquired a young wife, and later an infant son.

Coke had been guilty of other mismanagement. Wanting to concentrate his estates in Norfolk, he sold land in Lancashire, which was reasonable enough, but he forgot that there is coal in Lancashire and did not reserve his mineral rights. It nearly broke Blaikie's heart when he realised what vast wealth his employer had thrown away.

Then in 1821 and 1822 came a major depression in farming, so that the tenants could not pay their rents. There was no hope of meeting expenses, and Blaikie was scared his employer would die. It was not that he loved the man, but if that happened, the infant son would become a ward in Chancery, and the Chancellor would insist on the payment of the arrears to the sinking fund. They were £57000. Happily for the estate, Coke did not die and, happily for Coke, his steward and his London solicitor, P.A. Hanroth, had enough character to take him in hand. He was at the time more interested in preparing a will full of the most lavish bequests than he was in facing his financial problems. Blaikie and Hanroth saved him by selling lands in Buckinghamshire for £127000, and using the cash to reduce his debt.

Coke did invest in his estates. How much is not clear, but in his declining years he boasted of £500000, and this must have been no understatement. Spread over the sixty-six years that he held the estates, it is an annual average of about £7500. Assuming it is correct, we can compare it with the £12000 household expenses of 1822, and the 'personal spending' of £4000.

We have yet to mention the Dungeness Lighthouse, the lease of which came to Lord Leicester as part of his wife's dowry. In all the major ports around the coast there were men who, along with their other occupations, acted as the Earl's agents. Every ship that passed the lighthouse paid one penny for each ton of its weight, and was not allowed to discharge its cargo until it had done so. From about £2000 a year in the 1760s the tolls increased to something like £6500 a year by the 1820s. Coke was supposed to keep the light in good order, but one night in 1817 a certain Captain Popplewick found it was not burning. After investigation it turned out that the keeper was seventy-eight and his wife seventy-seven and that even when the aged pair managed to light their fire the rain sometimes leaked in and extinguished it. The scandal added to a growing dislike of privately owned lighthouses. In 1836 an Act of Parliament allowed Trinity House to buy out the leases. Coke accepted £21000 for Dungeness.

Parker says that because of the lighthouse, 'the Coke's shared in the advancing commercial prosperity of Britain and Europe'. So indeed they did, but how much of the money was squandered on 'household expenses' and 'personal expenses'? The income from the lighthouse was probably more than Coke spent on his estates, which means that measured in hard cash he contributed absolutely nothing to the economic life of the country.

PROBLEMS

1 Draw up a balance sheet for the enclosure movement. What were the gains and losses to the country as a whole, and to different social groups? Read what the Hammonds said about enclosures. How have their views been challenged in recent years?

2 How and why did the pace of parliamentary enclosure vary? How important was parliamentary enclosure in relation to the whole enclosure movement?

3 Estimate the importance of the landed aristocracy in promoting agriculture. How far did they influence the economy as a whole? Consider such men as the Duke of Bridgewater, as well as others like Coke of Norfolk.

4 Examine the causes for the increase in wheat production down to 1850. By what means was this achieved, at different periods?

5 Describe the changes which you would expect happened between 1700 and 1850 in (a) a Devonshire dairy farm, and (b) a Norfolk mixed farm.

6 Why did historians once give the second half of the eighteenth century as the first stage of the agricultural revolution? What evidence suggests it began much earlier?

7 Why was progress in agriculture slow compared with that in certain industries, like cotton? Is it correct to speak of a revolution in agriculture?

8 How far was the growth of agriculture a prerequisite of industrial growth? How far were agriculture and industry interdependent?

9 How did agriculture and population influence each other? Did the growth of agriculture stimulate population, or was it the other way round?

10 How was agriculture affected at different times by (a) a shortage of labour (How is modern farming technology affecting the rural population today?), and (b) a surplus (look at the working of the Old Poor Law)?

11 What links are there between the growth of agriculture and transport? Why did railways have more effect than turnpike roads or inland waterways?

12 Which was better for industrial growth, low food prices or high?

FURTHER READING

Caird, James. *English Agriculture in 1850–1851*. Cass, 1968.

Chambers, J. D. and Mingay, G. E. *The Agricultural Revolution*. Batsford, 1966.

Cobbett, William. *Rural Rides*. Everyman ed. 1941.

Ernle, Lord. *English Farming Past and Present*. 1st ed. 1912; Heinemann, 1951; Cassell, 6th ed. 1968.

Fussell, G. E. *The Farmer's Tools*. Andrew Melrose, 1952.

—— *The English Dairy Farmer 1500–1900*. Cass, 1966.

Hammond, J. L. and Barbara. *The Village Labourer*. Longmans, 1906.

Hasbach, W. A. *History of the English Agricultural Labourer*. 1908; Cass, 1966.

Hoskins, W. G. *The Midland Peasant*. Macmillan, 1957.

——. *The Making of the English Landscape*. Penguin, 1970.

Hoskins, W. G. and Stamp, L. Dudley. *The Common Lands of England and Wales*. Collins, 1963.

Jones, E. L. *Agriculture and the Industrial Revolution*. Blackwell, 1974.

Kerridge, Eric. *The Agricultural Revolution*. Allen & Unwin, 1967.

Orr, John. *A Short History of British Agriculture*. O.U.P., 1922.

Orwin, C. S. *A History of English Farming*. Nelson, 1949.

Orwin, C. S. and C. S. *The Open Fields*. 1938; Oxford, 3rd ed. 1954.

Parker, R. A. C. *Enclosures in the 18th Century*. Historical Association, 1960.

——. *Coke of Norfolk*. O.U.P., 1973.

Riches, Naomi. *The Agricultural Revolution in Norfolk*. 1937; Cass, 1967.

Tate, W. E. *The English Village Community and the Enclosure Movement*. Gollancz, 1967.

Thompson, F. M. L. *English Landed Society in the 19th Century*. Routledge & Kegan Paul, 1963.

Power

9 Windmills and water-mills

WINDMILLS

Windmills have done all manner of work, like fulling cloth and sawing timber, but generally they have not been much employed in the manufacturing industry. Their two main uses were grinding corn and pumping water to drain land. They first appeared in England in the twelfth century and, except in hilly or mountainous districts where there was plenty of fast-flowing water, almost every village soon had one.

The earliest was the post mill. So that the sails could face the wind, the whole body turned, being moved with a tail pole which the miller used as a lever. The post on which the mill pivoted was supported by four massive timbers, arranged like the sloping corners of a pyramid. They were often enclosed in a brick roundhouse which protected them from the weather, and also served as a store.

Later, perhaps from the fifteenth century, there were tower mills and smock mills. A tower mill is circular, built of brick or stone. A smock mill is octagonal. It may have a brick or stone base, perhaps several storeys high, but the upper part has a timber framework covered in weather-boarding. The tapering octagonal shape is said to look like a man in a smock. With both kinds the body of the mill and the machinery stay in place, so that only a cap at the top swivels to face the wind. Their construction is more demanding of the wheelwright than is a post mill, but it taxes the carpenter a good deal less.

There were two problems with the earlier mills. In the first place the working parts were almost all of wood, which wore out quickly, and secondly, tending the mill was a full-time job. We have already seen how the miller had to 'wind' his sails by hand, and that was not all. Wind varies in strength as well as direction, so he had to adjust his sails constantly. They were of canvas on a wooden framework and had to be reefed and unreefed, like the sails of a ship. Stopping the mill for reefing was inconvenient, but a sudden gale could

Post mill. With this mill, the whole body turns to face the wind. The four timbers on which the mill pivots are inside the roundhouse.

To turn the sails into the wind there is a fantail. When the fantail has its edge to the wind, it is still, but when the wind strikes it from the side it revolves, turning the wheels below it which are resting on the ground, and so moving the whole body of the mill. Before the fantail was invented, the miller had to swivel the mill himself with the help of a tail-pole, which meant he had to watch constantly for changes in the direction of the wind.

The sails are of the improved kind with variable pitch and with shutters that fly open and 'spill' wind if there is a sudden gust.

Tower mill. Here, only the cap of the mill turns, the machinery remaining in place in the tower. It is possible to see the 'spider', a complicated system of levers in the centre of the sails. This enables the miller to regulate the shutters from inside.

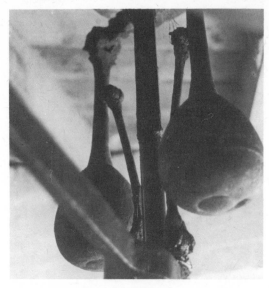

Windmill governor. As the machinery turns, the iron weights spin, like the chairs on a merry-go-round. Owing to centrifugal force, the faster they go the farther they fly outwards and upwards. As they do so, they raise the lever below them which closes the gap between the millstones.

mean disaster. If caught by one the miller had a choice: he could let the sails run away, wrecking themselves and the machinery, or lean on his brake, which would then send out a shower of sparks, perhaps starting a fire. Another unpleasant possibility was being 'back-winded'. A gust, striking the back of the sails, might blow the top off the mill.

From 1750 onwards there were improvements, which reduced the nervous strain on millers as well as making their mills more efficient.

Millwrights began to use cast iron in the cog-wheels and other working parts. Then there was the centrifugal governor. If the millstones began to turn too quickly, the gap between them was closed, so that they continued to grind thoroughly. In 1745 Edmund Lee patented the fantail which worked like a weather-vane, making sure that the sails always faced the wind. John Smeaton found that sails were more efficient if they were twisted, similar to a propeller, instead of having the same pitch along their entire length. In 1772 Andrew Meikle invented a sail that had shutters, like a venetian blind, instead of canvas. The shutter flew open if there was a sudden gust of wind, and all the miller had to do was adjust a spring from time to time, instead of reefing and unreefing canvas. Cubbitt's sails, patented in 1817, worked on the same lines, but were completely automatic.

WATER-MILLS

There were water-wheels in Britain in Roman times, and the Saxons built them as well. Domesday Book records no less than 5000. The early mills were for grinding corn, but water is such a good source of power that other industries began to use it. Long before Arkwright invented power spinning, men in the woollen industry had fulling mills. In mining they used water power to crush ores and, where possible, to drive pumps; it became essential for the iron industry, powering blast-furnace bellows, trip-hammers, rolling and slitting mills, and drills to shape the bores of cast-iron cannon.

The simplest wheel merely dips its floats in the current of a stream, and the miller hopes that the water-level will not rise or fall too much. If there is a small head of water then it is possible to hurry the stream along by sending it down a short slope, which gives the undershot wheel. Wherever they could, though, they had an overshot wheel. Here the water must be higher than the wheel and is carried above it in a wooden chute called a launder. The wheel has buckets instead of floats and it is the weight of the water in them that turns the wheel, not the force of a current.

Overshot wheels are the most powerful, but where there is not quite enough head of water for one, then a breastshot wheel is a good compromise. Here the water is caught between

Stream

Undershot

Breastshot

Overshot

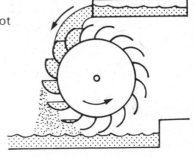

Pitchback

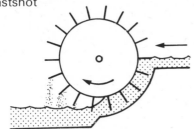

Types of water-wheel

the floats and the curved masonry that follows their circumference. As it is anxious to escape at the bottom, it turns the wheel with a fair velocity. A later type was the pitchback, which is a variation of the overshot. One advantage is that the launder does not have to dangle out so far over the top of the wheel, and another is that the wheel turns in the same direction as the flow of the stream at the bottom. This is useful if ever the water rises in time of flood and reaches the buckets. 'Backing up in the tail race' was a problem for many mills. Too much water can stop a wheel, as well as too little.

For centuries millers were able to squander water. They had far more than they needed, and their only problem was to make wheels big enough to work their machinery. Efficiency did not matter. During the Industrial Revolution, though, it was essential to use every horsepower the streams and rivers could give, so a lot of thought went to improving water-wheels.

One thing that concerned engineers was turbulence. Somehow the water had to be persuaded that its job was to turn the wheel and not waste its energy in a lot of spraying and splashing. With an undershot wheel, it first rebounded from the front of the floats as they came down, and then swirled and eddied behind them as they struggled upwards. In an overshot wheel it might shoot 6 feet high as it fought with the air in the bucket.

It was J.V. Poncelet who took the under-shot wheel in hand, increasing its efficiency from 20 per cent to over 60 per cent. He did it by curving the floats, so that the water, on striking, flowed up them instead of rebounding. Then, when their work was done, the floats left the surface at right angles to it, smoothly and gracefully, instead of being sucked back by a lot of turbulence. A similar curving to take the flow of the water improved the buckets of overshot wheels, but there was still the problem of the airlock. Sir William Fairbairn solved it by having a bucket within a bucket. The inner one had holes in the bottom and the air escaped through them so that both buckets filled smoothly.

A man who did valuable work on water-wheels was John Smeaton. He constructed models and carried out all sorts of experiments to find the best designs. Another earnest researcher was John Banks, who produced his *Treatise on Mills* in 1795. Here are 172 pages of mathematical formulae and descriptions of experiments, which show how thoroughly he investigated the problems of the water-wheel. Nor did he work alone:

I have not entrusted entirely to my own observations, but have been assisted in the whole by one or more gentlemen well acquainted with the subject, by my eldest son and by my wife who, THOUGH A WOMAN, is perhaps as accurate in making experiments in philosophy and some branches of chymistry as most men. (op. cit., p. x)

Improving the buckets and floats meant that wheels could generate up to 200 horse-power, so they had to be strongly made. Spokes were giant levers, wrenching away at their axle and, unless something was done, they would be sure to tear themselves loose. One answer was to have stronger shafts, so John Smeaton made them of cast iron with projecting sockets to house the spokes. In about 1800 Thomas Hewes found a better way, when he invented the suspension wheel. It had teeth all round its rim, so it was in effect a huge cog. The drive was taken from the rim, and provided it was placed where the water was doing its work, there was no strain on the spokes, other than the weight of the wheel itself so they could be made quite slender.

The sluice-gate was improved by John Rennie. The old type was pulled up like a guillotine, as on a weir today. Rennie's was opened by lowering it, the advantage being that it gave a higher head of water.

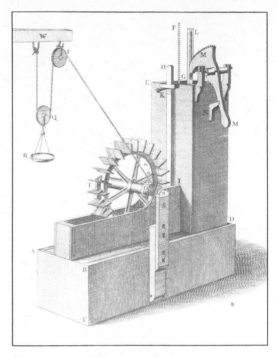

Smeaton's model water-wheel

Siting a mill was usually a problem, particularly if it had to process heavy materials that could not be carried long distances. Much valuable iron-ore remained in the ground because it was too far from reliable water power. None the less, a lot could be done to adapt a mill to its site. If there was a good flow to a stream, but no great head, then there could be an undershot wheel of some width. The Kennet and Avon Company built one at Claverton, near Bath, which was 24 feet wide; they used it to pump water from the river into their canal. On the other hand, if there was a good head of water but only a small flow, the wheel, though narrow, could have a large diameter. The largest in Britain is the 'Lady Isabella' on the Isle of Man, which is a pitchback wheel 72 feet across. The Great Laxey Company used it for pumping a lead-mine 2000 feet deep.

Another way was to adapt the site to the mill. The heroic Samuel Greg, who owned the Quarry Bank Mill at Styal in Cheshire, dug a tunnel three-quarters of a mile long, under several waterfalls. It lowered his tail race 15 feet, doubling his head of water to 30 feet. He then put in a 100 horsepower wheel, 32 feet in diameter and 21 feet wide. It all cost him £21000, but he doubled the capacity of his mill, and the wheel lasted from when it was built, in 1818, until 1904. Even then it was replaced not by a steam-engine, or by an electric motor, but by a water turbine.

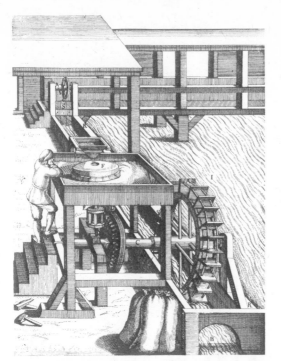

Corn mills with undershot and overshot wheels, seventeenth century. These are primitive wheels, of an elementary design and generating little power. Almost all the working parts are of wood.

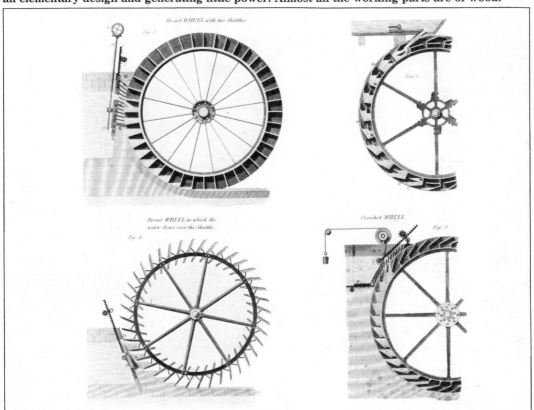

Advanced water-wheels. These wheels show some of the developments that had taken place by 1820 – for example, sophisticated sluice-gates, well-designed buckets, and the use of cast iron.

The Lady Isabella water-wheel on the Isle of Man

10 The steam-engine

It had been known for a long time that there is power in steam, and from as far back as the classical period there are stories like the one of the temple doors that opened mysteriously at the behest of a fire on the altar. Steam interested Leonardo da Vinci, while in the seventeenth century there were some important experiments. In 1690, for example, a Frenchman, Denis Papin, showed it was possible to use steam both to raise a piston and to create a vacuum. However, the first man to make an engine that worked for its living was an Englishman, Thomas Savery.

The late seventeenth century was a frustrating time for Cornish mine-owners, since they knew they were sitting on fortunes in the shape of tin- and copper-ores, but they could not reach them because, unless they had water power, they had no way of pumping deep down. It was to solve their problems that Savery made his 'Miners' Friend'.

As Papin had already shown, steam can be used in two ways. The first, and most obvious, is to raise it to a high pressure and then make it push something. The alternative is to fill a container with it, so that all the air is driven out, and then cool it so that it condenses into water. It will then occupy only 1600th part of its former volume, so there is an almost perfect vacuum. The atmospheric pressure on a vacuum is 14½ pounds to the square inch, which is a respectable source of power. Savery used both methods in one machine.

It had a large receiver, in which a vacuum was created, by condensing steam. The pressure of the atmosphere then filled it with water from the mine. Next, high-pressure steam forced the water the rest of the way to the surface. Unfortunately, the atmosphere could only lift the water 25 feet, which meant the engine had to be that height from the bottom of the mine. Also, Savery was unable to make a boiler that would stand more than two or three atmospheres, so he could only raise enough pressure to take the water another 60 feet. However, the Cornish miners already had pumps that worked to a depth of over 90 feet so they were not interested in Savery's invention. What Savery had done, though, was to show it was indeed possible to make a practical engine, and also to demonstrate that it was easier to use atmospheric rather than steam

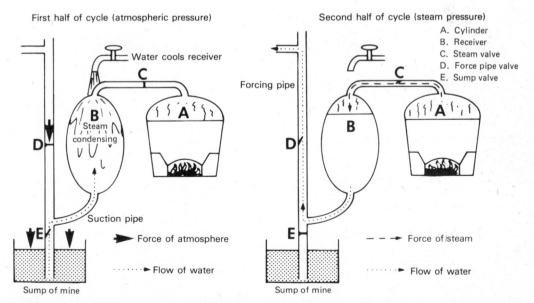

Savery engine. The engine has two receivers working their cycles alternately, so that pumping is continuous.
The engine is 25 feet from the bottom of the mine, which is the height to which air pressure will raise the water. High-pressure steam then forces it the rest of the way to the surface.

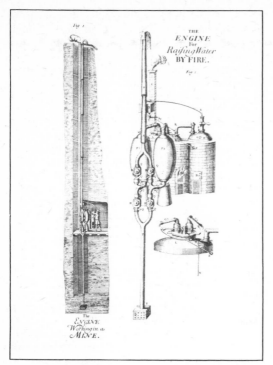

Savery engine

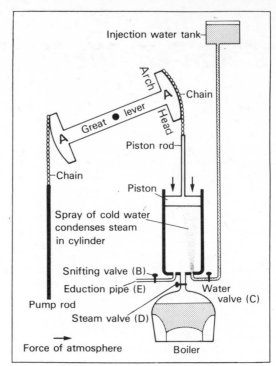

Newcomen engine

pressure. The man who acted on this idea was Thomas Newcomen.

We know little of Newcomen's life. He was baptised in 1663, and when he grew up he became a blacksmith and ironmonger. He had a partner called John Calley who was a plumber and tinsmith, so that between them they could handle a variety of metals. In 1705 they went into partnership with Savery, so presumably they had become interested in steamengines by then. In 1707 Newcomen settled at Dartmouth, which was near some tin-mines, but his first successful engine was probably the one he built for Tipton Colliery in Staffordshire. This was in 1712. He worked under the umbrella of Savery's patent, but when Savery died it went to a syndicate of London business men. They made a lot of money from royalties; the inventor died in poverty in 1729.

Why Newcomen did not take out a patent of his own is not clear, though it may be that he could not afford one. Not every inventor had the money, perhaps as much as £700, to pay for a patent, and even if he did he needed to be rich to fight legal battles with people who pirated his ideas. Even the great Arkwright lost, Crompton did not even try, and if James Watt succeeded it was because he had Boulton alongside him. Possibly, then, Newcomen thought Savery was the protector he needed but, if that was so, he made a mistake.

The figure above shows, in a simplified way, how the Newcomen engine worked. At the top there was a beam called the great lever, pivoted in the middle. It had two arch heads (A and A) so that, as it rocked, the piston rod and the pump rod remained vertical. Each rod ended in a chain which followed the curve of the arch head. The engine was adjusted so that the weight of the pump would almost, but not quite, raise the piston. There had to be a little help from the steam otherwise the piston might rise too quickly and draw air into the cylinder. As it was, the steam was able to build up enough pressure to raise the piston and also to drive out any air through the snifting valve (B). Valve C was now opened and a jet of water shot into the cylinder. The tank feeding it was over 30 feet high, so the jet hit the underside of the piston with some violence, breaking into a fine spray that quickly condensed the steam. Valve D was closed and the pressure of the atmosphere drove down the piston. This was the working stroke which raised the pump rods. Afterwards, the cycle began again. Water from the injection and the condensed steam ran away through the eduction pipe (E).

The most difficult part to make was the cylinder. In his first engines Newcomen used brass, because it is easy to work, but it was so expensive that he went over to cast iron. This

40

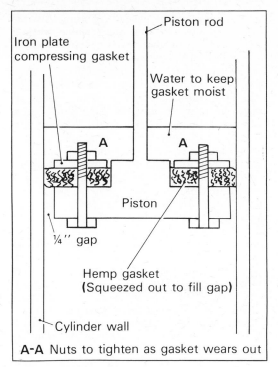

Piston rod

Iron plate
compressing gasket

Water to keep
gasket moist

A   A

Piston

¼″ gap

Hemp gasket
(Squeezed out to fill gap)

Cylinder wall

A-A Nuts to tighten as gasket wears out

Newcomen piston

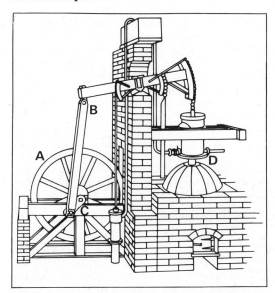

Newcomen engine adapted for rotary motion. The main problem was to compensate for the fact that the piston only worked on its downward strokes. This was solved by having a flywheel (A), and a heavy connecting rod (B), which fell under its own weight, so turning the crank (C) while the piston (D) was rising. Two problems were intractable: one was a tendency for the piston to hesitate at the top of its stroke while waiting for condensation to begin inside the cylinder, and the other was fuel consumption.

is extremely hard and difficult to bore. The implement they had was a wheel with cutters wedged in the rim and which they could not hold firmly enough to guide properly. The sides of a cylinder were never straight and parallel, so the piston had to compensate for its deficiencies. They made it the shape shown in the figure opposite and fitting loosely with about a quarter-inch gap all round. They then formed a gasket from layers of loosely spun hemp. An iron plate, clamped on top of the gasket, squeezed it out so that it filled the gap. It was kept soft and, as was most important, airtight, by floating water on top of the piston.

John Beighton improved the Newcomen engine as early as 1718. He made a system of catches which opened and shut the valves automatically, so that this vital job no longer depended on the uncertain attention of the engine-man – or worse, the engine-boy.

To increase power, they increased size. This was the dinosaur period of the steam-engine. For example in 1775 John Smeaton built an engine for Chasewater Mine in Cornwall which had a piston 6 feet in diameter with a stroke of 9 feet. There were three boilers, each 15 feet across, the great lever was 22 feet long, and the whole engine was 70 feet high. It generated 76 horsepower. Smeaton also made several improvements which greatly increased efficiency.

However, Smeaton's engines were exceptional. Most 'common engines' had cylinders that were badly bored, boilers that were too small, steam pipes that were the wrong sizes, injection cylinders that were not high enough to give a good jet of water, and working parts that were large and strong to be safe, but needlessly heavy. These engines were only 0.5 per cent efficient, but the owners fed their voracious beasts with all the coal they needed and were quite content with them as long as they did their job. Nearly all Newcomen engines belonged to coal-mines, and as they burnt the waste fuel no one would buy, it did not matter how much they used.

In addition to mine-owners, ironmasters found uses for Newcomen engines. With their pumping action they would work bellows to a blast-furnace and they could be invaluable during a drought, returning water to behind a dam. In a year of normal rainfall such an engine would only be needed for a few weeks, so fuel consumption was not too important. Moreover, all progressive ironworks of the Industrial Revolution were built on coalfields.

Away from the coalfields, however, those who bought a Newcomen engine had to be both rich and desperate, and this was true of only one group, the Cornish mine-owners.

41

There were some attempts to adapt the engine to rotary motion, so that it could drive machinery directly, without involving a water-wheel. Bateman and Sherratt of Manchester solved enough of the problems involved to manufacture engines for the cotton mills. However, they were never completely satisfactory. The Newcomen engine was an excellent servant as long as its owner gave it all the fuel it wanted and only asked it to do pumping. However, there were manufacturers who were thinking longingly of an engine that would give them the services of a water-wheel, without the problems of water supply. Eventually, they had one, thanks to a series of brilliant inventions by James Watt.

Watt was born at Greenock in 1736. He started work as an instrument maker in London, but soon moved back to Glasgow to become a technician at the University. His job was to look after scientific equipment. Here he was befriended by Dr Joseph Black, the Professor of Medicine and Lecturer in Chemistry, and by his successor, John Robinson. They saw that Watt was no ordinary technician and they gave him help and encouragement.

Watt first took an interest in steam when he had a model Newcomen engine to repair. He found he could only persuade it to do a few strokes at a time, so he looked for the reason. He was surprised to discover how large a quantity of cold water had to be injected into the cylinder to condense the steam. Accordingly he tried an experiment which worked the other way round, feeding steam from a kettle, down a pipe and into cold water. He found that a small amount of water in the form of steam would heat a considerably larger amount of cold water to an amazing extent, so much so that he doubted his figures, and checked them again and again. Fortunately Black was at hand, and he explained the mystery with his own theory of latent heat. It was clear, then, that every time the Newcomen engine condensed steam it wasted latent heat, and this was the prime reason for its inefficiency. How could the steam be condensed without cooling the cylinder and piston.

The answer, as Watt discovered, was to condense the steam in a separate vessel. Then the condenser was always cold, while the cylinder was always hot, so it was no longer necessary to waste latent heat by alternately heating and cooling large quantities of iron.

Such was the fundamental principle. Watt thought of it in 1765, but it was 1776 before he and his partner Matthew Boulton began to erect engines for customers, since there were difficult business and technical problems to be solved. Boulton overcame the business worries, while that irascible genius, John Wilkinson, discovered how to bore cylinders with the absolute accuracy the new engine required. Though Wilkinson made exaggerated claims, it is certain that without his help Watt would have failed. However, Watt must be given credit for a series of brilliant discoveries. First, with the aid of his separate condenser and the principle of expansion, he produced a pumping engine that used only a quarter of the fuel burnt by a 'common' engine. This was highly successful in the Cornish tin- and copper-mines, which were far away from the coalfields. Next, he adapted his engine for rotary motion, by inventing the double acting piston, parallel motion and the sun and planet gear, and by pressing into service the centrifugal governor. Here was a revolutionary source of power, economical, smooth in its action, steady, reliable and suitable for all manner of uses.

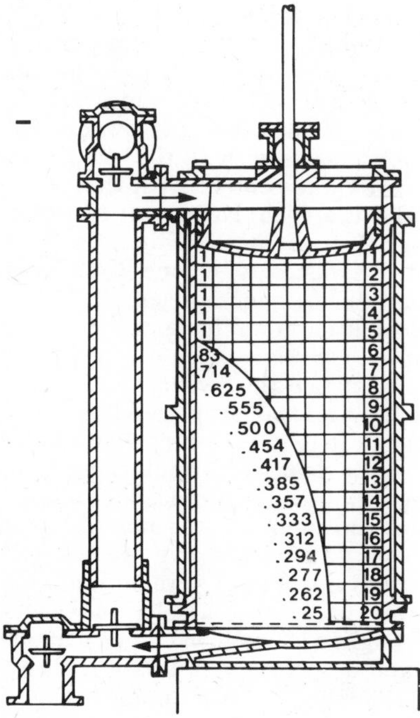

1
1
1
1
.83
.714
.625
.555
.500
.454
.417
.385
.357
.333
.312
.294
.277
.262
.25

2
3
4
5
6
7
8
9
10
11
12
13
14
15
16
17
18
19
20

Expansion engine. If steam is cut off before the piston has finished the stroke, steam which is left in the cylinder will continue to expand, and to drive the piston. Its force decreases, as the diagram shows, but there is a considerable gain in efficiency. If the piston finishes its stroke at full power, the rest of the mechanism has to act as a brake on it. The curve shows how the force of the steam decreases after cut-off, which takes place here when the piston has made a quarter of its stroke.

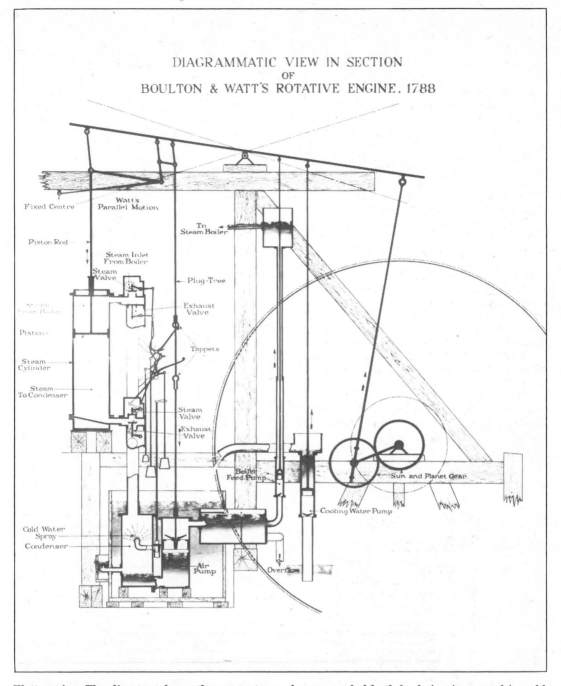

DIAGRAMMATIC VIEW IN SECTION
OF
BOULTON & WATT'S ROTATIVE ENGINE. 1788

Fixed Centre

Watt's Parallel Motion

Piston Rod

To Steam Boiler

Steam Inlet From Boiler

Steam Valve

Plug-Tree

Steam From Boiler

Exhaust Valve

Pistons

Tappets

Steam Cylinder

Steam To Condenser

Steam Valve

Exhaust Valve

Boiler Feed Pump

Sun and Planet Gear

Cooling Water Pump

Cold Water Spray

Condenser

Air Pump

Overflow

Watt engine. The diagram shows the separate condenser, cooled both by being immersed in cold water, and by the injection of a cold-water spray. The air pump emptied the condenser of water which otherwise would have rapidly filled it.

The engine is driven by steam, but only at atmospheric pressure or less. This avoided the problem of exploding boilers.

The piston is double-acting. The steam valve at the top is open, so steam is driving the piston down. For the up-stroke, the steam valve at the bottom will open.

Parallel motion was a system of levers that allowed the piston rod to remain vertical while moving the end of the great lever through the arc of a circle.

The sun and planet gear consisted of two cogged wheels, the 'planet' turning the 'sun'. It was better than the simple crank because it doubled the speed of the axle.

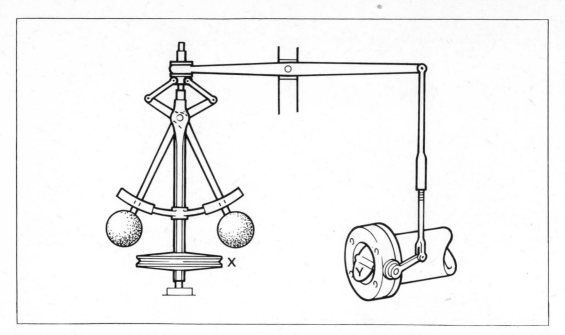

(Above) Governor. The balls are rotated by the pulley (X). If the engine turns too quickly, they fly outwards and the various levers close the steam throttle valve (Y).

(Below) Cylinder and valves of Watt's engine. These are accurate drawings. They show the complexity of Watt's engine and the high level of engineering that went into it.

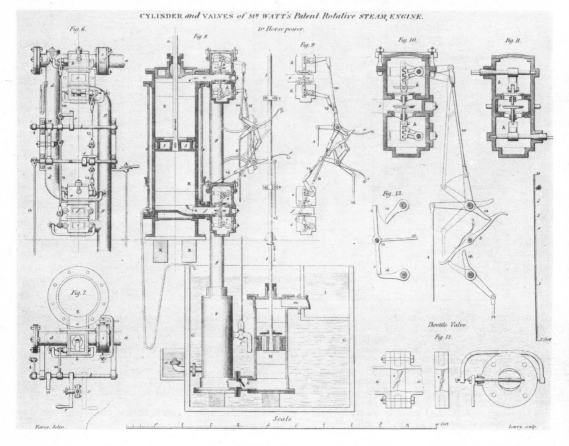

CYLINDER *and* VALVES *of* M.ʳ *WATT'S Patent Rotative STEAM ENGINE.*

When the patent expired in 1800 and Watt retired, he was at the peak of his influence: many people, including the inventor himself, imagined that the steam-engine had reached perfection. However, the story was far from finished.

The most important development in the first half of the nineteenth century was the use of high-pressure steam. Savery had tried to employ it but failed. Newcomen managed without it, and though Watt experimented with it, he decided it was not for him – indeed he roundly condemned anyone who favoured it. One of the pioneers who dared to break with the tradition was Richard Trevithick. In 1802 he patented an engine using a pressure of 45 pounds to the square inch and running at twenty-four strokes a minute. It was simple, cheap, compact and portable. He soon found customers in South Wales and Cornwall, where the miners called them 'puffer engines' because of the noise made by the steam exhaust coming out under pressure. 'Puffers' did not have condensers. There was a set-back, though, when in 1803 a boiler exploded at Woolwich. Admittedly Trevithick's safety-valve was not all it might have been, but he could hardly have anticipated that an engine-boy would jam it shut with a piece of wood and go away, still less that a workman would then come along and stop the engine. As the boiler was of cast iron 1 inch thick, the explosion was a big one. Three people were killed, three more were maimed, and the flow of orders came to an abrupt stop. Trevithick decided he must always provide two safety-valves, one of which would be in a box closed with lock and key. There were more explosions after that, but high-pressure engines made progress in spite of them.

The old-style beam engine was improved, and a new kind, the direct-acting engine, was developed.

One interesting invention was the grasshopper beam. It was half a great lever with both the piston and the connecting rod on the same side of the pivot. It had a curious motion reminiscent of a dog running or, as contemporaries thought, of a grasshopper hopping. An engine with a grasshopper was more compact than one with a great lever. Powered by high-pressure steam, it was just right for the early locomotives.

The full-size beam engine reached its prime in the 'Cornish' engines made by Trevithick and others. As they were for pumping they were single acting like Watt's first engines, but they were much more effective. In the first place they were huge. Cylinders were 7 feet in diameter, with piston strokes of 12 feet, and

Grasshopper engine

great levers were of cast iron weighing up to 30 tons. They used high-pressure steam at 40 pounds to the square inch, which had additional help from a condenser. As it was cut off after just one-tenth of the piston stroke, the engine delivered only a fraction of its possible power, but it was extremely efficient.

Beam engines were reliable, and since they were slow moving they lasted for years. They were manufactured throughout the nineteenth century, the last one being erected as late as 1919. However, they were bound to give way to direct-acting engines, which were more versatile and went at much higher speeds.

A direct-acting engine is one which has no beam; instead the piston is linked directly to the crank by a connecting rod. It will only work with high-pressure steam. Once again there was the problem of making the end of the piston rod travel in a straight line, but after 1820 this was easier to do because of the invention of the planing machine. Engineers could now make a flat surface that was nearly perfect, so it was possible to have a crosshead on the piston rod and run it in guide rails.

To raise high-pressure steam, engine-makers improved their boilers. Savery had made his of copper, which he found was not strong enough. As Newcomen was not interested in pressure, he made his boilers of copper, with lead tops. Copper and lead were expensive, so when wrought iron became more plentiful they used that instead. The boiler

45

shape they favoured was the 'haystack', with its domed top. They increased the heating surface by curving the underside, and also by passing the flue gases right round the lower section of the boiler before sending them up the chimney. For his engines, Watt preferred the longer 'wagon' boiler which took heat from the flue gases by passing them back over the fire to be burnt.

For high pressure, a much greater heating surface was needed. Trevithick built a cylindrical boiler which had a single large tube in the middle, holding the fire. Another way was to have the fire at one end and carry the heat through a number of fairly small tubes. The *Rocket* locomotive had such a boiler.

For extra strength, high-pressure boilers were made of cast iron.

Trevithick high-pressure engine. The engine is direct-acting, which means the piston turns the crank directly without the aid of a beam. The cylinder is inside the boiler to keep it hot.

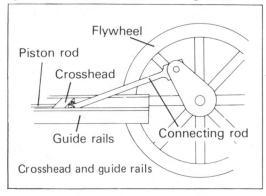

Crosshead and guide rails

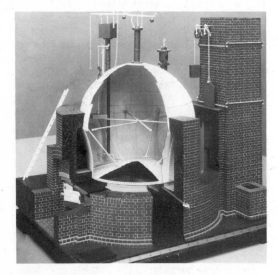

Haystack boiler

Wagon boiler

Trevithick's 'Cornish' boiler

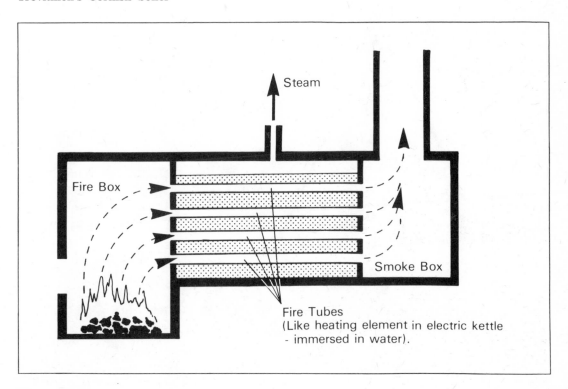

Steam

Fire Box

Smoke Box

Fire Tubes
(Like heating element in electric kettle
- immersed in water).

Tubular boiler

11 Power and the economy

It is a common belief that the Industrial Revolution was also the age of the steam-engine. In 1827 John Farey wrote:

In our populous towns a multitude of steam engines, of all sizes, are continually at work for a great variety of purposes, such as pumping water, grinding corn, sawing timber and stone, rasping logwood, expressing oil from seeds, grinding cutlery, forming lead or copper into sheets or hollow pipes, fulling and scouring woollen cloth, twisting ropes and cables, drawing wire and for every description of laborious employment. We find them also in all extensive breweries and distilleries, in tanneries, soap manufactories, iron foundries and in the national establishments of dock-yards and arsenals. Their number is daily increasing and they are continually applied to new purposes. (A Treatise on the Steam Engine)

Farey, however, was an enthusiast. In fact, traditional forms of power were important for a long time, while steam made only slow progress.

We must not forget muscle power. The horse gin persisted, for example in textile factories, breweries and in the smaller coal-mines, while in countless workshops and little factories, men, women and children worked the machines. Even the sewing-machines which boot and shoe manufacturers introduced in the 1870s were turned by hand or by foot.

As for windmills, in the early nineteenth century they generated more horsepower between them than all the steam-engines put together. There was a growing population, there was more corn to grind, but it was done, not by the new source of power, but by the old one used more efficiently. Windmills were built well into the nineteenth century, and the end came for them not because they were failures but because of other changes. After 1870 corn growing declined in Britain, and

Muscle power

48

there were bulk imports of American wheat. The economical way to grind this was in large, steam-driven mills at the ports.

Water remained important for a long time as well. The 'Lady Isabella' water-wheel, for example, was built as late as 1852. In the Potteries, water-wheels ground corn and mixed clay: at Sheffield they drove tilt-hammers and the cutlers' grinding wheels: in South Wales, they turned the rolling mills for the tin-plate industry: in Lincolnshire they fulled cloth, made paper, sawed timber and crushed bones for fertilisers: almost everywhere they ground corn. During the Industrial Revolution most manufacturers in most industries met their growing needs for power by building more and better water-wheels, not by installing steam-engines. In a few places water power lingered well into the twentieth century, either because the site was particularly good, or because the manufacturer was particularly old-fashioned. When the famous New Lanark Mills closed in 1968 they still had three water turbines that raised, between them, 1000 horsepower. Sticklepath edge-tool factory in Devon went on until about the same time. Here, still on display, are a forge, a grindstone, two trip-hammers and a pair of shears, all in working order and driven by three conventional overshot wheels.

Certainly water power had disadvantages. A flood might stop a wheel for a number of days, and a drought for much longer. To avoid these dangers manufacturers had to go where water supplies were reliable, and this was often in obscure places. The first cotton spinning mills, for example, were built in remote valleys in the Pennines. Also, there is a limit to the power which any one site can supply, and here was a problem that taxed the iron industry especially. For large-scale production it needed to be organised in large units: however, its water supplies decreed that it should be scattered in small works along the banks of the streams in the Weald and the Forest of Dean. As Professor T.S. Ashton said, the industry could not grow until it was freed from 'the tyranny of wood and water'. A new source of power was as important as a new fuel.

None the less, it was water power that made the Industrial Revolution possible. Wind was unreliable, there was not enough strength in human and animal muscles, and steam was still an infant. Meanwhile there were valuable inventions that could not be exploited without mechanical power. Water power filled the gap.

As the traditional forms of power were slow to decline, so steam was slow to grow. Steam-engines were unknown in many industries,

and rare in certain parts of the country. Apart from breweries, there were few in London, because most of its industries were handicrafts. It must have distressed Boulton and Watt to know that, outside their own Soho works, there were only two of their engines in the whole of Birmingham. Here, also, handicrafts were common. By the time their patent expired in 1800, Boulton and Watt had erected some 500 engines. Their average was only 15 h.p. and between them they gave a mere 7500 h.p. Today, a single turbo-generator produces twenty times as much. There were Newcomen engines as well, but probably there were no more than 1200 steam engines in all, giving together less than 20000 h.p. The table shows the growth of steam power through the nineteenth century:

	1800	1850	1870	1907
horsepower	20000	300000	1000000	9700000
(estimated)				

It is clear from this when the steam revolution took place in industry as a whole.

There are, however, important qualifications. In the first place these figures do not include steam locomotives and they were vital for the development of the railways. However, they were not too numerous until the late 1840s, while the railways themselves did not make a significant contribution to the economy until well after 1850.

More important during our period were the colliery engines, and they are not included in any of the figures in the table, save the estimate for 1800. Though the smaller coal-mines made do with horse gins, the larger ones had to have steam, and most employed at least two engines. Usually one was of the Newcomen type, for pumping, while the other was a rotative engine, for winding.

Finally, much of the steam power in manufacturing industry was concentrated in cotton:

Growth of Power in the Cotton Industry

	Steam horsepower	Water horsepower	Imports of raw cotton (millions of pounds)
1838	47000	13000	400
1850	71000	12000	620
1856	88000	9000	800
1870	300000	8000	1100

Clearly then, the importance we attach to steam power must depend to quite an extent on how highly we rate the contribution of cotton to the Industrial Revolution. We return to this point later (see pp. 93 and 194).

12 Case histories

Here we describe the use of water power at contrasting sites. One is on the upper reach of the River Teign, at Fingle Bridge on the eastern edge of Dartmoor. The valley is deep, so it was easy to build a weir a few feet high. It runs diagonally across the stream for extra length, because the longer a weir is, the more slowly water collects behind it during heavy rain. Ideally the water-level should not vary at all. From the weir runs a leat, now empty and in ruins. It is nearly level, so that, effectively, it gains height as the river drops in its valley. The remains of the mill are about a quarter of a mile below the weir. There are some bits and pieces of iron that once formed the shaft of the wheel and its flanges. What type it was is not obvious, though probably it was breastshot. Weir and leat between them gained a head of barely 6 feet, and not all that could have been used for the wheel, since a tail race must have a good fall to stop 'backing up' when there is a flood. There are no millstones and no remains of machinery. They could have ground corn there, crushed ore, or even sawn timber. The mill is typical of hundreds that are scattered, abandoned and forgotten, all over the country.

At the other end of the scale there were Jedediah Strutt's cotton spinning mills at Belper in Derbyshire. The weir was not a simple diagonal but a horseshoe shape, which gave even greater length for the width of the valley. It held back a lake of 14 acres. Between 1786 and 1813 six mills were built here. This is a description of the West Mill, completed in 1796:

The principal of these mills is 200 feet long, 30 feet wide, and six storeys high, and is considered as fireproof, the floor being constructed with brick arches and paved with brick. The two water-wheels which work the machinery in this building, are remarkable as well for their magnitude, as for the singularity of their construction, one of them being upward of 40 feet long, and 18 feet in diameter, and the other 48 feet long, and 12 feet in diameter. (J. Britten and E.W. Brayley, *The Beauties of England and Wales,* Vol. III, 1802)

These were breastshot wheels. There were two of them to allow for floods, the one with the larger diameter working when the river was at its normal level, and the one with the smaller diameter when it rose. The difference in lengths meant both wheels had the same power.

Here then were wooden wheels at their largest and most powerful, but the Strutts moved with the times. About 1810 they gave the West Mill a pair of iron wheels each 21 feet 6 inches in diameter and 15 feet wide. They were overshot, suspended wheels taking the drive from their rims. The water-wheels operated the sluice-gates automatically. The mechanism was connected to a governor and, as more or less machines were working in the mill, so the sluices opened or closed to give the right amount of power.

Belper was a good site, so good that a hydroelectricity generating station was built there in the twentieth century. In other places water gave problems.

We have some detailed accounts of the Coalbrookdale Iron Company in Shropshire. The graph opposite shows how iron output varied with the seasons.

Not only was low output a problem, for if the air blast to the furnace was not strong enough, the iron was of poor quality.

There was a crisis in the 1730s when the manager of the works, Richard Ford, was increasing his sales of steam-engine cylinders, and a partner, James Goldney, had found some good customers for iron at Bristol. Just when they wanted more output, they had two dry years, 1733 and 1734. While Goldney asked urgently for iron, Ford could only send letters of despair. In November 1734 he wrote:

Our Water here continues very Short wch at ye Close of ye year will prove much in our disfavour: there never was Such a Complaint at this time of ye year; I dont think there is a Forge in ye Countrey does half work, but there is no remedy but Patience. (Raistrick, op. cit., p.117)

He did find an alternative to patience, though, which was a horse-driven pump to return water to the pond. In 1742 they replaced it with a Newcomen steam-engine, which solved their problems for a long time. This brought about a much more regular output, with no seasonal changes:

However, when they tried to push production from about 90 tons a month to over a 100 tons, they put a strain on the system, and only managed their increase in the winter months. They must have had thankful hearts when Boulton and Watt sold them economical, reliable engines, and they finished for good with water power and its vagaries.

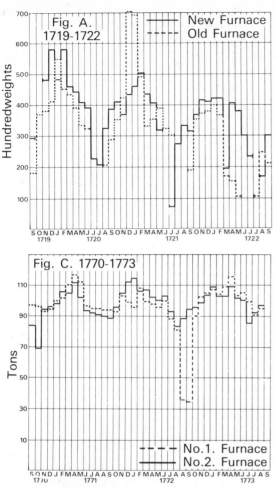

Fig A. Furnace output when entirely dependant upon water-wheel blast driven from Furnace Pool.

Figs. B and C. Furnaces blown by steam-engine and blowing machine.

SOURCE: Raistrick, *Dynasty of Iron Founders – The Darbys and Coalbrookdale*, p. 107.

Iron output at Coalbrookdale

PROBLEMS

1 Investigate animal-powered machines.
2 Why did it take so long to develop an efficient steam-engine? Why was industry even longer adopting steam power?
3 How much did James Watt owe to his associates?
4 How did the development of mechanical power affect transport?
5 How far was mechanical power important in agriculture?
6 Trace the development of the various forms of motive power from 1700 to 1850. Assess the importance of each for industry. Consider, among other things, investment, forms of organisation and effects on the labour force.
7 How did the developments in industry affect the growth of mechanical power?
8 Discuss the view that the importance of the steam-engine in the early nineteenth century had little relation to the total steam horsepower in the country.

FURTHER READING

Hills, Richard, L. *Power in the Industrial Revolution*. Manchester U.P., 1970.
Law, R.J. *James Watt and the Separate Condenser*. Science Museum, London, 1969.
Reynolds, John. *Windmills and Watermills*. Hugh Evelyn, 1970.
Storer, J.D. *A Simple History of the Steam Engine*. John Baker, 1969.

Industry

13 Coal-mining

Coal-mining was not the most progressive of industries. It had started in Roman times, so it was old – more than old enough for owners and workers to be set in their ways and unwilling to accept change. Indeed this showed, for in 1850 there were still many mines where the methods and equipment belonged to the Middle Ages. Also, as late as 1800, coal-mining added not more than 1 per cent to the nation's income and even in 1850 it was only 2 per cent.

However, even if coal itself was not a leading industry, then at least it was essential for others that undoubtedly were, like iron and cotton. Moreover, it is hard to believe that Britain would have been the first country in the world to have an Industrial Revolution, if she had been without her mines.

MINING TECHNIQUES

Having found coal, which was often quite a business in itself, the miners' first task was to reach it. During the Roman period and the Middle Ages they tunnelled into the ground wherever there was an outcrop, but by the sixteenth century much of the coal that was near the surface was worked out, so they had to sink shafts. In the nineteenth century writers were describing shafts as being four times as deep as the dome of St Paul's, or like seven London Monuments piled on top of each other. In the 1830s Staffordshire had a pit 2000 feet deep.

There was little indiscriminate burrowing by the eighteenth century, workings following set patterns. The most common was 'pillar and bord', or 'pillar and stall'. The 'bords' or 'stalls' were underground galleries, which ran at right angles to each other, like the street plan of an American city. Between them were the 'pillars', solid rectangles of untouched coal that supported the roof until the workings had been driven as far as the mine-owner wanted. The men then worked back towards the shaft, removing as much of the pillars as they dared. Sometimes that was not a lot, and two-thirds of the coal might remain in the ground.

Another problem was that, since there were so many galleries, they were difficult to ventilate. None the less, pillar and bord working was the best method when the roof was unsafe – that is, where the rock above the coal was soft or where the seams were at all thick.

An alternative was the 'long wall' method. Two parallel galleries were driven into the seam, and joined by a third running at right angles to them. It was here that the working face, or 'long wall', lay. The miners propped the roof and dug about 4 feet of coal. They then moved their props forward, flinging any unwanted rubble into the open 'gob' they left behind. With the long wall system all the coal was removed. However, it was only practical in mines, for example in parts of Yorkshire and North Somerset, where the seams were narrow and the rocks above the coal were solid.

At the coal-face was the man for whom the shaft and the miles of galleries had been built – the hewer. He needed strength and skill, although his equipment was simple enough. He started his work with a short-headed pick, and cut a slot, perhaps 4 feet deep, at the bottom of the seam. Next, he broke the coal above his slot with wedges, or, if there was no gas in the mine, with gunpowder. Finally, he took his shovel and loaded the coal into large baskets called corves. It was a method hewers had used from time immemorial, and which they went on using until coal-cutting machinery was introduced in the middle years of the twentieth century.

The problem now was to take the coal to the pit bottom, which might be more than 2 miles away. One difficulty was that no mine could pay its way if the workings were any deeper than the seams. The permanent roads from the pit bottom could be high enough for comfort, but the others were limited to the thickness of the coal. Where this was as little as 20 inches, only a child could do the hauling. Indeed, whatever the height of the 'gates', hauling was the duty of the hewer's family.

Hewing coal

Sledge for hauling coal

Haulage with pit ponies. The bucket of coal has been hauled from the working to the main roadway. The crane is lifting it on a 'rolly', and the pony will draw a train of these to the pit bottom.

Their corves might be mounted on a sledge, or on wheels. In the larger mines there were rails, but only in the main roadways. The plight of the 'hurriers' and 'thrusters' much excited the social reformers of the nineteenth century, like Lord Shaftesbury, and the Mines Act of 1842 forbade their employment. After that, youths did the work.

There were improvements in underground transport. Wooden rails were replaced with iron ones, and corves gave way to wheeled tubs holding up to 8 hundredweight each. For haulage in the main roadways, pit ponies became more and more common.

The next stage in the journey was the pit shaft. Here the most primitive gear was a series of ladders, or else a kind of spiral staircase. Women and girls carried loads of over a hundredweight each on their backs, which they were still doing in Fifeshire in the 1840s. Another way was the hand-driven windlass, like the one at the top of a well. However, with the increase in coal production, there had to be something better. Usually they had horse capstans which were still common as late as 1850, but deeper mines needed even more power. In the early and middle years of the eighteenth century they used water-wheels wherever possible and then, after the 1760s, Watt's rotary engine was gradually adopted.

Ropes were first of all of hemp, but by the end of our period many were of wire. Mathias Dunn, a mining engineer, calculated that a wire rope 2 inches in diameter, would carry a load of 8 tons. A hemp rope, doing the same work, would have to be 6 inches in diameter, and would weigh over four times as much.

The rope, whether of hemp or of wire, ended in a chain on which hung the 'clatch harness'. It was an iron bar which hung horizontally, like a coat-hanger, with hooks dangling at each end to hold corves. Full corves on their way up passed empties coming down, sometimes colliding, so it was an improvement when guide rods were introduced to prevent the loads swinging.

By 1850, in the larger pits, the clatch harness had given way to the cage, and the corve to the wheeled tub. The winding engines could raise four tubs at a time, each holding 8 hundredweight. Now, 32 hundredweight came up the shaft instead of 10 hundredweight by the old method.

Pit-head gear became quite sophisticated, as is shown by Dunn's diagram on page 55. This shows a plan of the shaft (1), looking down on the tubs. One set would be going down and the other coming up. At the surface, the tubs ran out on to a cradle which can be seen most clearly in (2). They were then tipped over the screens (3) which were made of iron bars half an inch apart. The small coal fell into the hoppers (4), while the larger pieces came to rest at (5). Here any stone was removed by hand, and the coal loaded into chaldrons.

From the smaller mines the coal went away on pack-horses or in wagons and carts. The larger mines had wagon-ways to link them to rivers or canals. As they were the forerunners of the railways they are described in Chapter 21.

Men and boys 'coming to bank'.

Model of pit-cage, with wire guides

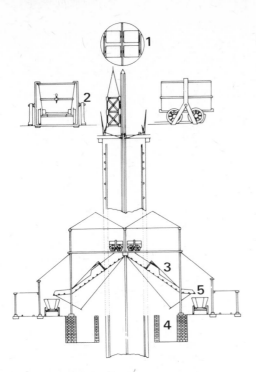

Pit-head gear (from Dunn, *Treatise on the Winning and Working of Collieries*)

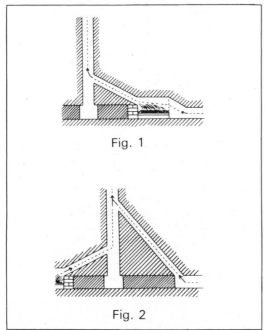

Fig. 1

Fig. 2

Ventilation with furnaces. In Fig. 1 the air from the workings passes over the furnace, so this method was used only in mines with no gas. Fig. 2 shows the arrangement for mines containing gas. Air for the furnace comes down from the surface, and the hot air rising from the fire induces a draught in the mine workings.

The miner's worst enemies were water and gas. One way to drain a mine was to use a chain and buckets, but it was not satisfactory. Water slopped out of the buckets, and sometimes the chain broke, with spectacular results. None the less, the chain and buckets were used in some pits until the middle of the nineteenth century. Better was a sixteenth-century German invention, the rag and chain pump. It was a pipe that went the depth of the shaft, into the sump at the bottom. Through the pipe ran a chain with knots of rag at intervals which just filled the pipe, and as it was pulled upwards it brought water with it. Wherever possible they drove these devices with water-wheels, but nearly always they had to use horses. After 200 feet, lack of power began to tell, and many coal-seams lay out of reach because they could not be drained. Demand for coal was growing, so the need for an efficient pump was desperate. The answer was, of course, the steam-engine.

There are two dangerous gases found in some mines, one which was called 'choke damp' and the other 'fire damp'. Choke damp is carbon dioxide, and is usually harmless enough. The trouble in a pit was that it collected in pockets, driving away the air, so that anyone working in it might die of suffocation. Usually, though, a miner had some warning because his candle burned more and more dimly, so that, with any luck, he would have time to escape. Fire damp was much more dangerous. It is the gas methane which will explode when ignited, if it is at all concentrated. It usually lies in small quantities in the coal itself, but often there is a fissure, or a 'blower' from which it will pour, sometimes for months, or even years. There was a third danger of which miners were only dimly aware, and that was coal-dust. It will explode if it is thick enough in the air, as sometimes happens in a domestic boiler.

The best answer to gas is ventilation. In the tiny drift mines they took little enough trouble. Sometimes they hung a sack over the entrance and waved it backwards and forwards to raise a current of air. They called this 'wafting'. As mines became deeper, though, they had to do rather better, so they constructed a furnace. The diagrams show two ways in which this could be done. A properly built furnace will move great quantities of air.

What was not so easy was to make sure the air did its work properly. Left to itself, it simply took the shortest route, leaving many places unventilated, so it had to be guided by partitions and doors.

The problem of lighting went along with ventilation, because all miners used candles

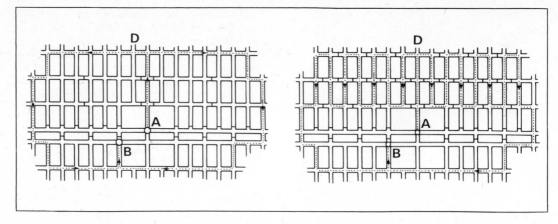

Ventilating pillar and bord workings. The left-hand diagram shows 'face-coursing' and the right-hand one coursing of some of the waste. The current of air divides at D because it is roughly the same distance to the upcast shaft either way. A = downcast shaft. B = upcast shaft.

whose naked flames often caused explosions. In the early days they sometimes sent in a 'fireman'. This brave fellow clad himself in wet sacks and went through the workings with a light on a long taper, exploding any pocket of gas that might have collected in hollows in the roof. When he had finished it was, with any luck, safe for a shift to work with candles.

In 1760 Carlisle Spedding invented a steel mill. A boy turned a handle which rubbed a toothed wheel against a flint. There was a shower of sparks which gave the hewers just enough light to do their work. Meanwhile the boy watched the sparks, and if they became big and bright, he knew it was time for everyone to go. The steel mill had disadvantages. The boy's arm must have ached by the end of the shift, and, more to the point for the hewers, he had to be paid. Also, though nothing

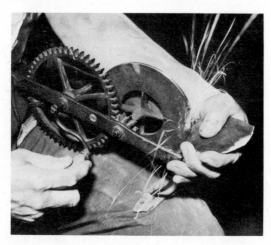

Steel mill

like as dangerous as a candle, the sparks from the mill could cause an explosion.

In 1812 there was an explosion at Felling Colliery in Durham which killed ninety-one miners, and the disaster led to the formation of the Sunderland Society for the Prevention of Accidents in Coal Mines. It was this Society which, in 1815, approached Sir Humphry Davy and asked him to produce a safety lamp. Within a few weeks he had done so. Though he worked quickly he was thorough, making careful experiments that included an analysis of methane gas and the conditions under which it would explode. He risked his own life by testing his lamp in a gas-filled mine.

The essential part of the Davy Lamp was the wire gauze that surrounded the flame. The flame could not pass through the gauze to the gas, but the gas could pass in to the flame. Mathias Dunn described what happened when the lamp was in a gas pocket: 'The upper part of the lamp becomes quite red, a continued rushing noise and a crackling of the gauze is heard, and the smoke and smell emitted from the lamp show the immense combustion that is going on.' (op. cit., p. 188) Here then was a danger signal clear enough for anyone.

Mine-owners did not improve ventilation and lighting just to save their men's lives; they were after more coal as well. They could now sink their shafts to seams that had once been too dangerous to mine, and they drove their workings far under the ground. Formerly many wastes had become enveloped in gas, so that the pillars had been left, but now they could be removed fairly safely. They even reopened old mines to clear the wastes, so that many tons of coal were raised that would otherwise have been lost. Gas was conquered, as well as water, and output rose.

14 The iron industry

Iron was as essential to the Industrial Revolution as coal. Demand grew and the iron-masters met it by increasing the scale of their works, and also by improving their methods. Their technology changed much more radically than that of the coal-owners.

TECHNICAL CHANGES

There were two main products: pig-iron, or cast iron, and wrought iron, sometimes known as bar iron. Steel was made, but not in quantity before the late 1860s. Until then it was expensive, so wrought iron usually took its place.

Iron-ore is a chemical combination of iron and oxygen, in its simplest form, Fe_3O_4. To make iron, the oxygen is removed with the aid of carbon. It is done in a blast-furnace, so called because air has to be blasted into it under pressure to make enough heat. The furnace is charged with a mixture of ore, fuel and limestone. The fuel is the carbon, and the limestone forms a flux, which, when liquid,

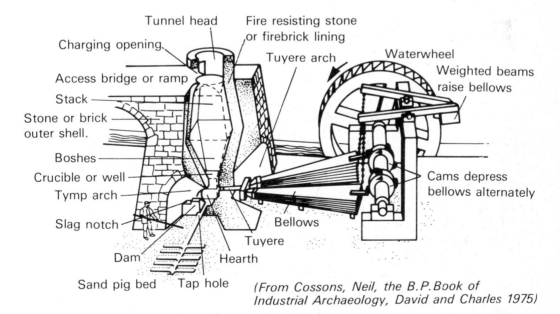

(From Cossons, Neil, the B.P. Book of Industrial Archaeology, David and Charles 1975)

Eighteenth-century charcoal blast-furnace. A comparison of the photograph with the diagram will explain the various features of the furnace, apart from the two small openings near the top, and the tiled roof. Probably the furnace was adapted for some other use when its working life was over.

57

G.B.E.—E

Ironfounder.

Casting

iron, so it has been used wherever possible. Because it is so hard, the usual way to shape it is to melt and cast it, which is why it is also known as 'cast iron'.

What makes pig-iron hard and brittle is carbon, which it absorbs from the fuel in the blast furnace, so to turn it into wrought iron, much of this carbon must be removed. As carbon took oxygen from the ore, so oxygen now takes carbon from the iron. In the early eighteenth century this was done by heating the pigs and then belabouring them with trip-hammers. The carbon on the surface combined with oxygen in the air to form carbon dioxide, while the constant hammering slowly turned the pigs inside-out, bringing every part to the surface in turn.

In addition to carbon there was a certain amount of slag in the pigs, and another result of the hammering was to beat out a good deal of it. Some remained behind in the form of minute threads, so that if a wrought-iron bar was bent until it broke, it looked fibrous, rather like a green twig. It was the slag threads that gave it its distinctive properties, for iron with a low carbon content and no slag is mild steel.

A third effect of the hammering was to improve the physical qualities. 'Wrought' iron is 'worked' iron and, like dough, the more it is kneaded the better it is. Presumably the working reduced the slag to fine threads so that it was not distributed in random shapes.

In the early eighteenth century the iron industry was backward. First of all there was competition from abroad. The ores of Sweden and Russia were purer than those of Britain, so their wrought iron was better. Steel-makers neither would nor could use British iron.

absorbs many of the impurities found in both the ore and the fuel. Under intense heat the carbon combines with the oxygen in the ore, and leaves the furnace as a gas, which is a mixture of carbon monoxide, and carbon dioxide. The molten iron flows to the bottom of the furnace, while the impurities, known as 'slag', float on top of it. They are drawn off first, and then the furnace is tapped at its base to allow the molten iron to flow. In the eighteenth century tapping was done about once a day. The furnace was charged continuously and did not go out until its lining had to be renewed, or until there was no market for its iron. To relight a furnace was a slow, costly business.

Today, molten iron goes directly to the steelworks, but formerly it ran into sand moulds in order to cool. The moulds were long channels called 'sows', with smaller side channels called 'pigs'.

Pig-iron is extremely hard, harder than many steels, so that it will resist compression. On the other hand it has little tensile strength – in other words it is brittle. In a vertical column, supporting a heavy weight, it is ideal, but in a crowbar it is useless. One great advantage is that it is the cheapest form of

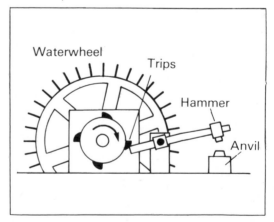

Trip-hammer. This hammer has too short a stroke to beat pigs, but the principle is the same.

Charcoal burning. The process is badly named because it was important *not* to burn the charcoal. The heap of timber is encased with clay to exclude air. A fire in the middle then heats it until it decomposes into gas, tar and charcoal. Exactly the same principle is used to make coke from coal.

Secondly, the industry had to work under what Professor Ashton has called 'the tyranny of wood and water'. Coal, or coal mixed with charcoal, was good enough for some of the later processes, but in the blast-furnace they had to have charcoal on its own. Estimates of the amount of fuel needed to make one ton of iron are of the order of one acre of oak woodland, presumably coppice, or six large trees. House builders competed for the timber, as did shipbuilders. The demands of the Royal Navy were paramount, and the charcoal-burners were sometimes accused of endangering the safety of the country. In spite of all, a blast-furnace might work in one place for ten or twenty years, but in the end it would burn all the timber near it, which meant its owners had to move.

Water power was also important. Water-wheels were needed to power the blast-furnace bellows, the trip-hammers and the slitting mills. Fast flowing, reliable streams are common enough in our climate, but they are not always where it is convenient, and the iron-master wanted his power near his fuel and his ore. He found all three in the Forest of Dean and the Weald, so they became the traditional areas for iron manufacture. In 1700 they were still flourishing, but that could only go on as long as iron production did not outpace the growth of oak coppice, which normally took twenty years. If there was to be a massive increase in production, then the ironmasters would have to use another fuel.

Some must have thought of coal, but it is a most impure form of carbon containing all sorts of undesirable chemicals like sulphur. This is one of the furnace man's chief enemies, for it makes iron 'hot short' – that is, liable to crumble and be unworkable when it is hot. However, if coal is heated with air excluded from it so that it cannot burn, it breaks into gas, tar and coke. Coke is reasonably pure carbon, and it was coke that they learnt, eventually, to use.

During the seventeenth century several men experimented with it and then, in about 1709, a Shropshire ironmaster, Abraham Darby, succeeded. Darby owned an ironworks at Coalbrookdale where he manufactured cooking pots. They were the round-bellied, three-legged kind and they came in all sizes, the largest being like cauldrons and known as 'missionary pots'. Casting them was difficult enough, but they were not made from iron of the first quality, so Darby was willing to experiment. He was successful, probably because the local Shropshire 'clod' coal contained little sulphur and made good coke.

In the short term Darby's discovery brought no revolution to iron-making, and fifty years later there were only seventeen coke-fired furnaces in the whole country. There are various reasons why the new technique spread so slowly.

There was the personality of Abraham Darby, who kept his knowledge to himself. Perhaps he was secretive, but, more likely, being a good Quaker, he was not given to boasting. However, we can be sure that if other ironmasters had been really interested they would have found what he was doing. There are more convincing reasons.

As we have seen, Darby made cooking pots, and while his coke iron was good enough for them, there were many things for which it would not do. It contained phosphorus which made it 'cold-short', or brittle and unworkable when cold. It would not convert to wrought iron, so Darby could not sell to forge masters. Secondly there were, for some time, no great pressures on the industry. From about 1710 to 1740 the economy was quiet, even stagnant, and as there was no mounting demand for iron, no one had any incentive to risk a costly failure by trying a new and uncertain technique. Thirdly it is clear that the fuel crisis cannot have been as great as has been suggested. Pictures of Coalbrookdale itself show the works surrounded by trees, and it is possible that Darby was not interested so much in fuel

saving as in higher temperatures. From a charcoal furnace the iron flowed, or rather oozed, like thick treacle, while for casting awkward shapes it was important it should flow freely, as it did when smelted with coke. Ironmasters were perhaps aware of a likely difficulty with fuel, but it was still over the horizon and would only become acute if they wanted to expand production. Eventually that was what happened. There was a further development in about 1748 when Abraham Darby II discovered how to make iron that was free from phosphorus, so the industry was poised for a big advance. It was only waiting on demand. That came soon afterwards and by the late 1780s was considerable. Timber fuel proved inadequate, so that by 1800 only a few charcoal furnaces remained. The number of coke furnaces, on the other hand, went from the seventeen of 1760 to around 170 in 1805.

With the increased output of pig-iron the old slow way of making wrought iron created a bottle-neck, so ironmasters looked for ways of

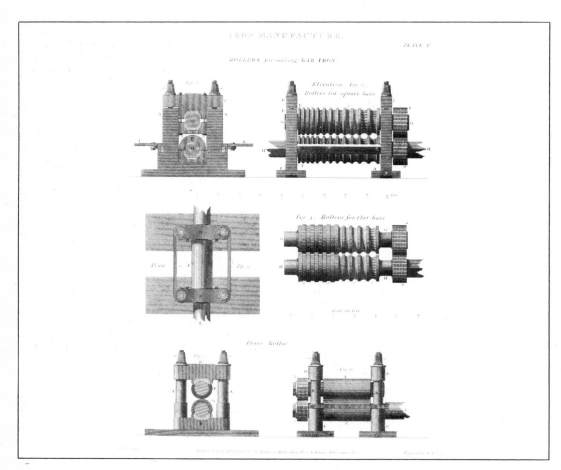

Rollers for making bar iron

removing it. Several realised it would be quicker to stir molten iron than to beat pigs, and two brothers called Cranage, who worked at Coalbrookdale, produced wrought iron in this way. However, it was only fit for nails. Peter Onions also did pioneer work at Coalbrookdale, and at Dowlais in South Wales. However, the man who finally succeeded was Henry Cort. He was a naval agent who had acquired a small ironworks called Fontley Forge, near Fareham in Hampshire. He undertook to supply Portsmouth dockyard with iron goods, and lost money. He also contracted to take old hoops and turn them into useful iron by heating them and beating them into solid bars. However, his forge did not work fast enough, the hoops piled up and Cort was again losing money. His despair drove him to invent rollers, which compressed the hoops much more quickly than his hammers. Smooth rollers were already being used to turn bar iron into sheets, but Cort's were different in that they had grooves ranging from large to quite small, so that a bar could gradually be reduced in size. They worked well, which encouraged Cort to try more experiments.

Ships of war had cast iron for ballast, so there was plenty of it in Portsmouth, and Cort decided he would try and convert some to wrought iron. Like the Cranage brothers and Peter Onions he first of all melted the cast iron and stirred it until almost all the carbon was gone, a process that was to be called 'puddling'. He used a reverberatory furnace which had a low wall to keep the metal from the impurities in the coal fire. The heat was reflected from the roof: it 'reverberated' round the furnace like noise in an empty room. As we have seen, puddling alone did not make good wrought iron, which is not surprising, since the beating had done more than remove the carbon. It had also driven out impurities and improved the iron's physical properties. Cort realised that his rollers would be just right to work wrought iron, so he followed the puddling with rolling, and made a product good enough to satisfy the fastidious Navy Board at Portsmouth. He patented his process in 1784.

Unhappily for Cort, he did not have the capital to buy equipment for large-scale production so he visited several wealthy ironmasters to persuade them to adopt his process and, of course, pay him a royalty for each ton of iron they made. The man who agreed to do so was William Crawshay of Cyfarthfa in South Wales. Crawshay made money quickly, and in view of a growing demand for wrought iron, other manufacturers were eager to copy him.

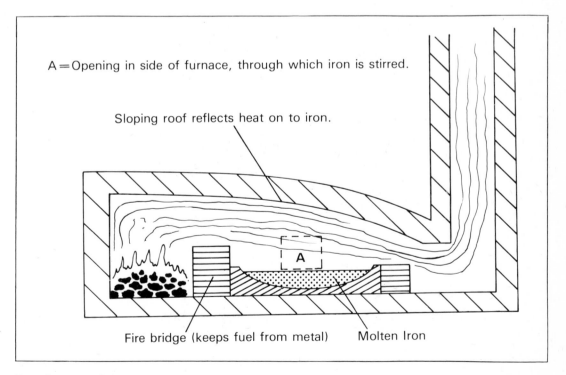

A = Opening in side of furnace, through which iron is stirred.

Sloping roof reflects heat on to iron.

A

Fire bridge (keeps fuel from metal)   Molten Iron

Reverberatory furnace

Puddling iron has been described as the hardest work ever devised for human beings. The furnace took a charge of 5 hundredweight which the puddler stirred for something like an hour and a half. The worst time was at the end, for, as the carbon burnt out and the iron 'came to nature', it was no longer liquid but a viscous mass. At the end the puddler divided it into blooms small enough to be lifted from the furnace. When the furnace was empty they charged it again, and would work through five charges in a shift of eight hours.

Puddling was not only hard work, it was also skilled. The iron had to be properly stirred, and it was most important to remove it from the furnace at just the right moment. Puddlers knew they were indispensable and they tried their employers sorely.

From the furnace a bloom went under the hammer to be beaten into the right shape for the rollers. These were worked by two men, one of whom fed in the metal, while the other caught it and passed it back to his mate. The iron went through each groove in turn, until it was drawn into a long bar. Its agony was not over, however, for it was reheated, folded, consolidated under the hammer and then passed through the rollers again. For the best results, this happened six times. 'Wrought' iron was indeed 'worked' iron. Certainly it was a tedious process, but even so, it was much quicker than the old-fashioned method. A rolling mill could do fifteen times as much work as a trip-hammer.

Another important innovation was steam power. A steam-engine was useful for driving

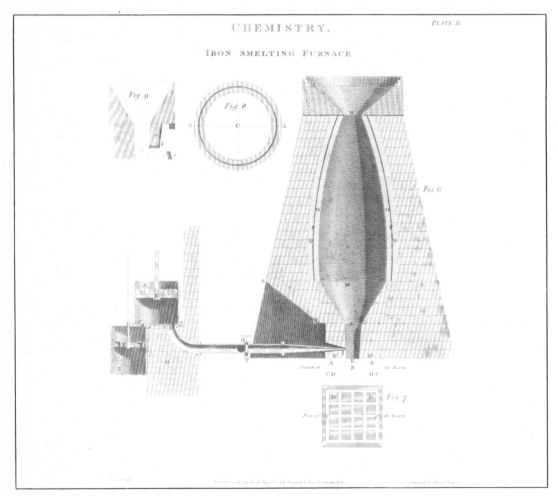

Improved blast-furnace 1820. Iron-ore, coke and limestone were fed in from the top. They expanded as they heated, so the furnace widened. Smelting began at level (M), whereupon the materials contracted rapidly.
   In place of water-powered bellows, there is a pair of steam-driven pistons, working alternately to give a continuous blast.

the bellows of a blast-furnace, or a trip-hammer, but for a rolling mill of any size it was essential. Fortunately Boulton and Watt were making their reciprocating engines, so ironmasters installed mills like the one John Wilkinson had at Bradley. His engine had a 24 foot flywheel, the rollers were 4 feet in diameter and the mill could process 18000 tons of iron a year.

By the end of the eighteenth century Swedish visitors began to be uneasy, for they saw they had competition of quite a new kind. They had reason to worry, since, by 1810, British iron was a good deal cheaper than their own. To keep a share in the British market, they had to specialise in a kind of wrought iron especially suitable for making into steel. The Russians, who were unable to change, were soon selling us no iron at all. Coal had freed the British ironmaster not only from 'the tyranny of wood and water' but from foreign competition as well.

There were further technical changes in the first half of the nineteenth century, most of them being improvements to the blast-furnace.

One way to make more iron was to have larger furnaces, and more of them. In the early eighteenth century they were about 25 feet tall, in 1815 anything up to 50 feet, and in the 1860s 100 feet. Their numbers increased from 170 in 1805 to 655 in 1852.

Another way to have more iron was to make the furnaces more productive, and this could be done by heating the air blast. James Neilson made the discovery in 1828. He was superintendent of Glasgow gasworks and, having had no formal scientific education, he went to evening-classes at the University. He made good use of his knowledge, for he found a way of purifying coal gas. According to one story he became interested in blast-furnaces when a local ironmaster asked him if he could also purify air. He imagined that in the summer it was contaminated with sulphur because the furnaces did not work as well then as in winter. Neilson knew better, but after looking at the problems the ironmasters were having, decided to try heating the air. He saw that if he did so it would expand as it left the bellows, so increasing the power of the blast. That was correct, but Neilson's discovery was a success for quite another reason. If cold air is blasted into a fire it has the same effect on it as on anything else – it cools it. Hot air will make the fire burn just as fiercely, but will not cool it nearly as much, so it takes less fuel. Ironmasters had not realised this before because, although the idea is simple, it is not obvious. Moreover, they saw their furnaces worked better in cold weather. Presumably it was because cold air contains less moisture than warm air, but they thought that it was the temperature that mattered. At first they refused to believe Neilson, but the evidence was clear enough, and indeed the more the blast was heated, the more fuel was saved. When it reached 600°F, fuel consumption was cut by two-thirds.

There was another advantage. Thanks to the higher temperature, smelting did not take as long, so the furnaces could be tapped more often than once a day.

In 1815 an average furnace made 60 tons of iron a week; in 1848 one of the larger furnaces, using Neilson's hot blast, would make 200 tons.

Nothing as spectacular happened in the manufacture of wrought iron, and it kept up with pig-iron mainly because there were more and more puddling furnaces and rolling mills. One discovery, though, was made by Joseph Hall of Tipton in about 1826. He found that if he flung some high-grade iron-ore into the puddling furnace, it made wrought iron much more quickly. Iron-ore is iron oxide, and adding it to the pig meant that there was more oxygen to take away the carbon. It did its work in the heart of the furnace, so that carbon monoxide came bubbling through the molten iron. Because of this, they called the process 'pig boiling'.

ORGANISATION OF THE INDUSTRY

The new techniques and growing output meant changes in organisation.

In the days of wood and water most firms were small enough to be run by one man and his family with perhaps a labourer or two. A diorama in the Science Museum, London, shows one of these works with its little blast-furnace and forge. Indeed, it was not unusual for the furnace and forge to be separate, and belong to different owners. In the days of coal and steam, on the other hand, works were much larger.

Ironmasters brought all the stages of manufacture under their own control. They had coke ovens, blast-furnaces, fineries, puddling furnaces and rolling mills. Next, they took out mineral leases with land-owners, so that they mined their own coal, limestone and ore. Thirdly, they turned their iron into goods. At Coalbrookdale they made steam-engines, the Carron ironworks in Scotland produced armaments, while Josiah John Guest of Dowlais sent his iron rails all over Britain and, indeed, the world. These were fully integrated concerns whose owners did everything from mining their raw materials to selling their finished products.

The changes in techniques also meant that the iron industry developed differently in different parts of the country. In the early days, as we have seen, most iron came from the Weald and the Forest of Dean. However, when the industry began to depend on coal it had to move to those coalfields which had deposits of iron-ore nearby. Down to 1850, the most important were Shropshire, its close neighbour South Staffordshire, South Wales and the Western Lowlands of Scotland. However, they did not all develop together, and it is interesting to see how the technical changes affected each of them.

The Shropshire industry was the first to grow, because of the pioneer work of the Darby family, and by 1806 this small coalfield was producing one-fifth of the country's pig-iron. Then came depression, particularly in 1812. In the 1830s Alfred Darby and Abraham IV revived the flagging Coalbrookdale works, but they had lost their technological lead. Once they had taught others, but now they were content to learn from them, adopting Neilson's hot-air blast, and Hall's pig boiling.

In South Staffordshire the source of everyone's prosperity was the famous ten yard coal-seam. There was a famous ironmaster, too, for John Wilkinson had one of his works at Bradley, where he introduced coke smelting as early as 1757. The Napoleonic Wars particularly brought prosperity, the number of furnaces increasing fivefold between 1793 and 1812. Later there was another boost, because it was at Tipton that Hall discovered pig boiling. By 1850 South Staffordshire produced half a million tons of wrought iron a year. Comparatively, the region was at its peak in the 1830s when it made one-third of British pig-iron.

South Wales had ample forests and water power as well as ore, so it had been an iron manufacturing area for a long time. There was less need to turn to coke smelting here than perhaps anywhere, but it was introduced at Tredegar in 1764 and spread rapidly enough. The industry was mostly at the north-east of the bituminous coalfield around Merthyr Tydfil. Here are names famous in the history of iron-making – Cyfarthfa, Dowlais and Pen-y-Darren. However, the boom really began not with the introduction of coke smelting but of puddling. Though Cort invented it at Fareham, it was Crawshay of Cyfarthfa who made it a success, and the fortunes of Guest's Dowlais company began when they adopted it soon after 1800. The speciality of Dowlais was iron rails. Orders from home and abroad kept it working when others were in difficulty, while the railway boom of the 1840s gave it a considerable boost. As we shall see, it was the South Wales ironmasters who made the bulk of the rails at this time.

Pig-iron production in the whole region rose from 317000 tons in the depression of 1842 to 707000 tons in 1847. Comparatively, South Wales was most important about 1830 when 45 per cent of British iron was made there.

Scotland had great advantages for iron-making. There was ample coal in Lanarkshire, while between the Clyde and the Forth were perhaps the richest deposits of ore in Britain. This was the famous 'black band' ore, some of which is 70 per cent iron. David Mushet discovered it early in the nineteenth century, but for the time being it stayed in the ground. In 1806 the Scottish iron industry was like a sleeping giant, accounting for only 9 per cent of British output. The reason was that neither Scottish coal nor Scottish ore could be used economically without hot-air blast, but everything changed when Neilson made his discovery. Output jumped from 40000 tons in 1830 to 200000 tons in 1840, it passed 1 million tons in 1862 and was to stay at around that figure for the rest of the century. From 9 per cent in 1806 Scottish output reached nearly 30 per cent of the national output by 1852, and it was this increase which meant the comparative decline of South Staffordshire and South Wales.

STEEL

Steel was essential for a few items, like clock springs and the cutting edge of tools, but it was much too expensive to be used in bulk before 1870. Wrought iron usually took its place. However, an account of the iron industry would not be complete without some mention of it.

Like wrought iron, steel started as pig-iron, which contains about 4 per cent carbon and many impurities. The problem was to remove all the impurities, and make the carbon content about 1 per cent. By heating and beating the pig they first made almost pure iron, which is quite soft, and then added carbon to the right amount. To do so, they packed bars of iron in a furnace between layers of charcoal, to be heated for several days. They came out covered in marks like blisters, so the product was called 'blister steel'. In that state it was not much use, because there was more carbon on the outside than the inside, so each bar had to be heated and go under the hammer until it was uniform all the way through. It was then called 'forged steel'.

In the 1750s Benjamin Huntsman made the first cast steel. Clearly, if blister steel was melted, the carbon would mix with the iron more quickly and more evenly, but steel melts at a high temperature and there was no furnace that would stand the heat. What Huntsman did was to find a recipe for a clay mixture that was strong enough. He made it into crucibles, so his product was known as 'crucible steel'.

However, Huntsman's discovery did not bring a revolution. In the first place it was a long time before British ironmasters could make bar iron pure enough for steel, and, as we have seen, the Swedes kept their monopoly of that branch of the trade. Secondly cast steel could only be made on a small scale. A Huntsman furnace produced only 20 pounds at a time, and when the Swiss industrialist Johann Fischer visited the works he was astonished to be led to it through the living-room of the house. Even in Sheffield, steel-making remained a backyard industry with no firm employing more than about eight men.

Everything changed following the discoveries of Bessemer and Siemens in the late 1860s. As steel replaced wrought iron, more and more unhappy puddlers had to stand humbly at the side of the new experts, learning how to operate open-hearth furnaces.

Making crucible steel. The size of the crucibles gives an idea of the scale of the industry. The men on the left are casting steel, a novel process in those days, for Huntsman was the first to discover how to work in temperatures that were high enough to melt steel.

65

15 The cotton industry

Welsh spinning-wheel. This was used for wool, but the principle was the same for cotton. The spindle sticks out at right angles. From it is dangling a carding, which has been drawn out to form a sliver. The spinner will turn the wheel one way to twist the sliver to make a roving, then reverse the wheel to wind the roving on to the spindle.

THE EARLY EIGHTEENTH CENTURY

In the early eighteenth century the cotton industry was unimportant. Woollen exports were worth £3 million a year, while cottons were a mere £10 000. Imports of raw cotton were around £1 million, as against £50 million in 1800 and £600 million in 1850.

Like many other industries in their early years, cotton depended heavily on London. It is true that spinning and weaving had started in Lancashire in the sixteenth century, and were well established there by 1700, but they are only two of many things that must happen between the day the raw cotton leaves the plantation and when the finished cloth appears in the shop. London had a vital part to play.

In the first place it was the centre of trade. The raw cotton arrived there and was sent to Lancashire by road. The woven cloth then came back to be sold in Blackwell Hall Market. It was the London dealer who could watch the changing fashions, who knew what foreigners wanted, and who could make a shrewd guess at how much should be produced. Secondly, there were important branches of the industry in London. The cloth left Lancashire still looking like a raw material, being quite plain and a dingy grey colour. It was in London that it was bleached and then printed with the colours and patterns of the latest fashions. Finally, the people who found the money were the London merchants. It was their capital which was tied up during the long wait between the arrival of the raw cotton and the sale of the finished goods. They not only financed their own buying and selling but allowed credit to the Lancashire manufacturers while they were doing their spinning and weaving. As we shall see in Chapter 31 this supply of working capital was essential for the progress of the Industrial Revolution.

The technology of the industry was still primitive. British manufacturers could not rival the delightful chintzes which the East India Company imported. Indeed, there was little true cotton cloth made in Britain at all. Spinners in this country could not produce a cotton thread that was both fine and strong, so

Saxony wheel. The bobbin and flyer meant that twisting and winding went on simultaneously, so spinning was continuous. The foot treadle meant the spinner had both hands free to manipulate the thread.

for warp the weavers preferred their traditional fibre, flax. They then wove in a cotton weft, to produce a cloth known as fustian.

Spinning was done on the one-thread wheel, which had evolved from the distaff and whorl. A sliver had to be drawn out, twisted into yarn, and then wound. With the earlier wheels the spinner had to stop to wind each length after she had drawn and twisted it, but by the late fifteenth century the Saxony wheel had been invented, which would do continuous spinning.

The work was done in two stages. First of all the woman made a loose thread, about as thick as a candlewick, and which was known as a 'roving'. The second stage, drawing out, twisting and winding the roving, was the spinning proper. It was difficult to produce fine yarn. The thickness of yarn is measured by the number of hanks, 840 yards long, that can be spun from a pound of cotton. A good hand spinner could make 20s, but by 1800 there were machines making 300s. Modern sewing cotton is usually No. 40, which gives some idea of the other counts. From the spinner the yarn went to the handloom weaver. Like the wheel, the loom had been much improved over the centuries, but using it was still a slow, laborious business. The weaver threw the shuttle from side to side by hand, which meant that unless he was willing to employ a mate, he could only make cloth of a limited width. It was also difficult for him to give his work an even texture, for he had to tap each shoot of warp into place with a blow from his lathe, and the strength of each blow was bound to vary.

The finishing processes were, if anything, even more long-winded. They are described later.

Spinning and weaving were organised on the domestic system. This was run by merchants, who had many complex duties. For one thing they maintained the links with London. It was from there they had the raw cotton, and it was there they sent the woven cloth for finishing and for sale. A man might have a partner in the City, or he might have a more or less permanent arrangement with a business house there. In Lancashire he had to organise production by 'putting out' materials to employees who worked in their own homes. His task was complicated because each weaver needed several spinners to keep him going. First of all the merchant had to distribute raw cotton for spinning and collect it as yarn. Next he had to apportion the yarn among his weavers and collect the woven cloth. This was done from a warehouse or from a number of depots that opened in the villages, perhaps one day a week. It could all become very involved. One

manufacturer, William Radcliffe, had 1000 weavers scattered over three counties.

It is not surprising that many merchants found they had enough to do marketing their goods, so they handed the supervision of the spinners and weavers to middle men, called 'putters-out'. They saved the merchants worry and responsibility and, since they delivered the materials to the workers, they saved them their weekly visits to the warehouse. However, the putters-out made problems of their own, as we shall see; indeed, the whole domestic system had weaknesses.

First of all spinners and weavers had little supervision. They saw their employer or his agent once a week, and how they used their time between the visits was their own affair. No merchant, when he gave out raw cotton, could say when it might come back as cloth, so he would be unwilling to promise his customers firm delivery dates. Spinners and weavers usually slacked during the first part of the week, and then might or might not make up for lost time by a frantic bout of overwork from Thursday onwards. Moreover, they usually found excuses for neglecting their textiles. Women spinners had homes to run, while during the hay and corn harvests they went to work on the farms. They could earn good wages and harvest was the traditional time for merry-making. As for the weavers, nearly all had gardens, and some of them small farms. Neither their weaving nor their farming was done well.

The workers were not the only problem. As we have seen, William Radcliffe's weavers were scattered over three counties, so he had troubles and expense with transport. Moreover, it was nearly impossible to co-ordinate the work so that spinners and weavers kept the same pace. Either there was a shortage of yarn or else a glut. The first often happened in the middle of the century, so that spinners gave themselves airs, and pushed up prices, and the second was likely towards the end when, according to legend, the weavers were going round with £5 notes stuck in their hats. The problem was made worse by the philosophy of the eighteenth-century workers, many of whom would use an improvement in their daily rates of wages to buy leisure time instead of extra comforts.

While the domestic system gave workers freedom, which they cherished and abused, it also gave them problems. Scattered as they were, their employers could play one group against another. Putters-out were quick to take advantage, for they had no salaries. Instead each one had a contract to deliver goods to the merchant at a stated price, and was free to pay as little as he needed to the workers. Lancashire people sometimes said of a misfortune: 'It 'ud melt th' heart of a whetstone, or what's harder a putter eaut.' (T.S. Ashton, *Industrial Revolution 1760–1830*, p. 42)

One victim of the domestic system was the consumer. In the early years of the eighteenth century an ordinary man had to accumulate six weeks' wages before he could buy a new suit of clothes. It was the direct result of the inefficiency of the domestic system.

It was not only the cotton industry that had a primitive technology and poor organisation. Others were the same, including the other textiles, linen and wool. If any one of them could escape these restrictions, then clearly it would have a brilliant future. Cotton, the most insignificant of them all, was the first to do so.

TECHNICAL CHANGES

The cotton industry was transformed, partly because of inventions made over a period of a hundred years.

The first was simple enough. It was the flying shuttle, patented by John Kay in 1733. In the older handloom the shuttle, which held the weft, was thrown from side to side of the cloth by hand. The weaver had to bend forward for every 'shoot', which took time, while the width of the cloth could be no more than the distance he could throw, usually about 27 inches. To make wider cloth he needed a mate to take the shuttle from him. What Kay did was to fit a pair of rollers to the shuttle and make it run on a track. At either end of the track was a loose wooden block, and from each of these a cord ran to a peg which the weaver held in his hand. By tugging on the peg, now to the left, now to the right, he jerked the wooden blocks in turn, and they tapped the shuttle from side to side. As the weaver no longer had to bend forward and reach for his shuttle he could work twice as quickly as before. Moreover, he could weave cloth 36 inches wide without any help.

Here was an ingenious invention, but unhappily for Kay he made it before anyone wanted it. In the 1730s trade and industry were stagnant, and as weavers could not find enough work for their traditional looms, they had no time for a gadget which might make numbers of them unemployed. They terrorised Kay, who fled abroad to die in poverty. It was not until the 1760s that demand was great enough to persuade the weavers to use the flying shuttle. Almost as soon as they adopted it, though, they created a bottle-neck. The spinners could not work fast enough to supply the weavers and, being much in demand, began to charge dearly for their services.

Bottle-necks are one of the main reasons for progress in technology. Certainly it was this demand for yarn which led to the invention of spinning machines by two men, James Hargreaves and Richard Arkwright.

Hargreaves was a weaver at Blackburn, who no doubt suffered from a shortage of yarn like the other members of his trade. According to legend, he one day saw his wife's spinning-wheel tip over and go on turning. The spindle was upright instead of horizontal, which gave him the idea of putting several in a frame to spin a number of threads at a time. His problem was how to draw out the rovings. On the ordinary wheel the spinner held the single thread between her finger and thumb and then stretched it. To imitate her action Hargreaves made a clasp on a moving carriage. It gripped the rovings and the spinner stretched them by drawing the clasp towards him. At the same time he turned a handle, which caused the spindles to revolve, so twisting the yarn. He then pushed the clasp back for another bite and turned the handle the other way to wind the spun yarn on the bobbins.

Hargreaves finished his first 'jenny' some time in the mid-1760s. At first he meant it only for himself and his family, but, being short of money, he made several machines for sale. News of it now spread quickly and a crowd of angry spinners invaded his house to smash his jenny. They made his life so unpleasant that in 1768 he moved to Nottingham, where he found a partner, Thomas James, a joiner. Between them they equipped a small mill, and in 1770 Hargreaves decided, at last, to protect his invention with a patent. It was too late, for others had already copied the machines which he had sold. Fortunately his mill prospered.

The first jennies had eight spindles, but soon they had sixteen and, in the end, 120. It was a typical invention of the Industrial Revolution. There was no new source of power, while any spinner would have quickly recognised almost all the moving parts, for they were copied from the one-thread wheel. However, everything was rearranged to be much more efficient, allowing one spinner to do the work of many.

The jenny did have its limitations. In the first place it would not take raw cotton, but only converted rovings into yarn. Rovings still had to be spun on the one-thread wheel, so here at once was another bottle-neck. Also, jenny yarn was no better than any that had been made before, so it was fit only for weft, and had to be woven into a linen warp. Furthermore, the jenny took up so little space that it could quite well be used in the home.

Spinning-jenny. The rovings were drawn out by the moving clasp, on the right. The rovings are on the bobbins which are in the frame at the top left. The spindles, for twisting and winding, are in the sloping frame in the centre. Twisting and winding were separate operations, so spinning was discontinuous.

Although it increased output, Hargreaves's invention encouraged two things that were traditional, the manufacture of fustians and the domestic system.

Another invention followed hard upon the jenny, being patented in 1769. It was the water-frame, the work of a Lancashire barber, Richard Arkwright. Here again was a combination of old ideas rather than anything new, and indeed in 1785 Arkwright's patent was successfully challenged. Twisting and winding were done by a flyer and bobbin taken from the Saxony wheel, while the rovings were drawn out by a device that Lewis Paul had patented in 1739. It had several pairs of rollers, the front ones moving faster than the ones behind, so that as the rovings passed between them they were stretched – but in a different way from the spinning-jenny. Presumably because they were also compressed they made a yarn, which, though it was still somewhat thick, was firm and strong. Paul's idea had languished for the same reason as Kay's, but when Arkwright copied it the economic climate was quite different and it was an immediate success.

In the first place water-frame yarn was strong enough for warp. Weavers used it with jenny weft, for the first time making pure cotton calicoes to rival those of India. Secondly, Arkwright found that his yarn was suitable for stockings. They had long been made of silk and worsted, but hand-spun cotton was no good for them. Arkwright took his

The water-frame. This is not a factory machine but a model, made in order to secure a patent. The front set of rollers can be seen at the top. Twisting and winding were done with the bobbin and flyer so that spinning was continuous.

Most of the machine, including part of the driving mechanism, is in wood. Like all early textile machines, this one was made by a turner, a joiner and a clock-maker.

69

invention to Nottingham, where a hosiery manufacturer, Jedediah Strutt, saw its possibilities and made Arkwright his partner.

A most important feature of the water-frame was that it needed more power than a human being could give it. At first Arkwright and Strutt used a horse capstan, but horses need feeding, a disadvantage which does not apply to water-wheels. Accordingly, in 1771, they went to Cromford on the River Derwent and built a mill that is famous in history as the first cotton factory to use mechanical power. Andrew Ure described it enthusiastically as 'the nursing place of the factory power and opulence of Great Britain' (*Cotton Manufacture*, p. 227). It was of course the use of water power that gave Arkwright's machine its name.

It may be that Arkwright copied other men's idea, but that does not detract from the importance of his work. First of all he set the cotton industry on its meteoric rise; in 1775 it produced 57 000 yards of calico, and, in 1783, over 3½ million. Secondly, Cromford Mill meant the doom, eventually, of the domestic system.

The last of this succession of spinning machines was Samuel Crompton's mule. Crompton was a yeoman farmer from Firwood in Lancashire who, like so many of his kind,

Sir Richard Arkwright was one of the few inventors who became rich. This was in spite of his patent being invalidated. Once he had made his fortune by spinning cotton, he turned his energies elsewhere. He was a social climber, currying favour with aristocrats by lending them money, buying vast landed estates, and seeking honours, like his knighthood.

Crompton's mule. The mule produced the finest of yarn, because it combined the methods of the water-frame and the jenny for drawing out the rovings. The rollers are on the left and the moving carriage is in the centre. It has been cut short for some reason, perhaps for demonstration. This machine is hand powered, unlike the factory models.

did spinning and weaving as a sideline. He was dissatisfied with his jenny yarn so he set to work in his spare time to make a better machine. In 1779, after several years of effort, he finished his first mule. It had this name because it combined the methods of both the water-frame and the spinning-jenny. The rovings were first of all stretched by rollers and then, as they were being twisted, were drawn out still farther by a moving carriage. The yarn was both fine and strong, so that Crompton caused a sensation when he sold his first samples. He started with No. 40, and then went to No. 80, just to prove it could be done. By the 1830s mules were spinning No. 350, or 167 miles of thread from 1 pound of cotton.

Crompton did not patent his machine, probably because his ideas were not new. He tried to keep it for his own use, but visitors plagued him, some even climbing trees to look through his windows. He dealt with them by charging them a guinea each to come in and make a proper inspection. He raised £50 in this way, and used it to build a bigger machine; he also found supporters who gave him £500 to expand a business he had started in Bolton. Meanwhile others quickly copied his machine, and soon there were hundreds of mules whose owners had not paid the inventor a penny. In 1830 Parliament recognised that the country owed him a debt, so it voted him £5000. He gave it to his sons to start a bleaching works and they lost the lot. He would have died in poverty if some friends had not bought him an annuity of £60 a year. He suffered, like many an inventor, because he had little business sense, little capital, and no Matthew Boulton or Jedediah Strutt to help him.

Crompton's mules were modest, hand-driven machines with 150 or so spindles, but by the early nineteenth century they had up to a thousand. The bigger machines were power-assisted. The delicate task of pulling back the carriage to draw out the threads still had to be done by hand, but it was safe to let the machine do the winding. The spinner could control two mules, drawing out the threads on one, while the carriage was retreating automatically on the other, so that he was controlling perhaps 2000 spindles. All he needed was a handful of children to mend any threads that might break and to keep the room clean.

Finally there was the 'self-acting' mule, patented by Richard Roberts in 1830. After that, few improvements were possible; there were mules working in Lancashire in 1976.

The mule gave textile manufacturers an abundance of yarn of whatever quality they wanted. They could produce coarse cottons for the slaves of a Louisiana planter, or the most

Power-assisted mules. On the right, the spinner has drawn out the carriage while the machine twists the rovings. He will now let it go and the carriage will run back of its own accord, winding the yarn as it does so. Meanwhile the spinner will be drawing out the carriage of the mule on the left. He is spinning 2000 threads at once, with the help of two children.

Carding, drawing and roving. Carding is taking place on the left. The carding proper is done by the large drum, while the cotton is stripped off by the 'doffer' which is the smaller drum.
The machine on the right converts the carding to a roving by drawing it out and twisting it.

delicate muslins for the finest ladies of London society.

The progress in spinning created bottle-necks in all the other processes of cloth-making. One by one they were removed.

Cotton arrived in Britain compressed in bales, so the first job was to loosen it. Workers unpacked the bales, shook the cotton apart and removed any foreign bodies like stones. This process was called 'scutching'. In the early days it was done by hand, but then machines called 'devils' were invented to do the work. Operating them was the worst job of all, because they filled the air with so much dust that it was sometimes impossible to see across the room.

The next stage was carding. The fibres had to be disentangled and laid in parallel rows, like a neatly combed head of hair. In the early days it had been done with teasles, or thistles, which was how the process got its name, since the Latin for thistle is 'carduus'. Later, cards were made by pushing numerous short lengths of wire through pieces of leather and then fixing them on boards with handles, like square table-tennis bats. The carder placed the cotton wool on one card and then stroked it in one direction with another until all the fibres were straight. He then changed the direction of his stroke and stripped off the cotton in a loose roll called a 'sliver'. Numbers

Arkwright's drawing-frame. Arkwright's attempts at spinning by machine all failed until he realised the importance of having rovings that were perfectly uniform. He invented this machine to produce them.

of these short slivers had to be joined end to
end to make one long enough for the spinner.
In 1748 Lewis Paul produced a carding
machine. It had a drum, turned by a handle,
and was covered on the outside with wire
spikes, just like those on the hand cards.
Under the lower half of the drum was a
stationary frame, curved to the same shape,
and also covered with wire spikes. The cotton
passed between the two and was stripped off at
the other side by a smaller toothed roller
called a 'doffer'. Later machines were driven
by power – first water, and then steam.

The next stage was roving, for which
Arkwright invented two machines. The first
was the drawing-frame, patented in 1775. The
trouble with a sliver that came from the carding machine was that it varied in thickness.
Arkwright put six slivers together, then
passed them between rollers, like those on his
water-frame, which drew them out to a little
less than their original thickness. This was
repeated three times, after which the sliver
was perfectly even. It was then fed into a
revolving can so that it could be carried away,
and which also gave it a slight twist.

After leaving the drawing-frame the cotton
went to another machine, very like the water-
frame, which drew it out and twisted it lightly
to make a roving. It was then ready for the
spinning proper.

After weaving, the cloth had to be bleached,
which was once a long and tedious business. It
was first steeped in alkaline, a process called
'bucking', and was then spread on the ground
to be exposed to the uncertain rays of English
sunlight. This was known as crofting. It also
spent a lot of its time in sour milk. To make
the dingy grey cloth that came from the loom
pure white could take up to eight months. In
the meantime there were thieves bold enough
to risk the death penalty by stealing it from
the crofts, and, even more important, capital
was lying idle. This was the money that had
been spent on the raw materials and all the
earlier processes. It would be hard to discover
a better example of a bottle-neck. When cloth
was produced in quantity it was essential that
bleaching should be done more quickly.

For once, the first discoveries were made
abroad. In 1774 a Swedish chemist, Scheele,
found that chlorine would destroy vegetable
colouring. He had the idea when he saw that it
turned the cork of one of his test-tubes white.
A Frenchman, Berthollet, realising that
Scheele's discovery could be useful in the textile industries, went on to prove that chlorine
would bleach cloth. As may be imagined,
manufacturers in Britain were delighted at
the news, but they were not so pleased when it

Crofting. Bleaching cloth in the sunlight.

came to making and using liquid chlorine, for
it is dangerous and unpleasant. Various
people experimented, until in the end Charles
Tennant discovered how to combine chlorine
with lime to make chloride of lime, or
bleaching powder. Tennant opened his St
Rollox chemical works at Glasgow in 1799.
Bleaching, which had taken weeks, could now
be done in a couple of days.

After bleaching came printing, which in the
early days had also been tedious. The printer
had a block of sycamore, about 10 by 5 inches,
with the pattern carved into it. He used it like
a library stamp, pressing it first on a wet pad,
then on the cloth. To print a piece of cotton 28
yards long took 448 applications of the block.

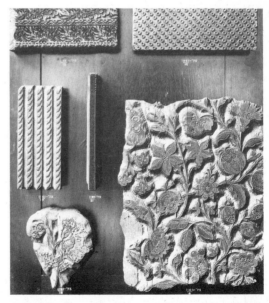

**Printing blocks. Separate blocks were needed
for separate colours. For some of the more
expensive silks there could be as many as sixteen applications to produce one section of the
pattern.**

73

Cotton printing by hand

This method was replaced by roller printing which first started in 1785 at the works of Livesey, Hargreaves & Co. The roller was of copper with the pattern etched on it. It dipped in the dye as it turned, a steel blade removing the surplus. The cloth passed over the roller, absorbed the dye from the parts that had been etched, and then went on to be dried. Printing 28 yards now only took two minutes.

While preparation, spinning and finishing were developing, weaving remained almost unchanged. Towards the end of the eighteenth century the weavers were much in demand and enjoying a golden age. Some bar doors had the notice 'Handloom Weavers Only'.

Though they could earn good wages, many weavers preferred to make do with fewer luxuries and work less hours. In 1840 one of them, looking back on the palmy days, described his week: 'Monday was generally a day of rest; Tuesday was not severe labour; Saturday was a day to go to the warehouse and that was an easy day to the weaver.' (*Parliamentary Papers*, 1840, Vol. XXIII, p. 218)

Here, then, was a bottle-neck, which should have given an incentive to make a new invention, and indeed in 1785 the Reverend Edmund Cartwright patented a powerloom. He had never seen a loom of any kind, so it was an extraordinary piece of equipment. He said:

You may readily suppose that my first loom was a most rude piece of machinery. The warp was placed perpendicularly, the reed fell with the weight of at least half a hundredweight, and the springs which threw the shuttles were strong enough to have thrown a Congreve rocket. (Baines, p. 230)

Cartwright then went to see some looms and, suitably humbled, came back to work on his own for a further two years. At the end of that time he opened a factory at Doncaster, but unfortunately his powerlooms proved no faster than handlooms and in 1789 he went bankrupt.

What happened now is interesting. For the time being no one attempted to improve Cartwright's invention but instead manufacturers employed more and more weavers. Indeed, even after an efficient powerloom had been developed, many manufacturers were loath to use it. The reason was that wages were falling so much that they saw no point in buying expensive machines. In the first place the weavers' prosperity had become notorious, so many people learned the trade. Secondly, weaving was crowded with refugees; they came from Ireland and also from other branches of the cotton manufacture that had been mechanised. Thirdly, and most important, the population was growing too rapidly for industry to employ all the labour that became available. Plain weaving was easy, so in the textile regions it was what the unemployed learned to do. The notices on the pub doors now read 'Mule Spinners Only'.

However, in the early nineteenth century the powerloom was made efficient, notably by William Radcliffe, Richard Roberts and William Horrocks. Other inventors even solved the problem of pattern weaving by machine. Jacquard had found the way to do this on handlooms about 1800, and in the 1830s his method was applied to powerlooms. With its punched cards, the Jacquard loom was the great grandfather of the computer.

Powerloom weaving

Power weaving did not bring such startling increases in productivity as power spinning, but the results were impressive enough. In 1823 Richard Guest calculated that 200 powerlooms manned by 25 adults with 100 young helpers would do the work of 875 hand-looms operated by 2000 workers. Guest took into account the inefficiency of the domestic system, with the women leaving the weaving from time to time to cook and keep house, and the men to waste their time.

Handloom weaving died slowly, none the less. In 1850 when there were a quarter of a million powerlooms in Britain, there were still 50 000 handlooms.

Two improvements took place to textile machinery of all kinds. One was the use of iron, and the other was mechanical power.

Spinning-wheels and handlooms were almost entirely of wood, and so were the earlier machines. Few of the inventors being either engineers or even mechanics, they were happier using wood, besides which, wrought iron was expensive. Arkwright, for example, made his first water-frames of wood, and employed a clock-maker to cut his gearwheels. Then, towards the end of the eighteenth century, machine-making became a specialised industry while, thanks to Henry Cort, wrought iron was plentiful and cheap. It was used more and more, for it was easier to clean than wood, lasted longer, and did not catch fire. It also needed less space, so that a mill-owner could buy more machines without extending his building.

At first men, women and children supplied all the power, but then came Arkwright's machines which needed something more, and horse capstans were quite usual, especially in small mills. However, when they could afford them, manufacturers preferred water-wheels. They were cheaper to run, gave a smoother, steadier drive and developed more power. Numbers of Arkwright-style factories were built in the remote valleys of the Peak District, some of which survived until 1850 and even later. Finally, there was steam. The cotton industry was one of the first to adopt Watt's engine, but even so it was a long time before it ousted the water-wheel.

COTTON MILLS

The mill buildings were as important as the machines which they housed.

The woollen industry had had mills since the Middle Ages, but only for finishing processes, like fulling, which could not be done in the home. Then, early in the 1720s, two half-brothers, Thomas and John Lombe, opened a silk mill at Derby. It was perhaps the first modern factory in Britain, but as silk was expensive its mass production did not progress. Cotton was the growing industry, and though it was the last to develop, it was the first to have mills in any significant numbers. Arkwright and Strutt were the pioneers with their Cromford Mill of 1771.

Some of the earlier mills did not even go as far as warp spinning on water-frames, but stopped at carding. They then handed their cotton to domestic spinners who turned it into weft on their jennies. It was not until the power-assisted mule replaced the jenny that all spinning was done in factories.

As we have seen, weaving took a long time to mechanise. During a boom in the early

1820s some of the more progressive manufacturers added weaving sheds to their spinning mills, but it was not until the 1830s that there were new factories, built to include weaving departments. However, in them at least, the gap between spinning and finishing was closed, all processes going on in one building, directly under the control of the manufacturer. Andrew Ure, writing in 1835, described one of these new mills at Stockport. It was 300 feet long, 50 feet wide and seven storeys high. On the first and second floors were throstles, which were improved water-frames used for spinning warp. On the fourth and fifth floors were mules for spinning weft. The preparation was done on the third floor, between the two spinning departments. Since the powerlooms needed a solid base they were on the ground floor, while the lightest work of all, the warp dressing, took place in the attics. At each corner was a staircase and a hoist.

A disadvantage of the early mills was that they made spectacular bonfires. There was plenty to burn, for not only was there a lot of timber in the building, but the machines, also largely of timber, dripped oil. To start a fire someone only had to be careless with a lamp or a candle – and there were no extinguishers. Manufacturers, prodded by their insurance companies, began to look for ways of making fireproof mills, so there was a revolution in building techniques. One of the pioneers was Arkwright's former partner, Jedediah Strutt. His mill at Derby, started in 1792, was probably the first to be fireproof, or nearly so. The main problem was to support the floors. Strutt had several rows of cast-iron columns running the length of the building, and each row supported a massive beam that also went from end to end. Next, brick tunnels were built, resting on the beams, so that the ceiling was corrugated. The top they made level with a filling of sand, and then they laid a floor of earthenware tiles. The pillars had only to resist compression, so cast iron was ideal for them. The beams, however, had to resist tension, and if made of cast iron would have fractured. Wrought iron was too expensive, so Strutt had to have timber beams, though he cased them in iron to make them safer.

In 1803 Charles Bage invented the girder, with its characteristic H-shape.

Heating methods varied. Strutt's Derby factory had a hot-air system, but by the 1830s it was normal to use steam, carried round the building in cast-iron pipes. The proper temperature is important in cotton manufacturing, especially spinning. As there were ample windows, ventilation was no problem, except that it was sometimes difficult to persuade the workers to open them. Cotton mills were among the first to have gas lighting, and it was this which allowed them to work the abominably long hours that upset the social reformers.

Mills could be cheap or expensive. Peak Forest Mill, built in 1792, cost £310. Stayley Bridge Mill, built in 1835, cost £87 000.

THE FACTORY SETTLEMENTS

Factory workers needed somewhere to live. Where mills used water power, and were miles from any town, the owners sometimes built 'apprentice houses', filling them with pauper children from the workhouses. Later, with the coming of steam power, the factories moved into towns and the workers lived in industrial slums. There is plenty about the evils of both these places in the *Parliamentary Papers*, but they were not always bad.

At Belper and at Cromford, for example, Strutt and Arkwright built new villages. Instead of having pauper apprentices, they attracted complete families by creating what Ure described as 'handsome towns, built of hewn stone, with streets flagged with the same and regular houses on the most commodious plans where the operatives with their families pass the even tenour of their lives' (*Philosophy of Manufactures*, p. 343). As adult cotton spinners were among the best-paid workers in the country, they furnished their houses well. An astonished visitor to one of them saw a mahogany table, a piano, a barometer and a painting of the Virgin and Child at Bethlehem. Employers who built villages made a problem for themselves, since their factories needed mainly women and children with just a few skilled men. They had to go to still more trouble to find work for the others. At Cromford, for example, there was lead-mining, and at Belper, nail-making.

Some employers built churches and schools as well as houses. The places of worship were usually nonconformist chapels, but at Haslingden Leonard Horner found 'a large and beautiful church, with a tower and bells'. The Strutts built a British School at Belper in about 1810, and there was a Sunday School as well. Anyone up to the age of nineteen could attend the British School for a penny a week.

The factory settlement shows clearly how much control the employers had over their workers. The owner's responsibility was total. He not only organised his people's working lives, but looked after their physical, moral and educational welfare into the bargain.

THE RAW COTTON

In the early eighteenth century Britain bought cotton from the Levant, Egypt, some of the West Indian islands and a little from the southern colonies, like the Carolinas, on the North American seaboard. The sudden rise in cotton output could not have taken place without an equally sudden increase in the supply of the raw material. It came from the United States of America.

The thirteen colonies won their independence in 1783 and, along with it, they gained the vast area of land that lies between the Appalachians and the east bank of the Mississippi. Twenty years later, by the Louisiana Purchase from France, they bought an even larger piece of territory on the western bank so that the huge flood plain of the river and all its tributaries belonged to them.

In the early nineteenth century settlers began to move into the new lands in large numbers. They went by several routes, but the one that interests us was in the Deep South, running from South Carolina and Georgia to Alabama, Mississippi and Louisiana. Cotton had been cultivated for a long time on the silty clay lands of the Atlantic coast, from Virginia southwards, and when the settlers moved into the Mississippi Valley they tried growing cotton there. It did well. The climate is subtropical, with no danger of frost for well over half the year; there is rain in the spring when the plants are growing, and there is hot, dry weather in the summer when the crop is ripening. Moreover, the soil is perfect. For thousands of years the Mississippi and its tributaries had been flooding and laying down a thick layer of warm, rich, black silt. The area it covers in the states of Alabama, Mississippi and Louisiana is known as the 'black belt'. Here was one of the world's regions of great natural resources and geologically it was as important for the Industrial Revolution in Britain as our own coalfields.

The cotton plantations needed many labourers. The plants are raised from seed every year, so the ground has to be prepared, while during the growing season there is weeding and thinning to do. Finally, there is picking, which, before machines were invented, went on from September until November. It was all hard, tedious work, to be done in the subtropical heat, and the only people that could be made to do it were Negro slaves. In 1800 the United States boasted 1 million, and by 1808 there were 1¾ million. In that year the trade with Africa ended, but the slaves already in America were encouraged to breed, so that by 1840 there were 2¾ million.

Cotton will make a cloth of virgin whiteness, but its production depended on the ruthless exploitation of three very black commodities – coal, soil and slaves. Two of these three were in America.

One vital piece of equipment was invented by an American. When cotton wool, or 'lint' as it is called, is picked, it is adhering, inconveniently, to a large seed. It can be stripped off by hand, but processing thousands of pounds like that was impossible, even with slave labour. Here was a bottle-neck which urgently needed some new invention. Rollers seemed a good idea, but they did not work and no one made any progress until, in 1784, Eli Whitney produced his 'gin'. It was simple enough, but it had the right principle in that it tore the lint from the seed, as a cat might with its claws. Whitney deserves a place alongside Hargreaves, Arkwright, Crompton and the other British inventors. He also suffered the same fate as many of them: his gin, being easy to make, was difficult to protect by patent.

Cotton gin

77

16 The woollen industry

During the early Middle Ages England produced raw wool in quantity and exported it to towns in the Low Countries like Bruges, Ypres and Ghent, where it was made into cloth. Then, in the fourteenth century, the manufacture of cloth was started in Britain, with some help from Flemish weavers who had been encouraged to settle here by Edward III. There was a minor Industrial Revolution in the fifteenth century, which continued into the sixteenth. Farmers produced far more wool, but exports fell from 30000 sacks a year to 5000. At the same time exports of cloth grew twentyfold. From the sixteenth to the early nineteenth century wool was Britain's most important industry. We must now see how wool was manufactured in the early eighteenth century.

The techniques of the woollen industry were much the same as those of cotton at that time, which meant almost everything was done with fairly primitive cottage equipment.

The first job was to unwind the fleece, which might be something of a surprise package. The second task was to sort the wool. A fleece is a complex garment, but in spite of all its variety, wool fell into two broad categories. There was the short-stapled kind that was made into woollens, and the long-stapled sort that was made into worsteds. Their manufacture was similar in some ways but different in others.

Both needed a good clean for a start. Most people used soap and water, though in Somerset they preferred stale urine. If there was a stream close by they did their rinsing there, putting the short wool in baskets, and holding the long between two crooks, so that they could wring it.

After washing, the short wool was carded, in just the same way as cotton, and a sliver prepared for the spinner.

Long wool was combed. A comb had teeth that were fewer and larger than those on a card. They were arranged like the tufts on a hairbrush with as many as six rows or 'pitches' for fine wool, or eight for alpaca. The worker stuck the handle of one comb into a post, and hung a tress of wool on it. He then pulled a second comb through the tress, drawing it out evenly and straightening the fibres. Where the tress joined the first comb some of the fibres remained tangled, and were relegated to the woollen manufacture, but with what remained a good comber could make a sliver over 6 feet long.

So far combing sounds pleasant enough, like hairdressing, but unfortunately the combs needed to be hot to make the wool soft and pliant. The worker had to move quickly, and he had to be near the stove that heated the combs, so that he was uncomfortably warm and plagued with charcoal fumes. As we shall see, wool combers were the most irascible people in the industry.

For both woollens and worsteds, spinning came next, sometimes with the distaff and whorl, sometimes the hand wheel, and sometimes the Saxony wheel. Following that came weaving on the handloom, after which woollens and worsteds again parted company.

Worsted had only to be washed to remove the warp dressing, and dyed, but woollen cloth straight from the loom was uneven and would unravel when cut. It had to go through a process called finishing, that sounds like a series of tortures. First of all there was fulling, in which the cloth was beaten by wooden stocks turned by a water-wheel. This matted the fibres together. The cloth was stretched on tenterhooks to dry and then, as if it had not suffered enough, it went to be teased. This meant scrubbing the cloth with teasle heads, held in a wooden frame, so as to remove loose fibres and pull up the nap. The teased cloth looked like a lawn after several weeks neglect in summer, so it had to be sheared. Cropping the nap with huge shears to be just the same length everywhere was highly skilled work. Finally the woollen cloth was dyed and was ready for the tailor.

Cropping

GEOGRAPHICAL DISTRIBUTION

Some spinning and weaving went on almost everywhere in Britain, but three regions were especially important.

One was the West Country, or rather a large part of it that included most of Gloucestershire and Somerset, and much of Wiltshire and Dorset.

The second region was East Anglia. Norwich, where they specialised in high quality worsteds, was the most important of the towns. The weavers there used yarn that had been spun not only locally and in Suffolk but as far away as Cheshire and Northumbria. At Colchester and in Essex generally they wove 'bays' and 'says', which were exported to Catholic countries both in Europe and South America. The clergy used them to make their habits.

The third region was the West Riding of Yorkshire. Yorkshire cloth was poor, because they did not take much care over their sorting, they included inferior wool, like lamb's wool, and their finishing was rough. In the main they exported to the more poverty-stricken countries like Poland and Russia. There was a story of a Russian regiment on parade in the rain whose uniforms shrunk before the eyes of the spectators. There was also an expression 'To shrink as northern cloths'. Anyone living at that time would have said that Yorkshire was the most backward of the three areas. However. when the Industrial Revolution overtook the woollen industry, it killed it in East Anglia, reduced it almost to nothing in the West of England, but made Yorkshire, for a time, the most important woollen manufacturing area in the world.

We must first see what happened in the West Country and East Anglia. Here, the industry used the domestic system, which meant problems of transport and organisation. Wool sometimes passed through fourteen pairs of hands and travelled up to 150 miles before it was finished cloth. There were problems too with spinners, weavers and wool-combers.

Spinners were not people to organise strikes, and they took low wages for long hours of work. Their trouble was that they were unreliable. Their yarn was often faulty, varying in thickness and weak in so many places that it kept breaking in the loom. Many of them embezzled the wool their employers sent them to spin. They found it difficult to finish work on time, since most of them were married women with homes to run, and who often had to help on the farms.

Many weavers were men, and they were indeed likely to form unions and demand higher wages, in spite of the disadvantage of being well scattered. Their work was sometimes faulty. They might have indifferent yarn, but they did not make the best of it. Through lack of concentration their weave was often tight in some places and loose in others, so that their cloth varied in thickness. The beginning of a roll was likely to be good; so was the end, but not the middle. Many were part-time farmers, so, like the spinners, they rarely delivered their work on time. Also like the spinners, they embezzled materials when they had the chance.

The really difficult people, though, were the wool-combers. Their tempers were frayed by working in charcoal fumes and intense heat, and, moreover, they had good opportunities to show their displeasure. They were highly skilled, so there was no hope of their giving work to anyone else, and also they roamed about in groups, going where they could find employment, so that they were able to form effective trade clubs. They restricted their numbers by ruling that no man should have any apprentice other than his eldest son; they bribed or bullied any stranger wool-comber who came into their area, until he left; they extorted high wages from their employers, and then took advantage of them to cut down their hours. James describes them as 'a powerful, organised body, who frequently by their commotions, strikes and insubordinate conduct, occasioned much difficulty to the masters' (op. cit., p. 250). The patron saint of woolcombers was Bishop Blaize, who had suffered martyrdom by being torn to pieces by iron combs. It was an apt choice in more ways than one.

Capitalists had long had control of the East Anglia and West Country branches of the industry. In some of the craft guilds of the early Middle Ages all the craftsmen may have been independent. Each owned his place of work, tools and equipment, bought his raw materials, and sold his finished goods himself. The spinner bought wool from the grazier and sold yarn to the weaver, while the weaver bought yarn from the spinner and sold cloth to the fuller, and so on. Yet for such a system to last, everyone must put back enough money from each sale to buy his next stock of materials, which was something the average working man could not do consistently. Sooner or later, because of misfortune or mismanagement, he was out of money, out of materials and looking for a loan. The person most likely to help was the merchant who sold the finished cloth, since he wanted those who supplied him to keep working. At first one or two craftsmen might come to him for short-term loans, but in the end they all depended on him permanently.

By the eighteenth century merchants in the West Country and East Anglia had become 'clothiers' and had taken heavy financial burdens with formidable problems of organisation. They had to find the capital for vast supplies of wool, and that capital had to pay interest while a none too diligent army of cottagers spent weeks, or even months, on their several tasks. Moreover, valuable stock was in homes scattered over several counties and had to be coaxed through as many as fourteen separate processes. At the same time the merchant was watching standards of work, guarding against embezzlement and hoping that perhaps, once in a while, he might meet his delivery dates. His compensation was a large share of the profits. He might be not just a 'clothier' but a 'gentleman clothier', a man of wealth and influence.

Most clothiers had taken one step towards direct control of the manufacture. As fulling needed water power, they usually owned the mills and employed the men who worked in them. Moreover, after fulling, a piece of cloth was too valuable to go back into some dubious cottage, so the cropping and dyeing were also done in the clothiers' workshops. However, there had been no progress beyond that.

Clearly the problems with the domestic system and its workers must have checked the growth of the woollen industry, but the cotton industry, too, had the same handicap. The difference was that the cotton manufacturers overcame them by building factories and buying machines. Why did the woollen manufacturers not do the same?

It is possible they thought their workers could not be made to accept changes. In the sixteenth century John Winchcombe, known as Jack of Newbury, built a large shed and put all his spinners and weavers to work in it. He anticipated the factory system by over two hundred years, for, apart from machinery, he enjoyed all its advantages. He was able to insist on regular hours and minimum standards of work, and he stopped embezzlement. Above all, he saved himself transport costs. The last did not interest the workers, but the other three were anathema to them, so they made sure his experiment failed. The workers had not changed their ideas by the early nineteenth century. In 1812 the Yorkshire Luddites smashed shearing frames and gig-mills; later the weavers attacked powerlooms; the wool-combers staged two vicious strikes, one in 1825 and another in 1832, the former lasting twenty-two weeks, and involving 20 000 men. The militia had to be called out in Frome in 1822 because the weavers objected – not, be it noted, to the powerloom, but to the flying shuttle. John James said of Norwich in the 1830s: 'In truth, for anyone at this period to set up machinery there, was to venture his life.' (History of Worsted Manufacture in England, p. 437)

Here were reasons for the slow modernisation of the woollen industry, but they are not entirely convincing on their own. After all, they were met and overcome in other industries, including cotton. We are left, then, with the men in charge, the clothiers. Those people were not fools; on the contrary, they had persistence and powers of organisation. Their trouble was that they were gentlemen first and clothiers second. John James gives this description of the Norwich clothiers, 'the acknowledged aristocracy of the city', taken from a writer of 1784:

Being opulent men and generally surrounded by their dependants, they had something of a lordly bearing, and a marked line of distinction was preserved between the merchants and shopkeepers. To improve their carriage, they were sometimes accustomed to learn the use of the small sword. This was, I suppose, a general practice, for an eminent dyer, being once waited on by a London traveller, before he would enter upon business took him to his back parlour for a fencing bout. From this, they probably derived their peculiar air on entering a drawing room. What with shouting, scraping, stamping and bowing, a well-bred gentleman made as much bustle at the door as if an ambassador had just returned from a foreign court. (op. cit., p. 261)

Such men were remote from the routine work of cloth-making. Their agents organised the progress of the wool through the tortuous labyrinths of the domestic system, but they themselves can rarely have seen a spinning-wheel or a loom in action. Even if they had, it would not have interested them unduly. Once yarn had gone to a master weaver it was his responsibility to make it into cloth, and the clothier had nothing to do with it until it was woven and ready for the fuller. Moreover, the gentlemen clothiers were the leaders of Britain's greatest industry. Being men of wealth and influence they were well satisfied and, like the king of the castle, they were more concerned to defend their position than to improve it. They misdirected their energies and abilities. While the cotton manufacturers were bent on improvement, anxiously seeking new machines, new organisation and new markets, the clothiers were employing private detectives to nose out illegal exports, or making sure that the wretched Irish had no industry of their own. It was as much in their interest as that of workers for things to remain unchanged.

Also, clothiers were still merchants, and they had the outlook of merchants, which included a love of high living. Adam Smith lumped them with land-owners:

The expense of a great lord feeds generally more idle than industrious people. The rich merchant, though with his capital he maintains industrious people only, yet by his expense, that is, by the employment of his revenue, he feeds commonly the very same sort as the great lord. (Wealth of Nations, Bk II, Chap. 3)

If one of them had money to spare, he would be more likely to build a fine house and employ what Adam Smith called 'menial servants' than to build a factory and employ productive workers. The follies around Bristol, like Blaize Castle, are good examples of misdirected merchant capital.

It was not in the nature of the gentleman clothier to turn himself into a Richard Arkwright. Even if he had felt inclined to sink his pride in order to add to his already considerable wealth, he would have been deterred by the fury any suggestion of change would have aroused in his workers. There was also another disincentive, perhaps more important than any of the others. We have already seen how the technology of even the cotton industry was checked when the population grew too fast in the early nineteenth century. East Anglia and the West Country had a surplus of workers long before then, which must have discouraged innovations.

Fortunately for the British woollen industry, Yorkshire was different from the other two regions. A Yorkshire clothier was so poor and uncouth that no West of England clothier would have invited him to dinner. Like his wealthier colleagues he bought wool from graziers and sold his finished cloth, but on average this took only a day a week. The rest of the time he was no organising merchant but a small manufacturer who employed at the most ten people. Moreover, he worked alongside them under the same roof, spending many hours on the loom himself. Quite probably he had a small farm as well as his workshop, so he was not even a full-time manufacturer. Clearly the domestic system had developed differently here. Instead of the wealthy men at the end of the line – the merchants – gaining control, individual craftsmen had prospered in a small way and each taken a few of their poorer neighbours into their direct employment.

Yorkshire had its labour problems, as the rising of the Luddites proved. It was not the workers but the clothiers who thought differently. They had not lost touch with manufacturing. Moreover, they had no social position to defend, they had modest incomes, and they led hard lives, all of which meant they had powerful motives for making improvements. What is more, they were as crude as their machinery, as rough as their cloth, and quite hardy enough to knock any opposition on the head, literally, if need be. In 1800 a clothier who was building a mill in Bradford heard that a mob was preventing a load of stone from going to the site, so he went to see for himself. Not being a gentleman, he stripped off his coat and cleared a way for the cart with his bare fists.

One final advantage the Yorkshire clothiers had was being near Lancashire. Their successful neighbours aroused jealousies and ambitions, but to do as well the woollen manufacturers had only to copy them.

By the mid-nineteenth century the Yorkshire manufacturers had accepted the fundamental ideas of the Industrial Revolution. They introduced new machines, built factories, developed new products, and found new sources of raw materials and new markets.

We will deal first with the technical changes.

For carding they were lucky, since all they had to do was adapt the machine the cotton manufacturers used. For combing, however, they needed a new invention. The first man to try was the same Edmund Cartwright who invented the powerloom. His device, nicknamed 'Big Ben', simply imitated the action of the hand comber, and it did not work well.

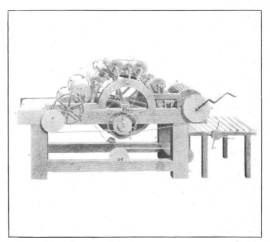

Wool-carding machine

81

There were other attempts, but no one had any real success until the 1840s when a Frenchman, Josué Heilman, invented the 'nip'. With hand combing, one end of the sliver became so entangled that it could not be used for worsted (see p. 78). In Heilman's machine a nip, rather like a pair of pincers, held the end of the sliver, while the rest was combed. The hold was then transferred to the other end, so that the part that had been in the nip could be combed in its turn. It was of course not tangled, as it would have been under the old system. There was no waste, the process was quicker, and it was possible to comb much shorter wool.

After carding or combing came drawing, known also as 'slubbing'. Following the hand processes, the individual slivers had been joined end to end, so there were bound to be differences in thickness. The new machines made continuous slivers, and the slubbers turned them into rolls of wool which, though still loose, were reasonably even and slightly twisted.

The final stage before spinning was roving. The slubbing was drawn out and twisted, then doubled, drawn out, and twisted again and again. It was just the same treatment that Arkwright gave cotton, save that he put six threads together instead of only two. The result was a perfectly even roving that could be spun into perfect yarn, at least in theory.

First of all woollen manufacturers took over cotton-spinning machines, the jenny, the water-frame and the mule, hardly changing them at all. The yarn was decidedly furry, lumpy and liable to break, all of which meant it was difficult to weave. However, by the 1830s there were machines making yarn that was fine, smooth and strong. Handloom weavers could at last use the flying shuttle.

When they tried powerlooms they found that worsteds were more difficult to weave than woollens, but unfortunately it was worsteds that they wanted to make in quantity. John Horsfall of Bradford solved the problem in the 1820s, and when the handloom weavers had been beaten into submission, the power-loom spread quickly enough. In 1840 there were about 11000 of them in the West Riding, and nearly three times as many in 1850. They became more efficient, too, for the early ones worked at eighty picks a minute, and the later ones at 170.

For finishing woollens, the gig-mill and shearing frame replaced teasels and hand shears. Being fairly simple they were the earliest machines to be used, and as such they took the brunt of the workers' anger (see P. F. Speed, *Social Problems of the Industrial Revolution,* pp. 81–2).

To house the new machinery there had to be factories, but to the disgrace of the West Riding the first mill to spin worsted was at Dolphin Holme, near Lancaster. It opened in 1784. Bradford, which was to be the centre of the industry, had no mill until 1800. In 1810 it had five, with a total of 120 horsepower, and in 1830 there were thirty-one, generating between them 862 h.p. Growth in the 1830s was rapid, so that by 1841 there were sixty-seven mills whose combined horsepower was 2058.

Some of these mills rivalled the ones of Lancashire, being fully integrated and costing up to £50000. Little mills were more typical, though. A small clothier would only carry out one process, like preparation, so he could manage with an old barn or corn mill equipped with second-hand machinery. Moreover, the change to the factory system was slow, for as late as 1856 half the workers in the Yorkshire textile industries were still domestic. Wool continued to limp behind cotton.

As the woollen industry expanded, English growers became unable to supply it. In the first place they did not produce enough, and secondly the quality of their wool was not what it had been (see Chapter 3).

For two reasons, then, the manufacturers had to look abroad. At first they bought from Spain and Germany, but then sheep-rearing began in Australia. In 1789 there were twenty-nine sheep in the colony, while in 1850 there were 17 million. Here was a development as important for the woollen manufacture as the cultivation of the Mississippi Valley was for cotton.

For sheep, Australia's temperate grasslands are ideal, and in the early nineteenth century a man could buy all the land he wanted from the Government at a few pence an acre. The mild climate meant the sheep

Shearing-frame

82

Woollen mill *c.* **1850**

needed no special care, so it was possible to keep large flocks with the help of a few Aborigines. There were, though, the problems of transport, and of the quality of the wool.

The cost of transport fell as ships improved, and the wool itself was so cheap that it made up for the expense of carrying it. In the 1820s importers were saying that they could sell Australian wool more cheaply than German.

Quality improved rapidly. The first sheep were a mixed lot that came from all over the place, including India, but in the early nineteenth century growers imported merinos and began to breed carefully. There was no question of selling mutton, so they concentrated on improving the wool alone. The climate helped them, and London merchants were soon praising the new wool. It was soft and fine and, they said, blended better with English wool than any other kind.

The table below shows how imports of Australian wool grew:

Imports from Germany reached their peak in 1825 when they were close on 30 million lb Spanish imports also reached a peak in the same year at 8.2 million lb. Thereafter they declined, but were still 21.8 and 1.3 million lb respectively in 1840. Australian wool did come into first place, but not until the days of the steamship.

With their new machines and new sources of raw wool, manufacturers turned to new products. The main problem was to destroy the

traditional image of the worsted, which was of a durable cloth, refusing to wear out, but thick with hair powder, snuff and tobacco smoke, misshapen, and green with age. The demand was for light, cheerful materials which could be discarded when there was a new fashion. The answer was to mix wool with other textiles. Even the Norwich manufacturers were willing to experiment, and made some exotic products from wool and silk. The most promising materials were Parisiennes, mixtures of wool and cotton woven in patterns. They were made in Bradford. 'Perhaps,' said James, 'there never was a more decided hit than this.' (op cit., p. 527)

Parisiennes were not alone. John James's book, published in 1859, gave an alphabetical list of Bradford's products. There were no less than eighty items, ranging from Amiens and Alpaca lustres to Pelliones, Ponchos and Yergas.

Along with new products came the quest for new markets. When Napoleon's blockade made it difficult to export to Europe, merchants found a new outlet in South America. Goods flowed back to Europe again after 1814, and in the 1820s Germany was the best customer. By the 1830s, however, the United States of America had taken her place, trade with that country having grown steadily ever since the War of Independence.

The story of woollen manufacture is instructive because it shows how a once great but moribund industry was brought back to life. There were new techniques, new products, new sources of raw materials and new markets. It all happened because there was a new spirit in Yorkshire. The clothiers there were bold in trying different ideas and in dealing with reactionary workers. They accepted change, so where they found obstacles they were quick to overcome them, and where they found opportunities they were quick to seize them. In East Anglia and the West Country, on the other hand, both employers and workmen decided instead that they would keep things as they were. Nevertheless, change could not be avoided, though it came to them in a different form. Instead of prospering, their industries died.

Imports of Australian Wool							
Year	*1810*	*1815*	*1820*	*1825*	*1830*	*1835*	*1840*
Pounds imported	167	73 171	99 415	323 995	1 967 305	4 210 301	9 721 243

17 Two Dorset industries: button-making, and hemp and flax

These two industries are worth studying because they were typical of many that were found all over Britain. Also, they make an interesting contrast, because when industrial change began in the Dorset countryside, one of them died while the other prospered, to continue until the present day.

BUTTON-MAKING IN EAST DORSET

In the Middle Ages buttons were for ornament only and clothes were fastened with tie strings or toggles. In Tudor times, however, something more elegant was needed, and buttons were adapted for the purpose. One of the earliest Dorset manufacturers of any importance was Abraham Case, who settled in Shaftesbury in 1622. He made his buttons by covering discs of sheep horn with linen and then embroidering them with thread to make patterns. Charles I had Case buttons on the silk waistcoat he wore to his execution.

As the industry prospered a bottle-neck appeared, because even in a county like Dorset there was a limit to the supply of sheep horn. Early in the eighteenth century Abraham Case's grandson found that wire rings were a good alternative. The first operation in making them was to wind a length of hot wire round a rod into the shape of a spring. Next, this was snipped along its entire length, so that it fell into a multitude of rings whose ends were joined by dipping them in molten solder. The invention was to button-making what the fly shuttle was to weaving, or the jenny to spinning, so here was an Industrial Revolution in miniature. There remained the 'casting', which was covering the rings with linen, and the 'filling', which was the embroidery. People could see no way of speeding those jobs, but there was progress in that they developed more and more types of filling. In the middle of the seventeenth century there were about thirty, and by the end of the eighteenth century over a hundred. They had names like High-Tops, Honeycombes, Yannells, Birds'-Eyes, Mites, Spangles, Dorset Knobs and Blandford Cartwheels. High-Tops were for hunting waistcoats, Mites and Spangles were very small buttons; Blandford Cartwheels had been designed by Huguenot refugees for the lace garments they made.

The industry was organised mainly on the domestic system, though the manufacturers produced the rings in their own workshops. Those belonging to the Case family were at Shaftesbury and Bere Regis, where wire arrived by the ton, hauled in broad-wheeled wagons from Birmingham. Children made the rings. The ones called 'winders' did the winding and snipping, and 'dippers' the soldering, both risking burns – and the latter lead poisoning as well. Finally, 'stringers' threaded the rings together in gross lots for transport. There were depots in the villages, rooms in public houses being quite good enough as, for example, at the St Peter's Finger in Lytchett Minster. They opened once a week, 'button day', when the workers brought their finished goods, and collected their pay and raw materials. The buttons were taken back to the workshops where women sorted and carded them. Seconds, those that were badly made or grubby, went on yellow cards, standard buttons on blue, and superior ones on pink. Pink and blue were for export only, local purchasers managing with seconds.

In the homes, children of eight, or even younger, did the casting, while women and girls did the filling. It was just possible to make a gross in a day, but six or seven dozen was more usual. Payment could be as low as 5d. a gross for seconds, or as much as 4 shillings for the best work, which meant a skilled woman could earn more than her husband did in the fields. Buttony was not popular with farmers, who expected women to work for them at harvest time for 9d. a day.

Button-making was also done in the schools and workhouses. When Lady Caroline Damers founded a Charity School at Milton Abbey, it was part of the curriculum. The children learnt a useful craft while helping to pay the expenses of the school. In 1770 there were three men and eleven women making buttons in Blandford workhouse. They must have been busy, because they usually produced ten gross a day between them. That model pauper, John Jenkins, once made ten dozen, but another time the unreliable Hannah Ellot lost nearly as many.

The industry was in the hands of merchants, some of whom had many workers, as for example Atchinson of Shaftesbury who was employing 1200 people in the 1790s. Being merchants, though, they paid more attention to selling their goods than they did to the way they were made. The Case firm had a permanent agent in Blandford, one office in London and another in Liverpool. The London office opened in 1743, in time for the upsurge in trade that was beginning then and lasted to about 1760. In Liverpool, Peter Case built Case's Street and Clayton Square, and it was typical of a merchant to spend his profits on show rather than plough them back into the manufacturing side of his business. Their buttons were sold all over the British Isles, as well as in Europe and North America. Clearly they were riding on the back of the cotton industry, since anyone buying cloth by the mile wants a suitable number of buttons to go with it. In 1807 Case had a turnover of £14 000, which was the highest the firm ever achieved.

The Dorset industry went on prospering in the first half of the nineteenth century, but competition was on its way. In the late eighteenth century Matthew Boulton was already making metal buttons, though they were mainly for heavy garments. No one wants steel buttons on his shirt. Something more ominous happened in 1810, for one Sanders, a Dane, opened a factory in Birmingham which mass produced wire buttons. However, since he covered them with pasteboard, they were hardly likely to have lasted many washdays. The trouble for Dorset really started in 1850, when Sanders's son-in-law, Ashton, patented a machine that would cover the rings with cloth. He showed it at the Great Exhibition. Henry, the last of the family to run the Case business, described its end:

Perhaps you would like to learn something of Ashton's patent machine button and its disastrous effect on the hand-made button. It was in the year of the Great Exhibition [1851] that it was whispered among the people of East Dorset, and the smash came at last, 1851–2–3, worse and worse. We employed in wire makers, paperers and button workers, from 800 to 1000; but they were soon in a state of poverty, some starving, and hundreds were sent off to Perth, Moreton Bay and Quebec by the noblemen of the county; about 350 left Shaftesbury. My uncle and father dissolved partnership, and in 1849 and 1850 there was on hand a stock of £14,500 worth of goods and buttons; but my uncle still continued his journeys to the chief towns. Ashton's buttons were becoming known everywhere, but I may state that in March 1859, I sold in the City £856 worth of wire and cloth worked buttons in five days, all to be delivered

within a month of purchase, and that was the last extensive sale of the hand-made button. My father was just upon being ruined, but the lords of the manors of Bere Regis and of Milborne stepped into the breach and saved him. (Bright, op. cit., pp. 73–4)

Case, then, blamed machinery for the disaster. The obvious question is why he and his colleagues had not developed machines of their own, or at least bought Ashton's. They might have feared labour problems, but hardly from women and children who made up the majority of their employees. More likely, since they were primarily merchants, and since theirs was a long-established industry, they lacked the imagination or enterprise to reorganise. Instead they waited until disaster was upon them, and then simply redoubled their efforts at marketing, inevitably to no avail. Their attitude was very like that of the gentlemen clothiers. There is a parallel, too, with certain modern industries that fail to modernise and then run to the taxpayer complaining of foreign competition and the hardships of unemployment. In the 1850s it was the landowners who came to the rescue of the buttonmakers, paying the manufacturers' debts and shipping the surplus workers to the colonies.

The old industry lingered for another fifty years, so there must have been a small demand for the more fancy handmade buttons. In 1912 a curious institution, the Mission House at Lytchett Minster, was still organising the remains of the domestic system, but there was no button day at the St Peter's Finger, since the goods went by post. That year they sold buttons worth £38, while wages and materials came to £36. Henry Case had already died in 1904, and Malachi Fisher, the Blandford agent, closed his draper's shop the following year. He ordered his staff to burn his entire stock of Case buttons.

THE HEMP AND FLAX INDUSTRIES OF WEST DORSET

Hemp and flax grow well on Upper Liassic deposits, and are equally happy on Inferior Oolite. Both rocks are common in West Dorset, so hemp and flax were cultivated there in the Middle Ages, and this led to their manufacture. It was certainly flourishing at Bridport by the early thirteenth century, since King John sent the town an urgent and important order for ropes to equip his fleet. By the sixteenth century Bridport manufacturers were supplying the Royal Navy with almost all its rope, which was something of a distinction, even though the Navy did not have many ships. They also sold to merchants and, indeed, to anyone who wanted ropes. There was a curious expression for being hanged, which was to be 'stabbed with a Bridport dagger'.

The technology of the industries was simple enough. The flax and hemp leaves were steeped in water or 'retted' so that the green matter decomposed, releasing the fibres. These were beaten, or 'scutched', to knock out the seeds, and then combed to prepare them for spinning. The flax was spun on an ordinary wheel, but rope-making was done in a walk, which was a long, narrow enclosure. Here two people worked – a child, known as a turner, and a man, who was the spinner. The turner stood at a wheel with a hook in the middle that took the combed hemp. The spinner drew it out as it was twisted by walking slowly backwards. He went up and back 160 yards four times in an hour, for ten hours a day. In a working life of fifty years he walked the equal of four times round the world. Some of the turners were parish apprentices who only had their board and lodging, and some were 'free' children who earned up to 2 shillings a week. Such were the joys of the domestic system.

Net-making was women's work. It was ideal for a domestic craft, since the goods were easy to transport and the equipment simple – a wooden needle and some hooks on the wall. Whenever possible they worked outside. As they did little more than tie knots, they must have been bored, but they did not look for variety, since each village specialised in its own kind of net and refused to change.

The citizens of Bridport were typical mercantilists. In the first place they looked for government protection. When rope-walks appeared in Burton Bradstock, 3 miles away, they petitioned Parliament for help. In 1530 it obliged them with an Act, saying there must be no rope-making within 5 miles of their town, and that all hemp grown in the same area had to be sold in Bridport market. Secondly, there were guild restrictions. In Queen Elizabeth's reign one Morgan Moore leased the town's beam and weights for £4 a year. He used them to check the quality of the ropes by seeing they weighed enough for their length. There were also the usual guild regulations governing prices, the number of apprentices a man might have, output and so forth.

Bridport had problems in the early eighteenth century. The Navy decided it would no longer buy its heavy cables there, since the largest ones were 25 inches in circumference and difficult to transport. Instead, they built rope-walks at Woolwich and Portsmouth, for which they imported raw hemp from Holland. Also, the Act of 1530, along with the guild restrictions, had driven the industry elsewhere, Bridport men going as far as Yorkshire to carry on their trade. To add to their worries, their harbour filled with silt. It is at West Bay, on the mouth of the River Brit, some 3 or 4 miles from the town and the Brit, being only a small stream, does not have the strength to scour its mouth clear. Finally, the times were bad for rope-makers, for trade was flagging and the shipping industry along with it. After 1740, though, Bridport, like the rest of the country, became more and more prosperous, so that by the end of the century its industry was transformed.

In the first place communications were improved. The River Brit was diverted into a better course, the piers were rebuilt and the harbour dredged. Apart from helping industry back in the town, this encouraged shipbuilding, which flourished until the 1870s. Also, the roads were turnpiked. Bridport was on the main road from London to Exeter, which was useful, but more important, good roads made it easier for merchants to use other local ports like Poole and Lyme Regis. At times business was too brisk for West Bay alone to handle it.

The Bridport manufacturers produced more varied goods. They still made ropes, though only enough heavy ones for their own ships, and they also spun string, pack-thread and twine. From 1750 there was a new industry, sail-making. The best place to make sails, it was thought, was West Coker, in Somerset, owing to some quality in the water there. Bridport manufacturers described their sails as 'made at Bridport near Coker', relying on their customers' ignorance of geography. The two places are 15 miles apart. However, it was net-making that became the main occupation, chiefly fishing nets of all kinds, drift, seine and trawl. They gave them their own names, like Lance, Caplin, and Dongarbin, and even had a special Bridport knot for making them.

Their goods had a wider market than before, but they sold most of them in Newfoundland. The fisheries there reached a peak during the Napoleonic Wars when the Royal Navy blockaded the European ports, and as they prospered, so did Bridport. The ships took out nets and returned with salt cod. As a sideline they carried Madeira wine which, so it seems, makes better drinking after a long sea voyage. It was best to send it round the world, but four trips to Newfoundland were nearly as good.

There were changes in the organisation of the industries. By tradition rope-making was a family business, but in the eighteenth century capitalists took control. From the sixteenth century there had been middle men buying from farmers and selling to manufacturers, and as they gained wealth, so they gained influence, just like the wool and cotton merchants. As early as 1665 Samuel Gundry was purchasing hemp and putting out work. In 1670 William Hounsell opened a spinning mill. It was just some traditional rope-walks, with no new machinery, but they were grouped together and worked by Hounsell's employees, under Hounsell's supervision. Gundry's method of 'putting out' was the one that became general, though. Hounsell's mill was very like Jack of Newbury's unsuccessful experiment in the woollen industry. Netmaking, too, was run in the usual way for domestic crafts, the employers putting out twine, and the cottagers working in their own homes.

An unusual feature of capitalist control at Bridport was its extension backwards, to the production of the raw material. There were flax jobbers who paid farmers so much for each acre of flax, supplied them with seed and labour, and then sold the crops to manufacturers.

The old guild restrictions went. How or why is not clear, but the result was that instead of having stagnant industry in Bridport, and a barren no man's land 5 miles wide, the countryside for 10 miles around was busy, while the town itself hummed with life.

Such, then, was the first stage of the Industrial Revolution in Bridport. It is interesting in that it came about without any new technology, for, although water power was used a little in the 1790s, it was not general until after 1820. However, the Bridport manufacturers had met problems and overcome them. They were willing to make changes, and this ensured that their industries would not die.

In the nineteenth century the Bridport industries found more new markets, new sources of raw materials and, at last, developed new techniques.

After the Napoleonic Wars ended, Dorset's trade with Newfoundland declined, so Bridport traders looked elsewhere. They went to the mainland of North America, selling their goods in the seaport towns from Quebec down to Florida, and then on to the West Indies. They also exported to Europe. All the time, British shipowners were good customers.

While Dorset flax and hemp might have been the best grown in England, it was not of the highest quality, so Bridport manufacturers took advantage of their improved communications to buy from the Baltic countries. The raw materials came first to London, Hull, Newcastle or Dundee, and then finished their journey in coastal vessels. In 1825 the port of Lyme Regis handled 1200 tons, enough to make large quantities of sails and nets.

The imported flax and hemp improved the quality of Bridport's goods, but their coming was unfortunate for local farmers. The two crops occupied 4000 acres in 1814, but they dwindled to none at all over the next hundred years. There was no longer a geographical reason for the industry being in West Dorset, but it remained because the plant and workers were there. This is called 'geographical inertia', although where it is found it means that an industry has shown anything but inertia; rather, it has adapted to meet new conditions.

Technical changes came slowly. The first was simply to use water power instead of children for turning, while the spinners still worked in the same old way. There were more rapid developments just before 1850. They had hackling, combing and rope-making machines, and powerlooms to weave sails. For nets they had the jumping loom, so named because at the end of each cycle the operator had to jump with his full weight on a pedal.

Machinery meant larger firms. Gundry's, for example, mechanised and opened works at Campbelltown on the Moray Firth, and at Rochdale. However, the cottage industry lingered. The women left the heavier nets to the machines and worked on finer goods, like pockets for billiard-tables. Some of this 'braiding', as they call it, is real artwork. A special order will still go to some trusted outworker. Wimbledon nets and those for the 1966 World Cup were made in Dorset cottages.

In the twentieth century the changes continued. There were new materials, artificial fibres; there were new products, like camouflage nets during the war; transport improved, being now by lorry; techniques have improved, one net factory having machines that tie 30 000 million knots a year. Firms have continued to grow and amalgamate. Most joined together in 1947 to form Bridport Industries, and Gundry's joined them later to form Bridport–Gundry Ltd. It is a pity that in the 1960s they met those twin horrors, government taxes and Japanese competition, although the company still survives.

CONCLUSION

The buttons and the hemp and flax products of Dorset were quite unimportant in the national economy. However, they are worth studying for all that. The leading sectors like cotton attract a lot of attention, and rightly so, but the cotton mills were the wonders of the Industrial Revolution, not its norm, so we need to look at something like the Dorset industries as well, in order to keep a balanced view.

18 Industry and the economy

To ask how important a role industry played in the Industrial Revolution may seem like asking how much of the work in a restaurant is done by the customer. He is there to be served, while waiters, cooks, delivery men and suppliers minister to his needs. Similarly, it might be thought that the Industrial Revolution was a revolution in industry which agriculture, transport, trade, financial institutions, population growth and so on, all assisted. A few moments reflection, though, will show that this is too narrow a view. There were most complex relationships between all sectors of the economy: each acted and reacted upon the others. Manufacturing industry was just one of those sectors.

As we have seen, there was no large-scale mechanisation before the latter part of the nineteenth century, save in cotton, metallurgy and, to a lesser extent, coal. Most industries were like the ones in Bridport, making significant progress, but by reorganising their existing resources rather than by adopting new technologies. Thinking of the slow growth of steam power, Chapman said, 'British industry had not been revolutionised by the mid-nineteenth century' (op. cit., p. 435).

The figures below show the importance of industry relative to other activities. They give the percentage contribution of each to national income:

Industry is in the lead by 1821, but for most of our period we would do better to speak of a revolution in agriculture, supported by industry, rather than the other way round.

However, what these general statistics conceal is the rapid growth of some individual industries, notably cotton. In this there was indeed a revolution, whether measured in capital formation, output, exports or level of mechanisation. Though but a small proportion of the whole economy, it may have been the yeast without which all the rest would have been a heavy, unresponsive dough.

We will now look at each of the major industries in turn.

COAL AND THE ECONOMY

The industry did not grow smoothly. Progress in coal-mining is never smooth. A detailed graph would show seasonal changes, with more production during the winter months, and even more important fluctuations over five- or six-year periods, because of the trade cycle. However, in the long term, there was considerable expansion. Output was perhaps 2½ million tons a year in 1700, it was 11 million tons in 1800, 22.4 million in 1830 and 49.4 million in 1850. Incidentally 1913 still has the record, which is 287.4 million.

The mines produced more coal because their owners employed more men and used improved techniques, but these changes would never have come about had there not been a growing demand.

In the early eighteenth century most coal was burnt in the home, nearly all of it for heating and cooking, but some also for domestic crafts like nail-making and other metal trades. Outside the home the only industries that could use it were those where smoke and sulphurous fumes did not matter, such as glass and brick-making, soap boiling, lime burning and, for some of its processes, brewing. All these together did not need much coal, and even domestic demand was not high outside London. Most people lived in the country and

	1688	1770	1801	1821	1851
Agriculture	40	45	32.5	26.1	20.3
Manufacture, mining, building	21	24	23.4	31.9	34.3
Commerce	5.6	13	17.4	15.9	18.7
Housing	5	3	5.4	6.2	8.1
Government, domestic, professional and others	28.4	15	21.3	19.9	18.6
Total %	100	100	100	100	100

no villager would buy coal when he could gather fuel on the common.

By the end of the eighteenth century there had been changes. Domestic demand grew. The agricultural revolution meant that many villages lost their commons. Cobbett found farm labourers in Wiltshire who were burning straw or bean haulms, sometimes sharing one fire between several families. They would have welcomed cheap coal. At the same time the towns were growing, so that most of their inhabitants had to burn coal or go without heat.

Also, during the eighteenth century, demand grew from the iron industry. It did not come suddenly. Abraham Darby of Coalbrookdale discovered how to use coke for smelting in about 1710, but forty years later hardly any other ironmasters had copied him. Progress was more rapid after 1750, however, so that by 1800 only a handful of charcoal furnaces remained. Further, there were new processes in other parts of the industry also needing more and more fuel. The fortunes of coal and iron were firmly linked.

In the early nineteenth century over a half, and perhaps as much as two-thirds of coal output was still burnt in the home, iron took between 10 and 15 per cent, exports were a mere 2 per cent, and miscellaneous industries had the rest.

By 1840 the picture had changed again:

	%
Iron industry	25
Domestic	31.5
Miscellaneous industries	32.5
Mining	3
Steam transport	1.5
Gas	1.5
Exports	5
	100

There was no absolute decline in domestic demand; rather, there was an increase. For fuel, people living in the new industrial cities depended entirely on coal, and with real wages rising after 1815 they had more to spend on their comforts. Just as much as before was needed for domestic crafts, since only a few industries had moved into factories. What had happened was that industry had increased its demands so much that instead of taking less than half the 11 million tons produced in 1800, it needed two-thirds of the 33 million tons produced in 1840. By 1870 it had increased its share to three-quarters of a total output of over 110 million tons.

Prices do a great deal to influence demand. Until well into the nineteenth century coal was expensive, except in places close to mines. This was partly owing to government taxes but mainly to the cost of transport. The one way to carry coal over long distances was by sea, so the only fields that were at all important nationally were Northumberland and Durham and, to a lesser extent, South Wales. From both it was relatively easy to take coal from the mines, down rivers and so into ships. South Wales coal was sold along the coasts of the Bristol Channel, and right round to Exeter. The market for the north-eastern coalfields was even greater. It covered the whole of the east coast of Britain, and the south coast as well, as far as the Dorset ports of Poole, Weymouth and Lyme Regis. Most of it went to London.

London was favoured but, even so, in 1814 coal retailed there at £2.8s. a ton while its pit-head price was 13 shillings. Inland, and more than 15 miles from a pit, it was too expensive to buy, which was why the Wiltshire labourers went on shivering.

In the 1830s the coal taxes were removed, but improvements in inland transport were more important. Canals helped a little, but it was the railways that made the real difference. They turned the whole country into one large market for coal, so that the inland coalfields could compete with those near the coast. Prices fell as a result.

The coal industry, then, provided rapidly increasing supplies of fuel, at falling prices, which was bound to give a fillip to the economy. Coal-mining was, moreover, at the centre of a revolution in technology. Railways were first built for coal-mines and then, when the national network was finished, they greatly stimulated demand, both because of what they burnt themselves and because of the much wider market which they opened. Coal made it possible to produce iron in quantity, and iron returned to the pits as rails, ropes, tubs, engines and equipment of all kinds, greatly increasing efficiency. Steam-engines first appeared at coal-mines. They drained them, and later raised the coal, so helping output. They burnt coal and were constructed of iron made with coal, so they increased demand. The stationary engine led to the steam locomotive, which in turn made the long-distance railway possible. There was also gas making, which had widespread ramifications, especially in chemicals.

Here are just a few of the obvious interconnections with only a handful of other industries. It would be easy to list many more. When it is said that the coal industry con-

G.B.E.—G

tributed only 1 or 2 per cent to the national income, we must not think of it as just another fraction of a potato in the country's dinner, but rather as the pinch of salt that changes the taste of everything.

THE IRON INDUSTRY AND THE ECONOMY

The demand for iron changed a good deal. In the early eighteenth century much of it went into the home, the craftsman's forge, the farm, the shipyard and the armaments works.

A modern house contains a fair amount of steel, but if we discount one or two major fixtures, like the central heating system and the bath, it is possible that a prosperous eighteenth-century home contained an equal weight of iron. The front door key, for example, might have had enough metal in it to make an entire lock today. In the living-rooms and bedrooms there were firebacks and fire-bars, while the kitchen held a clutter of iron-work – dogs, spits, hooks, chains, oven doors and round-bellied pots like the ones Abraham Darby made. There were all sorts of 'irons' that could be heated and used, some to press clothes, some to crimp them, and some to curl

hair. There were knives, scissors, corkscrews, candle snuffers, lanterns and a multitude of knick-knacks that are bewildering in their variety, quaintness and ingenuity. Unfortunately there is no way of measuring domestic demand, but it must have grown as the population increased in numbers and prosperity.

Craftsmen like blacksmiths, farriers and wheelwrights were to be found in every town and village. They shod horses and made and repaired vehicles, becoming more and more important as transport improved. Even the railways brought them extra work, for, as we shall see, they encouraged the use of horses over short distances. It was only the long-distance coach traffic that they killed.

Farmers used a lot of iron, so much so that many found it worthwhile to have their own forges. At first, implements were mostly of wood – the plough, for example, having only its share made of iron. Later, ploughs were of iron entirely, as were other pieces of equipment. Rich farmers owned threshing-machines powered by steam-engines. A new industry, agricultural engineering, appeared, needing growing quantities of iron.

During our period most ships were made of

Early uses for iron – fireback and lock

wood. However, even wooden ships needed iron for anchors, bolts, chains and numerous fittings. Men-of-war also needed ballast, but as they could spare but little space for it they took on iron, or 'kentledge' as they called it.

The other traditional use of iron was for muskets and cannon, and as the eighteenth century had more than its fair share of wars there was a brisk demand. The Seven Years War from 1756 to 1763 was a grand time for ironmasters, but it was as nothing compared with the Napoleonic Wars.

As time went on, iron found new uses. In the first place there was building. We have already discussed ordinary fittings, but in the Regency period wrought-iron railings and balconies were popular. However, what was revolutionary was the use of iron in construction. Possibly the first time it was tried was at St Anne's Church, Liverpool, where there are iron pillars supporting the gallery. Later there were fireproof mills. Jedediah Strutt went a long way with his Belper mill of 1792, though the first mill with a complete iron frame was Jones's Maltings on the outskirts of Shrewsbury, built in 1796.

In the nineteenth century they learnt how to use iron with glass. The Crystal Palace of 1851 was the most ambitious project, but there were plenty of others that came before it, such as conservatories in the gardens of big houses. More important were the railway stations. Here they needed to span wide areas to admit as much light as possible, and to save space on the ground by having slender supports. Iron and glass construction was ideal.

Along with building went civil engineering. The new cities needed so much water that it was useless trying to supply it through hollow elm logs. Instead, from about 1800, they used iron mains. At around the same time William Murdock found how to use coal gas for lighting, so gasworks multiplied, and they too needed iron. There were bridges as well. Abraham Darby III built the first iron bridge in 1779 to connect his works at Coalbrookdale with the other side of the Severn. More bridges followed, like the one over the Wear at Sunderland, built in 1796. Telford used iron for his famous Pont Cysyllte Aqueduct, and for his graceful suspension bridge over the Menai Straits. The early builders sometimes ran into trouble because they used the cheaper cast iron which is satisfactory only for vertical

Later uses for iron – Crystal Palace and Britannia Bridge

supports. One or two nasty accidents, like the collapse of the Dee Bridge, convinced them they must use wrought iron. It was from this material that Robert Stephenson made his famous Britannia Bridge of 1850. It is incredible, but until Stephenson and his colleagues made their experiments for this bridge no one had bothered to test cast and wrought iron in order to discover their relative qualities under tension and compression.

Yet another growing industry was mechanical engineering. Iron replaced wood in textile machines, and it has been estimated that in 1850 these took one-sixth of total output. Obviously the steam-engine could not have developed without iron. Boulton and Watt would have had to manage with brass, which was expensive, wore out quickly, and could not be cast in large pieces. As it was, they had Wilkinson cylinders that would last for a hundred years, were up to 6 feet across, and yet were bored accurately. The iron industry was itself one of its own best customers, for it needed massive equipment such as furnaces, rolling mills, steam-hammers and steam-engines.

Coal was closely linked with iron. By 1800 iron depended entirely on coal, but it had plenty to give in return, as has already been shown.

Finally there were the railways, which probably made more demands on the iron industry than everything else put together. By 1848 there were 6000 miles of track in Great Britain, each mile of which needed over 150 tons of iron. Moreover, foreigners were building railways as well, and their own ironmasters could not supply them. As one American remarked, rail iron from South Wales had no equal, so there was no point in buying elsewhere. It all meant a great increase in output, with good profits, but it did make the industry too dependent on one kind of customer. It is also curious that the demand for railway iron did not encourage any improved techniques. G. R. Hawke has tried conscientiously to find some, but he says that the only change was an increase in the size of the South Wales blast-furnaces, which might have come anyway because of competition from Scotland (*Railways and Economic Growth in England and Wales*, 1970). As new industries cease to be new and pass into maturity, their output is at its highest, but, like human beings, they lose their ability to change.

Turning from the demand side to supply, we can find no reliable figures before 1820, but the general trend is clear enough. In 1720 the industry produced perhaps 25000 tons of pig-iron, and by the late 1750s output had crept up

to about 30000 tons a year. The Seven Years War gave a powerful if temporary boost, after which civilian demand grew, output doubling between 1757 and 1788. After that, progress was rapid. Coke smelting with puddling and rolling on the one hand, and the growing number of uses for iron on the other, were changes enough, but on top of them came the Napoleonic Wars with government orders for armaments on a scale not known before. It is possible that the Navy alone took one quarter of an output which quadrupled between 1788 and 1806, by which time it was 250000 tons a year. Immediately after the war there was depression, followed by growth until 1830, more or less in step with the rest of the economy. As with cotton, falling prices stimulated demand, and manufacturers were able to increase their profits by increasing output. Then came the railways and output again quadrupled in twenty years, rising this time from just under 700000 tons a year to over 3000000.

For convenience, this information is summarised in a table:

Output of Pig-iron in Britain

Year	Thousands of tons
1720	25
1757	30
1788	60
1806	250
1830	700
1850	3000

It would give a wrong impression, though, to plot these figures on a graph and join them with a smooth curve. Like all other industries, iron suffered from the trade cycle, and was, moreover, especially unfortunate in its choice of friends.

In the first place there was cotton, whose demand for machines and iron-framed factories varied with its sudden changes of fortune. Secondly there were armaments. During wartime the government was importunate, but as soon as peace came, it was prompt in cutting its orders. The end of the Seven Years War left the ironmasters wondering what to do with their surplus furnaces and forges, and after the Napoleonic Wars things were even worse. The industry was in a depression that lasted for several years until civilian demand grew enough to revive it. Finally there were the railways. They brought much prosperity, but were not built at an even pace. Instead there were two 'mania': one, relatively small, from 1836 to 1837, which produced 500 miles of track, and another, much more important, from 1845 to 1848, which produced 6000 miles of track. When each of them ended, and particularly the second, the iron industry again went into a depression.

The problem was that most iron products were capital goods, things like powerlooms, winding engines, threshing-machines and railway locomotives. Business men only bought them when they had heavy investments to make, which was not often. A man would want to open a new factory, or extend the one he had, only if he was making exceptionally good profits. Even the peak of a normal trade cycle was not usually enough to encourage him: it had to be a major boom, and one of these only came every nine years or so. Thus it was that the iron industry had to face inordinate demands over short periods, while the rest of the time it worked well below its capacity.

The industry added much to the wealth of the country. Without it iron would have been imported at considerable cost, but in fact Britain virtually ended her imports by about 1800, and began exporting. A mere 34 000 tons went abroad in 1806, yet by 1850 the figure was over 780 000 tons. How much iron added to the national income in precise terms it is impossible to say, but it may have been in the region of 6 per cent in 1805 and the same in 1851, though somewhat less in the period between.

COTTON AND THE ECONOMY

In the hundred years from 1740 to 1840 the cotton industry grew more rapidly than any other. Unlike most eighteenth-century industries we can measure its progress reasonably accurately because we have the figures of imported raw cotton:

Retained Imports of Raw Cotton (millions of pounds)

1700	1	1800	50
1740	2	1820	141
1760	3	1840	452
1780	5	1850	621

It is significant for one theory of the Industrial Revolution that the rate of growth was most rapid between 1780 and 1800 (see Chapter 38).

People at that time were amazed, some being lost in admiration, while others were uneasy or even hostile. No one, though, doubted the importance of the cotton industry. In the first place it added directly to the national wealth; secondly it gave an impetus to other industries; thirdly, it had a psychological effect which, though it cannot be measured, was perhaps the most important of all.

In their invaluable study *British Economic Growth* (1967) Phyllis Deane and W. A. Cole tried to calculate just how much the cotton industry contributed to national income. They say it was insignificant as late as 1770, but was 5 per cent at the turn of the century and over 7 per cent by 1811–13. S. D. Chapman (op. cit.) has since pointed out that Deane and Cole may not have included the cost of bleaching, dyeing and printing, which would mean their estimates are low. In about 1800 a roll of calico straight from the loom was worth £1. 6s., whereas when it left the printers it could be worth anything up to £5.

It is just as difficult to estimate the increase in fixed capital, but obviously the total value of mills, machinery, factory settlements and warehouses must have been considerable. Manufacturers ploughed back their profits consistently, but especially from 1825 to 1850, which was when they were building large integrated factories with powerlooms and steam-engines.

Statistics of overseas trade are more precise. In 1700 two-thirds of British exports were wool and there were practically none of cotton. In the early 1790s wool was twice as important as cotton, but by the end of the Napoleonic Wars it was the other way round, with cotton twice as important as wool and accounting for 40 per cent of all exports. By 1830 this figure was 50 per cent. We must remember that, unlike wool, all the raw materials for cotton manufacture were imports and that by 1830 they came to 20 per cent of the national total. None the less, the industry made a handsome contribution to the balance of payments.

There were advantages for ordinary people. The price of clothing fell, so they could dress better, and still have more money to spend on other things. Also, the factories gave work to women, youths and children who, without them, would have had no jobs.

In such ways cotton added directly to the wealth of the country, but it had indirect results as well. While it shot ahead, other textiles at first lagged behind, but its example was too good to be ignored and, eventually, wool, linen and silk were following it. Cotton machinery was adapted to suit the other fibres, and their manufacturers went over to the factory system. They hated their upstart competitor, but they had a stimulus from it that they badly needed.

Textiles could not grow in isolation. Other industries had to grow with them, like coal, iron, engineering, chemicals, building and transport, as well as commercial activities like banking, insurance, shipping and trade.

93

As we shall see in Chapter 38, W.W. Rostow believes it was the cotton industry that led the British economy in its 'take-off into self-sustained growth'. That may be too extravagant a claim for it, but there is no doubt that cotton was a leading growth sector, and a highly important one.

Finally there were the psychological effects. A revolution, whether it is political or industrial, means, as much as anything, a change in the way people think, and the cotton industry certainly gave food for thought. It would be wrong to suggest that people of the early eighteenth century did not exert themselves, or that Britain was an underdeveloped country. None the less, many folk were happy to accept their position in society and jog along at a modest pace. The countryman was content if, during his lifetime, he could add a few acres to his farm, and accumulate a little linen and pewter. The ordinary worker asked for no more than a leisurely existence, and if he had the choice of more money or more free time, would usually take the latter. The explosion in the cotton industry did much to destroy the traditional pattern of life and the traditional way of thinking. For the first time people could see what progress meant and, having seen, they believed. The new faith was one of the driving forces of the Victorian age.

WOOL AND THE ECONOMY

There is, perhaps, a tendency to point a finger of scorn at the woollen industry. Its growth rate fell as the Industrial Revolution progressed. Its share in the export market declined: from 1700 to 1770 it accounted for two-thirds of domestic exports, but at the end of the century its share had sunk to a quarter, and by 1830 to 12 per cent. The industry was slow to mechanise, with no real progress until after 1850. Above all, there was the contrast with cotton, for the venerable woollen industry was outstripped by its upstart young rival in a few decades.

The woollen industry, though, had its handicaps. Not the least of these was its age. As we have seen, the attitudes of employers and workers in both the West of England and East Anglia had hardened so much that change was impossible. New growth depended on Yorkshire. Here the social constraints were less, but there were economic ones also connected with the age of the industry. Even before the Industrial Revolution began, the market was already well supplied with woollen goods. As it progressed, the population grew and *per capita* consumption of wool probably grew as well, but there were limits to the rate at which demand could increase. For

cotton, though, the market was wide open. The new fibre had all sorts of exciting possibilities, so manufacturers exploited them, and people were eager to buy. Thanks to the rise in real incomes, they were able to spend more money on textiles, but they wanted more variety as well as greater quantity. Consequently, while they went on buying about the same amounts of woollens as before, most of the extra cash was spent on cottons. Much the same thing happened in the twentieth century with the introduction of rayon and nylon. Then it was cotton's turn to be eclipsed. If during a period of innovation a traditional fibre can keep pace with the growth in population, then it is making fair progress: wool did marginally better than that in the first half of the nineteenth century.

Not only was demand relatively inelastic, but so was the supply of raw materials. It was during the Napoleonic Wars that Britain had the best opportunity to expand her trade. At that time there was no problem of trading with America, while farmers there had slaves and virgin soil, so they were able to supply all the raw cotton that Lancashire needed. The woollen industry was much less fortunate. Nine-tenths of its raw wool came from Britain, where there was no virgin land to exploit, and where the pressure of population combined with movements in prices to make it more profitable for farmers to grow food. There was no question of converting tillage to pasture, and though sheep were valuable livestock, they were bred more for their mutton than their wool. A certain amount of raw wool came from Europe, but as in England an increase in production could only come at the expense of some other agricultural product. It is possible, too, that the war interfered. Imports from Spain, Britain's largest supplier, were £6.9 million in 1805 and £5.9 million in 1810. Next in importance was Portugal which sent £1.7 million in 1800, but only £0.2 million in 1805. The importance of elasticity of supply is shown when the woollen industry in its own turn was able to draw from tracts of virgin soil, the temperate grasslands of Australia. The industry gained momentum in the 1840s, while from 1850 to 1875 it doubled the amount of raw wool it used. At that time it was probably growing faster than the cotton industry.

We can do more than simply excuse the woollen industry for failing to show the same spectacular progress as cotton, for it made a valuable contribution to the national economy throughout our period.

From Gregory King's survey in 1688, it seems that the value of woollen goods then produced each year was £3 million, and that was one-third of the total of all industries put together. At the same time woollen goods accounted for two-thirds of domestic exports, as we have seen. A contemporary estimate put the numbers employed at close on 1 million, or nearly one in five of the population. That may not have been far wrong, if every child who gave a hand, and all part-timer spinners and weavers were included.

There can be no doubt, then, of the importance of the woollen industry in the early eighteenth century. This, moreover, was the time when the economy began to stir, in preparation for the great surge forward that came later in the century. The woollen industry earned foreign exchange; it encouraged shipping and transport; it led to the growth of commercial institutions and the use of credit; it boosted farming; it increased the purchasing power of countless families, who would otherwise have depended only on agricultural wages. More than any other industry, wool helped to carry the economy forward to the point where the Industrial Revolution became possible.

Furthermore, the rate of growth of the woollen industry increased from 8 per cent in the decades between 1700 and 1740, to 13 per cent or 14 per cent between 1740 and 1780. Some authorities date the beginning of the Industrial Revolution at 1780, but there are good arguments for 1740. If the latter date is correct, then wool played an important part in the early stages of the Revolution, as well as in the period leading to it.

As the century wore on, the rate of growth declined to 6 per cent and there were no changes in technology or organisation. The leaders were cotton and iron. However, if we ignore rates of growth and exports and look instead at the total value of goods produced, we find that wool compared not unfavourably with cotton.

Net Output of Wool and Cotton
1770–1850

	Woollen and worsted (£m)	Cotton (£m)
1770	7.0	0.6
1805	12.8	10.5
1821	16.6	17.5
1836	16.7	21.8
1845	21.1	24.3
1850	20.3	21.1

SOURCE: P. Deane and W.A. Cole, *British Economic Growth, 1688–1958* (1967).

Moreover, cotton imported all its raw materials, while in the the first half of the nineteenth century wool imported only one-third. Probably wool was making as great a contribution to the national income as cotton, down to 1820. In the third quarter of the century, as we have seen, large supplies of Australian wool became available and the industry was mechanised. By 1905 it was using 700 million pounds of raw wool a year compared with 100 million pounds in 1805.

In sum, then, we can say that no other industry could match wool in the period leading to the Industrial Revolution, and it compared favourably with the leader, cotton, while the Revolution was in progress. It had its own period of rapid growth after 1850, and that might well have come earlier had it enjoyed the same abundant supplies of raw materials as cotton.

PROBLEMS

1 What changes in mining technology depended on progress in other industries?

2 To what extent were coal-mines a breeding ground for technologies that could be applied elsewhere?

3 Examine the links between the coal industry and transport.

4 What created the increasing demand for coal down to 1850?

5 How far did the mining industry meet growing demand by increasing efficiency, and how far by increasing the units of production and the labour force?

6 In what ways did the demands of the iron industry stimulate other industries?

7 What demands were made on the iron industry, and how were they met?

8 Assess the relative importance in the iron industry of new technologies and the increase in size and number of units of production.

9 What demands did the iron industry make on (a) capital, and (b) labour?

10 Explain the growing importance of wrought iron down to 1850.

11 What changes did the growth of the iron industry make in society?

12 What Quaker families were engaged in the iron industry apart from the Darbys? What attracted Quakers to this industry?

13 What were the linkages between the cotton industry and the rest of the economy? Were they strong enough and numerous enough for cotton to produce what Rostow has termed the 'take-off into self-sustained growth'? (Rostow's views are given, in outline, in Chapter 38.)

14 Why was foreign trade vital for the development of the cotton industry?

15 Examine the pattern of population growth in Lancashire. How was it different from other parts of Britain, and why?

16 How far and in what ways was cotton ahead of the rest of British industry by the 1840s?

17 In what ways did the woollen industry help establish what Rostow terms 'the preconditions for take-off'?

18 Explain why there was constant friction between wool growers and woollen manufacturers.

19 What were the main overseas markets for British woollens, and what goods were imported in exchange?

20 How far did social attitudes rather than economic factors influence progress in the woollen industry?

21 How did changes in technology affect the location of industries? Show how bottlenecks have stimulated changes in technology. How far does this support Rostow's theory of 'leading sectors'?

22 How far did changes in technology depend on progress in pure science? How far could an industry progress without changes in technology? Consider the roles of the inventor and the innovator. What motives influenced each?

23 Why did so many inventors fail to make money?

24 What were the social and economic problems created by the domestic system? Why did it persist for so long?

25 What social attitudes hindered the growth of the factory system?

26 Why will workers sometimes accept changes in industry, such as new machines and new organisation, and sometimes resist them?

27 Why do old-established industries find it more difficult to make progress than new ones?

28 Assess the importance of elasticity of supply and of demand for industries.

29 How far did war affect industry?

30 Assess the importance of London in the Industrial Revolution.

FURTHER READING

Ashton, T.S. *Industrial Revolution 1760–1830*. Home University Library, Manchester U.P., 1948.
_____. *Iron and Steel in the Industrial Revolution*. Manchester U.P., 3rd ed. 1963.
Ashton, T.S. and Sykes, J. *The Coal Industry of the Eighteenth Century*. Manchester U.P., 1929.
Bowden, Witt. *Industrial Society towards the End of the Eighteenth Century*. 1925: Cass, 1965.
Cardwell, D.S.L. *Technology, Science and History*. Heinemann, 1972.
Chapman, Stanley D. *The Early Factory Masters*. David & Charles, 1967.
Checkland, S.G. *The Rise of Industrial Society in England, 1815–1885*. Longmans, 1964.
Cossons, Neil. *Industrial Archaeology*. David & Charles, 1975.
Fitton, R.S. and Wadsworth, A.P. *The Strutts and the Arkwrights*. Manchester U.P., 1958.
Gale, M.K.V. *Iron and Steel*. Longmans, 1969.
Harris, J.R. (ed.) *Liverpool and Merseyside*. Cass, 1969.
Hudson, Kenneth. *Industrial Archaeology*. Methuen, 1965.
——.*Industrial Archaeology of Southern England*. David & Charles, 1965.
Lipson, E. *The History of the Woollen and Worsted Industries*. A. & C. Black, 1921.
——.*A Short History of Wool and Its Manufacture*. Heinemann, 1953.
Nef, J.U. *The Rise of the British Coal Industry*. Routledge, 1932.
Raistrick, A. *Dynasty of Iron Founders: The Darbys of Coalbrookdale*. Longmans, 1953.
Schubert, H.R. *History of the British Iron and Steel Industry*. Cass, 1957.
Singer, C., Holmyard, E.J., Hall, A.R. and Williams, T. *A History of Technology*. O.U.P., 4 vols, 1959.
Wadsworth, A.P. and Mann, J.L. *The Cotton Trade and Industrial Lancashire 1600–1780*. Manchester U.P., 1931.

Inland Transport

19 Turnpike roads

ORIGINS AND DEVELOPMENT

In the Middle Ages every town and village had a duty, under the Common Law, to maintain its own roads. The law was reasonable, because there was not much long-distance travel, and the roads were used almost entirely by local people as they went about their farming. The problem with the Common Law was the difficulty of enforcing it, so in 1555 the care of the roads was made a statutory obligation by an Act of Parliament. It stated that each parish was responsible for its roads, and laid down procedures. The ratepayers at the vestry meeting had to elect one of their number to be surveyor of highways for one year. He could dig the stone and gravel he needed without payment, and he could demand help from everyone. Those who owned or rented land worth more than £50 a year had to send horses, carts, tools and workmen; the poor came empty-handed but ready, in theory, to use the equipment others had provided. The surveyor could call on anyone at any time, save during the hay and corn harvests, for a maximum of four days in the year. In 1563 the number of days was increased to six. All these services had to be given free of charge. They were called 'statute labour'. As one would expect of the sixteenth century, the Justices of the Peace supervised. If they decided a parish was neglecting its roads, they presented it at quarter sessions and spent the money from the fine on repairs.

Here was a system that could have kept the roads in order, but it did not work. Magistrates were too busy or indifferent, while surveyors were unpaid amateurs on temporary appointments, each one counting the days until his year should be over. Their colleague ratepayers, who should have known better, often failed them:

Sometimes the worst horses are sent, at others a broken cart, or a boy, or an old man past labour to fill; they are sometimes sent an hour or two too late in the morning, or they leave off much sooner than the proper time. (*The Complete Farmer,* 1807, quoted in Searle, op. cit. p. 87)

The ordinary villagers caught the mood:

They make a holiday of it, lounge about and trifle away their time. As they are in no danger of being turned out of their work, they stand in no awe of the Surveyor. It is a common saying among us, that if a drop of sweat should happen to fall from any of them, it would infallibly produce a quagmire. (*St. James's Chronicle* [5 January 1768], quoted in Searle, p. 86)

Statute labour was barely good enough to maintain local cart-tracks, and by the seventeenth century some villages were unlucky enough to find themselves on important routes carrying heavy through-traffic. The Hertfordshire section of the Great North Road was especially busy, because a tributary of the Thames, the Lea, had been made navigable, and wagons converged on the little river port of Ware carrying grain for London. The road repairs were more than the villages could manage, especially Stanton. That unhappy place was presented regularly at quarter sessions, and its inhabitants were doing double statute labour, but all to no avail. They argued that the men whose traffic ploughed their roads should pay some of the expenses, and joined with other villages in petitioning Parliament for the right to levy toll. Accordingly, Parliament passed an Act in 1663, which allowed gates at Wadesmill, near Ware, at Stilton, 50 miles away in the north of

Huntingdonshire, and at Caxton, which is between the two in Cambridgeshire. The Justices in the three counties were to appoint surveyors, whose duty it was to keep the road in repair. The parishes still gave statute labour, but the surveyors had the toll money as well. Here, then, were two new principles. In the first place there were wider authorities than the parishes, and secondly the road users had to pay a share. The plan seems to have worked, and it would have been even better if the people of Huntingdon had allowed the Stilton gate to be erected. Here was a new dilemma. It was good to milk the through-traffic, but not so pleasant to pay toll oneself.

Probably for this reason, thirty-two years went by before there was another Act to authorise tolls. However, Parliament had thought of an even more unpleasant alternative, for the Highways Act of 1662 allowed Justices to levy a rate whenever statute labour was not enough. It only needed an increase in traffic to make tolls the lesser evil, and this came in the 1690s when French privateers drove goods from the seas, and on to the long, difficult overland routes. Statute labour, with rates, placed the whole burden on the parish; statute labour, with tolls, extracted something at least from the through-traffic. There were several Acts after 1695, all like the one for the Great North Road.

It was soon clear, however, that Justices were not the men to care for roads, so Parliament looked to others. In 1706 there was an Act which placed the road from Furnhill to Stony Stratford in the charge of thirty-two trustees. They had the duty to keep it in repair, and to do so they could call on statute labour and collect tolls. This was the first of the many turnpike trusts that were to bring a slow but useful improvement in road transport.

Down to 1836, Parliament passed over a thousand Turnpike Acts, but there was no attempt by the Government to guide development. It was left entirely to local people, like land-owners, farmers or town councils, to obtain their Acts and organise their trusts, and consequently road improvement was haphazard.

Activity came in bursts, the most important being from 1750 to 1770 when more than a third of all Turnpike Acts were passed, and there was another, smaller boom in the 1790s when the cotton manufacturers were putting the Lancashire roads in order. The length of road any trust maintained varied. Barnet to Galley corner was one mile, and Newcastle upon Tyne to Buckton Burn was 51 miles. The average was only 10 or 12 miles. Often, improvements were made to disconnected stretches. For example, in 1720 a traveller on the Great North Road found a turnpike from Holborn to Barnet, a gap from there to Stevenage, more turnpike to Biggleswade, and then another gap to Alconbury.

What did dictate some sort of pattern was London, for most through-traffic was going to or from that city. We have already seen how the first tolls were collected on a road that pointed towards London, even though the last part of the journey was along the River Lea. When turnpiking began, it was mainly the roads to London that were improved. Dr Albert has identified thirteen and, up to 1720, three-quarters of all Turnpike Acts were for these roads, and within 40 miles of London. By 1750, they were almost finished along their full lengths, making a total of 1400 miles.

However, what happened over most of the country was that numerous local networks were built. The Bristol Trust, for example, managed 173 miles of road radiating from the city. The little port of Poole, with its trade in Newcastle coal and Newfoundland pine, also had its modest network, built under a series of Acts from 1755 to 1836. Something that looked like a national system appeared when the local systems extended outwards until their extremities joined. Not surprisingly, the finished result was a little shaggy.

ADMINISTRATION OF TURNPIKES

The founder members of each trust were listed in its Act of Parliament, and they filled any vacancies by co-opting. They were men who were interested enough in good transport to go to the trouble of petitioning Parliament and then giving at least a little time to their trust. In the main they were land-owners, farmers, manufacturers and merchants. They had to be men of substance, for there was a property qualification of £100 a year, which was raised to £200 after the inflation that came with the Napoleonic Wars. Parliament liked to see a few J.P.s on the list, because it was their work the trusts were doing. There had to be about thirty members in order to prove to Parliament that there was a good measure of support, but trustees had no liking for humdrum meetings, which the Act usually anticipated by fixing a quorum as low as three.

The trustees appointed officials – a clerk, a treasurer and a surveyor. The clerk's duties were to minute the meetings, not an arduous job, to write letters and solve legal problems. Usually he was a solicitor. Since the work was not heavy he found the time easily and, indeed, one man could be clerk to several trusts.

Pub. by Price & Nattes 1807

Paying toll. The variety of vehicles, travelling under a variety of conditions, created vexing problems for gatekeepers, and caused many arguments.

The treasurer might be a solicitor, too, but it was better to have a banker. His good name would add lustre to the trust, and if they were ever short of money he could be expected to make a loan. It did not always work. George Grote, treasurer of the Marylebone–Finchley Trust, refused a loan of £1000 from his bank, so they sacked him.

It was difficult to find a good surveyor. A farmer, publican or tradesman might take the job and earn himself £5 a year for comparatively little trouble. Macadam remarked: 'Surveyors are elected because they can measure; they might as well be elected because they can sing.' (Albert, op. cit., p. 79) The problem was that at first there were no professional road engineers. They appeared in the nineteenth century, Macadam and Telford being the two most important.

Like the parish surveyors and Justices before them, trusts had the right to call on statute labour, but they knew it would be useless, so they usually compounded for money. Statute labour contributed less and less as time went on, and in 1835 Parliament abolished it.

The collection of tolls was fraught with difficulties. Sometimes drivers made off without paying, and toll-keepers were known to climb on the back of a wagon or cling to the spokes of a wheel. One jumped into a load of clean linen. They could be just as single-minded about defrauding their trusts, and it was almost impossible to check that they handed in all they collected. In 1848 *Punch* complained that the keeper of the gate by St Paul's was collecting tolls from women walking alone, which was probably his own ingenious way of living on immoral earnings.

Fortunately for the trusts, there was a simple answer to all these problems, and that was to farm the tolls. They let their gates at auction, and then knew exactly how much their income would be. There were people who made a good living by renting tolls, and receipts at a gate invariably increased when one of these professionals managed it.

Trusts were not allowed to make profits. They paid their expenses and were supposed to spend every remaining penny on their roads. Why, then, did men become trustees? In the first place there were the advantages the turnpike road gave them. Farms near a turnpike commanded higher rents for their owners; farmers could sell their produce over a wider area; traders and manufacturers no longer had expensive goods lingering on journeys. Secondly, trustees could lend money to their trusts. They had to put their roads in order on taking responsibility for them, and before they had any income, so they had to mortgage their tolls. Taking the interest on the loan was not much different from taking a dividend on capital invested in a factory or a trading company, save that the rate was fixed by the usury laws.

Private carriage – early eighteenth century.
The picture shows why coach-builders in any
particular area always kept to the same gauge.
It was not usually possible for a carriage to go
too far from home because a change of district
usually meant a change of gauge.

A well-managed trust would spend less
than 10 per cent of its income on administration, pay 20 per cent in interest on loans, and
have 70 per cent left for road repairs. However, in the 1830s the Wiveliscombe Trust was
paying 98.6 per cent as interest and, feeling
bound to spend 7.4 per cent on repairs, was
running even further into debt.

The average trust incurred a quarter of its
debt by paying the legal and parliamentary
expenses of its Act. In other countries the state
has normally given active help in the provis-
ion of this vital social overhead capital, the
public transport system. In Britain the men
who wanted to do the work were not only
unaided, but had to pay enormous sums to
lawyers and politicians merely for permission
to begin. Moreover, each Act had to be renewed every twenty-one years, at additional
cost. That at least ended when Parliament
began passing a Turnpike Renewal Act each
year, which dealt with all the trusts together.
However, the first was not until 1831.

ROAD BUILDING

During the eighteenth century turnpike trusts
made little attempt to find new techniques of
road building. To prevent their materials
sinking into soft ground they first laid faggots,
and then covered them with anything suitable
they could find, such as flints, pebbles, gravel,
or broken stones. They realised that water was
their most serious enemy, so they dug ditches
beside their roads, and drains under them,
also piling the metal high in the middle to
give a camber that was sometimes alarmingly
steep. Another solution, and one travellers
heartily disliked, was to make a series of
switchbacks, with a drain running across the
road at the bottom of every dip. By the early
nineteenth century, though, traffic had increased so much that roads had to be built
more scientifically. Two men who did good
work were Thomas Telford and John
Macadam.

Telford believed in solid foundations, so,
having prepared his ground, he laid a course
of heavy stones. On top of that came a 6-inch
layer of broken stone and then a surface of 2
inches of gravel, laid to form a gentle camber
of 1 in 60. Telford's roads lasted well, showing
that his principles were as sound as his foundations, but they were expensive. He was
concerned mainly with some of the few roads
on which the Government spent money, like
the Glasgow to Carlisle, and the famous Holyhead Road. In 1815 he became General Surveyor to the Holyhead Road Commission and
was directly responsible for the Welsh section.
He carried out some marvellous road engineering in the mountains, and also built
suspension bridges over the Menai Straits and
at Conway.

Macadam concentrated on his surface. He
held that if the subsoil was dry it would
support the road and its traffic, without foundations, so, as well as good drainage, there
had to be a waterproof surface. First the soil
was made convex, to correspond with the camber of the road. Next came a 10-inch layer of
broken stones, none of them more than 2
inches across. The road was then left for a few
weeks to let the traffic consolidate it. Finally
there was a further 6-inch layer of the same
size stones. They were broken to be rough and
angular, so that the iron-shod wheels ground
them together, making a fine powder that
filled the gaps and compacted the whole into a
waterproof mass. The theory was as sound as
Telford's, but in general the roads were not,
because it was difficult to create the ideal
conditions Macadam wanted. However, his
roads were popular because they were cheap,
cheaper even than the old ones, since they
took less material. Another reason why people
liked Macadam's methods was because he employed feeble paupers, like old men and
women, for whom the Poor Law authorities
could rarely find work. Macadam gave them
long-handled but light hammers, and made
them sit for their stone-breaking. He claimed
that a woman working as he instructed could
break as much stone in a day as two navvies

Telford's Menai Bridge

wielding sledge-hammers. Many trusts employed Macadam, and many more copied his ideas. In 1816 he became General Surveyor to the Bristol Trust, the largest in the country, and having proved himself there, found plenty of work around London.

Telford, Macadam and all the better road engineers built their roads with the easiest gradients possible. 'Nimrod' wrote:

Great things have been done in cutting through hills and altering the course of roads; and it is no uncommon thing now-a-days to see four horses trotting merrily away down hill on that very ground where they formerly were seen walking up hill. (Thomas Cross. *The Autobiography of a Stage-Coachman*, 1861)

Improvements in roads led to improvements in vehicles. A coachman wrote:

Instead of the old, heavy lumbering vehicle, with a boot fixed on the fore-axle, and a large basket on the hind, with a license to carry six inside passengers and as many as could well be crowded on the outside, the new and elegant Telegraph coaches made their appearance. (Cross, p. 70)

These smart vehicles, light and well sprung, could run at 20 m.p.h. and keep an average speed of 12 m.p.h.

With the help of several Acts of Parliament, trusts encouraged owners of wagons to fit broad wheels, so that they acted as rollers. The wagon that gave most pleasure to turnpikes had broad wheels, carried a light load, and was drawn by few horses. Such a vehicle paid little toll, and sometimes none at all. Others, with narrow wheels, heavy loads and numerous horses, paid high tolls, or even fines. However, many wheels, though broad

The pack-horse. Before roads were turnpiked this was usually the only way to carry goods.

YORK Four Days Stage-Coach.

Begins on Friday the 12th of April 1706.

ALL that are defirous to pafs from *London* to *York*, or from *York* to *London*, or any other Place on that Road; Let them Repair to the *Black Swan* in *Holbourn* in *London*, and to the *Black Swan* in *Coney-ftreet* in *York*.

At both which Places, they may be received in a Stage Coach every *Monday*, *Wednefday* and *Friday*, which performs the whole Journey in Four Days, (if God permits.) And fets forth at Five in the Morning.

And returns from *York* to *Stamford* in two days, and from *Stamford* by *Huntington* to *London* in two days more. And the like Stages on their return.

Allowing each Paffenger 14l. weight, and all above 3d. a Pound.

Performed By { Benjamin *Kingman*. Henry *Harrifon*, Walter *Baynes*,

Alfo this gives Notice that *Newcaftle* Stage Coach, fets out from *York*, every *Monday*, and *Friday*, and from *Newcaftle* every *Monday*, and *Friday*.

Handbill for stage-coach, 1706. This illustrates the problem of coach travel before roads were improved.

enough, were shaped like the base of a cone, so that they could slope parallel to the sides of the wagon. There was a lot of argument about what they did to the road, but since the inner rim moved faster than the outer, they ground the surface with a scuffing action.

STEAM CARRIAGES

A promising invention which came to nothing was the steam-carriage. The pioneer was Goldsworthy Gurney, who made his first long trip in 1829. It was from London to Bath and took six days. In 1831 he ran a service from Gloucester to Cheltenham which, during four months, covered 4000 miles at an average speed of 10 m.p.h., and carried 3000 passengers. Fares were half those charged by stagecoaches. There were problems with the vehicles, but no doubt they could have been solved; the real difficulty was that the steam-carriage made enemies. Farmers disliked it because it consumed coal instead of oats, while coaching companies were afraid of competition. That being so, turnpike trusts were bound to be hostile as well, since many of their members were farmers, and coaching companies provided most of their income. They claimed that steam-carriages were destroying their roads, and charged them tolls that were quite prohibitive. John Herapath was sure that they only caused one-seventh of the damage that coaches did, while Macadam said they would actually do good and, moreover, there were no horses to kick the surfaces loose. The turnpike trusts would not be persuaded, and kept the high tolls. For example, a steam-carriage that ran the 5 miles between Liverpool and Prescot had to pay £2. 16s., while a coach paid only 4 shillings. Such charges drove out of use the invention which might have saved long-distance road transport from its long, sad decline during the railway age.

20 Inland waterways

EARLY DEVELOPMENTS

At first the only inland waterways were rivers, and they have disadvantages for transport. Each one is a dead end; in their upper reaches they are shallow and fast flowing; in their lower reaches they have long meanders, with sandbanks and bars; in their estuaries they are tidal. Anywhere they are likely to have crumbling banks or receive tributaries, so, before they were improved, towing had to be done by gangs of men instead of horses. This method was still used on the Upper Medway as late as 1838. However, in their natural state, there were many English rivers, like the Thames, that were tolerably well behaved. They had few obstacles, while the tides in their estuaries made a natural dam twice a day that helped to keep their levels high. When they were hardly needed for trade, in Saxon times, they were good waterways, as the Danes were pleased to discover. However, just when commerce began to grow in the Middle Ages, man-made obstacles appeared. Monks built fish weirs so that they could eat as their vows required, and millers also built weirs. A town might contrive a barrier deliberately, like a low bridge, so that it made itself the head of navigation rather than a rival town upstream.

In the sixteenth century, though, traders began to assert themselves and there were at least eight Acts of Parliament empowering groups of 'undertakers' to improve rivers for navigation. One was the River Lea, the work there encouraging heavy traffic on the Great North Road, as we have seen. Progress continued, so that by the late seventeenth century there were 700 miles of navigable river, and by 1725 close on 1200. There was, for example, the Aire and Calder Navigation which, with its tow-paths, cuts and pound locks, was a highly developed waterway. It linked Leeds, an important centre of the woollen industry, with the Humber.

The first canals in this country were built by the Romans for carrying East Anglian grain to their legionary fort at York, but there were no more until the reign of Elizabeth I, when the Exeter Canal was built. A local aristocrat had made a weir across the Exe, to the annoyance of the town, so the citizens dug a canal running parallel with the river. It had a wharf at Topsham. There was another long pause until 1740 when the Newry Canal opened in Northern Ireland, but after that the pace began to quicken. Liverpool needed coal, so its merchants and salters commissioned Henry Berry, who had worked on the Newry Canal, to join St Helens and its mines to the River Mersey. Originally they were going to make the Sankey Brook navigable, but Berry built a true canal alongside it. Completed in 1757 it was a success from the start. For some reason, though, the canal age is usually said to date from the year 1761 when the Bridgewater Canal opened. The inspiration of a lovelorn duke, it was the work in part of a semi-literate millwright who solved his problems by thinking in bed, and it had some spectacular features, like the Barton Aqueduct. Certainly it excited the imagination more than had any earlier waterway.

The Duke of Bridgewater owned coal-mines at Worsley, and though they were only 7 miles from Manchester, the journey by pack-horse was tedious and costly. They were drift mines, with a lot of water in them, which gave the Duke the idea of floating the coal to the entrance by underground waterways and then taking it to Manchester by canal. He set his agent, John Gilbert, to work and, from time to time, asked James Brindley to advise. Brindley was a millwright whose interest in watermills had led to his interest in water transport. He had been ruminating on the possibility of a link between the Mersey and the Trent when the Duke of Bridgewater invited him to help with his own scheme. The main obstacle was the Irwell, a canalised river that linked Manchester with the estuary of the Mersey at Runcorn. The first plan was to join it with a flight of locks, but the proprietors proposed such high tolls that Brindley thought again, and spanned the river with the Barton Aqueduct. It was a massive structure for those days, having three wide arches and a height of 48 feet. The canal was an immediate success, delighted Mancunians finding that the price of their coal was halved.

The Duke then rubbed more salt into the smarting wounds of the Irwell Navigation by extending his canal to Runcorn. From here the barges made their way down the estuary of the Mersey to Liverpool.

THE GROWTH OF THE CANAL SYSTEM

As with turnpikes, no one had an overall plan for canals, but economic conditions and the geography of the country did produce some sort of pattern.

The canal builders' aim was to complete the work God had begun so well with the rivers. They were still useful, even when the boats had to leave them, for they had cut valleys which sometimes made excellent routes for canals. An early canal that followed rivers was the Trent and Mersey. The Trent is not navigable above Nottingham, but the canal uses its valley until it reaches the watershed at Harecastle, just north of the Potteries. On the other side, it follows the Weaver down to the Mersey. The Kennet and Avon Canal leaves the Avon at Bath, but it is able to go beside the river which has obligingly cut a deep valley, almost a gorge, at Limpley Stoke.

However, canals did more than accompany rivers back to their sources; they joined them together to provide through-navigation. It was this idea which led Brindley and others to plan what L. T. C. Rolt calls the 'canals of the Midland cross' (op. cit., p. 33). In the first place there was the Trent–Mersey Canal, otherwise known as the Grand Trunk, authorised by Act of Parliament in 1766 and completed in 1777. Secondly there was the Stafford and Worcester Canal that ran from the Grand Trunk at Haywood to the Severn at Stourport. Its Act was passed on the same day as the Grand Trunk's, but it was completed in 1772, five years sooner. It had a short but highly important branch, the Birmingham Canal, that also

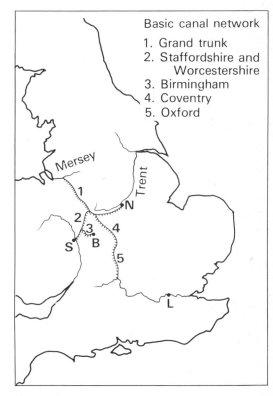

Basic canal network
1. Grand trunk
2. Staffordshire and Worcestershire
3. Birmingham
4. Coventry
5. Oxford

Basic canal network

opened in 1772. Finally there were the Coventry and Oxford Canals, both authorised in 1783 and opened in 1790. They joined the Grand Trunk to the Thames at Oxford. Between them these canals linked the four main river systems of the country – the Mersey, Humber, Severn and Thames.

Rivers were sometimes linked together to make coast-to-coast routes. There are a number of canals that did this, from the Caledonian down to the Kennet and Avon. On the whole they did not do well. The Caledonian Canal was built for strategic reasons which never applied and, apart from the Forth and Clyde, the commercial canals made only modest profits. The heroic proprietors of the Leeds and Liverpool spent forty-six years driving their canal over the Pennines, only to find it was hardly used except at its two extremities.

In two senses, then, the canals completed the river systems. They extended them inland, and they joined them together. When Brindley was asked what he thought was the use of rivers he said he supposed they had been created to feed canals, but that is just making the same statement from the other point of view!

Obviously no one built canals simply to make the river system tidier. The reasons were economic. As with the turnpikes, centres of industry and trade spread their tentacles in search of raw materials and wider markets. The Duke of Bridgewater built his canal to take coal to Manchester. Josiah Wedgwood backed the Grand Trunk so that he could have easier transport for his Cornish china clay that was shipped to the Mersey, and for his flints that came out of the chalk hills around the Humber. Crawshay, the South Wales ironmaster, wanted canals to serve his works when he began using Henry Cort's puddling process. The outstanding example is Birmingham which, having no navigable river, became the centre of the canal system; a canal map of the Black Country looks like the work of an inebriated spider.

Canal companies had less of a Dick Whittington complex than turnpike trusts. We have seen that the Oxford and Coventry Canals joined London to the Midlands and the North, but it was not a direct route. That came with the construction of the Grand Junction Canal which joined London with the Midlands network in Northamptonshire, cutting the journey to Birmingham from 227 miles to 138. However, the Grand Junction was not completed until 1805. Four canals also extended the Thames navigation to the west, the Kennet and Avon, the Basingstoke, the Wilts and Berks and the Thames and Severn. They were none of them particularly early or particularly successful. This is not to say that London was unimportant as a centre of waterways. There was the Thames itself, one of the best navigable rivers in Britain, and it had three useful tributaries – the Wey, the Lea and the Medway. The Thames below Staines was in the care of the Corporation of the City of London; the Lea was improved in the 1570s and given one of the first pound locks built in Britain; in the 1650s Sir Richard Weston made the Wey navigable for its last 15 miles, digging cuts that totalled 7 miles; the Medway Navigation had its first Act in 1664, others following in the early eighteenth century. The fact was that London had organised its inland waterways before the canal era began.

These river navigations did not extend far inland. When the long-distance canals were built, they might have done London a service if they had opened the city to the inland coalfields, so allowing them to compete with the one in the North-East, with its advantage of sea transport. They did not do so. The valuable London market remained at the mercy of the Newcastle coal-owners until the coming of the railways.

When, finally, the canal network was complete, it was far from uniform. Engineers thought primarily of their own areas and their own immediate problems. If, like the Kennet and Avon, a canal ran through tolerably easy country, with plenty of water, then it was a generous width. On the other hand if the country was rugged, or if water was short, then the canal had to be as narrow as practicable, sometimes no more than a large ditch. Gauges varied, but there were four main types of craft. There were the river barges which, in the estuaries particularly, could be quite portly. On the wide canals there were craft, also called barges, which were up to 60 feet long and 14 feet wide. On narrow canals there were 'narrow boats', about 70 feet long, but only 7 feet wide. Finally, there were tub boats which were found, mainly, in Shropshire. They were about 20 feet long and less than 6 feet wide, rectangular and made of iron. They could be hauled on a wagon way where the slope was too great to construct a canal. When there was little through-traffic, these different gauges were unimportant, but it was another matter when the canals had to compete with railways.

Like the turnpike roads, the canal system did not grow steadily. The Duke of Bridgewater's success inspired a short boom in the 1760s. Next, there was the so-called 'mania' of the early 1790s, followed by a quieter period during which few new canals were started, but the more ambitious ones of the mania

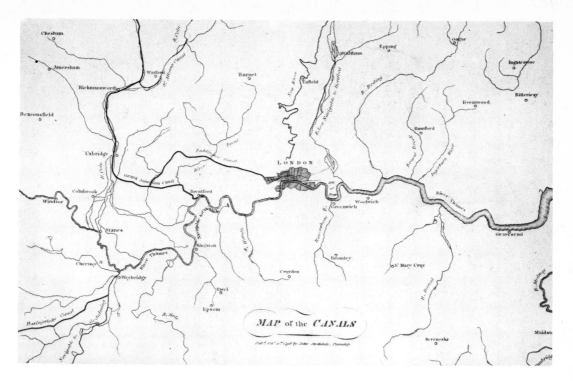

London's waterways. Even before the canal age London was well served by navigable rivers – the Wey, the Lea, the Medway and the Thames itself.

were completed. Finally there was a minor boom in the 1830s when the canals linked themselves to the railways. Dean and Cole estimate that about £3 million were spent between 1755 and 1790, up to £6 million during the mania, and £11 million from 1801 to 1835 (op. cit., p.238). It was unfortunate that so many canals were built during a time of inflation, for the high capital costs played havoc with the profits.

CANAL BUILDING

Canal building created a new profession, that of civil engineer. Brindley was one of the first, in fact if not in name, and others followed, like Smeaton, Rennie and Telford. The engineer was the man the canal company employed to take responsibility for the entire work. He surveyed the route and then divided it into sections, placing a resident engineer in charge of each. He in turn kept an eye on the contractor who built his section. There were massive quantities of earth and rock to shift, and as all the work had to be done by hand, contractors assembled large gangs of men. They were 'navigators', who were to spread consternation wherever they went, and rivet the attention of

moralists and social reformers until the end of the railway age. There was no place for Macadam's decrepit paupers, for navvies had to be brawny sons of toil. Some were local men who left as soon as their task was finished, but others were migrants who went wherever canals were built. Many were Scottish or Irish.

Although canal building was a new science, engineers did have some experience on which they could draw. The Fen people had been making drainage ditches for a long time; miners knew about tunnelling; much was learnt from river improvement which had involved digging cuts, and building tow-paths and locks.

None the less, there were problems enough. For a start, there were no suitable maps. Canal engineers could hardly work from those highly inaccurate eighteenth-century works of art that showed hills as pimples. Geology was another difficulty. They took borings at intervals, but there were usually some unpleasant surprises when they started work. For example, when building Blisworth Tunnel on the Grand Junction, they met clays and rotten oolite so full of water that work had to stop. Jessop, the engineer, wanted to abandon the

G.B.E.—H

tunnel, but the company called in Rennie, who advised a new line at an angle to the one first planned.

They did not know the answers to many problems of construction, and there were quite enough just taking a canal over level ground. A canal is a ditch with earth piled on either side, which sounds simple enough, but can the water-level be made higher than the ground level, and if so, how wide must the banks be to contain the weight? Clearly the sides must slope, but at what angle? What soils need 'puddling' – that is, lining with clay? If so, how thick must the puddle be? Should it be thicker at the sides or at the bottom? Nor are there final answers to any of these problems, for they vary in every place and with every soil. The only way of learning was by doing, and then profiting by mistakes, and it is easy to imagine the heartache and expense this caused, especially when the works were at all complicated.

The two most important problems were to overcome gradients and to make sure the canal stayed full of water.

Often it was possible to cross a small hill with a cutting or an embankment, but more was needed for larger obstacles. The usual way was to build a lock. Locks had been developed for rivers, the earlier kind being 'flash locks'.

They had but one gate, so that when it was opened there was a rush of water and a boat going downstream had to shoot the rapids, while one coming up had to be winched. On a canal such a device was out of the question, but fortunately the pound lock had also been developed. It has two pairs of gates and the barge is imprisoned in the pond, or pound, between them, so that it can rise or fall, according to the way it is going.

Often one lock was not enough, so others were built above it to form a flight. It saved expense if the bottom gate of one lock was also the top gate of that below it, a series so made being called a staircase. The longest flight in Britain is at Tardebigge on the Worcester and Birmingham where thirty locks raise the canal over 200 feet.

Alternatives to the lock were the inclined plane and the lift. With both, the barge was floated into an iron caisson for its journey. Inclined planes and lifts saved water and time, but were expensive to run. At Foxton in Leicestershire an inclined plane was replaced by a staircase of ten locks because a shortage of traffic made it uneconomical to keep the engine in steam.

When the canal reached a watershed there often had to be a tunnel. The earliest of any consequence was Brindley's tunnel at Hare-

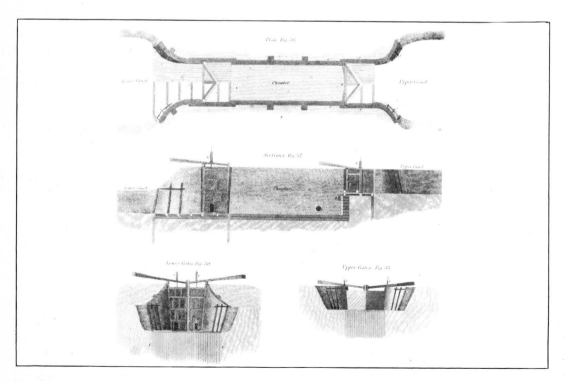

Pound lock

castle, which linked the valleys of the Trent and Weaver. It was some 2800 yards long and took eleven years to build. The longest tunnel, 5698 yards, is at Standege on the Huddersfield Narrow Canal. The first tunnels caused a lot of worry and expense, so builders made them without tow-paths. Men called 'leggers' lay on projecting boards and walked the barges through, pushing against the sides of the tunnel.

The most impressive works on the canals are the aqueducts. Brindley's Barton Aqueduct on the Bridgewater Canal was the first, and was remarkable enough, but much finer ones followed, like John Rennie's handsome structure over the River Lune. It has five arches, is 51 feet high and 350 feet long. The most famous of all is Telford's masterpiece that bears, for an Englishman, the unpronounceable name of Pont Cysyllte. It carries the Ellesmere Canal over the River Dee. It is 120 feet high, has nineteen spans, and is 1000 feet long, not including the embankments either end. The most serious problem was weight, so Telford made his trough of cast iron and it was because of this, above all, that his aqueduct was a thing of wonder. He had already shown it was possible to use cast iron when he built a much more modest aqueduct at Longdon-on-Tern in Shropshire, and where he learnt some valuable lessons. One was that if an aqueduct is only a few inches wider than a boat, then it is almost impossible to haul the boat against the pressure of water. Pont Cysyllte is nearly 12 feet wide, so that there is plenty of room for the water to flow round a boat. The trough sides are of sections bolted together, and they are wedge-shaped, like the voussoirs of a stone arch. Telford used a stone-

Pont Cysyllte Aqueduct

mason's technique to build in iron, but Pont Cysyllte, opened in 1805, is standing today – proof that his principles were sound.

As time went on, engineers improved their methods. As we have seen, Brindley's Harecastle Tunnel took eleven years to build, and it was only 12 feet high and 9 feet wide. In the 1820s Telford made another tunnel alongside it, with a tow-path. His was 16 feet high, and 14 feet wide, and took only three years to build. Engineers began to take more direct routes. The Ordnance Survey map shows that Brindley's Oxford Canal follows the contours exactly wherever it can, so it wiggles about, putting miles on the journey. The boatmen said that as they travelled around Brinklow they heard the church clock strike all day long. In later years this canal was shortened from 91 to 77 miles. Then, in 1835, the Birmingham and Liverpool Junction Canal opened which, with its massive cuttings and embankments, showed a splendid disregard for contours. Its engineers, Telford and Cubitt, were trying to prove that a level canal, taking a direct route, could compete with a railway.

There were several answers to the water problem. One was to have a long summit level and make it perhaps twice as deep as the boats needed, so that it would be a reservoir for the rest of the canal. If that was not enough, then separate reservoirs had to be built. Sometimes water could be pumped from a river. The Kennet and Avon Company had a pumping station at Crofton in Wiltshire, where they installed Boulton and Watt engines, and another at Claverton.

It was most important to puddle carefully, and if the contractor neglected this work, there could be serious problems. The Thames and Severn Canal lost 3 million gallons a day where it crossed the oolite of the Cotswold Hills.

Staircase of locks – Foxton, Leicestershire

CANAL FINANCE

Unlike turnpike trusts, which were not allowed to have profits, canals belonged to public companies which hoped to make money and pay dividends to their shareholders.

First the promoters drew up a scheme, organised public meetings and collected promises of subscriptions. Then they had to petition Parliament for an Act, which they needed for two reasons. In the first place, since the fiasco of the South Sea Bubble, either Parliament or the Crown had to give its authority for the formation of any corporate body selling shares to the general public (see Chapter 30). There was no other way of raising the money, since canals were too expensive for individuals or even groups of partners. The one exception was the Duke of Bridgewater, but he was rich and dedicated, and the first leg of his canal was only 7 miles long. The second purpose of the Act was to define the Company's powers, saying, for example, what tolls it might charge and giving it the right to make compulsory purchases of land.

Obtaining the Act was always expensive, and could be very expensive if there was much opposition. This could come from a turnpike trust, a rival navigation, or perhaps a landowner whose farms were to be cut in two. The company had to hire lawyers to state its case before a Committee of the House of Commons. Both groups charged heavily for their unnecessary services so that the legal and parliamentary expenses were a formidable item in the budget of any chartered company.

When the Act was passed, the company could raise its capital. The Act stated how much this was to be, usually the company's own estimate of the cost, and authorised a further amount in case it should be needed. It invariably was. The Leeds and Liverpool Canal had an authorised capital of £260 000, with £60 000 more, if needed, and cost in the end £1 200 000. The Grand Junction was allowed to raise £500 000, with a further £100 000 if required, and the total bill was £1 800 000. Initial estimates were so consistently wild with optimism that there must have been some reason for it, but what it was is not at all clear.

Shares were normally £100 each, and there was little enough fuss in selling them. The company would place a subscription book in a local shop, and anyone who was interested could inscribe his name, stating the number of shares he wanted. So far it was relatively painless because there was little to pay, but as work on the canal proceeded, the company made 'calls' on the subscribers until it had collected the full amount promised. By then the canal should have been finished, but none

ever was, even when the extra capital allowed by Parliament had been raised by selling additional shares. Subscribers who had put forward their names in the happy spirit of sign now and pay later, found they were under pressure. The company could raise money by borrowing, but a loan carried interest, fixed by the usury laws, so in that respect it was less attractive than shares on which, hopefully, the dividends would be higher. However, loan interest had to be paid before dividends were declared, as the companies were quick to point out, so it was usually the subscribers who found the money. The company might also obtain another Act, allowing them to make further calls on each share over and above the original £100. Then the only escape for a harried subscriber was to sell his shares for what they would fetch. When in 1808 the Barnsley Canal Company obtained the right to call for a further £60 on each of its £100 shares, there were plenty of people ready to part with them at £5 at time.

One advantage of being a public company was indeed that proprietors could sell their shares freely. However, there was no organised market. They were sold as one would sell a second-hand washing-machine today, perhaps to a trusting friend, or perhaps through the advertisement columns of a local newspaper. The exception was the Grand Junction Canal Company, whose affairs were ably handled by its auditor, Thomas Homer. Its shares were properly quoted in London, and exchanged hands in a business-like way. Homer was one of those men with a certain genius for finance who appear in any age. From being auditor of the Grand Junction he graduated to Superintendent of the Regent's Canal, and ended his career with seven years' transportation for embezzlement.

J.R. Ward has done much useful work, finding who shareholders were and why they invested their money (op. cit., especially Chaps. 3 and 5). A man might want a canal to help his firm, but if most canal proprietors had been business men concerned for the transport of their own goods, then the companies would have kept their charges low and been content with modest returns. In fact they fixed their tolls as high as they dared in order to pay maximum dividends, so it seems clear that the majority of investors were speculators who were after the best profits on their capital that they could find. Business men did indeed subscribe, but little more than anyone else, in relation to their wealth.

The part played by land-owners was interesting. The Duke of Bridgewater was known as the 'father' of the canal system, but by no means all aristocrats were as paternal. Canals were mixed blessings for them. Like turnpike roads they might widen the market for their tenants' produce, so increasing rents. On the other hand they could divide farms, so that the tenants demanded lower rents as compensation. Moreover, every mile of canal needed between 5 and 8 acres of ground, which some land-owner was made to sell by Act of Parliament. This was unlikely to endear him to the canal company, and he might take his revenge by insisting on a fancy price. Such was the system of arbitration that he was likely to have it. The attitude of a land-owner depended on what the canal would do to his estate and on his temperament. Some were as obstructive as they could be, while others were positively benevolent, taking modest prices for their land or even settling for a rent. Most were simply business-like. Land usually sold at something less than thirty years' rental, but canals usually had to pay a little more because of the inconvenience they caused.

As for making investments, it seems that land-owners bought shares in the same proportion to their wealth as any other class.

As well as business men and land-owners, almost every social group in the country bought canal shares except the poor. Professional men found money from their fees and salaries, clergymen from their stipends, and widows and spinsters from their legacies. At one time Oxford dons invested heavily and, at another, for some reason, so did Liverpool doctors. The inhabitants of Bristol showed a lot of interest in the 1790s, for trade in the port was declining and they wanted somewhere else to place their capital. All these people were speculators pure and simple; they had no mixed motives like manufacturers or land-owners, since they owned neither businesses nor estates that would benefit from canals. None the less, they usually put their money into local canals because they liked to see what they had bought.

One period was different and that was the brief 'canal mania' of the early 1790s. Here was a curious phenomenon. The mania afflicted people in the East Midlands, its symptom being a determination to buy any canal shares that were for sale. They started by snapping up everything that was going in their own area, and then emerged from Birmingham, Leicester or even unlikely places like Market Harborough, to wander the country seeing what they could find. Usually they were as welcome as a flock of vultures, and where any canal looked a reasonable proposition, the local people sent them packing. They had most success where investors were thin on the

ground and where they had doubts about the canal anyway. The Ellesmere Canal attracted a fair amount of East Midlands capital; it ran through sparsely populated country on the Welsh borders and was so uncertain a project that, as Hadfield says, 'it was promoted to carry goods in one direction and ended by carrying them in quite another' (op. cit., p. 102).

It was fortunate that so many people were willing to invest in canals. Without good transport the country could not have prospered as it did, but business men were unable to meet any more than a share of the cost. They had enough to do building up capital for their own needs. The state, which should have given help and encouragement, did just the opposite by saddling each and every company with a huge debt for its parliamentary expenses.

The dividends canals paid varied considerably. Some projects, like Southampton–Salisbury, were never completed, so that any money invested in them was lost. On the other hand the Loughborough Navigation paid a dividend of 154 per cent in its best year, 1829. Few could match that, but the Oxford Canal paid 30 per cent or more between 1811 and 1844. The Grand Junction did less well, but paid up to 13 per cent and never less than 6 per cent from 1811 to 1846. In those days of low interest rates such returns were impressive. However, an important, and in some ways successful canal, the Kennet and Avon, brought its investors little return. The most it ever paid was 3¾ per cent, and that was for two years only. Sometimes there were no dividends, and after 1842 they were never more than 1 per cent.

Given reasonably efficient management, the financial success of a canal depended on its original cost and on its tolls. The Loughborough Navigation scored on both counts. It was just a series of improvements to the River Soar, that came to a mere £10 000, but it had heavy traffic, for it ran from Leicester to the Trent. The Oxford Canal cost £300 000, but mile for mile it was much cheaper than the later canals. The Grand Junction and the Kennet and Avon were built during the Napoleonic Wars and, owing to inflation, cost over £1 million each. The Grand Junction could still pay respectable dividends because it joined London to the prosperous new industrial towns in the Midlands, but the Kennet and Avon led through agricultural areas to the insignificant North Somerset coalfield and the declining port of Bristol.

Broadly speaking, anyone who bought his shares at par in the early days, and in a busy canal, had a good return. On the other hand those who waited until the early 1790s, and the beginning of wartime inflation, gained little, unless they were very lucky. The eager share hunters of the canal mania would have done better to have stayed quietly at home and put their money in consols.

All canals charged tolls, but some owned boats as well, so they had a second income from freight. However, most carriage was done by independent firms. Some had just a boat or two, but there were others with such large fleets that it was worth their while to lease their own wharfs and warehouses. Pickfords, already an important road haulage concern, took to the canals in the 1790s.

21 Horse railways

In Britain the first railways were built in the sixteenth century. They were wooden timbers placed on the ground to make a smooth surface for wagons, just as the gardener's plank does for his wheelbarrow. To hold the rails to gauge they used wooden sleepers, and to keep the wagons on them they fitted flanged wheels. So much was easy, but they had problems because both rails and sleepers wore out quickly. The rails were soon damaged, and replacing them frequently played havoc with the ends of the sleepers. Sleepers suffered in the middle as well from the hoofs of horses.

A well-known wooden line was the one Ralph Allen built in 1731 for the quarries at Combe Down, near Bath. The rails were 4 inches square, the sleepers were six inches by five inches, and the gauge was 4 feet. It was a self-acting incline, which meant that loaded wagons doing down, pulled up the empties.

Wooden rails were still being laid in 1800, but after 1750 iron was becoming more and more usual. The first step was to cover the rails with iron strips, especially on bends, which was where the wheels did most damage. They were not a great success, as they were easily knocked loose and then broken. It is possible that the first all-iron rails were made at Coalbrookdale in 1767. They were simply cast-iron bars, laid on edge for extra strength, and for that reason called 'edge rails'. In the early 1790s they were given 'fish bellies' to make them even stronger. The fish-bellied edge rail is said to have been invented by William Jessop, a famous railway engineer and partner of Butterley Ironworks near Leeds. However that may be, he was probably

Ralph Allen's railway. A self-acting incline does not need a double track the whole distance, only at half-way, so that the full trucks going down can pass the empty ones coming up.

the first man to lay such rails, which he did on a line he engineered for the Leicester Navigation Company in 1791.

In that same year John Smeaton published an account of a line he had laid in 1759 for the building of Eddystone Lighthouse and in which he described L-shaped rails. Jessop's partner, Benjamin Outram, took up the idea with enthusiasm. Having the flange on the rail gave two advantages. In the first place the wagon could have smooth wheels which would run on roads, and secondly the flange strengthened the rail.

These rails were called plates, so the men who fitted them were 'platelayers', and the lines were 'plateways'. Most of the lines in the south were converted to plateways, including the considerable network in South Wales, but in the north they kept their edge rails.

It was the edge rail which won in the end, an important date in its history being 1820, when John Birkinshaw of Bedlington in County Durham patented a fish-bellied rail, with a special shape, and made of wrought iron. Wrought-iron rails had been used since about 1800, but it was Birkinshaw who made best use of the new material. When he convinced George Stephenson of the worth of his rails, their future was assured. One advantage they had was that they could be made longer than cast-iron rails and, much more important, they could carry a locomotive without shattering.

Sleepers were still a problem, because there was no way of preserving timber, and they rotted. Instead of wooden cross-sleepers they began, therefore, to use single blocks of stone, usually granite. They had to be flat top and bottom, but apart from that their shape could be irregular. So that they stayed in place they had to weigh about 200 pounds each. Holes were drilled in the top, 6 inches deep, and wooden plugs driven into them. Cast-iron chairs to hold the rails were then spiked into place. One advantage was that the space between the rails could be made into a good gravel road, or even cobbled, for the benefit of the horses.

The making of the lines also improved. Engineers learnt to avoid sharp bends, steep slopes and uneven gradients. The first caused derailments; the second meant the horse was working too hard when going up, and in danger of being run over by the wagon when coming down; the third prevented the animal from keeping a good, steady pull, so squandering his energies. Most lines led to waterways, which was fortunate, as the loaded wagons ran downhill. Outram said the ideal gradient was 1 in 100, since it meant the horse made the

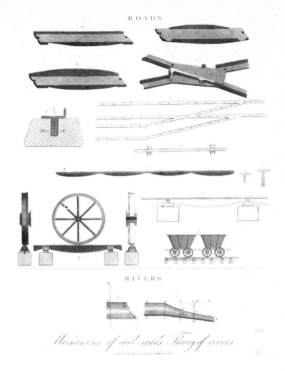

Iron rails. The rails at the top are for plateways: the lower ones are the wrought-iron, fish-bellied kind, developed from the edge rail. The diagram also shows a granite sleeper.

same effort both ways – down with the full wagons, and back with the empties.

To keep gentle gradients they built cuttings, embankments, bridges, viaducts and tunnels. Some of these were impressive. An embankment at Pandy in Herefordshire was over 40 feet high; the Forest of Dean Railway had a tunnel a mile long; at Risca the Monmouth Canal Company had a viaduct of thirty-two arches. There is a sad story about a bridge near Newcastle. A local mason, one Allen, built it of wood, and to his dismay it collapsed. He replaced it in stone, then committed suicide for fear it might go the same way. He need not have worried, because his arch is still standing.

When it was impossible to avoid a steep gradient, they built an inclined plane with an even slope. If the loaded wagons were running downhill they could haul up the empties, and the incline was self-acting. On the other hand, if the loaded wagons were coming uphill, there had to be a stationary engine to haul them. The diagram shows the sequence for taking

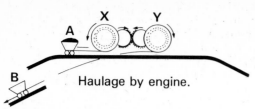

Haulage by engine.

1. A loaded set of wagons *A* is hauled to the crest of the slope by drum *X*, whilst an empty set *B* decends, controlled by drum *Y*. (The drums are interlocked by large gear wheels.)

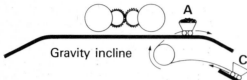

Gravity incline

2. The loaded set *A* is now disconnected from the haulage cable' and attached to the cable of the gravity-controlled system. *A* is now allowed to descend the incline to the docks, thus drawing up empty set *C* to the crest

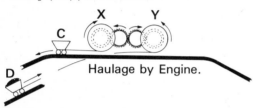

Haulage by Engine.

3. Set *C* is then connected to the cable-link from which *A* was disconnected. By this time the empty set *B* will have been exchanged for a loaded set *D*. The engine is now put into reverse motion so that loaded set *D* is hauled to the crest, from the colliery, whilst lowering empty set *C*.

Taking loads over a hill – use of stationary engine and gravity incline (from F. Atkinson, *The Great Northern Coalfield 1700–1900*)

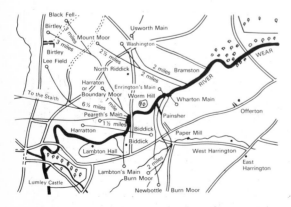

Network of horse railways on the North-East Coalfield

loads over a hill at Warden Law Colliery, County Durham.

Building the lines was not cheap. The Hay Railway in Brecknockshire cost £2700 per mile and came to a total of over £63 000.

Horse railways were of three kinds. The earliest belonged to mines or quarries. We have already mentioned Ralph Allen's at Bath, but much more important were the complex networks that grew on the coalfields of South Wales and the North-East. The map shows some of the lines in County Durham, each one connecting its colliery to the River Wear.

Later, canal companies built a great many lines. If they met a serious obstacle that was going to take years to overcome, they built a temporary railway. The Somersetshire Coal Canal Company did so at Combe Hay, while they were making a staircase of twenty-two locks, and the Grand Junction Canal Company employed Outram to engineer one for them while they dug Blisworth Tunnel. Such lines were taken up when the canal was finished, but there were permanent ones as well to act as feeders. They were used where the country was too difficult to build a branch canal, or where there was unlikely to be enough traffic to justify the expense. Usually such lines were no more than a mile or two long, but the Cromford and High Peak was 34 miles. It linked the Cromford Canal to the Peak Forest Canal, and carried limestone to both.

The third kind was the public railway. It was not an appendage to a mine or a canal but belonged to its own independent railway company. The first, and the best known, was the Surrey Iron Railway, which opened in 1803. The engineer was William Jessop. It ran from the company's own dock at Wandsworth, to Croydon, 9 miles away, and was later extended to Merstham, a further 7 miles. The plan was to take it, eventually, to Portsmouth. There was quite a spate of Acts for lines of this kind, including fifteen in the two years 1825 and 1826, though by no means all of them were built.

It is difficult to judge the economic value of the horse railways. In all there were perhaps 1500 miles of them, which compares not unfavourably with the 4250 miles of navigable waterways, though it must be remembered that the railway horse could pull only 8 tons, compared with the 50 of the canal horse. However, we must also remember where the lines were. In South Wales they carried coal to the canals, and in Northumberland and Durham to the rivers. Indeed, almost everywhere they formed a vital link between mines and water transport.

22 Steam railways

THE STEAM LOCOMOTIVE

Before the horse railway could develop into the modern railway an important invention was necessary: the steam locomotive. There was, literally, no hurry. Railways were for carrying coal short distances, and a gain of a few miles an hour meant nothing, so although serious experiments began as early as 1800. it was not until 1830 that a fully efficient locomotive was built. In those thirty years around seventy were made, or an average of only about two a year.

One of the most important of the early pioneers was Richard Trevithick, whose main contribution was to break with the Watt tradition. Watt was convinced, with good reason, that he had brought the steam-engine to perfection, but one has only to see his creations in the Science Museum in London to realise that, with their great beams, huge cylinders and bulky condensers, they could never have driven locomotives. Trevithick's answer was to use high-pressure steam, which allowed him to build a much more compact engine. In 1803 he drove a steam carriage up the Tottenham Court Road; in 1804 he built a locomotive for a railway at Samuel Homfray's Pen-y-Darren Colliery; in 1808 at Euston Square he demonstrated his *Catch-me-who-Can*, which was an engine that ran round a circular track, giving joy-rides and proving that the railway locomotive was a practical possibility. Yet just when he should have persevered, Trevithick gave up his experiments. He had other things to do and was discouraged by a number of set-backs, notably from rails that kept breaking under the unaccustomed weight. Others took up his work.

Early locomotives. The first picture shows a model of the *Rocket* as she was in 1829. The second picture shows the *Rocket* as she is today in the Science Museum. Later in her working life she was modified in several ways, e.g. her cylinders were adjusted so they were almost level. It is possible to see the ends of the tubes which carried heat from the fire into the heart of the boiler. The other photographs shows (from left to right) *Salamanca, Puffing Billy* and *Locomotion No. 1.*

Colliery locomotive

One problem that taxed them was 'slip'. They had visions of a loaded train failing to pull away because the locomotive's wheels did not grip the track. Blenkinsop solved the difficulty when in 1812 he built his *Salamanca*. The drive was to a cogged wheel that engaged pinions on the side of one of the rails. It certainly meant there could be no slip, but there was a good deal of friction. None the less, the *Salamanca* was a success, for it hauled twenty wagons at a time along the 3 miles from Middleton Colliery to Leeds, and remained in service for many years. In 1813, though, William Hedley produced his *Puffing Billy*, which ran with equal success on a smooth track, showing there was no need to worry about slip, as long as gradients were gentle and loads reasonable.

A more real difficulty was lack of power. It was no use connecting the piston directly to the driving wheel, for it could not have turned it, so there had to be a series of cogs, which meant a loss of speed, and a loss of efficiency because of friction. They still thought in terms of the beam engine, with its vertical piston and driving rod, but so that the mechanism was more compact they made use of the half-beam with its grasshopper motion (see Chapter 10).

The man who did most to develop the locomotive was George Stephenson. He was born in 1771 to poor parents and had no formal education. He began his working life stoking the boiler for a colliery engine, but he showed such good mechanical aptitude that he became engine-man at Killingworth Colliery and then, in 1812, engine-wright at High Pit Colliery, with a salary of £100 a year. This meant he was well established as a skilled engineer. Incidentally, he invented a miner's safety lamp in 1815, the same year as Sir Humphry Davy, but not surprisingly the reward and the recognition went to the gentleman.

Stephenson's work with pit engines led to an interest in locomotives, and in 1814 he built the *Blücher*. He went on to build several more colliery locomotives, but his great opportunity came when he was given the task of engineering the Stockton to Darlington line, opened in 1825, and for which he supplied that famous engine, the *Locomotion*. In 1829 he and his son Robert built the even more famous *Rocket* for the Liverpool and Manchester line.

Three things made the *Rocket* efficient. In the first place it had a tubular boiler. The fire did not operate like the gas under a kettle, but instead the heat passed through the heart of the boiler in a number of tubes. Next, the steam exhaust from the piston was sent up the flue, so drawing air through the fire to make it burn more fiercely. Both improvements gave a better head of steam, and so more power to the piston, which could now be connected directly to the driving wheel. There was no longer any need for the levers and cogs that had once intervened, so the engine lost friction and gained speed. None of these ideas was new, but no one had ever combined them so efficiently, or reached such a high standard of workmanship, as the Stephensons.

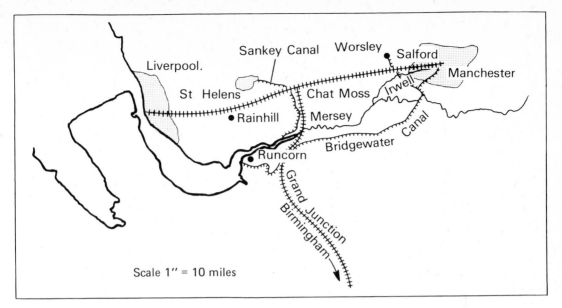

Liverpool and Manchester Railway

THE RAILWAY SYSTEM

As the locomotive was developing, so too was the railway system.

One of the best known of the early steam railways was the Stockton and Darlington, which is described in some detail in Chapter 24. All we need to note here is that it was a hybrid, being neither a modern railway nor a traditional wagon way. There were locomotives, but there were stationary engines and horses as well: the company owned most of the vehicles, but they also allowed private individuals to run coaches. If we define a modern railway as one that uses only locomotives for its motive power, and whose traffic is owned and controlled entirely by the company, then the Liverpool and Manchester was the first.

By the 1820s there were good reasons for improving the communications between these two towns. As this table shows, their population was growing:

	Liverpool	Manchester
1790	56000	57000
1821	119000	134000

There was coal to be carried from St Helens, farm produce from Ireland, and, above all, cotton. In 1800, 450000 tons of shipping docked in Liverpool, and in 1825 1¼ million tons. Most of these vessels carried goods for Manchester, but the only links were a turnpike road and two waterways, the Mersey and Irwell Navigation and the Duke of Bridgewater's Canal. The pressure on these was intoler-

The Liverpool and Manchester Railway – constructing the Edgehill Tunnel

The Liverpool and Manchester Railway – the Sankey Viaduct

115

The Liverpool and Manchester Railway – Chat Moss. Opponents of the railway had claimed that it was impossible to cross the Moss. Certainly, stone poured into it just vanished. Stephenson adopted a well-tried device, sandwiching layers of stone between hurdles: the hurdles prevented the stone dispersing. So far from being impossible, this section of the line was the cheapest of all.

able. To remedy matters the Liverpool and Manchester Railway Company was formed in 1824. Liverpool merchants took the initiative, and provided most of the capital, Manchester's share being insignificant. The company obtained its Act in 1826, at the second attempt, and appointed George Stephenson as its engineer.

Stephenson had a number of interesting problems. The Common Council of Liverpool refused to allow the railway through their town, which meant digging a tunnel under it, some 2200 yards long. Even when it emerged, the line had to have a cutting made for 2 miles in solid rock. Half-way to Manchester there was the valley of the Sankey Brook, which was wide enough to need a viaduct. Finally, towards Manchester, there was a marsh, Chat Moss. Stephenson dealt with all these problems efficiently, showing that railway engineers could overcome all likely obstacles.

One important question was whether to use stationary engines or steam locomotives. Accordingly the company organised the Rainhill trials in 1829, offering a prize of £500 to anyone who could design a locomotive that met their requirements. Robert Stephenson & Co. won with their *Rocket*, which beat the favourite, Braithwaite and Ericsson's *Novelty*.

The organisation of the railway was important. The Act of Parliament allowed private individuals to run their own vehicles on the line, and they would have been bound to cause confusion. However, the company had its own carrying department, with numerous locomotives, first- and second-class carriages, goods wagons, cattle wagons, warehouses and depots. No outsider could compete, so the company had the line to itself.

The official opening, on 15 September 1830, was marred by two incidents. Firstly the company had invited the Duke of Wellington, and a rowdy mob showed their dislike of his politics. Then tragedy struck when the *Rocket* ran over the M.P., Huskisson, as he stood on the track talking to the Duke. Despite these things, the railway was an immediate success. What amazed the company was the number of passengers, and indeed it was unable to spare a train for freight until the end of the year. After that, though, goods traffic grew fast enough:

	Passengers	Merchandise (tons)	Coal (tons)
1831	445 000	43 000	11 000
1835	474 000	231 000	116 000

Financially the line was a success as well. For years its shares paid 9½ per cent which, at a time when government stock yielded about 3 per cent was remarkable. The dividend could have been more, but one of the peculiarities of the Act was that if the dividend was over 10 per cent the company had to reduce its charges.

The Liverpool and Manchester was the first

116

modern railway. It was as important for passengers as it was for freight, it used steam locomotives along its entire length, and its organisation was modern as well. Here was no private track linking a coal-owner's mines to a waterway, and carrying his goods exclusively, but instead the public could use it at will. On the other hand it was no glorified turnpike road where all and sundry ran their vehicles, causing confusion and disorganisation.

The opening of the line was the beginning of the railway age. Many people had been waiting to see how it fared, and when it was a success the 'mania' of the early 1830s was the result.

However, none of this had been intended by the original committee, which had embarked on a local project to satisfy local needs. There were people who had grandiose dreams – but anyone can have dreams. Those who provided the inventive skill and and the hard cash for the Liverpool and Manchester Railway were thinking of the trade and industry of those two towns.

By 1850 Britain had close on 7000 miles of railway, and, for the first time, a national system of transport. Complex networks served the main industrial areas, the North-East, the West Riding of Yorkshire, South Lancashire and the Midlands. In addition, lines radiated from London, three of which were especially important. They were the London and North-Western that ran to Lancashire, the Great Western that ran to Bristol and then on to Exeter and Plymouth, and the London and South-Western that ran to Southampton. Other lines led to the East Midlands and East Anglia, while the London and Greenwich was the nucleus of a system that served the South-East. Scotland and Wales were less fortunate. Scotland had a modest network in the Lowlands, and two lines to England, one running from Edinburgh to Newcastle along the coast, and the other from Glasgow to Carlisle. In Wales there was the Chester to Holyhead, which was really England's railway to Ireland, and the Taff Vale, which ran inland from Cardiff. The agricultural counties of the South Midlands and South-West England also had few lines. However, apart from providing for Scotland and Wales the main network was complete. Later additions, and there were many, were largely those unprofitable branch lines that were to be the despair of Dr Beeching.

The first 7000 miles were built, for the most part, in three bursts of activity called 'mania'. This is an unfortunate term because it suggests that railway building was a form of madness, whereas most lines were properly planned, carefully built and made profits. The only thing that resembled madness was the willingness of some investors to buy any railway shares available on the market, because they were sure that every railway was bound to make money. It was much the same phenomenon as the canal 'mania' of the early 1790s. Indeed, the peak of every trade cycle caused a certain fever among speculators, whether railway shares were for sale or not.

The first boom came in 1824. As many as 3000 miles were planned, but few companies obtained their Acts, and fewer still built their lines. The ones that were completed were fairly modest, like Stockton and Darlington, and Canterbury and Whitstable.

The second boom was from 1836 to 1837. By that time the Liverpool and Manchester was paying a steady 9½ per cent. Also, four major companies had obtained their Acts, the London and Birmingham and the Grand Junction in 1833, the London and South-Western in 1834 and the Great Western in 1835. So many people spending so much, spread confidence. Finally the economic climate was favourable. Investors had plenty of money, but as interest rates were low they were frustrated because they could not put it to good use. The railways, with their hopes of high returns, were just what they wanted. Even so, only about 500 miles of track were laid.

It was the third boom that created the railway network. The middle of the 1840s saw a return of the same economic conditions as ten years before, added to which the railways had more than proved themselves. While enterprising promoters rushed to form companies, investors poured out their money. The peak year for Acts was 1846, when Parliament sanctioned 4540 miles. Building was at its height in 1847 when there were a quarter of a million men laying some 6000 miles of track.

The railway 'mania'

BUILDING THE RAILWAYS

The key men among the railway builders were the engineers, and it is interesting to learn how they acquired their skills. It is sometimes said that they profited from the experience of the canal builders but, if that is so, it is odd that no canal builder of note made a railway. Telford, for example, tried instead to prove that canals were the better form of transport. In fact most railway engineers gained their experience building and maintaining the wagon ways for the coal-mines.

As well as railway engineers, another new group was the railway contractors. They were the men who organised the gangs of navvies to build the lines according to the engineer's plans.

The most famous of the railway contractors was Thomas Brassey. He was the son of a Cheshire farmer and, as a boy, he was articled to a land agent at Birkenhead. Brassey saw the town was going to grow, so he bought a brickworks and some limekilns. He prospered and saved money. Later he met George Stephenson, who encouraged him to try his luck with railways; so, when the Grand Junction was planned, he tendered, successfully, for the Penkridge Viaduct. He gave such good service that when the engineer, Joseph Locke, went on to build the London and South-Western, he entrusted Brassey with much of the work. Here he firmly established his reputation as a first-rate contractor. He had three assets – an ambitious wife, a capacity for hard work, and the abilty to choose good assistants. He built railways the world over, having at one time 100 000 navvies in his charge. By 1850 he had made £1 million, and then went on to make £2 million more.

The problems the railway builders faced were many. Even before work started they had opposition, some of it informed and intelligent, some of it stupid. Environmentalists, who now fight to keep railways, then fought to prevent them. Many were country gentry who took a pride in their estates. Parks which had been laid out with loving care in the eighteenth century were coming into their prime, so that a land-owner would welcome a railway no more than would a painter having his canvas slashed. Some towns, like Northampton, objected to railways, and it is easy to understand why. Apart from the noise and dirt, they usually strode through on viaducts, which no one who loved his native place would wish to see.

As well as environmentalists, there were people who were concerned about the effect travel at 30 m.p.h. might have on health. There were worries, too, about farm animals, many of them quite reasonable. It is indeed true that sheep which are often frightened, quickly lose weight.

Naturally turnpike trusts, coach companies and canals all made difficulties, but the most ruthless enemy any new railway could meet was a rival line. It cost the Great Northern over £400 000 to obtain its Act, because of the opposition of George Hudson of the North-Eastern.

There were natural obstacles that were nearly as intractable as the human. Tunnels usually caused problems, a particularly difficult one being at Kilsby on the London and Birmingham. When Robert Stephenson was surveying his line to avoid Northampton, as its inhabitants required, he met an unwelcome hill. He made borings, which showed

Railway viaduct

118

oolitic limestone, but soon after work began the men found quicksands. The contractor went home, went to bed and died. Stephenson brought in steam pumping engines, whereupon the work went on steadily, until they hit a spring which flooded the tunnel so quickly that the men in it barely escaped. Apart from abandoning the tunnel, the only answer was even more pumping. Eventually there were thirteen engines taking out water at 1800 gallons a minute. To finish the task took more than 1000 navvies thirty months, while the total cost was £300000, against the £90000 agreed with the first contractor. It also cost twenty-six lives. Other problem tunnels were the Box Tunnel on the G.W.R. and the Woodhead Tunnel on the Sheffield, Ashton and Manchester. At Box, a hundred men lost their lives, and at Woodhead thirty-two, or 3 per cent of the work-force. A Royal Commission on Railway Labourers was appointed because of the Woodhead scandal, and Edwin Chadwick calculated that a higher proportion of men were killed or injured there than in any of Wellington's battles. Most of the accidents during tunnelling were from explosions, but there were other reasons. At Kilsby some of the navvies used to relieve their boredom by jumping over the mouths of the shafts.

A wide stretch of water was difficult to cross, and became even more so if it was dear to the Lords of the Admiralty. At Saltash, on the Tamar, they decreed that the bridge to carry the Great Western Railway had to be 100 feet above the high-water mark for its entire length. Brunel decided on a suspension bridge, but with a difference. Above each of the chains was a wrought-iron tube, curved to form an ellipse. The two of them stopped the chains from pulling their piers inwards, and at the same time helped them support the roadway of the bridge. Their lordships also stated that the safety of the realm required that the Chester and Holyhead line should pass 100 feet over the Menai Straits. Stephenson built his Britannia Bridge as a huge square tube through which the trains ran.

Not the least of the difficulties the railway builders faced came from the lack of power of the early locomotives. Henry Booth explained: 'If a locomotive engine is exactly able to draw after it 30 tons of weight on a level, the same engine will draw only 7 tons, at the same speed, up an inclined plane rising one yard in a hundred.' (op. cit., p. 82) This meant that lines had to be as level as possible, therefore needing long tunnels, deep cuttings and high embankments. Brunel's 'billiard table', the G.W.R., is at its steepest gradient of 1 in 100 in the Box Tunnel; for 40 miles out of Bristol it is, at the most, only 1 in 750, and the rest of the way to London it is never more than 1 in 1000.

TECHNICAL CHANGES
Technical changes went on faster than ever. For example, in the late 1840s Daniel Gooch designed the 'Iron Duke' locomotives for the G.W.R. Their boilers had a heating surface of 2000 square feet, and raised a steam pressure of 100 pounds per square inch. There were many improvements – for example, to couplings, signals and points, and the electric telegraph was introduced. Stations became larger and better. At Nine Elms in London they found the best plan for a terminus as early as 1838. It had two widely spaced platforms running parallel with each other, whose

The Saltash Bridge

Construction of embankment

Cannon Street Station

ends were joined by a range of buildings that included the waiting-rooms, booking-office, administrative offices and, sometimes, a hotel. At first there were sidings in the area between the two lines, but in most places it was soon needed for extra platforms. Station buildings had monumental façades in every style of classical and medieval architecture, while behind them were the latest nineteenth-century structures of iron and glass. Such prestige buildings were expensive. Philip Hardwick's Doric arch at Euston cost £35 000.

INTEGRATION

Turnpike roads and canals had not made a national system of communications. London, it is true, reached out a long way into the provinces, but for the most part local people built to satisfy local needs. As they extended their own systems, they met others doing the same. This gave the finished map the appearance of a national system, but in fact it was a patchwork of local ones. To give an example, neither turnpikes nor canals could move bulk supplies of coal into the agricultural south, or even to London. Railways, too, began in the traditional way. There were a few lines that connected London to places like Bristol and Birmingham, but the remainder were for local use, such as the Stockton and Darlington. They then pushed outwards, just as turnpikes and canals had done, but when they met other systems, they behaved differently. Instead of loosely knotting the ends, as it were, they integrated with each other. This integration took three forms. In the first place all railways were, eventually, the same gauge; secondly they made efficient arrangements for through traffic; thirdly companies amalgamated.

Probably the early lines kept the same gauge by accident. The Stephenson's dominated, and they had brought their 4 ft 8½ in

gauge from Darlington to Liverpool and Manchester. Events then moved quickly, for by 1833 the London and Birmingham and the Grand Junction began the construction of their lines, so the 4 ft 8½ in gauge, already well established in the North-East and the North-West, was also in use on an important trunk route. It was certain it would then spread to much of the country

However, almost anyone could have seen that the best gauge for a short Northumbrian coal-track was not right for an important railway. It only needed an engineer with the character to defy the Stephenson tradition and serving a company with large enough resources to be independent. As everyone knows, Brunel decided on a 7 foot gauge for the Great Western Railway, and was proved right, because his carriages were roomier and his trains were more stable at high speed. John Braithwaite, engineer of the Eastern Counties Railway, also went his own, rather more timid way, and built the London to Colchester line to a 5 foot gauge.

At first the differences did not matter, but in 1845 broad gauge and narrow gauge met at Gloucester, so that passengers and goods had to change trains. Further, the Great Western had plans for lines running to South Wales, and even into the very heart of narrow gauge country, the Midlands and Lancashire. The problems at Gloucester were going to arise at many more places unless something was done, so in 1846 Parliament passed an Act stating that 4 ft 8½ in was to be the standard gauge for the country, and that all lines built in the future must adopt it. Existing lines could stay as they were – the G.W.R. was powerful enough to ensure that. Parliament would have done the country a service if it had acted a year or two sooner, when there were still only 500 miles of narrow track, and settled for 7 feet, but by 1846 it was too late. The expense of widening track would have been enormous, with major works at every station, cutting, embankment and tunnel. It was so much easier for the G.W.R. to conform, which it did, eventually, of its own free will. It began by putting down a third rail, between the other two, so that it could take standard gauge trains as well as its own, and by 1892 had abandoned the broad gauge entirely.

The railway system, in the early days, was made of a multitude of fragments, many of the lines being like the old turnpike roads, no more than about 10 or 12 miles long. This caused problems for long-distance travellers until companies co-operated to provide through trains.

To divide the revenue from them, there was

The Railway King

a Railway Clearing House. It opened in 1842, and by 1849 forty-seven companies were members, having between them 648 stations.

As well as co-operating, companies also amalgamated. Frequently it was the way to end tiresome competition. In the 1840s the Midland Counties and the Birmingham and Derby Junction were fighting for the traffic between Derby and Rugby. They cut their charges so low that they were heading for ruin, until George Hudson intervened. Thanks to him the two companies amalgamated to form the Midland Railway. It was the first of Hudson's big strokes and he then went on until he had control over hundreds of miles of track, earning himself the title of 'Railway King'. The North-Eastern, which devoured the Stockton and Darlington, was his greatest creation. Hudson was a determined, ruthless man, and he was not honest. Among other things, he sometimes used money invested in one project for something quite different, and which the subscribers would never have dreamt of supporting. Eventually he was discovered and had to flee the country. However, this was only a temporary set-back to the process of amalgamation that ended in 1948 with the creation of British Rail.

23 Inland transport and the economy

In an industrial society there are three kinds of capital. There is working capital, which is a manufacturer's raw materials and his customers' debts. Next there is fixed capital which is, for example, a manufacturer's factory with its machines. Finally there is social overhead capital: this includes a wide variety of things, such as hospitals, schools and public houses, but the most important part of it by far is the transport system.

Social overhead capital is different from the other two. Usually it is possible to obtain credit for working capital, perhaps from a bank, while a prosperous business man can add to his store of fixed capital by ploughing back some of his profits, year by year. Social overhead capital, however, is difficult to accumulate. A railway or a canal costs far more than most individuals are able to pay, so there has to be some form of organisation enabling numbers of people to pool their money. Next a transport project takes a long time to construct, and an even longer time to show a profit. Investors, therefore, have to be either very optimistic, very patient, or desperate for somewhere to place their money. Finally social overhead capital benefits the whole community to a greater degree than the other two. Anyone may use a road for his own profit, but he can hardly enter another man's factory to make what he chooses.

However, once a country has acquired a transport system, it may expect good returns from it, though these do not come automatically. In the late eighteenth century Arthur Young was bemused to find splendid roads built by the French Government almost unused. The British made an excellent railway network in India, but the peasants showed as much interest in the passing trains as did their sacred cows. However, in Britain during the Industrial Revolution, progress in transport was an integral part of progress in the economy as a whole. We will deal with each kind of transport in turn.

ROADS

From contemporary accounts it is difficult to say how well the turnpike trusts did their work. Arthur Young described the road from Salisbury to Romsey as having an excellent surface, firm and dry, with no loose stones. He added: 'It is everywhere broad enough for three carriages to pass each other: and lying in straight lines, with an even edge of grass the whole way, it has more the appearance of an elegant gravel walk than of an high road.' On the other hand he complained of the 'Execrable muddy road' from Bury to Sudbury which, he said, was no better than certain neglected tracks he had found in the Welsh mountains.

However, Dr Albert has drawn some significant conclusions from the rules which Justices of the Peace made for carriers (op. cit., Chap. 8).

In the first place, by the nineteenth century there were no longer any differences between winter and summer charges, which can only mean that transport was possible in bad weather as well as good. Secondly, charges were lower on main roads than on side roads, showing that travel was easier on the main roads, and they were the ones that had been turnpiked. Thirdly, prices remained low for a long time, in spite of toll charges. Indeed, in the middle of the eighteenth century, they were lower than at the beginning. They then stabilised until the Napoleonic Wars, when the high price of grain drove up costs – but even so, freight charges did not rise as much as other prices. Turnpikes were still holding down the cost of transport. It was only after 1815 that they came under strain. Traffic increased so much that, although grain prices fell, freight charges still increased, showing that by then something better than roads was needed for long-distance transport. Fourthly, loads became much greater. In 1662 the maximum was 30 hundredweight, and a carrier was allowed a team of seven horses to draw it. By 1765, the load was 120 hundredweight, but the number of horses was only five. Turnpikes

had increased the efficiency of the wagon horse by 600 per cent.

Also, the travelling time of coaches improved. In the seventeenth century the journey from London to Edinburgh took ten days, but by the 1830s it was only two, and this reduction to about one-fifth was general on all main roads. Turnpike roads, then, had done almost as much for the coach-horse as for his colleague that drew a wagon.

How far did people take advantage of these improvements? We know, for example, that farms near turnpikes commanded higher rents, so their tenants must have been selling over a wider area. We know, too, that the number of passenger coaches increased. In 1756 one coach a day went from London to Brighton, while in 1811 there were twenty-eight. In 1820, 1500 coaches left London every twenty-four hours.

Along with the passengers went mail. In 1784 John Palmer started a mail-coach service to replace the notoriously inefficient post 'boys' who, only too often, were middle-aged drunks working in league with highwaymen.

Mail is obviously important for business, but easy travel for people is more valuable than it might seem at first sight. It is difficult to have confidence in someone you have not seen, and a personal visit could make all the difference. Boulton and Watt would not have made nearly as much money in Cornwall if Boulton had not travelled there from Birmingham. The steam-engines could not sell themselves, and Watt, who erected them, was from the business point of view a positive liability. It was Boulton's personality which made a success of the venture into Cornwall.

All this, though, is impossible to quantify. We do not know how many goods and people travelled, nor do we know how far they went. Simply because it was possible to go from London to Edinburgh in two days, it does not follow that large numbers did so. Were the coaches used like inter-city services, or more like stopping trains? Two things are certain, however. One is that the roads did not carry that most vital of bulk materials, coal, over any great distances. The second is that fares were too high for ordinary people to travel regularly.

We must remember also how the turnpike system grew. It was a patchwork of local routes with the main roads to London superimposed upon them.

It would seem, then, that the turnpike roads did only a limited amount towards dissolving the local economies and making one national economy.

Other effects which turnpikes had were

Changing horses

even more limited. Labour was needed to build the roads and maintain them; there was work for toll-keepers; coaching inns prospered; there were many horses to tend and feed. All these, though, can have amounted to little when measured against the economy as a whole.

How much the roads cost it is difficult to say. Apart from tolls on the turnpikes, money was spent from the county rates, and the Government too made a modest contribution. Expenditure was at its peak in the first quarter of the nineteenth century, when it may have amounted to £3.5 million a year. This was approximately 1 per cent of the national income.

CANALS

It is possible to draw up an impressive list of the changes brought by canals. We can start with Smeaton's calculations that a canal horse could do the work of 400 pack-horses. Here, then, was an increase in efficiency that must imply a revolution in transport.

The inland waterways meant easy and therefore cheap transport for bulky low-cost goods. If a business man trades in, say, watches, his transport costs per ton of merchandise will hardly matter. Coal is quite different. In the eighteenth century it was cheap enough at the pit-head, but if it had to go on pack-horses, its price rose steeply for every mile it travelled. After 10 or 15 miles it

was too expensive for people to buy. However, the Industrial Revolution depended far less on the production of small high-cost luxury items than it did on cheap bulky goods. It is easy to understand, then, why the canals had a vital part to play.

Canals helped a number of towns to grow and change. When the canal from Lancaster to Kendal opened, the people of Kendal built wharfs and warehouses, and widened some of their streets for the extra traffic. Stourport, on the Severn, became an inland port when it was made the terminus of the Staffordshire and Worcestershire Canal, while farther down the river, Gloucester itself was busier because of the link with the Midlands canals. A seaport would become more prosperous if it had a canal, like Ellesmere, which was at the end of the Chester Canal, or Goole, on the Aire and Calder Navigation.

Canals helped agriculture. Barges carried grain: they delivered materials for soil improvement like marl, sand, lime and chalk: they took loads of manure from the towns into the countryside, to the advantage of both. However, it is not likely that canals did much for farms, save perhaps some that were near their banks. No canal prospered that ran through rural areas only.

Canals helped the building trade, for sand, bricks and timber were ideal cargoes. Yet, as with farming, it is unlikely that they served more than their immediate areas. Buildings of

Stourport. Here the Staffordshire and Worcestershire Canal joined the Severn. The canal basins, with their warehouses, formed the nucleus of a little town.

the eighteenth century are made of local materials.

There was more help for manufacturing industry. M.W. Flinn's map shows how the early waterways served a major industrial area (*An Economic and Social History of Britain since 1700*, 1963, p. 53).

A later example comes from Glamorganshire:

Goods Carried on the Glamorganshire Canal

	Iron (tons)		Coal (tons)
1817	39500	1819	35000
1827	85,000	1829	84000
1837	125000	1839	211000

SOURCE: Hadfield, op. cit., p. 167.

That is not to say, of course, that the Glamorganshire Canal created the South Wales iron industry. What it did was to help it to grow. Many a manufacturer must have felt that, with the opening of a canal, someone had taken a foot off his windpipe. He had easier, cheaper transport for his raw materials and finished articles, and he could sell over a wider area.

Without doubt the most important cargo was coal. The two earliest canals, the Sankey and the Bridgewater, had been built to carry it, and indeed no canal prospered without it. As we have seen, the opening of the Bridgewater Canal halved the price of coal in Manchester, and much the same happened elsewhere. At Oxford they rang the church bells when the first barge arrived carrying Midlands coal. Without cheap coal the towns could

not have grown as they did, while industries needed it more and more, particularly for the manufacture of iron. The Industrial Revolution could not have made much progress without coal, and the canals took much of it where it was needed.

Unfortunately there was some wastage of capital, for certain canals were never finished, never carried a cargo and never paid a dividend. The unlucky Dorset and Somerset Canal, for example, was planned to run from the Kennet and Avon Canal, near Bath, to Blandford Forum. The short feeder which was to have joined the collieries at Nettlebridge with Frome was the only section which was started, and not even that was finished. This little project swallowed some £60000, and there were other, similar failures. That centralised planning by the Government would have saved capital wastage, as Phyllis Deane suggests, is open to question (*The First Industrial Revolution*, p. 80).

Whether successful or not, canals were, in the economist's language, 'capital intensive'. As a result of canal building, were other enterprises starved of capital, and would the money have been better spent on them? It is impossible to say, but it is likely that, without canals, some at least of the money might have been worse spent. Two groups who bought canal shares were land-owners and merchants, both of whom had expensive tastes, particularly in building. Even if a canal, like the Kennet and Avon, paid no dividends, an investor was no poorer than if he had built a folly, while the community benefited. Nor were the canals too expensive for the country to afford. About £20 million were invested in

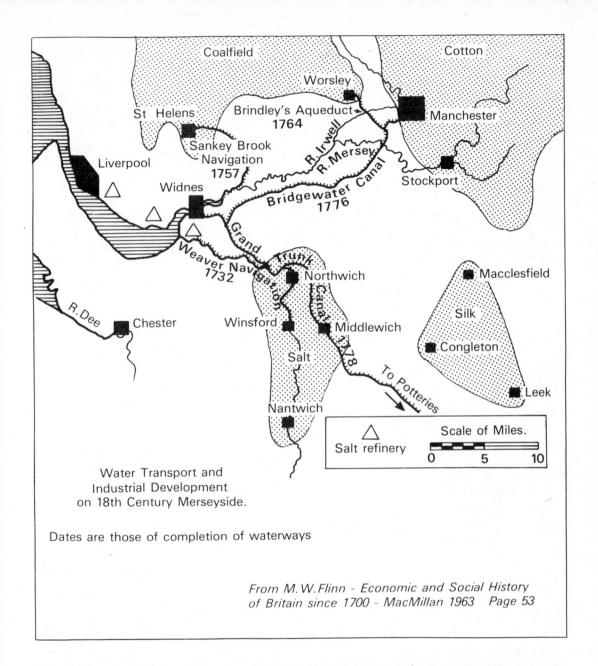

Water Transport and
Industrial Development
on 18th Century Merseyside.

Dates are those of completion of waterways

From M.W.Flinn - Economic and Social History
of Britain since 1700 - MacMillan 1963   Page 53

Water transport in south Lancashire and north Cheshire. The rock-salt deposits of north Cheshire began to be worked intensively from the late seventeenth century, coal being used to evaporate the brine. The nearest coalfield was in south Lancashire, and Liverpool merchants engaged in the export of refined salt built the Mersey salt refineries in the 1690s. As a first step towards reducing the cost of transport of rock-salt and coal, the Liverpool merchants secured an act in 1721 for improving the navigation of the River Weaver to Winsford. Later, in the 1750s, they built the Sankey Brook Navigation to make cheap coal available for salt-making. As a result of the development of these new waterways, the output of salt from north Cheshire rose from 14000 tons in 1732 to 28000 tons in 1752, to pass the 100000 ton mark by the end of the century. The original Bridgewater Canal of 1764 brought coal cheaply to the textile manufacturing centre of Manchester, and its extension in 1776 made possible the immense expansion of the cotton industry by the cheap water carriage of American raw cotton from Liverpool and the finished cotton goods from Manchester to Liverpool for export. The Grand Trunk Canal of 1778 gave the Potteries and the silk towns of the Cheshire–Staffordshire border access to the port of Liverpool. (from M.W. Flinn, *Economic & Social History of Britain since 1700*) them between 1755 and 1835 which was roughly one-third of 1 per cent of national income.

The canals saved working capital. A manufacturer who is sure of regular supplies does not need to carry large stocks, so some of his money is freed. He might use it to expand his store of fixed capital or he might invest it in other enterprises.

Canals helped the accumulation of capital by educating the public. Joint stock companies were not new, but they attracted investment from only a limited public. However, more and more people were introduced to them as the canals criss-crossed the country. Most families had already given up keeping their gold in an oak chest, preferring to put it on deposit in a local bank, or to buy government securities. The Funds, particularly, were quite safe, but investing in them meant a quiet life with no rich returns. The excellent dividends paid by the more successful canals, though, showed that glittering prizes awaited the adventurous investor, and many rushed to buy canal shares.

All learnt from their experience – some never to do anything like it again. Yet many profited, and they and their friends and acquaintances saw the advantages of the joint stock company.

During their construction, canals gave work to thousands of labourers and even some craftsmen. When they were finished men were needed to maintain them, and handle the barges and their cargoes.

It is time now to look at the other side of the balance sheet.

Water transport is slow, so it did not attract the passenger traffic that the railways were to find so profitable. It is true that on the Forth–Clyde Canal there were passenger boats drawn at 10 miles an hour by galloping horses, but they were unusual. Mostly people travelled by road. However, turnpikes and canals complemented each other. While the roads carried people, mail and lighter goods, the canals carried heavy, bulky loads. It was a good division of labour.

The most common criticism of canals is that with their varying widths, depths and charges they were not as efficient a system as they might have been. Again, as with capital wastage, it has been suggested that intelligent planning from the centre would have avoided most of the problems. However, this shows a misunderstanding of the nature of the canal network. Like the turnpike roads it was not built as a national system, but as a number of local systems. Through-traffic was insignificant, so the gauge of the Shropshire canals mattered nothing to the merchant using the wide Kennet and Avon Canal.

It followed from this that the canals did not turn the country into one market for coal. London still had its coal by sea from Newcastle, and went on paying Newcastle prices. In the enclosed villages of the south, labourers hunted farther and farther afield for odd pieces of wood, or made do with fires of wheat stubble.

In short, the canals must have strengthened and enlarged the local economies, but what they did not do was to create a national economy.

RAILWAYS

The changes brought by railways were, in some ways, broadly similar to those made by canals. However, there were striking contrasts as well.

Many towns grew, some of them from nothing. Certain ones, like Middlesbrough, prospered because of railway traffic. Others sprang up around railway workshops. Swindon, on the G.W.R., was one, and the pleasant terraces of cottages that were its nucleus are still there. The London and North-Eastern Company developed Crewe. In 1849, it had over five hundred houses, public baths for washing, a mechanics' institute, a church and a town hall, all of which were railway property. The company employed teachers, a clergyman and a doctor. Here then was the same paternalism as in the factory settlements, though on a larger scale.

There was help for agriculture. Soon after the Liverpool and Manchester line opened there were some remarkable changes to Chat Moss. Cuthbert Johnson describes how the railway brought clay and lime, which the farmers had spread on the peat, turning it into fertile soil: 'The traveller by railway now sees, in the very middle of this great Bog, well cultivated and neatly arranged fields, and the Ploughman profitably employed where, a few months since, silence reigned undisturbed.' (op. cit., p. 8) Most farmers used the railways more for the transport of live cattle, fresh meat and fresh milk than for soil improvement. As an aid to marketing, railways were much better than canals, and played their part in the 'golden age' of British agriculture. However, that belongs to the third quarter of the nineteenth century, after the railway network was completed: the gains in South Lancashire were, in our period, exceptional.

Railways helped the building industry. Local materials may be the most picturesque, but they are not always the most convenient. For

Railway village at Swindon – houses from front and back, the public house at street corner.

cheap houses, builders needed bricks, Scandinavian softwoods and Welsh slate. The railways carried these unattractive goods all over the country, the towns continued to grow, and the Industrial Revolution maintained its momentum. Again, this was a development that came when the network was complete. Railways did stimulate building during our period, however, because of the demands they made themselves. There were stations, bridges and viaducts to be built, and tunnels to be lined.

Brick-making flourished, appearing almost anywhere that there was clay and good transport. Building the viaduct for the London and Greenwich Railway, with its 878 arches, kept the Kentish brickfields in a fever of activity during the 1830s. The railways together used 740 million bricks in 1845 alone, and that was by no means a peak year for construction.

Railways stimulated iron and engineering. These industries needed and produced heavy, bulky goods, and railways halved the cost of their transport. Yet once again, during our period it was the demand the railways made themselves which was more important. Between 1844 and 1851 rails alone took 18 per cent of iron output, and rolling stock and other equipment 12 per cent more. Most of the rails came from South Wales. From the beginning, firms there supplied railway companies in the south, but had to compete with others for sales in the Midlands and Lancashire. As the railway network grew, though, they lost the disadvantage of distance and dominated these markets as well. Only in the North-East did the local ironmasters hold their own. The wife of Sir Josiah John Guest of Dowlais, Lady Charlotte, watched with nervous excitement. In 1845 she entered in her diary:

We have sold the Great Western 10,000 tons of Rails at £12 a ton, which is now a great price. But people are wild at this moment about Railways and speculations, and they say that Iron will still further advance, which if the bubble do not too soon burst, may probably be the case. (op. cit., p. 615)

The bubble did not burst, for 1845 was only the beginning of the boom.

In the late 1840s railways took 20 per cent of the output of the engineering industry. There were locomotive works in Lancashire, the West Riding and the North-East, as well as in the specially built railway towns like Swindon and Crewe. The proprietors of the London and Greenwich Railway found that the best-known locomotive makers, Robert Stephenson & Co., were too busy to supply them, so they did their shopping in Tipton, Liverpool, Birmingham, Southampton, Deptford and London. All this was within eight years or so from the opening of the Liverpool and Manchester line, so the manufacture of railway locomotives must have spread rapidly.

Especially significant were the effects on the coal industry. Again there were the demands made by the railways themselves. By 1850 locomotives were burning 1 million tons a year, which was 2 per cent of national output, while an unknown amount went to make the iron and bricks that were needed. Even more important, the railways opened new markets for the inland coalfields. They did what the roads and canals had never done, and carried coal to London.

For the capital, that meant cheaper fuel, since the mine-owners from the North-East found they had competition from the Midlands. For much of the rural south, it meant a blessed relief from a fuel famine they had suffered since the enclosure of the commons. Everywhere the railways went, they carried coal, and even the smallest station had its coal-yard where the local merchants could come with their carts.

There were far more passengers than the railways expected. The Stockton and Darlington line was built for freight, and passengers travelled in coaches hitched to goods trains. The London and Greenwich was for passengers only, which made it quite exceptional. Most lines were like the Liverpool and Manchester, which was built for freight but hoped to attract enough passengers to make a useful contribution to the company's income. In fact here, and on most railways, passengers were more profitable than freight until about 1850.

The railway companies knew that it was the rich who travelled, so at first they were the people they did their best to attract. It was true that they carried coal and working men, but there was no need to go near either, since first-class passengers had separate entrances to stations, separate waiting-rooms, and of course separate carriages. Railway companies, in general, showed their contempt for the poor by making them ride in open trucks, sometimes even without seats.

Gladstone came to the rescue. In 1844 he sponsored a Railways Act which, among other things, laid down certain rules for third-class travel. Companies had to run one train a day, in each direction. It had to include some covered third-class carriages, and it had to stop at every station. Fares had to be no more than a penny a mile and, so that it could not be shunted into a siding and forgotten, the average speed had to be no less than 12 m.p.h. Such

were the 'Parliamentary Trains' of The Mikado's song. They were used by working men, morning and evening, which was what had been intended, but they had an evil reputation with wealthier travellers, and the supercilious staff of the G.W.R. called the 6 a.m. from Paddington the 'Plymouth Cheap'.

After a time the companies were surprised to find that third-class passengers were contributing handsomely to their profits, so they improved their carriages, giving them roofs, sides and seats. To help family outings they allowed babies to travel free, and children at half fare. They also offered special rates for excursions. One of the first of these was organised by a certain Thomas Cook who, in 1841, took a party from Leicester to Rugby for a temperance meeting. The Duke of Wellington had opposed railways because, he said, they would enable the lower orders to move about, but the companies paid no attention to him and went on encouraging the social revolution which, quite unintentionally, they had begun.

Freight traffic began to grow rapidly from the middle of the 1840s. Receipts from it were £1.4 million in 1843 and £7.7 million in 1852, by which time they were roughly the equal of passenger fares. The most important item was coal. By the middle of the 1850s receipts from minerals, mainly coal, were 30 per cent of all freight, and they accounted for 60 per cent of the tonnage carried. The railways had already taken most of the inland carriage of coal from canals, and were going to do what the canals themselves had never done, which was to challenge the coastal shipping.

It must be stressed, though, that by 1850 traffic was only just beginning to grow:

	1850	1870
Passengers carried (millions)	50	300
Ton/miles of freight (millions)	650	5000
Percentage of London coal supplied by rail	1.6	56

Railways made their demands on capital. In fact they took it on a scale that no enterprise had ever done before. They were expensive to build and nowhere more so than in Britain. In 1884 it was calculated that they had cost £42 000 a mile on average, compared with £21 000 in Germany and £11 000 in the U.S.A. There are various reasons for these differences.

In the first place the British Government, so far from helping rail transport as other governments did, handed each company to social vampires as soon as it was born. Objections to a new line, instead of being heard by salaried professional men, had to be argued by lawyers before a Parliamentary Committee. Both lawyers and M.P.s charged enormously for their services. The London and Greenwich thought they were lucky to have their Act for £22000, while the Great Northern had to pay £433000. The London and Birmingham paid £73000, which was not unusual. However, even though these amounts were utterly unreasonable, they did not account for more than 2 per cent of the expense of the average line.

Next, there was the cost of the land. Many land-owners overcharged, like Lord Petre who made the Eastern Counties pay £120000 for land they thought worth £5000. However, this was exceptional. Normally the railways received fair treatment as the canals had done, paying a little over the market value. Generally the cost of the land was about 14 per cent of the total.

Thirdly the railway companies were extravagant. There was no need for the London and Birmingham to spend £35000 on a triumphal arch at Euston; the openings of railway tunnels did not have to look like entrances to baronial castles any more than stations needed to resemble classical temples or Tudor manor-houses. However, it is unlikely that having prestige buildings instead of functional ones added more than 1 per cent to the total costs.

Certainly the fact that Britain pioneered the railways made a difference. There had to be a lot of digging to make easy gradients for the early locomotives, while the industry, being a new one, had not learnt how to cut its costs.

However, when all these things are added together, we are still a long way from explaining the vast differences between costs in Britain and those in Germany and the U.S.A.

Paying for the railways took a good slice of the national income. From 1844 to 1846, that is during the first three years of the major boom, £16½ million were spent, amounting to 3 per cent of the national income. During 1847, the peak year for investment, £52 million were spent, which was 10 per cent of the national income and equal to the total value of exports. According to Dr Hawke, this must have meant a 'decline in consumption, not just a re-direction of income' (op. cit., p. 250). In other words there were men who, in order to buy railways shares, were willing to deprive themselves, or their familes, of some of life's luxuries. It was not until the late 1850s that profits were equal to investments.

There were two features of this flood of investment that had not been seen on the same scale before.

In the first place much of the money came from investors all over the country. For the most part early transport projects, including railways, were financed locally. It is argued that investors had a good idea of the plans and were able to make a shrewd guess at their chances of success. During the railway boom, however, people bought shares in lines being built miles from their homes, guided only by a faith in railways in general. The London and Greenwich is a good example. Londoners were sceptical, so most of its capital was raised in Liverpool. As it happened, the people of London were right, for, apart from one year when

Tunnel entrance – London and Birmingham Railway. The elaborate classical ornamentation must have added substantially to the cost of the building.

its shares yielded a modest 3½ per cent, the company paid no dividends at all. Clapham is scathing about 'Blind capital, seeking its 5%, a totally different thing from the clear-eyed capital of the Quaker businessmen from the Midlands and the North' (*Economic History*, Vol. 1, p. 388).

Secondly there was speculation in railway shares. In other words some people bought them to sell at a profit soon afterwards, rather than waiting to draw dividends on their investment. Miss Deane seems to suggest this was not a 'respectable' thing to do (*The First Industrial Revolution*, pp. 159–60).

The argument is that the railways encouraged a wastage of capital as well as dubious business activity. Certainly there was a wastage of capital, for some lines duplicated each other needlessly, and others failed to attract enough traffic to make profits. However, most lines proved their worth, and by 1850 the network was coherent and sensible. This was without any centralised planning. Moreover, we do not know how much 'clear-eyed' capital was wasted on earlier projects, and how much 'blind' capital was wasted on railways. Without the two figures to compare, we are in no position to judge. As for speculation in shares, it is hard to see how buying them to sell at a profit is any more immoral than buying and selling other articles.

Dividends varied. The Liverpool and Manchester paid 9½ per cent from 1836 to 1845. The Stockton and Darlington usually paid 11 per cent and 14 per cent in its best year, 1837. On the other hand the London and Greenwich managed 3½ per cent in one solitary year, and for the rest of its life, nothing. The average was about 5½ per cent in 1845, falling to 3⅓ per cent by 1850. Railway shares were no longer for those afflicted with a 'mania' but rather for people who wanted a quiet life, with a safe, steady income.

Railways provided a good deal of employment. In 1847 a quarter of a million men were building them, while close on 50 000 were operating the ones that were finished. At that time the working population was only 12 million.

However, the most striking thing about the railways is that, unlike the roads and the canals, they were a national system of transport. We have already seen that they integrated, by keeping the same gauge, by organising through traffic and by amalgamating companies. When they were completed, the country became one economic unit, with the products of every industrial area being everywhere available. We have also seen how agricultural produce, building materials, iron and above all, coal, travelled freely. This description of Camden Station in the early 1860s adds detail to the picture:

In the grey mists of the morning, in the atmosphere of a hundred conflicting smells, and by the light of faintly burning gas, we see a large portion of the supply of the great London markets rapidly disgorged by the night trains; fish, flesh, and fowl, Aylesbury butter and dairy-fed pork, apples, cabbages and cucumbers, alarming supplies of cats' meat, car loads of water cresses, and we know not what else, for the daily consumption of the metropolis. No sooner do these disappear than at ten minute intervals arrive other trains with Manchester packs and bales, Liverpool cotton, American provisions, Worcester gloves, Kidderminster carpets, Birmingham and Staffordshire hardware, crates of pottery from North Staffordshire, and cloth from Huddersfield, Leeds, Bradford and other Yorkshire towns, which have to be delivered in the city before the hour for the general commencement of business. At a later hour of the morning, these are followed by other trains with the heaviest class of traffic; stones, bricks, iron girders, iron pipes, ale, (which comes in great quantities, especially from Allsopps and the world famous Burton breweries), coal, hay, straw, grain, flour and salt. (Railway News, 1864, p. 343, quoted in Hawke, op. cit., p. 59)

Are there any reservations we must make? Dr G.R. Hawke has shown that there are, at least in our period.

It has been suggested that since railways carried goods more quickly than canals, they allowed merchants and manufacturers to hold lower stocks, so freezing capital for other uses. However, the average haul was only 30 miles and, though a railway could cover it in a couple of hours, a canal needed no more than a day. Saving ten hours on a journey does not release much capital.

Another thing that has been assumed was that the railways, by making heavy demands on the industries that supplied them, encouraged technical changes in those industries, which then allowed them to produce more cheaply for all their customers. In fact the only likely improvements brought in this way was an increase in the size of the South Wales blast-furnaces, and the ironmasters there might have done that anyway to meet Scottish competition.

The railways certainly helped to supply cheap labour, for they encouraged Irish immigrants in their thousands, and then sacked them when their work was finished. However, unskilled labourers were a thing the country did not lack, so finding yet more was a service to no one.

Dr Hawke also measures what he calls the 'social saving' made by the railways. He means the amount extra the country would have had to spend on transport, to carry the same increase in passengers and goods, if there had been no railways. He arrives at the respectable figure of 10 per cent down to 1870, but to do so he has to make a curious comparison. A load of coal does not mind how it travels, but passengers do, and how do you compare travel by rail with travel by coach? D. R. Lardner in his *Railway Economy* of 1850 suggested that going first class by rail was like travelling inside a coach at 4d. a mile, while second and third class were like travelling outside at 2½d. a mile. On the other hand the Royal Commission on Railways of 1867 likened first class to travelling post at 2 shillings a mile, second class to travelling inside a coach, and third class to travelling outside. Dr Hawke accepts the second of these, and calculates that the 'social saving' on passenger traffic was 6 per cent of the national income, which, with 4 per cent for freight, makes up his total of 10 per cent. However, if Lardner's view is correct, then the social saving on passenger traffic was a mere 2 per cent. Further, even if we accept the higher figure for social saving, there had been practically none of it by 1850 – perhaps 1 per cent for passenger traffic, and something less for freight.

Down to 1850, then, railways were to the country what growing children are to their families – they mattered more for what they took than for what they gave. The most significant thing about them was the strength they revealed in the country's economy, namely that it was able not only to meet their enormous demands, but to do so, for the most part, in the few frantic years between 1845 and 1848.

We must now see how railways affected roads and canals.

Coaches could not compete with trains. To travel 40 miles from Leeds to York, for instance, took a coach four hours, and the fare outside was 3 shillings – which was cheap for a coach. The train took only eighty minutes, and the fare was 2s. 6d. Overall, though, the railways brought an increase in travel by horse, not a decline. Passengers and goods had to reach the railway stations, so that people bought their own vehicles, especially small two-wheelers. Many folk led a horse and ignored the existence of railways until the day of the motor car. It was not just private horse transport that grew, however, for coaching companies did well, provided they could act as feeders to the railways and did not have to compete with them. Taxes from coaches were £212000 a year on average between 1845 and 1850, and £198000 a year between 1850 and 1854. Clearly the railways had only brought a loss and not disaster. As for turnpikes, those that happened to be useful cross routes found their takings from tolls increased. They had all indeed vanished by 1892, but their going was the result of the reorganisation of local government, not of railway competition.

Many canals took fright too easily and offered themselves for sale, while the railways, anxious to remove dangerous rivals, were eager to buy. However, in 1850 the Bridgewater Canal was still carrying two-thirds of Manchester's goods, while in the country as a whole canal freight was still as important as railway freight. After that, railways shot ahead, so that by 1900 canals only carried one-tenth as much as their rivals. It was only a comparative decline, though, for canal traffic continued to grow until 1914. It was much the same story as with the roads. If a canal was in competition with a railway, it lost, but if on the other hand it followed a route not taken by a railway, or better still, could act as a feeder, then it prospered.

Broadly speaking, what happened was that the canals gave up their long-distance traffic, which had not been unduly important for them, but increased their short-distance work. They have been blamed for not amalgamating, standardising and fighting the railways with cheapness and efficiency, but that is to misunderstand their nature. They were not national thoroughfares but local means of transport, and the railways left many of them to carry on their traditional work, sometimes even helping to increase it.

We must remember too that the great age of the railways was the second half of the nineteenth century. Before 1850 anyone on a journey would most likely be travelling by horse and, quite possibly, by stage-coach. Also, if a merchant was dispatching goods, the chances were that he would be sending them by boat or wagon.

24 Case histories

THE THAMES AND SEVERN CANAL

The dream of joining the two most important rivers in southern England was an old one, going back to the early years of the seventeenth century. The Act for a canal was finally passed in 1783 and it opened for traffic in 1789. It ran from the Thames at Inglesham, on to the escarpment of the Cotswolds, through the remarkable Sapperton Tunnel, and then down to Stroud. Here it joined an older canal, the Stroudwater Navigation, which led to the Severn at Framilode.

The men who built the Thames and Severn Canal intended it to carry long-distance traffic. We know this because in the first place they announced in the *Gentleman's Magazine* that they were going to make 'an inland communication from the capital with Bristol, Gloucester and Shrewsbury, as also with the manufactories in Worcestershire, Staffordshire, Warwickshire, Cheshire and Lancashire' (Vol. 60, p. 109, quoted by Household, op. cit., pp. 39–40). Secondly the money for the canal came mainly from men living at either end of a system of waterways that were to be, between them, something over 300 miles long. They were a number of the proprietors of the Staffordshire and Worcestershire Canal, and some London merchants. It is true that after they had bought their shares the Londoners did little, but the proprietors of the Staffordshire and Worcestershire Canal not only found 30 per cent of the capital for the Thames and Severn, but took an active part in running it. Clearly they were looking for a wider market for Staffordshire coal. Finally there was the anxiety of the proprietors of the company to complete their canal in good time. When they obtained their Act in 1783 work had already been in progress on the Coventry and Oxford canals since 1769, but was dragging. They were going to make a side door into the Thames Valley, and the newcomers saw they had a chance to push through the back door before them. In this they succeeded, for they finished their own canal just one year before their rivals. This proves that they were interested in at least the middle reaches of the Thames.

We can compare the completed waterways to a chrysanthemum plant. The flower, drawing nourishment from the rest, corresponds to London. The stem, a long one, is the Thames,

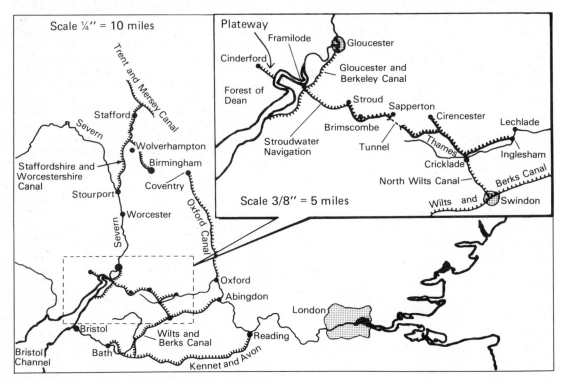

Waterways linked by the Thames and Severn Canal

the Stroudwater Navigation leading off from the Severn, and, joining them together, the Thames and Severn Canal. The main root is the River Severn, running more or less at right angles to the stem, with side-roots sprouting from it. At first the most important of these was the Staffordshire and Worcestershire Canal, which joined the Severn at Stourport. As we have seen, the main reason for building the Thames and Severn was to carry Staffordshire coal into the Thames Valley. By 1798 the company had made arrangements with other carriers so that goods could be dispatched to Bridgewater, Newport, Hereford, Shrewsbury, Birmingham, Manchester and Liverpool. They also sent their own boats into the Bristol Channel to trade with south and south-west Wales. By the turn of the century the Forest of Dean coalfield was being developed and in about 1808 some of the mine-owners built a plateway from Cinderford to Bullo Pill on the Severn. This is only 6 miles from Framilode, and the plateway was to be an important feeder to the canals. In 1819 the North Wilts Canal opened, which, if we want to keep our analogy, was more like a side-shoot than a root. It ran from the Thames and Severn at Cricklade to the Wilts and Berks Canal, which in turn joined the Thames at Abingdon. It was then possible to avoid the upper reaches of the Thames, which were not easy to navigate. Finally there was the Gloucester and Berkeley Canal, which opened in 1827. Its main object was to allow ships to avoid an awkward stretch of the Severn, so that they found it easier to reach Gloucester from the Bristol Channel, but it also connected with Framilode.

Here then was a system of waterways that looked impressive. It joined the capital to the two most important ports in the West of England, Bristol and Gloucester, to three important coalfields, Staffordshire, South Wales and the Forest of Dean, and to two rich agricultural areas, the Vale of Gloucester and the dip slope of the Cotswolds. All this had become possible because of the imagination and enterprise of the men who built the Thames and Severn Canal.

Unhappily, when we look more closely, the picture vanishes like a mirage. However great their variety, the volume of goods that went the whole distance to London was insignificant. When the canal first opened, the proprietors were dismayed that hardly anyone wanted to travel along its full length, and even after three years, in 1792, only about two boats crossed the summit level in every three days. After war broke out in 1793 there was more activity, possibly because the coastal trade suffered. In 1795, 450 boats passed the summit level and in 1800, 723. However, this is no more than two for every working day of the year, and by no means all of them would have been going to or from London. Humphrey Household in his admirable book on the canal says that 502 tons of goods reached London from Gloucester in the whole of 1828, which was barely enough cargo for nine Thames barges. For the rest, he is very vague, so presumably there are no accurate figures available. However, he speaks of the company and later, private carriers, sending one boat a week from Brimscombe to London and he also mentions an advertisement for 'Thames and Severn canal boats which leave Cirencester every quarter day of the moon'. As to what came from London, it hardly mattered at all, since goods travelling westwards on the canal were less than one-fifth the volume of those travelling east.

There were good reasons why there was so little through-traffic. The Thames and Severn had all the natural hazards of canals, along with more than its fair share of problems with water. For several miles its summit level

Year	By Frost	For maintenance	By other causes	Total
1809	21	16	14 (Thames floods)	51
1822	0	127	—	127
1826	20	26	70 (Stroudwater–Berkeley Canal junction)	116
1827	19	at least 39	—	58
1828	0	40	—	40
1829	4	Tunnel 63	—	67
1830	40	5	35 (Stroudwater repairs)	80
1839	0	28	—	28

SOURCE: Household, p. 161.

crosses the Great Oolite of the Cotswolds, which is porous, and full of cracks and fissures. The canal could be made watertight, temporarily, by careful puddling, but during heavy rain, springs burst through from below, and when they subsided they left gaps. The table on p. 133 shows the days lost for various reasons in particularly bad years.

Apart from natural hazards, the canal had obstacles of its own. From the Thames to the summit was 130 feet, with fifteen locks, while on the other side the rise from Stroud was 350 feet, with twenty-eight locks. The summit level itself was over 7 miles long, but that was no clear run because of the Sapperton Tunnel. Building this tunnel was an achievement in which the company took much pride, and showed it with a magnificent classical portal on the east side, and another in the Gothic style on the west. None the less, the tunnel was a thorough nuisance, for it was over 2 miles long, it took single-line traffic only, and it had no tow-path. Vessels had to be legged through by their crews who contracted, some of them, a nasty complaint they called 'lighterman's bottom'.

On top of the water problem and the delays caused by the locks and the tunnel there were dishonesty and incompetence. The boatmen were experts at helping themselves to cargo. For example, they could open a bag of sugar, remove a few handfuls, and close the bag again so that it looked as if it had never been touched. They replaced what they took with earth, so the entire sackful was ruined. The journey from Brimscombe to London took nine or ten days, and no merchant wanted to entrust valuable goods to professional thieves for that length of time.

The incompetence was on the part of the company. They had to start their own carrying department because at first there was no one else to do the work, but they did not manage it efficiently. The chief problem was faulty accounting. They failed to include a great many hidden expenses, like the depreciation of their boats, so in the end they found they were losing money. Soon after 1800 they handed the work of carrying to private boat-owners, having decided it was beyond their powers to manage 'so complicated and difficult a concern as the trade between London and the Ports on the River Severn' (quoted by Household, p. 110).

There was of course no comparison with the Great Western Railway, but even before that was built, the coastal traders were more efficient than the canals and charged less. It was cheaper to send goods from Gloucester all the way round Land's End than along the inland waterways. Certainly there was no question of the barges competing with the collier brigs from the Tyne, which not only delivered coal to London in vastly greater quantities, but did so about 10 per cent cheaper.

Finally the waterways which the Thames and Severn linked made no system at all. They were a complete hotchpotch.

The River Thames was not fully improved for navigation until after the Thames Conservancy was established in 1866. The river was particularly difficult in its upper reaches because of weirs and flash locks. The pound locks that had been built were designed to take Thames barges which were up to 12 feet wide and 88 feet long. One of these ponderous craft could be towed downstream by a single horse but needed a team of up to eleven coming the other way – that is, if it had been lucky enough to find a return cargo. Each had a crew of three who were given their keep and from £5 to £7 a man for the trip from Port Brimscombe to London and back. Tolls between Lechlade to London were over £25 and, for a time, a barge returning empty paid as much as one returning full. Not only was the journey expensive, but it took a long time, at least three weeks, quite apart from delays in London.

The Severn was at least free from tolls and weirs, but it had every other encumbrance, especially in its upper reaches where there were, according to the weather, either sandy shallows and rocks or floods. Above Gloucester the boatmen waited until a fall of rain in the Welsh mountains sent them a 'fresh'; below Gloucester, they sailed on the high tide that came once a fortnight. As there was no tow-path, they used the current, the wind, or the tides, and when they failed, the crew themselves towed, either from the bank or from a small boat. The boatmen were a wild, independent lot who resisted any improvements to the river because they could not bear the thought of paying tolls. There was a variety of craft on the river, but the most typical was the trow. Unlike a Thames barge, which was the shape of a punt, a trow had curved timbers like a ship. Also it was partly decked and carried a square sail. What was more important was that its dimensions were different as well, for it might be up to 20 feet wide, but no more than 68 feet long.

The other waterways were very miscellaneous. In spite of its name, the Stroudwater Navigation was a proper canal, and was of a piece with the Severn in that its locks were the correct size for trows. It did, however, have one important weakness, for its tow-path had obstacles such as stiles, so that towing had to be done by men, save when the wind was exactly right and the trow could hoist its sail. As we have seen, the company traded with South Wales, which meant navigating the Bristol Channel. This is virtually open sea, so the vessels had to be built like small coasters and rigged as ketches or schooners. Since they had keels they could not sail on the canals. The Gloucester and Berkeley Canal was for ships of up to 600 tons, which were of course much too big for the Stroudwater Navigation. The Staffordshire and Worcestershire Canal and the North Wilts Canal were both designed for narrow boats, over 70 feet long, but only 7 feet wide. Finally a most important feeder to the system was not a waterway at all, but the railway from Cinderford to Bullo Pill.

To sum up, then, there were two rivers with different characteristics, and quite different craft, two broad canals, but with locks of different sizes, two narrow canals, but separated by the River Severn so that they could not exchange boats, an area of open sea and a railway.

The only real success the canal had was a purely local one. During the eighteenth century the Forest of Dean coalfield had been exploited by independent miners working little pits with the help of their wives and children, so output had been low. However, towards 1800, capitalists began mining scientifically and produced large amounts of coal. To carry it to the Severn, they built plateways including, as we have seen, the one to Bullo Pill, a few miles from Framilode. Forest of Dean coal now found its way in considerable quantities up the Stroudwater Navigation and the Thames and Severn Canal. From practically nothing in 1805 it amounted to 36000

tons in 1825 and remained at about 40000 tons a year in the 1830s. In 1828 it amounted to 60 per cent of all goods carried on the canal. The market, though, was restricted. In the 1830s, 40 per cent of cargoes did not reach the summit level from the west, 30 per cent were discharged on wharfs along its length, and only the remaining 30 per cent came down the other side to the Thames or the North Wilts Canal. Practically no goods travelled the other way. Household says: 'The Thames and Severn Canal, far from developing into the artery of east-west trade envisaged by its projectors, had become principally a distributor of coal from the Forest of Dean to the homes and factories of the Stroudwater Valley.' (op. cit., p. 137)

In the classical portal at the east end of the Sapperton Tunnel are two niches, one of which was intended for Sabrina and the other for Father Thames. It was somehow fitting that the statues did not arrive, for the canal was never an effective link between the two rivers. Indeed, the sad ruins of the portal are a reminder of the failure of canals in general to create a national system of transport.

THE STOCKTON AND DARLINGTON RAILWAY

The men chiefly responsible for this line were a group of Quakers from Darlington, which included a woollen manufacturer, Edward Pease, his son Joseph, and a banker, Jonathan Backhouse.

In the early nineteenth century Darlington was a small town whose chief industry was textiles. There was huckaback, made from linen, and a whole collection of worsteds – camblets, wildbores, bombazets and tammies.

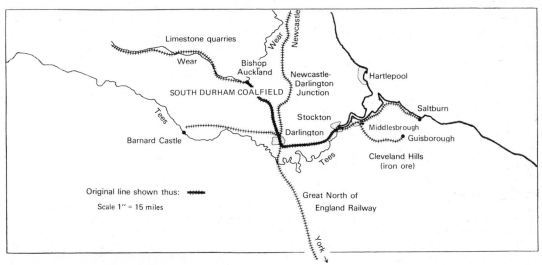

Stockton and Darlington Railway system

Opening of Stockton and Darlington line

Several of the firms belonged to Quakers, like the Pease and Backhouse families, and it was there that they learnt the business skills which they used later to run their railway with such success. The town is on the South Durham coalfield, but before the 1820s mining was not unduly important because the River Tees, unlike the Tyne and the Wear, was not a good waterway, and its port, Stockton, was a poor little place compared with Newcastle or Sunderland. The story is that lack of communications became especially frustrating when a Darlington woollen mill burned down, putting four hundred people out of work. Although it was not his mill, Edward Pease decided something should be done to bring coal more easily to Darlington and its neighbourhood, so helping the local industries.

This was in 1818, when the obvious way to improve transport was to build a canal. However, it did not look as if a canal would pay. Someone Jeans described as a 'clever statistician' wrote scathingly:

Look at the country all the way between the two places, Auckland and the Tees. Take its manufactures of woollen, cottons, earthenware, iron – its coals for the supply of the different manufactories, and all those in active employ from the very beginning of the project. Then look at the project; we have a most unfavourable country to pass over; there must be 50 locks in less than 30 miles. Then look at the population. Where are the inhabitants? A few thinly scattered farm-houses; no manufactories; little commerce; and when we get to the collieries, what are they? (op. cit., p. 18)

This 'clever statistician' calculated that a canal would cost £300 000 and they would be lucky if it paid a dividend of 1 per cent. Such arguments convinced most people that they had better be satisfied with a horse railway, the poor man's alternative to the canal. This was agreed at a meeting in Darlington in November 1818.

The next stage was to obtain an Act of Parliament, because the railway was to belong to a public company, and also they were going to need powers of compulsory purchase. At once there was trouble, since they had planned the line to run through some of Lord Hartington's fox covers, and his lordship saw that the Bill was thrown out. However, the Darlington Quakers were not men to accept defeat. They found another route, avoiding the foxes, and went sedulously to work, winning over local land-owners and even trying to influence the parliamentary elections which were then taking place. At the same time they had to collect promises of subscriptions, since there could be no Act unless they were able to show where they were going to find at least 80 per cent of their capital. Backhouse worked hard, but not hard enough, because at the end they were still £10 000 short. Edward Pease saved the day by promising the money, though he could ill afford it. However, all their efforts were worthwhile, for in April 1821 the second Bill was passed.

The company now appointed an engineer, who, as is well known, was George Stephenson. Jeans says there was a tradition that 'Stephenson tramped from Newcastle to Darlington with a bundle on his back for the purpose of seeing Mr. Pease and offering his services for the construction of the new line' (op. cit., p. 37). However, at this time in his life, Stephenson had no need to tramp anywhere looking for work and, as Jeans says, the Company probably employed him because his colliery railways were well known. There is another story, which tells of a disagreement. Stephenson suggested that the railway should run directly from the collieries to Stockton, since, like a good Newcastle man, he held that coal was for export. Clearly he had not understood the purpose of the railway. Pease chided him: 'George, thou must think of Darlington; thou must remember it was Darlington sent for thee.' (*Diaries of Edward Pease*, 1907, p.91) This was not unreasonable, for Darlington supplied almost all of the capital for the line.

The company had to decide on their track, and on the means of drawing their wagons.

Although Stephenson had patented a rail of his own, he recognised that Birkinshaw's was better, so four-fifths of the rails came from Bedlington. For some reason the remainder were of cast iron; perhaps they were for the sections where they used horse traction. They had two kinds of sleeper as well, most of them being stone blocks and the remainder oak timbers. For railway history the most important decision was the gauge. Stephenson felt he should see what suited the area best, so he took an average of all the local horse railways and arrived at the unlikely measurement of 4 ft 8½ in. It was to become the standard gauge of all railways in Britain, as well as of many the world over.

For traction, the company was happy to have horses, self-acting inclines and stationary engines, but when it came to locomotives it hesitated. Possibly it knew that they tended to end up as stationary engines – one of Trevithick's was even then pumping air into a cupola furnace in Newcastle. However, Stephenson settled the argument by taking Pease and some other directors to Killingworth to see his own locomotives in action. They came back convinced. The final plan was as follows. First, horses should bring the wagons along the feeder lines from the collieries. Next, stationary engines should draw the loaded wagons up Etherley and Brusselton hills, with self-acting inclines on the downward slopes. Finally, locomotives were to work the railway along the easy gradients of the valley of the Tees, between Darlington and Stockton. The stationary engines saved a lot of expense at the beginning, building cuttings and tunnels, but in 1839 a tunnel three-quarters of a mile long was completed at Shildon, which saved a lot of delay on the Brusselton inclined planes.

The first engine was Stephenson's famous *Locomotion*, which moved its own weight and 75 tons at about 5 m.p.h. The company were pleased with their investment, for they calculated, with commendable precision, that while it cost £163.8s.10d to move 4263 tons of coal by horse, the locomotive did the same work for £70.6s.6d. Others were not so happy about locomotives, like the frightened horses on the turnpike road, or plantation-owners who saw their pines showered with red-hot cinders. Running empty and downhill, the drivers delighted in going at their maximum speed of 12 m.p.h., so they had to be restricted to 8 m.p.h., and 5 m.p.h. near plantations.

There were few clear ideas on running public railway lines, but the company saw they would have to be the carriers and could not, like a Turnpike Trust, provide the road and then leave it to others to run traffic on it as they pleased. Consequently they bought locomotives and wagons for themselves, while one Chaytor, who asked if he could run his own locomotive, was turned away. They did, however, lease a horse-drawn passenger coach to Richard Pickersgill, and by 1831 there were also six privately owned coaches. Even they caused confusion, so in 1833 the company bought them all.

From the beginning the company meant their railway to carry heavy goods, like limestone and manure for agriculture and, more especially, coal for industry. Even on the day of the official opening, the train included loads of flour and coal, while visitors rode in open goods wagons. Passenger traffic was an afterthought. They did, however, build a coach which they named, doubtfully, *The Experiment* and, as we have seen, others followed. Before the railway a solitary coach had run between Stockton and Darlington three or four times a week, its four horses drawing ten or so passengers when it was lucky enough to have a full load. A railway coach carried twenty-six passengers and only needed one horse. Furthermore, as there were six within a few years, passenger traffic must have increased considerably due, no doubt, to the low fares. However, when the company bought out the private owners in 1833, they dismissed their horses, and hitched their coaches behind the goods trains, thus putting the passengers where they belonged. Pease had meant his line to carry coal, and that was what it did.

The history of the Stockton and Darlington line did not end with Stephenson's departure. By 1861 the original 25 miles had become 125, there were links with other railways, and the

137

whole economy of the area had changed (see map on page 135).

The South Durham mines had produced little coal because of lack of transport, but the railway opened them not just to Darlington and Stockton, as was intended, but also to the sea. The company had indeed built a wharf, expecting some modest exports, but were unprepared for the amount of coal that appeared. They installed new staithes, designed by Timothy Hackworth, and other improvements followed, so that Stockton became an important coal port until about 1850. Then the opening of the main railway lines to London made it decline again. The main problem was that the estuary of the Tees was difficult to navigate, so Pease determined to build a new port. In 1828, much to the distress of the Bishop of Durham, he and some friends bought 500 acres of swamp, about 4 miles down the river, obtained an Act of Parliament to extend the railway, and thus created Middlesbrough. It was the first town to owe its existence to a railway. In the early years 'Pease's port' was only a limited success. Its population grew from nothing in 1830 to nearly 6000 in 1841, and it exported quantities of South Durham coal, but other lines, farther north, took the bulk of it to another new port, Hartlepool. Middlesbrough's great days were yet to come.

The railways also pushed inland. Other companies built the extensions, but the name of Pease was usually on the list of directors. One branch was built, by stages, along the valley of the Upper Wear. It carried some lead ore but mainly limestone, which was burnt and sold to farmers. Another branch was built to Barnard Castle, against the will of the Duke of Cleveland, who was that same Earl of Hartington who had opposed the original Act of 1818. It was a pity, this time, that he did not succeed, for the line to Barnard Castle lost money. The population of the town refused to grow, while its staple industry, making carpets, hardly needed the railway. It did not automatically create an economic miracle wherever it went. Finally, there was a much more ambitious plan to take a line over the Pennines to join the one from Lancaster to Carlisle. This, the South Durham and Lancashire Union Railway, obtained its Act in 1858.

Running as it did, roughly east and west, the Stockton and Darlington Railway lay in the path of others that were being extended northwards. By 1841 it was joined to York by the Great North of England Railway, and in 1844 to Newcastle, by the Newcastle and Darlington Junction Railway. By then the little local line had become a small but busy fragment of the growing national network.

Then in 1849 came a link of another kind, for the Quaker railway amalgamated with the North-Eastern, which was the empire of the notorious George Hudson. Jeans, whose jubilee history of the Stockton and Darlington praises it all the way through, could hardly avoid mentioning the North-Eastern, but the name 'Hudson' does not sully his pages.

In the 1850s there were important developments, following the discovery of iron-ore in the Cleveland Hills. Joseph Pease was one of the first to open a mine, so it is no surprise to find that he pressed for another railway. An Act for a branch from Stockton to Guisborough was passed in 1852, and it became one of the most prosperous lines in the area. Middlesbrough turned into an important iron manufacturing town, while the Wear Valley and its railway came into their own. The limestone that had been quarried for local farmers was now needed in large quantities for the blast-furnaces.

To round it all off, an Act of Parliament of 1858 authorised a branch to Saltburn. Here Henry Pease, M.P. for South Durham and Mayor of Darlington, turned an empty piece of coast into a seaside resort for the people of Middlesbrough. Among the buildings he thoughtfully provided was the Zetland Hotel, with 100 bedrooms.

In the minds of old Edward Pease and his friends the Stockton and Darlington line was little more than an extended colliery railway. It was a modest local scheme, financed by local capital, and intended to meet local needs. As such it was the same as many of the lesser transport projects of the eighteenth and early nineteenth centuries and not nearly as ambitious as, say, Brindley's Trent and Mersey Canal. However, the railway exceeded all expectations. From 25 miles it grew to 125; it encouraged several established industries, especially mining and quarrying, and it helped the creation of a new one, iron manufacture. It also resulted in two new towns, Middlesbrough and Saltburn-on-Sea. The most important fact about the railway, though, is that it was a local transport system that became an integral part of a national system.

PROBLEMS

1 What factors led to the construction of turnpike roads?

2 What were the economic effects of turnpikes?

3 Describe the changing uses of roads between 1700 and 1850.

4 How far did canals meet the needs of the British economy down to 1850?

5 Could the canals have made a national system of transport?

6 Why have some continental waterways been more successful than those in Britain?

7 What economic changes led to the building of canals?

8 Why did railways make a national system of transport while turnpike roads and canals did not?

9 Could the railways be described as a leading growth industry?

10 How did railways affect industry? In what ways did the growth of industry stimulate railway building?

11 How did railways affect urban development?

12 Why did environmentalists object to the building of railways in the early nineteenth century, and why do they resist their closure today?

13 How did the problems connected with the building of the railways affect their development?

14 What was the importance to the economy of the railway boom of the 1840s?

15 How far were the changes of the 1840s beneficial to all forms of inland transport?

16 How was finance raised for inland transport?

17 How did improvements in transport affect investment?

18 How far could agriculture have developed without improvements in inland transport?

19 Was transport the key to economic growth during the Industrial Revolution? Consider ports and shipping as well as inland transport.

20 Explain the equivocal attitude of the landed aristocracy to improvements in transport.

21 Why did the British Government do so little to help provide a transport system during the period 1700 to 1850? What influence did it exert?

FURTHER READING

Albert, William. *The Turnpike Road System in England 1663–1840*. O.U.P., 1972.

Bagwell, Philip S. *The Transport Revolution from 1770*. Batsford, 1974.

Baxter, Bertram. *Stone Blocks and Iron Rails*. David & Charles, 1966.

Carlson, Robert E. *The Liverpool and Manchester Railway Project 1821–1831*. David & Charles, 1969.

Hadfield, Charles. *British Canals*. David & Charles, 1974.

Hawke, G.R. *Railways and Economic Growth in England & Wales 1840–1870*. O.U.P., 1970.

Household, Humphrey. *The Thames and Severn Canal*. David & Charles, 1969.

Jackman, W.T. *The Development of Transportation in Modern England*. 1916.

Rolt, L.T.C. *Navigable Waterways*. Longmans, 1969.

Simmons, Jack. *The Railways of Britain*. Routledge & Kegan Paul, 1961.

Walker, Charles. *Thomas Brassey, Railway Builder*. Frederick Muller, 1967.

Ward, J.R. *The Finance of Canal Building in Eighteenth Century England*. O.U.P., 1974.

Shipping, Ports and Trade

25 Shipping and ports

THE SAILING-SHIP

The eighteenth- and early nineteenth-century shipbuilders produced no vessel that was as spectacular as Brunel's *Great Eastern*; there were no technical improvements to compare with the compound engine or the steel hull; there was not even a ship to match the *Cutty Sark* for pure romance. However, there were important changes, even so.

In the first place there was an increase in tonnage:

Year	Tonnage of merchant ships
1700	300 000
1770	600 000
1830	2 200 000
1850	3 600 000

Next, ships were bigger. Builders had been quite capable of making large vessels, but owners had not wanted them. The East India Company, for example, learnt a hard lesson in 1609, when the *Trades Increase* of 1000 tons sank on her maiden voyage, taking a valuable cargo with her. Nor was it just a question of spreading risks. Any vessel might have to wait weeks for a full cargo, and the larger she was, the longer she had to wait. In the early eighteenth century the East India Company was content with ships of around 500 tons, and these were by far the largest afloat. Few ships sailing the Atlantic were over 200 tons, and 350 tons was considered large. With the growth of trade, though, it became easier to secure a full cargo, so owners began, cautiously, to order larger and larger ships and, in

1787, the East India Company once again had a vessel of 1000 tons, the *Ceres*. However, she was still exceptional. In the year she was launched three-quarters of the merchant ships afloat were 200 tons or less.

The increase in trade brought efficiency of another kind. Ralph Davis tells the story of the voyage of the *St Quinton* in 1727, which started when she went from London with cargoes for Lisbon, Alicante and Leghorn:

From Leghorn it got a small freight for Palermo, and a short journey in ballast took the ship to Jurgento, where a corn cargo for Lisbon awaited it. It went back in ballast to Jurgento, and took another corn cargo to Libson. Bringing cocoa from Lisbon to Cadiz, it found little business there, and went on to Genoa. Here, too, nothing was offered, so the St Quinton *went off in ballast to the Gulf of Negroponte to collect a corn cargo for Genoa. There was no return lading at Genoa, and the ship had to sail in ballast again, this time to Leizat in Sicily, where a cargo of salt for Ostend was found to bring her home.* (Davis, p. 249)

Spending so much time hunting for cargo and sailing in ballast was costly, and the way to make money was to put a ship on a regular run to the same port, carrying the same cargo year in, year out. That could not be done though, until there was enough trade to make it possible.

Finally there were changes in the design of ships. As by far the largest single expense was paying and feeding the men, they found ways of managing with smaller crews. In ships trading to Spain, for example, there was in 1686, on average, one member of crew for each 7.9 tons; by 1766 this had gone up to 12.6 tons. For ships going to Virginia the figure increased from 9.8 tons in 1686, to 14.4 tons in 1766.

What improvements there were in design is not entirely clear, because we do not know enough about eighteenth-century shipbuilding. A few points are obvious, though.

The typical merchantman of the seventeenth century was expensively built on the Thames. She had to face Barbary corsairs, enemy privateers and pirates of all nationalities. Consequently she had fine lines to make her manoeuvrable, was heavily armed and carried a large crew. All these things took cargo space and cost money. Most of her sails were square, including the awkward spritsail topsail that stuck above the bowsprit. To adjust the sail area involved a lot of work, since they had 'bonnets' – strips of canvas that were laced to the foot of the sails.

The typical eighteenth-century ship, on the other hand, was built more cheaply in the new yards of North-East England or North America. She was shaped something like a floating shoe-box, which made her slower and less manoeuvrable but increased the size of her hold. Save in time of war she had few enemies, so she carried few guns and few men to serve them. She had a greater spread of canvas, with topgallant sails and, for light winds, studding sails. She also had jibs and staystails, which meant a much greater fore and aft element in her rigging, so she could sail closer to the wind. To take in sails they reefed them, which was much quicker than unlacing bonnets. They also had more two-masted vessels – brigs and snows. In about 1700 most ships above 60 tons had three masts, but by 1800 the average two-master was 200 tons. There were many such ships in the coal trade. Beating against the wind in an estuary was especially tricky. Usually they went forward on one tack, then, instead of going about for the other leg, let the wind blow the ship backwards, relying on the tide to make some way. Clearly the fewer sails there were for such a difficult manoeuvre, the better. While a three-masted ship in the coal trade needed a crew of ten, a brig could manage with six.

Here were improvements that compared with the ones taking place on the turnpike roads and inland waterways.

STEAMSHIPS

The first commercial steamer was Henry Bell's *Comet* which began carrying passengers on the Clyde in 1812. Two years later there were eight more keeping her company. They proved ideal for estuaries, where it was difficult to tow barges or manoeuvre sailing-ships, and steamers soon appeared on the Tyne, the Mersey, and of course the Thames. Here the *Margery* was in service between London and Gravesend by 1815. Dickens wrote some lively accounts of holiday trips down the river.

It was not long before steamers ventured into the open sea. In 1815 George Dodd took the *Thames* 750 miles from Glasgow to London, via Dublin, in sixteen days.

All steamers carried passengers, and the privileged ones mail, but there was no cargo of any consequence. They were popular because fares were low. The *Monarch* that sailed between Leith and London in the 1830s had berths for 140 and carried an indefinite number of deck passengers. Cabin passengers paid 4 guineas, and deck passengers £2.10s. including food. The coach fare was £6.15s. inside and £3.10s. outside, added to which the traveller had to buy his meals. There were 188 steamers by 1821, which was nine years before the Liverpool and Manchester line opened, and before railway competition began to bite in the 1850s there were around 600 of them, making a total of over 200 000 tons.

The first steamers were wooden; then, in the 1840s, they were of iron. Langland's *Royal Sovereign*, for example, was the first iron ship on the Liverpool and Glasgow run. Until the

Collier brig

Passenger steamer

1850s they were all paddlers. Then, in 1852, the *John Bowes* was launched at Jarrow. This marked the beginning of a new era, because not only was she screw-driven but designed to carry coal. The railways were beginning to drive the coasters back to their traditional work of transporting bulk cargoes.

Steamships were run by companies, the first being the London and Edinburgh Steam Packet Company of 1821. The traffic across the Irish Sea was particularly important, and there were numbers of firms operating services between Liverpool, Glasgow, Holyhead, Dublin, Belfast, Cork and the Isle of Man. It was rather like the early railway network, because there was no plan. Companies often competed with each other until, faced with ruin, they either merged or came to agreements.

Economically, ocean-going steamships were unimportant until the 1860s, but Brunel had completed his pioneer work before then. In 1838 his *Great Western* reached New York and fulfilled his dream of travelling all the way from London to Bristol, and then to America, by steam. In 1843 he launched his *Great Britain*, important because she was the first ocean-going ship to be made of iron and driven by screw propellers. Finally, in 1858, came his *Great Eastern*. The problem with the long-distance steamer was that she burnt so much fuel that she had little space for passengers and cargo. Brunel thought, with good reason, that if he made a ship big enough he would achieve economies of scale, so the *Great Eastern* was nearly 20 000 tons. The ship was a failure, and in the end it was shown that the answer to Brunel's problem was to have the much more efficient compound engines in much lighter, steel hulls.

PORTS

A ship arrived in port at high tide, and then she had a choice. She could stay in mid-stream and remain afloat, but then she had to discharge her cargo into lighters. It had to be handled twice, which cost money, while the opportunities for pilfering, already good, became excellent. Alternatively she could go alongside the wharf, but there the tide dropped her on the river bed twice a day. For a large vessel a visit to Bristol was especially trying. First she had to make her way, as best she could, up the Avon Gorge and then, when she arrived, she was at the mercy of extreme tides. The rise and fall at Avonmouth is something over 14 feet, a world record the Bristol Channel disputes only with the Bay of Fundy. As it could take four months to turn her round, the unfortunate vessel might be deposited on the Avon mud well over two hundred times. Owners who traded regularly with Bristol had their ships strengthened specially, but many broke their backs.

The answer to the problem is the wet dock, which is a long, narrow basin, dug out of the river bank. Ships enter it at high tide and gates close behind them, imprisoning the water, so that its level stays the same. London had its first wet dock at Rotherhithe in 1700, but only a few were added until the early nineteenth century, when there was a dock boom, with well over £5 million being spent between 1799 and 1815. This was because of the massive increase in trade during the Napoleonic Wars. Similarly Bristol had a wet dock at Sea Mills in 1712, but the main development had to wait until 1809, when William Jessop built the Cumberland basin. Bristol's rival, Liverpool, also had a wet dock early in the eighteenth century, and here nothing important happened until Jesse Hartley became dock engineer in 1824. He was responsible for a magnificent series of docks. For protection against thieves and vandals they are nearly all behind a high stone wall, with entrances that would do justice to a baronial keep. Hartley died in 1860, so his work spans the early years of the railway age. His docks were built for the same reason as the railway line to Manchester.

The traditional plan for a port was a wharf, with transit sheds, a road running parallel with it and then, fairly well back from the water, a row of warehouses. Thomas Telford improved this considerably when in 1825 he built St Katharine Dock, near the Tower of London. The warehouses were right at the water's edge, so goods were hoisted out of the ships' holds and went directly to whatever floor was appropriate. They were no longer dumped in transit sheds and then hauled across a road. There still had to be a road along the side of the wharf, so Telford made an arcade on the ground floor. Cast-iron Doric columns supported the five storeys above.

26 Trade

THE COASTAL TRADE

Adam Smith explained the importance of sea transport: 'It requires only six or eight men to bring by water to London [from Scotland] the same quantity of goods which would otherwise require 50 broad wheeled waggons, attended by 100 men and drawn by 400 horses.' (*Wealth of Nations*, Bk II, Chap. 5) It is not surprising, then, that transport by ship played an important part in Britain's internal trade. In 1841, 12.5 million tons of coastal shipping entered the ports, while shipping in the overseas trade amounted to 4.6 million tons. The two were not equal until the early twentieth century.

The coastal trade was varied, but three aspects of it were especially important – the trade with Ireland, the Newcastle coal trade, and the passenger traffic which came with the steamship and lasted until the railway age. The last of these was described in the previous chapter, so we have only to consider the other two.

Ireland was mainly an agricultural country, while the rest of Great Britain was becoming a great commercial and industrial power, so there was bound to be a growing trade between them. In the early eighteenth century Britain re-exported colonial goods to Ireland, especially sugar and tobacco. Later she sent coal, first from Whitehaven and then, as demand grew, from Liverpool and South Wales as well. Another bulk cargo was Cheshire salt. Britain's need for Irish food grew with her population. She exported grain herself until about 1750, but after that began to import it, and Ireland supplied a great deal. In the early 1820s it amounted to 230000 tons a year, and ten years later 390000 tons. There were also dairy produce, eggs, pork and beef. Some of the meat was salted, but there were live cattle as well.

A most important Irish export was labour. At first, men came to help with the hay and corn harvests, and returned home for the winter. Later they settled permanently to work as navvies or general labourers. In the late 1840s unwelcome hordes arrived, fleeing from the potato famine.

Ireland's only major industry was linen – the British would not allow any others to develop. At one stage Ireland exported yarn, but when Arkwright and the rest developed spinning machines, she imported from Britain for her own handloom weavers.

The trade in Northumberland and Durham coal was, along with fishing, Britain's oldest. The coal was carried to places all along the coast as far as West Dorset. Some was landed in harbours, large and small, some was carried up rivers, and some was discharged on open beaches, the ships being deliberately stranded at low tide. Most of it, however, went to London. Here it was used in limekilns, in blacksmiths' forges, but most of all in ordinary houses. The city could not have grown to the size it did without this unlimited supply of fuel for heating and cooking.

We saw in the last chapter how ships were improved. By the end of the eighteenth century they had found that the ideal collier was a two-masted brig of about 200 tons, but there remained the problems of loading and unloading the coal. On both the Tyne and Wear it was brought to the ships in barges known as 'keels'. They were ugly but solid, and would carry about 17 tons each. A keel would be loaded from a spout, which was easy enough, but when she reached the collier the unlucky keelmen had to cast their load on board her. In the early eighteenth century it was not too bad, but colliers doubled in size, so in the end the men were flinging the coal a height of 8 feet which, as they made very plain, was far too much. To discharge a ship, the crew

Coal whipping

143

erected staging in the hold, and flung the coal from one level to the next. On deck it had to go into a vat so that an official called a 'coal meter' could measure the cargo in order to tax it. Finally it was tipped over the side into a lighter.

In the early nineteenth century both loading and unloading were made easier. On the Wear they kept keels, but they carried their coal in iron tubs which were hauled on board the ship by crane. On the Tyne, when they opened mines below Newcastle and its low bridge, they loaded directly from the wagons into the ships by means of coal drops. A coal drop worked like a see-saw. It was perched on a high river bank so that a ship could moor beneath it. The loaded wagon ran to the end of it, and it then dropped under its own weight until it was just above the open hatch of the ship. Here the driver discharged the coal by unlatching the bottom of the wagon. It was then much lighter, so the counterpoise raised it and it ran back to the shore.

To unload the brigs in London they used an amusing system called 'coal-whipping'. Four men worked in the hold, shovelling the coal into a large basket. From the basket a rope went through the hatch, then over a pulley high up in the rigging and back again. Part of the way down it divided into four, and one man took hold of each end. They stood side by side on a wide ladder until the basket was full, whereupon they all jumped together to the deck. The jerk whipped the basket through the hatch, where the foreman caught it and emptied it into the vat. In this way nine men unloaded as much coal as sixteen had done before.

Here were two characteristic inventions of

East Indiaman, the *Earl Balcarres*

the Industrial Revolution. Both achieved remarkable economies, but both were made from traditional materials and both used the oldest form of power there is, the force of gravity.

The coal trade grew considerably. London imported half a million tons a year in 1700, 1 million in 1800, and 4 million in 1850. Leifchild wrote in 1853: 'If you take your station at Tynemouth Priory, you will see many hundreds of vessels, mostly colliers, put to sea together. On one occasion, some 300 vessels, all laden with coal, were observed making sail in a single tide.' (op. cit., p. 79) It was unfortunate that the colliers could find no return cargo, which meant that the vessels came back in ballast. By the 1850s they were carrying home each year close on 1 million tons of unwanted Thames sand.

OVERSEAS TRADE

In the middle of the eighteenth century Britain was a great trading power, but she had not always been so. In the 1560s there were, for example, about fifty English ships trading to the Baltic, but close on 1200 Dutch, while the entire English merchant navy was smaller than those of some individual Mediterranean cities, like Venice and Genoa. Only the coal trade and the fisheries prospered.

Progress began in the late sixteenth century, helped by Britain's own wars and those of Britain's rivals. During the revolt of the Netherlands Britain captured their eastern Mediterranean trade, and much of their Baltic trade as well. Her war with Spain gave Britain the excuse to trade with her colonies. The Netherlands recovered when they gained their independence, which led to friction with England, and so to the First Dutch War in Cromwell's time. The English won, and doubled the size of their own merchant navy by helping themselves to something like 1000 Dutch ships as well.

As well as war there was colonisation. During the seventeenth and early eighteenth centuries Britain occupied the entire eastern seaboard of North America as far south as Florida, together with numbers of West Indian islands. Of these Jamaica, Barbados and St Kitts were the most important.

There were two periods of expansion in trade, from 1580 to 1640 and from 1660 to 1690. During that time merchant shipping grew from some 50 000 tons to well over 300 000 tons. Progress was not rapid in the first part of the eighteenth century, with only modest gains that averaged about 1 per cent a year, but by the 1740s the country was in the early stages of the first of the two important booms that were to do much to change the whole economy. We must see what the pattern of trade was at this time, on the eve of the Industrial Revolution.

The Southern colonies and the British West Indies were good trading partners. In the first place they were well populated, with 2 million people on the mainland alone. There were plenty of wealthy planters with a taste for European luxuries, like fine textiles, furniture and tableware. Even slaves had their needs, though these were mainly for clothing and the more humble household goods. Secondly the climate of these places is quite different from Britain's, enabling them to grow all sorts of crops that were impossible to cultivate in Britain. Finally the Navigation Acts kept the colonial trade a British monopoly.

From the West Indies came sugar, in the main, but there were also rum, coffee and mahogany. Virginia sent tobacco, and the Carolinas rice, pitch, tar and hardwoods.

In exchange, Britain exported her manufactures – woollens, cottons, linens, silks, leather articles and metal goods. Even when they had loaded as many of these goods as they could hope to sell, ships usually had room for more cargo, so they often called at Irish ports for salt meat, butter and cheese. However, Britain was greedy for tropical goods and, on top of that demand, her merchants wanted even more for re-export to other European countries. British manufactures and Irish food were not enough to pay for it all, so they made up the balance with people. Some of the first were children who had lost their parents during the Civil War, and they were followed by other orphans, all sent to be 'servants' of the sugar and tobacco planters. Bryan Blundell, a Liverpool merchant, carried on this traffic with crocodile tears in his eyes, and in 1718 used some of his profits to found a Blue Coat Charity School. As well as orphans they sent criminals. The most useful slave, though, was the Negro, so trade with America led to trade with West Africa. Ships went out with cargoes of coarse textiles, knives, hatchets, firearms and spirits, which they gave to the coastal tribes in return for Negroes captured inland. It is possible that between 1680 and 1786 as many as 2 million slaves were taken to the British colonies. At the beginning of the eighteenth century they fetched on average £15 each, but by the 1750s the planters were paying up to £40. Slave-trading was big business. This was the famous triangular trade – manufactured goods to West Africa, slaves to the West Indies or the mainland colonies, and sugar and tobacco back to Britain.

There was another less profitable triangle, but one that suited those who disliked the slave-trade. Some Liverpool merchants took Cheshire salt to Newfoundland, exchanged it for cod, which they sold in the plantation colonies, and then returned, like their colleagues, with sugar and tobacco.

Occasionally British merchants invited trouble, since, in order to keep their customers, they were too free with their credit. Planters had the aristocratic outlook of most great land-owners. They enjoyed high living and were happy to run up debts, in the confident belief that next year's harvest would be a bumper one. Frequently, of course, it was not, which brought unhappiness both to themselves and their creditors. However, these were not general problems, and all in all the trade with the plantations was most lucrative.

The northern colonies were different. They were voracious for manufactured goods, as anyone would have been who was trying to scratch a living from the soil in that part of the world. They needed textiles, boots, pottery, cutlery, saws, axes, farming tools, saddles and firearms. Since their houses were of wood, they used a phenomenal number of nails. Their problem was payment, for they produced little that was needed in Britain. They traded furs with the Indians, fished, and supplied masts for the Royal Navy. These goods were not enough, so to make up the balance of their payments they looked to the plantations. They sent them grain, timber and horses, and went across the Atlantic to fetch them slaves. In such ways they built up credit and, in effect, paid for their imports with the sugar and tobacco that they had earned.

Nearer home the countries around the Baltic supplied many of the goods that Britain could not produce herself. In the first place there was softwood. Tall, straight pines made masts and spars, or, sawn into deals, they were used for the interior work in ships. They were also important for building, since oak beams and oak panelling were out of fashion. The timber came from Norway and Russia, the port of Riga being especially famous for masts.

Flax for sailcloth, and hemp for ropes, were imported from the lands to the south of the Baltic where they grew well. Sweden supplied bar iron, which was essential because Britain's own bar iron was at that time of poor quality and could not be used, for example, to make steel. Finally there was potash, made by burning waste timber from the sawmills. In the eighteenth century it was their main source of alkali, and they used it to manufacture soap and glass.

It was the Russian trade which grew the most rapidly, especially after Peter the Great signed a treaty of commerce with Britain in

1734. Russia supplied the same goods as all the other Baltic states, including iron.

Payment was a problem. J.S. Watson mentions imports from Russia worth £950000 and exports of only £70000 (*Reign of George III*, p. 24). British woollens, Cheshire salt and re-exports of colonial goods were welcome everywhere, and Norway wanted coal. There were indirect ways of paying too. Ships went to Holland with coal, then to Norway in ballast, and back with timber. The coal earned bills of exchange on Amsterdam which paid for the timber. At that time Britain had a surplus of grain, and in the South of France this could be exchanged for wine, which was in turn carried into the Baltic. Even with all these efforts, though, the big timber ships sailed out in ballast far too often, and the Baltic trade remained in deficit. The only way to pay the balance was in gold coin which, in the eighteenth century, was considered an unfortunate thing to do.

The Mediterranean countries were ideal for British trade. Their climate is different from Britain's, and they were fairly well populated – some, like northern Italy, thickly populated. Spain and Portugal both had large colonial empires.

Spain was the first country to send wine in quantity – sherry, or sack as they called it, being popular in Elizabethan England. However, in 1704 the Methuen Treaty was signed, whereby England agreed to take Portuguese wines at a low tariff, and Portugal agreed to do the same for English woollens. From then on port became more popular in England than sherry. Fresh oranges and lemons also came from Spain and Portugal, and currants from the central Mediterranean and the Levant. There were as well raw materials for our industries, iron-ore and merino wool from Spain, and olive oil from both Spain and Italy. An especially valuable commodity was silk, both raw and spun. It came from Italy, Turkey and Persia via the Levant ports. Ships returning from the eastern Mediterranean could hardly bring full cargoes of silk, which was worth something like £2000 a ton, and even currants were not enough, so they laded raw cotton and mohair as well.

Britain had no difficulty in paying for these imports. Spain and Portugal were our best customers for woollens, and indeed people bought them everywhere, because there were many that were light enough to wear in a warm climate. It was the Roman Catholic clergy who kept the weavers of Colchester in business. Catholic countries needed a lot of fish, so swarms of little Cornish vessels delivered their pilchards to northern Spain;

Newfoundland cod was sold all over the Iberian Peninsula, and North Sea herrings in Italy. From 1700 Britain exported most of her surplus corn to the Mediterranean.

Exports were so valuable that they more than paid for imports, especially from Spain and Portugal, and those two countries had to make up the balance in silver and gold. Another reason why the Mediterranean trade was profitable was because the British acted as carriers. Their ships were safe, partly because they were well armed, and partly because few wanted to attack them: Britain was neutral in most of the local squabbles, while Blake's bombardment of Tunis and Algiers in 1655 had taught the Moorish pirates a lesson they were to remember for a long time. By moving bulk cargoes round the Mediterranean, British ships earned their owners good profits and added to the country's 'invisible exports' which then, as now, were necessary for its balance of payments.

North-Western Europe has a climate like our own, but Germany, the Netherlands and France were wealthy and thickly populated, so it was not difficult to find goods to trade. The river mouths faced each other invitingly across the water. On the European side the Rhine and the Gironde led to great wine-growing areas, while on the English side the Tyne supplied coal, the Mersey salt, and the East Anglian rivers grain. Other, more valuable goods were also exchanged. Germany and Holland provided linens, and France both linens and silks. In return, Britain sent woollens, her most valuable export by far, and re-exports of sugar and tobacco.

Unhappily this trade was marred to some extent by hostility with France. Easily the most powerful country in Europe, she menaced Britain with her army and her navy, and she harboured Jacobite pretenders. For safety's sake it seemed only right to weaken France, so during the wars against Louis XIV trade with her was forbidden, and afterwards both sides imposed such high duties that it was all but impossible. What did happen, though, was that the high duties encouraged smuggling, so that French silks, wines and brandies were still exchanged for English woollens, albeit illegally.

The trade which had the most romantic aura about it was the one with the Far East. It was the dream of making fortunes from spices that inspired the first explorers, like Columbus, but when finally the ocean routes were opened, it was the Dutch who had possession of the coveted East Indies. The English turned for consolation to the mainland of India, where they held their own, not only against the

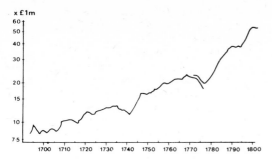

The growth of foreign trade (Net imports and domestic exports: three-yearly moving averages.)

Left curve - England
Right curve - Great Britain

Growth of foreign trade (from *The First Industrial Revolution*, p. 66, Phyllis Deane)

Dutch, but also the French and the Portuguese. By the early eighteenth century they were also doing business with those most difficult of trading partners, the Chinese.

The goods that were brought home were, for their weight, expensive. The Indians could spin finer yarn than was ever made in Britain before the invention of Crompton's mule, and it was woven into muslins that European women coveted greatly. There were also calicoes, chintzes and many other cottons, and silks as well. From China came porcelain, and again silk. Ships in the Far East trade needed to be large in order to defend themselves, and to fill them with such merchandise was not sensible. Fortunately there were some bulk cargoes as well. Tea from China and pepper from the East Indies took a lot of room, while saltpetre from northern India was ideal to fill a large hold.

Paying for the imports was a problem. The English took hardware to India, and opium from there to China, but ships on the outward journey carried mainly ballast, and paid for most of their purchases in bullion. According to the theory of the times this was bad for the economy of the country.

The Far Eastern trade has attracted a lot of attention. In the first place it was the monopoly of the greatest of the chartered companies, the East India Company. Secondly the ships were the best built merchantmen of their day, and so powerfully armed that they would fight with men-of-war. They were favourites with artists then, and have been favourites with admirers of sailing-ships ever since. Finally, the goods were exotic – muslins, silks, spices, tea, porcelain. Certainly the trade was valuable, but in a normal year more goods were exchanged with Ireland, whether measured by volume or value, than with the whole of the mystic East.

Such, then, was the pattern of trade in the early eighteenth century. From then on it developed in three ways. In the first place it expanded. There were set-backs from time to time, but overall, the rate of growth was higher than ever before. Secondly there were changes in direction. Some old markets contracted, while others expanded, and all the time there was a successful search for new ones. Thirdly there were changes in exports and imports.

Usually it is hard to find reliable statistics of the eighteenth century, but those for overseas trade are remarkably accurate and complete. They are in the ledgers of the Inspector General of Customs, and Mrs E. B. Schumpeter has used them to compile useful sets of tables (*English Overseas Trade Statistics*, 1960). However, it is unusual for economists to agree, and different writers have interpreted the tables differently.

M. W. Flinn in his *Origins of the Industrial Revolution* says they show four distinct periods. From 1700 to about 1735 trade grew slowly and eratically. From 1735 to 1760 growth was so rapid that the volume was doubled. From 1760 to 1785 there was stagnation. The American War of Independence brought depression, but even more important was the loss of the corn exports. They ceased because of the growth in population, and it was some time before manufactured goods filled the gap. Finally, from 1785 to 1800, there was another period of rapid expansion, with trade doubling in volume again, but this time in the short space of fifteen years. In her book *The First Industrial Revolution* Phyllis Deane divides the century into five. First came forty years of slow growth; next, between 1740 and 1750, there was rapid expansion; this was followed by twenty-five years of steady growth until the slump caused by the American War of Independence, which lasted from 1776 to 1782; and finally there was exceptionally rapid growth until the end of the century.

There are broad similarities between these two views. Both writers speak of a long, slow start, and of two periods of rapid expansion, separated by one of decline. Flinn thinks this decline was a quarter of a century of stagnation, but Miss Deane says it was just a temporary set-back caused by the American War, a brief interruption in what was otherwise continuous growth from 1740.

147

Whatever else, there can be no doubt that trade increased enormously, especially towards the end of the century. Miss Deane's graph is shown on p. 147. The vertical scale is logarithmic, so it indicates rates of change rather than real values. If it were pulled out, so to speak, to its full height, some of the slopes on the graph would be precipitous indeed. What is even more remarkable is that the growth was sustained. There had been periods of expansion in earlier centures, but they had all fizzled out, to be followed by decades of stagnation or decline. Now, apart from the swing of the trade cycle, growth was continuous, certainly from 1782, and indeed, if Phyllis Deane is right, from 1740.

The Napoleonic Wars were a wonderful time for British traders, since most of their rivals were chafing behind the blockade. They emerged when the war ended and caused a depression in Britain, but it was soon over and growth resumed even faster than before. We will now look at markets during three different periods: before the Napoleonic Wars, during them, and then when they were over.

In 1776 there was trauma, for the American colonies rebelled and by 1782 they had, with French help, won their freedom. To lose the war was bad enough, but to lose such close and valuable trading partners was a double blow. However, although the Americans did not want British rule, they did want British goods, and were anxious that trade should go on as before. The British, for their part, were sulking, feeling that if the Americans wanted to be foreigners, then they must take the consequences. They applied the Navigation Laws to them, and ordered them out of the West Indies. This hostility could not continue, though, and in 1795 the two countries signed the Jay Treaty, giving each other most-favoured nation terms. In 1800 the U.S.A. took a quarter of British exports, and in 1803 one-third.

In Europe something remarkable happened – a serious flirtation between France and Britain. In 1786 they made the Eden Treaty, agreeing to lower duties on each other's goods. It made the cotton manufacturers of northern France unhappy, because the British industry was already expanding rapidly, but the wine growers of Bordeaux were delighted. The treaty lapsed, of course, with the outbreak of war in 1793.

With other European countries, Britain was beginning to have difficulties. They saw the progress British industries were making and, in order to protect their own from such dangerous competition, they increased their tariffs. Trade with Europe did go on growing, but it lost its relative importance.

The Napoleonic Wars caused problems. The enemy captured ships, and insurance companies raised their premiums. Then there was Napoleon's Continental System. The Berlin Decree of 1806 and the Milan Decree of 1807 were intended to end Britain's trade with Europe and ruin her economy. Thirdly the British habit of searching neutral shipping for contraband led to war with the United States. However, trade was profitable enough to stand some loss of shipping and higher insurance rates; wholesale smuggling made nonsense of the Continental System; the American war did not start until June 1812 and was over by December 1814. Gains on the other hand were enormous, for the Royal Navy took command of the sea and the trade of the world was a British monopoly. It is sometimes said that Napoleon forced Britain to look for new markets, but the only compulsion was greed. The new markets were there for the taking, and taken they were. One thing which happened was that Spain and Portugal became virtually client states of Britain, because Napoleon had invaded them, and without Wellington's army to defend them they must have succumbed. Under the circumstances their governments could not refuse Britain's request for them to open their jealously guarded colonial empires to trade. As for Europe, trade there did not decline – quite the contrary. Continental people still wanted their tobacco and sugar, but now they could only have them by courtesy of Great Britain, so there was a boom in re-exports.

At the end of the war the European nations went back to normal trading, causing a depression in Britain. Also, more than ever, they protected their industries with tariffs. Britain watched the progress of the Zollverein with particular dismay. This was a customs union

Rates of growth of International Trade –	Compound Rates Per Cent Per Annum
1770–1800	2.3
1801–1831	2.7
1811–1841	3.4
1821–1851	4.4
1831–1861	4.5

SOURCE: Deane and Cole, p. 29.

Shipbuilding

which Prussia organised among the north German states, and whose members enjoyed free trade with each other, while keeping foreign goods out with tariffs. There was every justification, for Britain kept her Navigation Acts and had, moreover, passed the Corn Laws of 1815 and 1828 to protect her farmers. Prussia pointed out that she was an agricultural country with grain to sell, but if Britain would not buy it, then she had no choice but to develop her own industry, sheltering it with tariffs. Eventually Britain did become more liberal in her policy. She introduced free trade by degrees, then in 1846 repealed the Corn Laws and in 1849 the Navigation Acts. She hoped other countries would follow her virtuous example by removing their own tariffs, and some indeed did. Germany and Belgium, though, at once increased theirs. Presumably they were wondering what trick Britain was about to play.

If Europe was difficult there were compensations elsewhere, as in North America. Canada's population was only 76000 in 1760, but by 1828 it was 1 million. Canada sent Britain grain and supplies of timber and potash, which meant Britain could import less from the Baltic. The Canadians also opened the St Lawrence to the Great Lakes so that it was possible to trade with the new, growing areas of the United States. Following the war of 1812 there was, at first, some bickering with that country, but in 1818 she and Britain signed a Treaty of Commerce. Relations were especially good after the repeal of the Corn Laws and the Navigation Acts. All the time trade grew, particularly imports of raw cotton from the Southern States.

After 1815 the Spanish colonies in South America, and Portuguese Brazil, became independent. Most of these new states offered Britain commercial concessions in the hope that she would support them in their struggle, though, much to the disgust of the merchants, the British Government was usually reluctant to accept. It did not want to annoy Spain. However, this valuable market, which had been opened during the war, increased after it. By 1835 a Liverpool firm, the Pacific Steam Navigation Company, was even operating a pair of wooden paddle-steamers on the west coast of the continent.

In West Africa the profitable slave-trade came to an end. Not only were the coastal chiefs unhappy, but it took a long time to build a new commerce in palm-oil, cocoa and timber. Britain took Cape Colony from the Dutch during the Napoleonic Wars, but while the Boers wanted industrial goods they had nothing to give in exchange. Trade with South Africa was not important until the discoveries of gold and silver much later in the century.

Australia began to be important as settlers started sheep farms to supply the reviving Yorkshire woollen industry, but there was no rapid expansion until the gold-rush of the early 1850s.

There were interesting developments in the Far East. The British were disenchanted with colonies after the American revolt, so instead they looked for small, easily defended places, such as islands, that were near thickly populated areas, and which would be entrepôts for trade. During the war Malta was one such place, even though it was a centre for smuggling rather than legitimate commerce. After the war Britain acquired Penang, which was not a success, but in 1819 Sir Stamford Raffles persuaded the East India Company to lease Singapore from the the Sultan of Johore. In 1823 Singapore's trade was already worth £2.5 million, and was spreading far and wide. By 1840 the city had a fleet of steamers.

There had always been difficulties with the Chinese, whose attitude was one of fear mixed with disdain. They had no wish to be conquered, and knew that their weapons were no match for those of Europeans. At the same time they viewed traders much as perhaps we would dustmen – that is, as people whose work was useful but hardly to be admired. As the only Britons they met were traders, they assumed they must all be alike and scorned the entire nation. They did allow trade, but only through the one port of Canton, and even here they were obstructive. The British felt they were dealing with petty bureaucrats, and that if only they could reach the Emperor he would be sure to see reason. Eventually, in 1792, a mission under Lord Macartney did see him and presented him with some of the wonders of British technology, such as scientific instruments, textiles, hardware and jewellery. These irresistible treasures, they explained, were what his people could have in exchange for their tea and silk. The Emperor replied: 'We possess all things. I set no value on objects strange or ingenious and have no use for your manufactures.' (Judith Blow Williams, op. cit., p. 340)

The British went on trying diplomacy in the early years of the nineteenth century and then, after some bickering about the opium trade, they blockaded the coast of China and bombarded Canton. By the Treaty of Nanking of 1842 China agreed to open four more ports, including Shanghai, also ceding Hong Kong which was, eventually, to have the same success as Singapore.

The goods traded changed with the British economy. In 1700 two-thirds of Britain's exports were woollens, so that British prosperity in world trade depended on one industry. It is not surprising it was coddled by the state. During the first period of expansion, in the 1740s, there was more diversity, perhaps because the American colonists and planters were setting up home and needing goods of all kinds. There was also an increase in exports of coal and grain. After 1750 grain exports fell away and Britain began to import. The second period of expansion, the one after 1780, had a much narrower base than the first. Between 1785 and 1800, 92 per cent of the increase in exports was due to six commodities – wool, cotton, linen, copper and brass, iron and refined sugar. Wool and cotton alone accounted for 71 per cent.

During the Napoleonic Wars there was a striking change in the fortunes of wool and cotton. Before the war cottons exported were worth half the woollens; at the end, they were worth double. They were also 40 per cent of all exports, and rose to a peak of 50 per cent in 1830. After that there was more diversity, as the table shows:

Principal Exports as a Percentage of Total Domestic Exports

	1830	1850
Cotton yarn and manufactures	50.8	39.6
Woollen yarn and manufactures	12.7	14.1
Linen yarn and manufactures	5.4	6.8
Silks	1.4	1.5
Clothing	2.0	1.3
Iron and steel manufactures	10.2	12.3
Machinery	0.5	0.8
Coal	0.5	1.8
Earthenware and glass	2.2	1.7
Chemicals	—	0.5

SOURCE: Deane and Cole, p. 31.

Iron and steel progressed; indeed they had doubled their share of exports since 1815 when it was only 6 per cent. The traditional textile industries also made gains as the Industrial Revolution reached them.

SMUGGLING

With certain countries, and at certain times, smuggling was the normal method of trade. At its peak during the Napoleonic Wars, it went on whenever duties were high enough to make the risk worthwhile. The British Government was vigorous enough attacking it at home, but took the view that if other countries were wrong-headed enough to impose high tariffs or prohibitions, then smugglers, like Pharaoh's plagues, were justifiable chastisements. Britain encouraged them, or used the threat to do so, when negotiating commercial treaties.

After the war France was particularly obstructive over legitimate trade, so she attracted smugglers. The French people wanted colonial products and cutlery, while their weavers were anxious to have the excellent cotton yarn that was spun on British mules. Many goods went directly by sea, but usually it was safer to send them through Belgium. At one time they were carried by dogs that were trained to dash over the frontier and bite any Customs men who might be fast enough, and foolish enough, to intercept them. In a good year over £2 million worth of smuggled goods entered France in various ways.

27 Shipping, ports, trade and the economy

Like the various kinds of inland transport, ports and shipping were industries in their own right, providing work, and stimulating other activities.

Building the docks needed large numbers of men. Moreover, unlike the canals and railways, which only needed unskilled men when under construction, the docks found them employment when they were finished. We hear of Irish navvies, and later of Irish dockers, but not of Irish engine-drivers or even Irish railway porters.

Shipping gave employment to thousands of sailors. At the same time shipbuilding became a flourishing industry, first on the Thames and later in the North. We have seen, too, how the Dorset hemp and flax industries were encouraged. There were also demands on the iron industry, for although hulls were of wood, ships needed large amounts of iron for bolts, fittings, anchors, cannon and so forth. The proportion of iron to wood in a ship must have compared with that found in many farm implements, a stage-coach or even some of the early textile machines.

Shipping was also important for military reasons, since sailors were trained, however unwillingly or unintentionally, to man the vessels of the Royal Navy. Much has been made of the part played by the Navy in ensuring Britain's commercial supremacy. However, the fleet was always well below strength in time of peace and could only come rapidly to a war footing because it was able to press-gang large numbers of merchant seamen. While Britain's commercial strength depended to quite an extent on the success of the Royal Navy in time of war, equally naval power depended on the success of the merchant navy in time of peace.

As with land transport, ships carried a growing volume of goods with increasing efficiency and it is strange that their contribution is so often overlooked. The coastal trade is especially neglected. However, every major industrial region in Britain, save the Midlands, is either on the coast or on a large estuary. Before the railways the obvious way to exchange goods was by sea. The merchants of Gloucester, for example, preferred to send their wares to London by ship rather than accept the doubtful services of the Thames and Severn Canal. Even after the building of the railways the coastal trade held its own, being greater than the overseas trade until the twentieth century. The contribution of the passenger steamers is even more neglected. In the early eighteenth century the only sure way to travel was on horseback, so one horse carried one passenger. Thanks to the turnpike roads, four horses could draw twelve passengers. However, with the growth of population, industry and commerce, people needed to travel, not a dozen at a time, but in their hundreds. The coastal steamers filled an awkward gap, until the railways were finished.

We must now turn to the interesting and complex role of international trade in the economy.

In the first place trade helped towns to grow, and it was these heavy concentrations of population that were the breeding grounds of industry. First Bristol, then, later, Liverpool and Glasgow became large cities, but the outstanding example was of course London. London's story is too complicated to be explained by saying that the town grew because it was a port, but it is certain it would not have developed as it did if it had not been one. There were, for example, banking and insurance, while many varied industries prospered as well. The story of communications is also significant. Other towns spread their tentacles for 50 miles or so, but London's went the length of the country. It would be interesting to know how much London owed to its port, and how much the British economy as a whole owed to London.

Next, foreign trade provided capital for investment at home. Not enough is known about the flow of capital to say how much of the profit from trade found its way into other enterprises. Like most business men, merchants preferred to plough their profits back into their own firms, while if they had a surplus they were more prone than most to spend it on high living. However, plenty of men made themselves rich by dealing with merchants, so profits that came, at any rate indirectly from trade, found their way into industry. Merchants themselves often invested in transport. It was Liverpool merchants like Charles Lawrence and James Cropper who found the energy to plan the Liverpool and Manchester Railway, as well as the money to pay for it. The cotton manufacturers of Manchester stood to gain quite as much from the line, but they did little for it.

151

Trade stimulated other economies. Outstanding examples were the plantations of the American South and the West Indies. Britain enriched them by buying their tobacco, sugar and cotton, while they in turn were able to purchase British goods. The wealth of all the trading partners grew, each feeding on the other. It was not all gain, however. The growth of the British economy had a great deal to do with the slave-trade, which played havoc in the interior of Africa and was of doubtful benefit even to the coastal tribes.

Trade supplied Britain with raw materials, food and luxuries. The British Isles themselves can produce many of these things, but it was trade that brought an improvement to the drab life of earlier centuries. Let us take a simple example. During the eighteenth century the British, in most years, grew enough cereals for all the bread they needed. However, since they wanted cake as well, they imported sugar from the West Indies, and dried fruit from the Levant. A more important item was cotton. Woollen and linen goods made from materials grown at home were valuable enough, but thanks to overseas trade, the cotton industry developed as well. Again we see how trade increased both the variety and the quantity of the country's products.

Foreign trade also gave access to export markets. Demand is essential for economic growth, and the greater the demand, the greater the growth will be. A country like the United States can make advances, relying on her domestic market alone, but had Britain tried to do the same her growth must have remained stunted. As it was, industry developed because merchants were selling British products all over the world. Moreover, this growth was not only the result of the crude process of multiplying existing units of production, for there was greater efficiency as well. Adam Smith showed how industrial efficiency depends on the division of labour, and how that in its turn is limited by the extent of the market. In a remote Highland village one man may be a shoemaker, another a blacksmith, another a carpenter, but none of them will be able to give more than a few hours a week to his craft, because there are few people needing his goods. Instead, everyone has to spend most of his time farming, so the division of labour hardly exists. In a small town there will be work for a full-time shoemaker, so he will be more efficient than his colleague in the village, but he will, however, have to do all the processes of shoemaking himself. A larger town needs several shoemakers, so they can divide the different tasks between them and the output per man is much greater. As the market widens, the division of labour increases, and so too does wealth. Certainly manufacturers who were selling the world over were able to divide their work into a multitude of processes. That, in turn, made it much easier to make use of machinery.

Clearly foreign trade was an indispensable part of Britain's economic development. Moreover, at the end of the eighteenth century when trade expansion was at its most rapid, so also was the growth of the economy as a whole. Is it possible, then, that it was foreign trade which, in Dean and Habakkuk's picturesque phrase 'ignited the Industrial Revolution'? If that was so, then something must have stimulated trade. Two possibilities are naval power and cotton growing in the United States.

Britain had a more powerful fleet than any of her rivals. It protected and helped increase her empire: it enforced the Navigation Acts, making sure that at least the bulk of her colonies' trade came her way: during the Napoleonic Wars it swept her enemies' ships from the seas, so that her own merchantmen took their trade instead. There is certainly some truth in Napoleon III's remark that 'the volume of a country's exports is always in direct proportion to the number of broadsides it is capable of firing at its enemies'.

Next, the most vigorous industry in the British economy was cotton, and it depended on trade. It imported all its raw materials, and by 1815 was exporting three-quarters of its products. It accounted for some 40 per cent of the phenomenal increase in trade that took place between 1790 and 1810. W. W. Rostow suggests that it was cotton which led the 'take-off' of the British economy into self-sustained growth, but it was overseas trade that made the growth of the cotton industry possible.

There are, however, pointers in other directions. For example, trade with America grew as never before after the War of Independence. It is hardly likely, then, that naval power was decisive in maintaining trade with the thirteen colonies beforehand. Secondly the boom in European trade which the Royal Navy made possible during the Napoleonic Wars was mainly in re-exports. Goods like sugar and tobacco came to Britain, but after a brief sojourn went on their way. Such trade can have had little value for the British economy as a whole, though it kept the chief ports busy, and earned merchants handsome profits. Certainly some of those profits were invested in worthwhile projects, but we do not know what the proportion was. As for cotton, it is doubtful whether that industry exerted as powerful an influence as Rostow says (see p. 192). Finally there is the evidence we have from movements in the terms of trade. As we have seen, both British overseas trade and the British economy grew rapidly after 1780. That might indeed have been because trade was stimulating the economy, but, equally, the economy could have been stimulating trade. The movements in the terms of trade will give an indication. Let us suppose that something happened outside Britain, say a sharp increase in the amount of cotton produced in the United States. The American planters would have pushed the sales of their cotton in Britain, thereby lowering its price: at the same time they would have demanded more British goods, thereby raising their prices. Britain would have gained an increasing volume of imports in return for her exports, or, in other words, the terms of trade would have been moving in her favour. Let us suppose now that the opposite happened, and that Britain increased her output of goods. She would then have demanded increasing supplies of raw cotton in return. The prices of British goods would have fallen, and that of raw cotton would have increased. In other words the terms of trade would have been moving un-favourably for Britain. It does seem that at those times in the eighteenth century when trade was growing most rapidly the movement of the terms of trade was unfavourable. This was in the late 1740s, the late 1750s and, more especially, in the last fifteen years of the century. The table below shows not only the dramatic increase in trade but an equally dramatic deterioration in the terms of trade.

It would appear, therefore, that it was the British economy that stimulated Britain's overseas trade and not the other way round.

We can now summarise the argument. If foreign trade stimulated the British economy, we must find something outside the economy that stimulated trade. We have considered two specific possibilities – naval power and cotton growing in the United States. There is no conclusive evidence for either. Further, the movement in the terms of trade seems to show that neither these two nor any other outside factor was the driving force. The prime cause of the Industrial Revolution, if there was one, lay within the British economy.

This, of course, is not to deny the importance of foreign trade. It played a vital part, even though it seems unlikely that it took the lead.

	Imports (£000)	Re-exports (£000)	Exports (£000)	Gross Barter Terms of Trade (1785 = 100)
1786	21744	4476	11830	97
1800	42347	18848	24304	141

28 Case history: the Glasgow tobacco trade

A planter, William Lee, said that Scottish merchants were 'something like the stinking and troublesome weed we call in Virginia wild onion. Where one is permitted to fix the number soon increases so fast, that it is extremely difficult to eradicate them, and they poison the ground so that no wholesome plant can thrive'. This was both unkind and unfair. The Virginians produced little but tobacco, so they relied on Scottish merchants to buy their crop and bring them other goods in exchange. Our purpose here is to follow the growth of this trade to its abrupt end, and to see how it affected the economy of Glasgow and west central Scotland.

In the seventeenth century the tobacco trade was based in London. The method was for a planter to consign his crop to a merchant. The merchant provided transport, sold the tobacco in London, and used the money to buy goods that the planter wanted. The planter had to bear all the risks and expenses, but he remained the owner of the tobacco until its sale in London, so he received its full market price. However, planters often quarrelled with their agents, accusing them of taking too little for their tobacco, and paying too much for the goods they bought in exchange.

The trade was difficult to organise. There was some loose tobacco in late August, but the first hogsheads were not ready until October. Most of the packing was done in the winter, but it was not finished entirely until May or June. On arrival, the captains had to tout for business, lading at various places along the banks of Chesapeake Bay. Sometimes the sailors themselves had to trundle hogsheads along 'rolling roads' that ran from plantations miles inland. If the crop was good, then freight charges were high, and the ships' holds were full. If the crop was poor, many a captain had not only to cut his charges but to return with his ship half empty. In either event the ships were away a long time, for they left in the early autumn and did not return until the late spring. They then needed to refit, so there was no chance of sending them on another voyage before they returned to Virginia. During the early eighteenth century there were changes. In the first place the Virginians began to cultivate the Piedmont Plateau. There was a marked increase in the tobacco crop, but it came from beyond the Fall Line and was, therefore, out of the reach of the ships. Secondly Glasgow merchants began to take part in the trade, and, before long, had the lion's share of it.

The Scots had a windfall advantage, since transport was improving at just that time. Planters used larger hogsheads and packed them tighter, so that their weight rose from an average 350 pounds to over 1200 pounds. A ship with her hold full of these larger barrels had as much weight as she could carry, whereas previously she had sailed much too light. There were also the improvements in the ships themselves, which we have already described. (see pp. 141–4)

However, the Scots made advantages for themselves. They organised their shipping well, and were prepared to do what the Londoners were not – that is, to go into the Piedmont area and develop a new system of trading suitable for it.

One task which the merchants' factors had to do was to estimate the supply of tobacco and then prepare a schedule of ships. That meant an end to many of the old uncertainties. Also, since the factors bought the tobacco and warehoused it, there was no need for the ships to leave early in order to tout for cargo. They left much later, to load in the spring instead of the winter. This meant a quicker turn-round, so that each voyage was much less expensive. This, along with the improvements in tobacco packing and in ship design, reduced freight charges from 7 shillings a hundredweight in 1670 to 3 shillings a century later.

Instead of acting as agents for the planters, as the Londoners had done, the Scots bought the tobacco and sold imported goods themselves. To carry on the business, each merchant had a chief factor who opened stores. Every store was expected to purchase about 300 hogsheads of tobacco a year from 12 or 14 miles around, so it had to be in good farming country and not too close to any rivals.

A store would have a salaried manager, earning about £100 a year. Firms preferred Scots, because they were easier to train and less likely to go their own way than Americans. Their chief, and indeed their only loyalty, had to be to their work. One young man was dismissed for marrying. The manager had a staff of clerks, assistants and slaves. For example, there were fourteen slaves at the Cuninghame store at Falmouth: five of them were house servants, two unloaded the ships, four crewed the store's sloop, and three its schooner.

The store manager had not only to buy tobacco but to sell imported goods. There were the products of other colonies – tea, sugar and coffee, as well as manufactured goods from Britain – cloth, hats, gloves, stockings, gunpowder and ironware of all kinds. The merchants regarded the sale of these goods as especially important. To encourage the planters to buy, they were given better prices for their tobacco if they took goods. They were often allowed credit as well, though store managers were instructed to give this only to reliable men, to obtain security, and to ensure that accounts were settled annually. The last was not always easy to secure.

The Scots, then, penetrated both the territory and the economy of the tobacco colonies. By 1774 Cuninghame, for example, owned seven stores in Maryland and fourteen in Virginia. On an average they were worth £1000 each, not counting goods, slaves, small craft, wagons and horses. They also owned ocean-going ships and imported into Glasgow 5000 hogsheads of tobacco a year.

As the tobacco trade grew, so did Glasgow's share of it; it was 10 per cent in 1738, but well over 50 per cent in the 1770s. The 'tobacco lords' made their fortunes, but the town was relying on one article of commerce: tobacco accounted for 38 per cent of its imports and 56 per cent of its exports. Moreover, the trade depended on the Navigation Acts, which forbade the colonies to sell their wares to any country outside the British Empire. Of all the tobacco that came to Glasgow, only one-fifth remained. The rest stayed briefly in the warehouses, the Customs officials collected their duties on it, and then it was on its way again to ports all over Europe. Not surprisingly there was consternation in Glasgow when,

Glasgow Trade with the West Indies				
	Sugar Imports	Cotton Imports	Value of Imports	Value of Exports
1786	107000 cwt	846000 lbs	£236000	£140000
1790	135000 cwt	2700000 lbs	£372000	£319000

in 1774, its people realised the American colonies were likely to revolt. The merchants at once bought all the tobacco they could but, after war broke out, the trade was soon bypassing Glasgow. The Americans traded directly with the Europeans.

When peace came, merchants tried to re-establish their links with America, and it was not entirely a lost cause, for the Americans still wanted British goods, while the British still wanted tobacco. However, it was the re-export trade that had been really lucrative, and that was gone for ever. Here was a vacuum Glasgow had to fill if she was to regain her prosperity.

There had always been some trade with the West Indies, so merchants looked there for compensation, dealing in sugar and sea island cotton. The table above shows how successful they were.

At the same time that these vast supplies of cotton arrived, machines like Crompton's mule became available. Glasgow's cotton industry, which had been modest before the war, now boomed. By 1796 there were thirty-nine water-mills, including New Lanark, and hundreds of spinning machines having between them over 300000 spindles. There were related industries too. George Macintosh manufactured 'turkey red', an especially good dye for cotton, and Charles Tennant built his St Rollox Chemical Works to make bleaching powder.

The decline of the tobacco trade, then, did no lasting harm, since by the 1790s Glasgow was prospering as never before. Moreover, the new prosperity depended not so much on trade as on a flourishing new industry which spread its benefits more widely in the community.

We must now see how far Glasgow's industrial growth depended on merchant capital.

Throughout the eighteenth century it was usual for Glasgow merchants to hold industrial investments. Between 1740 and 1790 there were 163 merchants trading with America, and eighty-five of them were partners in manufacturing or mining concerns. One of them, John Dunlop, had no less than seventeen partnerships. There were various reasons for these investments.

In the first place there was vertical integration. Merchants needed goods to export to America, so they involved themselves in their manufacture. They invested in firms that tanned leather and made boots and shoes. They had complete control of the manufacture of glassware. Iron goods were much in demand, so in 1734 a group of traders opened a slitting mill for the production of nails. In 1769 Cuninghame and the Murdocks opened another mill 'for the manufacturing of hoes, bills, axes, spades, nails, hinges, anchors, bolts and every kind or species of ironware'. (Devine, 'The Tobacco Lords', *Economic History Review*, Vol. 30, 1977) Merchants also owned three-quarters of the shares in the Muirkirk Iron Company, which produced pig-iron. They invested extensively in linen and bleaching as well, since America was a good market for textiles.

Apart from supplying goods for export, investments in industry spread risks. The Atlantic trade was hazardous, so it was unwise to depend on that alone. Manufacturers were short of capital, while merchants were glad to supply it. They were content to be sleeping partners, allowing the experts to manage the works, an arrangement which was easier and safer to make under Scottish law than English.

Finally, merchants owned landed estates, and on many of these coal was discovered. Some just leased their mineral rights, but others exploited the coal themselves. The Dunlops and the Houstons were so vigorous that people accused them of aiming at a monopoly of the coal trade in the Glasgow area.

However, the great success story of the eighteenth century was cotton. That came immediately after the collapse of the tobacco trade, so it has been assumed that the merchants made massive transfers of capital to the infant industry, so ensuring its rapid growth. This theory has since been tested. Numerous cotton firms held policies with the Sun Fire Office, and their total valuation in 1795 was £292000. Among them we can identify the firms that were financed, in part, by merchant capital, and their total valuation was only £50100, or little more than one-sixth. Moreover, merchants did not have a majority holding in any one of those firms: the average was about one-third. Nor does it follow that because a merchant was investing money, it was necessarily mercantile capital. Most merchants owned land, and many of them industrial investments as well.

Clearly, then, there was no massive transfer of capital from the tobacco trade to the cotton industry. Indeed, during the crucial decade, the 1780s, the merchants' hearts were still in Virginia, where they were investing heavily to regain some at least of their former prosperity. The cotton industry was in fact the creation of master weavers like David Dale, the Buchanans and the Monteiths. They were already producing linen goods before the American War of Independence, so that when it was over they were well placed to take advantage of the sudden appearance of the sea island cotton and of the new spinning machines.

How far did mercantile capital stimulate the Industrial Revolution in Glasgow? The answer depends on what we mean by the 'Industrial Revolution'. If it includes the steady, unspectacular growth of a wide range of industries over a long period of time, then merchants had a great deal to do with it. If on the other hand the Industrial Revolution in Glasgow was the boom in cotton from the 1780s, then the part the merchants played was insignificant.

PROBLEMS

1 What was the relative importance for the economy of improvements in shipping and improvements in inland transport?

2 Did improvements in shipping keep pace with improvements in inland transport?

3 Assess the importance of the coastal trade for the development of the economy.

4 How much did Britain owe her success in trade to natural advantages, e.g. the form of her coastline and her geographical position?

5 What changes took place in the nature and direction of British overseas trade between 1700 and 1850? How were these movements related to changes in the British economy?

6 Consider how each of Britain's main trading areas contributed to the rise in the standard of living of the British people.

7 Explain why eighteenth-century governments attached particular importance to the possession of an overseas empire. What problems did the colonies create for the mother country?

8 How far is it possible to speak of an Atlantic economy during the late eighteenth century and early nineteenth century?

9 Why did cotton assume an increasing importance in British overseas trade?

10 How far did British economic prosperity depend on the slave-trade?

11 Assess the influence of war on overseas trade. Consider particularly the effects of the American War of Independence and the Napoleonic Wars.

12 How far did overseas trade depend on British naval power?

13 Why is merchant capital often held to be of somewhat dubious value in the economy?

14 Discuss the view that the growth of overseas trade was the prime cause of the Industrial Revolution.

FURTHER READING

Blow Williams, Judith. *British Commercial Policy and Trade Expansion 1750–1850*. O.U.P., 1972.
Chandler, George. *Liverpool Shipping*. Phoenix House, 1960.
Davis, Ralph. *The Rise of the English Shipping Industry in the Seventeenth and Eighteenth Centuries*. David & Charles, 1962.
Finch, Roger. *Coals from Newcastle*. Terence Dalton, 1973.

Capital

29 Money and the money market

Most people hold money of two kinds, currency and credit. Currency is the visible money we have in our pockets, for the ordinary person coins and banknotes. Our credit on the other hand is shown by no more than entries in such documents as bank ledgers. It can be turned into currency, but most people keep as much of their money as they can in the form of credit, because it is safer that way. In simple terms they prefer to have their money in the bank. Certainly all honest transactions of any size are made by credit transfer, which usually means paying by cheque rather than by drawing and handing over wads of notes.

In the early eighteenth century Britain had a highly developed currency, and important and useful institutions were also appearing for the handling of credit.

CURRENCY

Currency was of three main kinds: coinage, banknotes and bills of exchange. The coinage had an unhappy history, partly because of counterfeiting and clipping by criminals, but mainly because of debasement by governments. However, the invention of the milled edge in the seventeenth century checked the criminals, while by the eighteenth century governments were at least honest enough not to mix base metals with the gold and silver. There was also a variety of coins of all values so that, in theory, it was possible to buy and sell goods needed for everyday life quite easily. However, there were still problems.

In the first place there was often a shortage of coins. An employer might not have enough small change to pay his men and would have to give them, say, a note for £10, and tell them to divide it among themselves. As like as not the division would start with drinks all round in a public house. Another way was for the employer to make his own coins, or tokens as they were called. He then arranged for local shopkeepers to accept them and return them to him in bulk for banknotes. Such an arrangement did not suit the workers, because it was unusual for a shop to give goods to the full value of the tokens; they might only give as little as two-thirds. Copper coins were particularly short in the second half of the eighteenth century, until Matthew Boulton developed a machine that minted them by steam power.

Another problem arose because they used three different metals – gold, silver and copper – in their coinage, and the market price of those metals varied. It was all very well to say that twenty silver shillings must equal one pound in gold, but silver became scarce and

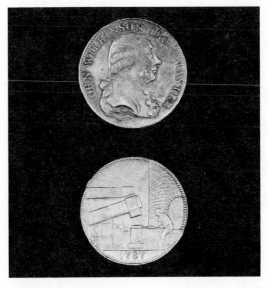

Employer's token coin

157

dear so that no one would make the exchange. It was more profitable to melt the shillings and sell the silver or, if you were a merchant, to export them and receive goods to their true value. They overcame this difficulty after 1819 by issuing 'token' coins whose face value was a good deal more than the metal from which they were made. Modern coins are like this, of course. Those we call silver contain no silver at all, and anyone who melted them for the value of their metal would be sadly disappointed.

Coins are only suitable for small transactions because, in any quantity, they weigh heavily. Consequently people found it more convenient to use pieces of paper acknowledging debts. A modern note still does recognise a debt, with the Bank of England's promise to pay the bearer, and the Chief Cashier's signature to prove the promise is good. Today the Bank will only make payment in token coins, or with another note exactly similar save for its number, but up to 1931 the bearer could claim a gold sovereign for every £1 note. Actually, it was hardly worth the trouble because the coin bought no more in the shops than the note did.

In Britain the first people to issue notes were the London goldsmiths of the seventeenth century. They had strong burglar-proof vaults so that anyone who had surplus gold was happier if it was in their care. On accepting money the goldsmith issued a receipt. Supposing, then, the depositor decided to spend his money, he might go back, hand over his receipt, collect his cash and make his purchase. There was a much easier way, though, which was to endorse his receipt and give it to the shopkeeper. He in turn might use it to settle one of his own debts, and it could go through several hands before it was presented to the goldsmith for payment. At first a receipt was for the exact amount deposited, which might be an awkward figure, so after a while goldsmiths made their receipts in round figures – £1, £5, £10 and so on. A depositor then took not one receipt but several 'notes', in whatever denominations suited him.

In the eighteenth century there was an increase in banknotes, mainly because there was a growing number of banks. The first, and most famous, was the Bank of England, founded in 1694. It accepted deposits and issued notes just as the goldsmiths had done, but on a bigger scale. Country banks also issued notes. They were modest little organisations, however, and though their notes circulated happily enough in their immediate areas, they were none too welcome if they strayed far from home.

At first the law said that notes had to be for £10 or over, but after 1797 they could be for as little as £1. Usually they were in round figures, but odd ones did appear. Pressnell mentions one of £87.17s.6d. (op. cit., Chap. 6)

By the end of the eighteenth century notes were common – and a small party of French soldiers made them even more important. During the Napoleonic Wars a frightened British nation was waiting for the dreaded news that the French had landed, and in 1797 it came. It was true enough, for the enemy was indeed in South Wales. It did not seem to matter that there was only a handful of them, and that the sight of some Welsh women frightened them into surrender. What did matter was to change paper for gold, and there was a run on the banks that they could not meet. The Government came to their rescue by releasing them from their obligation to convert their notes into gold, and the best anyone could hope to have was Bank of England notes. 'Inconvertibility' lasted until 1821. By then the market price of gold had fallen to what the Mint was willing to pay for it, so the country went on to the gold standard, but in normal times the notes of any reputable bank circulated with coin on equal terms.

In 1844 Peel's Bank Charter Act gave the Bank of England the monopoly of note issue throughout the country, though it was to come about gradually. No new banks could issue notes, and existing ones had to give up the right when they merged. The last to do so was Fox, Fowler and Co. of Wellington, Somerset, in 1921.

Another form of currency was the bill of exchange which, like the banknote, was a recognition of a debt. It had been used for international trade since medieval times, but in the eighteenth century the 'inland' bill became common. A merchant or manufacturer who took delivery of goods had the bill along with them. He was not expected, though, to pay it at once, for a supplier usually gave three months' credit. The purchaser endorsed the bill, accepting his liability to pay, and sent it back. At the end of the three months it was returned to him, and this time for payment. Quite possibly the supplier would want his money before then, so he would look for someone who would buy the bill from him. Provided it had been endorsed by someone reliable it might not be too difficult to sell, though no purchaser paid the full value, since he had to wait for his money. He would buy it at a discount, the transaction being called 'discounting a bill'. It might happen that a bill would change hands several times, each vendor endorsing it before parting with it. In

Lancashire, where the practice was especially common, bills sometimes had as many as a hundred endorsements, and pieces of paper had to be pinned on to carry them all. The people who most frequently discounted bills were bankers and, as we shall see, it was one way in which they fed their depositors' money into trade and industry.

Finally there was the cheque, which is an order a man sends to his banker instructing him to make payment on his behalf. Cheques can be 'negotiable instruments'; that is, they can pass from hand to hand like banknotes or bills of exchange, but while they originated in the Middle Ages they were not in general use until after 1850.

Such, then, were the visible signs of money; that is, the coins and paper in circulation. However, they were only a fraction of the total, since most 'money' consists of credit entries in the ledgers of a wide variety of institutions. We must now see what they were.

GOLDSMITH BANKERS

Banks not only accept money from depositors and lend it to others but they also create it. The first bankers of any importance in England were the London goldsmiths of the seventeenth century, whom we have already mentioned. They found that if they had a good amount of gold in their vaults they were in a position to earn themselves a large income. If one of them held, say, £5000 of gold from a hundred depositors, it was most unlikely they would all demand it on the same day. He would have issued notes to the value of £5000 to depositors, but it would almost certainly be quite safe to issue a further £10000 as loans to other people, and collect interest from them. He would then have created twice as much money as he had been given originally. A goldsmith took securities. A borrower might hand over the deeds of his house, or he might sign a paper promising to pay when his ship came in, so that the whole of the £10000 would be covered, and probably more than covered. However, houses take time to sell, and ships take time to reach port, so such securities were the banker's 'fixed' assets, while the gold and silver in his vaults were his 'liquid' assets. The advantage of the fixed assets was that money loaned on them earned interest. The disadvantage of the liquid assets was that the goldsmith had to pay interest on them himself to his depositors. If he was too cautious with his lending, then he paid more interest than he collected. If he was too ambitious, then he faced the possibility of a queue of depositors at his door, presenting his notes and demanding more gold than he had in his vaults.

Usually it was possible to calculate how much gold there should be in reserve, but sometimes there was a panic, perhaps because of a bad harvest, a threat of war, or the failure of an important company. People then wanted to turn their paper into gold, and if a bank could not pay them, it broke, or, in other words, went bankrupt. The problem of controlling the money supply by banks is still with us, and in a much more serious form.

THE BANK OF ENGLAND

An important step in the development of the banking system was the creation of the Bank of England. A group of Whig financiers led by William Paterson wanted to find 'Dutch' William the money to win the war against Louis XIV and so prevent a restoration of the Stuarts. Accordingly, in 1694, an Act of Parliament gave authority for a charter for 'The Governor and Company of the Bank of England'. The Bank was to raise £1200000 and lend it to the Government in return for £100000 interest a year. In addition, it could carry on the normal business of a bank, accepting deposits, making loans and issuing notes. It was a joint stock venture, anyone who subscribed over £500 being a member of the Company.

There was no problem in finding the £1200000 for the Government, other business followed, and the Bank prospered. In 1709 it won a most important privilege when an Act of Parliament ruled that no other partnership of more than six people could issue notes. That meant that no ordinary bank could hope to rival the Bank of England. If it were to issue notes, it would have to stay small; if it had many partners and was wealthy, then it would be under the control of the Bank in the all-important business of issue. The Bank of England now developed in two ways, as the Government's bank and as a banker's bank.

For the Government it continued to make loans, and also circulated exchequer bills; from 1751 it managed the Government's accounts and the National Debt. In short, it did the same kind of work as for a private company. Such business meant revenue for the Bank and, more important, prestige and confidence. The Government maintained that the Bank had no special status, but the ordinary man refused to believe it would ever be allowed to fail, and several crises were to prove he was right.

It is easy enough to see why the Bank of England became a banker's bank, but the results were complex and important. A bank must lend money in order to make profits, but it must also keep a reserve of cash in hand to satisfy customers who come to claim their deposits. Reserves used to lie idle in the vaults, but the Bank of England gave a new opportunity. It was large, respectable and, apparently, completely safe. Any London banker, then, placed his reserve there, so it accumulated at least some interest, and all he kept was enough cash to supply his tills for day-to-day business. A three-tier system developed, the country banks placing their reserves with the London banks, and the London banks placing theirs with the Bank of England. During a panic people demanded their gold from their local bank, which drew on its London bank, which in turn went to the Bank of England. The Bank of England had become the holder of the country's gold reserve, and the 'lender of last resort'. It was not a position it wanted. The Government refused it any special status, saying it should make its profits by lending money, but how could it do so in competition with others when it was the only one that had to keep a vast reserve lying in its vaults? None the less, while strenuously denying it was any such thing, it did act as the nation's central bank.

The Bank of England could, if it had the resolution, do much to stay a financial panic. Economic depressions were real enough, but like human illnesses, they were made worse by psychological problems like worry and loss of confidence. At such times people felt their gold would be lost for ever if it stayed with their banks, so they wanted to have it in their hands. It was then for the Bank of England to open its reserves and pay all that was demanded. There had to be no hesitation, and no sign of uncertainty – even the regular meeting of the directors had to close promptly at the end of its customary one hour. Such actions would give people the impression they could have their money when they wanted, and they would cease shouting for it. The interesting thing from the Bank's point of view was which would vanish first – the panic, or its reserves?

Maintaining the reserves, then, was vitally important, but it depended on the country's balance of payments. As long as exports paid for imports there was no problem, but if they did not, the balance had to be met in gold. Merchants appeared with their bills asking to have them discounted in gold, and the Bank's stock dwindled. It could refuse to discount, but that would destroy business morale, so usually it increased the Bank Rate, which was the rate of interest it asked for its loans. If it was high enough, people did not borrow, the supply of money fell, bringing down prices which, in turn, encouraged foreigners to buy our goods. Exports increased, the balance of payments improved, and gold flowed back into the country through the hands of the merchants and then, via the ramifications of the banking system, into the vaults of the Bank of England.

Such was the theory, but the country continued to be plagued with regular economic crises. They were the result of the trade cycle, which was an illness afflicting much of the economic life of the country, but the most conspicuous symptom was that of banks failing. For example, between 1820 and 1825, over three hundred went out of business to the loss and unhappiness of their depositors. It was felt that, by treating this symptom, the disease could be cured, and its cause seemed simple enough – the banks issued more notes than their reserves warranted. The cure, then, seemed simple as well, and it was to tie the issue of notes to the reserve. This was attempted by Peel's Bank Charter Act of 1844. We have already seen that the Act gave the Bank of England a monopoly of issuing notes, but it did much more than that. The Bank itself was divided into two departments, Banking and Issuing. In this way the all-important duty of issue was separated from the other business and was, moreover, closely regulated. The Bank could make what was called a 'fiduciary issue' of £14 million, provided it held government securities to that value, but any notes above that amount had to be backed by gold. If, therefore, there was a run on the Bank's gold reserves, it had to take an equivalent number of notes out of circulation. This would mean there was less money available, prices would fall, exports would increase, the balance of payments would right itself and the gold reserves would build up, as has already been described.

These were the ideas of the then Governor of the Bank, Horsley Palmer, who was one of the leaders of what they called the 'currency school'. Peel liked the system because it was self-regulating so, in theory, there should never be any need for the Government to interfere. A rival group, known as the 'banking school', pointed out that the balance of payments depended on far more than the amount of credit British banks were giving, and this in any case was much greater than the value of Bank of England notes in circulation. What about country bank issues, bills of exchange and, above all, the vast number of credit transfers? Nearly all important payments are made without a coin or a note changing hands. The currency school worsted the banking school but, inevitably, lost to the trade cycle. There was a crisis as soon as 1847, then another in 1857 and yet another in 1866.

Each time the Government had to release the Bank from the restrictions of the 1844 Act, allowing it to issue notes beyond those limits in order to allay the panic.

COUNTRY BANKS

Country banks were few in 1750, they increased steadily in numbers to 1785 when there were perhaps 120, and then very rapidly, so that by 1815 there were around 700. They began in all sorts of ways.

Some of the first bankers were industrialists. As a business grew, its owner needed a bank, and if no one else had started one locally, he might do so himself. He would open it to other people and carry on all the normal business of accepting deposits, making payments, making loans and issuing notes. Sometimes the bank became more important than the original business, as happened with the Lloyd Iron Company of Birmingham. Not surprisingly it was the leading growth industries of the day, textiles and iron, that produced most banks, though a good many were offshoots of breweries.

Other men who started banks were wholesale traders. They dealt in credit all the time, so the change to banking was easy. At the ports there were merchants who became bankers, the men who imported wine, cotton and timber. Inland, there were dealers in coal, iron and grain. Drapers made good bankers, perhaps because their trade was steady and reliable.

Yet another group were tax-collectors. They had no salaries, so the Government allowed them to keep the proceeds of certain taxes, like the land tax and stamp duty, for up to two years. They lent the money at interest, and from doing that it was but a short step to accepting other deposits given in a more friendly way, and becoming bankers.

Finally there were the lawyers. A country attorney knew about the business of all manner of people, and he readily involved himself, to become what was called a 'money scrivener'. He was able to bring together people who needed money with those who were wanting to lend, because he knew them all. Someone might ask him about raising a mortgage, and it could well be that the widow of a client was asking nervously what she should do with her legacy. Alternatively an attorney might invest clients' money for them, usually buying something safe and sensible like government securities or shares in one of the larger trading companies. Should there be any enclosures to be made, or turnpike roads or canals to be built, then there were all sorts of legal and financial problems. Many an attorney was

A money scrivener

called in to solve the immediate difficulties of a turnpike trust or a canal company, and was kept on as treasurer. With clients' money passing freely through his hands, the temptation to become a banker was strong. As a money scrivener the attorney took other people's capital and invested it for them. As a banker he accepted deposits, undertook to pay interest on them, and then lent the money in his own name. The difference was not great.

Many bankers were Quakers. Elizabeth Fry, for example, married a banker and she herself was a Gurney. The firm of Overend and Gurney was highly respected, dominating banking in East Anglia until its bill-broking branch in London ruined it with a spectacular crash in 1866. Like the iron industry, banking attracted Quakers. Paul Emden remarked unkindly, 'The silence in Meeting is such that a fall of one eighth of a per cent in Consols is clearly audible' (Alan Jenkins, *Stock Exchange Story*, p. 47).

A country bank started with money subscribed by its partners, and they could give more than hard cash, since, if they were well-known, respected citizens, their bank too would have a good reputation. For the rest, they attracted deposits by paying interest on them. People in business, traders and manufacturers, opened accounts, as did others with savings or legacies, such as widows, clergymen

161

and retired officers. Institutions like charities, hospitals, churches and turnpike trusts also used banks. Almost everyone who had spare money, banked it, and the family gold was no longer locked in an oak chest in the master's bedroom.

The banks lent at interest whatever money was deposited with them as well as a great deal more they created in the way we have described.

LONDON BANKS

The London banks between them carried on the whole business of the capital, which was important enough in itself, and they also linked the country banks, both with each other and with the Bank of England.

Every country bank needed a London agent, in order to operate in the London money-market. Sometimes one would open its own London branch, an arrangement called 'pig on pork', but usually it would make an agreement with an existing bank. Quite often one or two of the partners of the country bank would join the London bank, and the other way round. The London bank acted for the one in the country as it would for any other business, accepting its deposits, making its payments, giving it a loan in time of need, and sending it letters, often strongly worded, if it was overdrawn.

The country bank started by sending its reserves to its London agent and collecting a modest interest. When the reserves were large enough it would go on to buy government stock, which was as safe as could be, though the interest was low. Consols usually yielded 3 per cent. The final stage was to enter the bill market where there were risks, but, on the other hand, the profits were good. The country banker would already have been discounting the bills of local tradesmen, but now his London agent opened the entire country to him.

JOINT STOCK BANKS

A joint stock company is one that offers its shares for sale to the general public, so it can attract far more capital than a small group of partners could hope to provide. For a long time the Bank of England was the only joint stock bank in the country, but in 1826 an Act of Parliament made it legal to form others. Some established private banks became public, such as Barclays and Lloyds, and there were new ones as well, like the London and Westminster, the Midland, and the National Provincial. The banking community did not like the joint stock concerns and feared them, with good reason, for there followed a long, and sometimes painful, process of amalgamation.

It was necessary that this should happen, none the less. The little country banks went well enough with turnpike roads and domestic industries, but bigger businesses needed bigger banks.

MERCHANT BANKS

Merchant banks first appeared in the early nineteenth century. As their name suggests, they were banks for merchants. Each specialised in one particular trade and gained a thorough knowledge of the people who engaged in it. This allowed them to deal in international bills of exchange. Payment by bills of exchange was convenient for merchants, but it was risky when they belonged to an unknown, foreign firm. However, a merchant banker knew whose bills were good and, for a fee, he would back them. This was called 'accepting' bills, and if it were done by a reputable merchant bank, they became 'prime bank bills' and almost anyone in the world would take them. The 'bill on London' was an international currency, and helped the City to become the financial capital of the world.

THE STOCK EXCHANGE

So far we have been looking at short-term debts, acknowledged by bank notes and bills of exchange, but there were long-term debts as well, mainly government securities and shares in joint stock companies. They were handled by the Stock Exchange.

By the late seventeenth century there were already men who made a living buying and selling stocks and shares. Some were 'brokers', who acted as agents for other people and collected commission, while others were 'jobbers', who bought and sold on their own account, hoping to make profits. At first they were allowed into the Royal Exchange, but in about 1700 they were put out because of the noise and disturbance they caused. They then managed as best they could in the open streets and coffee shops, their favourite being Jonathan's. In 1773 they at last had a building of their own in Threadneedle Street, and in 1802 moved to a bigger one in Capel Court, which is still part of the Stock Exchange today. Respectability came to them sooner than the rolled umbrella and the bowler hat, for they were giving an essential service by the middle of the nineteenth century. There were already many firms that were public companies and so offering their shares for sale to the general public. Foreigners, both business men and governments, also sold their securities through the Stock Exchange, and between 1815 and 1914 Great Britain lent £4000 million overseas.

The Stock Exchange

GOVERNMENT SECURITIES

Then, as now, the most profligate spender was the Government. In 1748 the national debt was £71 million; in 1783 it was £238 million; and in 1815, thanks largely to the Napoleonic Wars, it was £820 million. This was higher than it was ever to be again until the First World War.

However, the debt was administered well. In the first place there was the Bank of England to handle the Government's affairs. Secondly all the miscellaneous long-term debts that had accumulated over the years were rationalised as 'Consolidated Bank Annuities', or 'Consols' for short. Thirdly the public had the choice of long-term or short-term investments. The long term were Consols and the short term were Treasury bills, or similar paper issued by the Army and the Navy. They were promises to pay a stated amount on a stated date, usually three months after issue. They were sold by auction, though of course they always fetched less than their face value. A man who gave £98 for a £100 bill collected his full £100 when the bill matured, the £2 difference being , in effect, his interest. There had been a time when lending to the Government was much the same as giving a personal loan to the King, and a hazardous undertaking it was. By the eighteenth century that had changed, as a modern writer explains:

The new government securities were very different from the dubious loans issued by needy monarchs in the past. Parliament, which had gained undisputed control over expenditure, also assumed full responsibility for revenue, and the national debt was secured, not on the yield of some particular tax, but on the consolidated revenue of the kingdom. Interest was paid regularly, maturing loans were promptly repaid, and the 'funds' were regarded, after land itself, as the most desirable form of property. (Morgan, op.cit., p. 116)

Government spending affected the rest of the economy. In the first place it stimulated several industries, especially those concerned with armaments and other war materials. Iron did particularly well. It was government business that gave Henry Cort the encouragement and the means to develop puddling and rolling, the Carron works in Scotland prospered, as did John Wilkinson's concerns. Only the Quakers, like the Darbys, held aloof, because of their religion. As well as weapons, the Government bought ships, clothing for servicemen and food.

Next, the sale of government securities helped the growth of the London money-market. We have already seen how a country banker would make his first cautious ventures there by purchasing government stock, which was completely safe, and would graduate from that to the riskier, but more profitable business of discounting bills. Ordinary investors behaved in much the same way. At one time they had left their money in their strong-boxes, but such good securities encouraged investment. The habit of lending money at interest became national, and the anxiety was not so much whether the capital was safe, but whether it was earning enough. 'John Bull,' it was said, 'can stand a very great deal, but he cannot stand 2 per cent.'

Finally the Government built and maintained the Royal Navy, and it is quite possible it was the Royal Navy which ensured that the first Industrial Revolution took place in Britain. The French, whose economic growth had been as rapid as our own, decided to indulge themselves with a political revolution and close on twenty-five years of war. During that time English merchants, under the protection of Navy warships, filched their overseas markets, and enjoyed a trade boom the like of which had never been seen before. The £820 million debt was money well spent.

30 Business organisation

SOLE TRADERS AND PARTNERSHIPS

The simplest form of business organisation, and the most common, was that of the sole trader. A man on his own had the advantage of freedom, but he had his problems as well, the main one being a lack of resources, physical, mental and financial. If he fell ill, there was no one to do his work; if an opportunity came his way he might miss it, because he did not have the wits to recognise it; even when he did see a good chance he still might have been unable to take it because he did not have enough money.

A sole trader could overcome these problems if he found a partner or two, men who would bring new ideas and extra capital. An excellent example was the partnership of Boulton and Watt, where business genius joined mechanical genius to create a great and famous firm. However, partnerships had their problems, especially if they were at all large.

In the first place there was no limited liability. Anyone who was a partner in a business was responsible for its debts to the full value of everything he owned, however much or little he had put into it. One man might find £100 or so, while his partners invested thousands, but if the firm went bankrupt he lost not just his £100 but all his other money as well. His house was sold over his head, and his property was taken to pay the creditors.

Secondly it was difficult to withdraw from a partnership. One member could not sell his share to an outsider, because it might mean foisting someone unknown or unwelcome on his colleagues. All had to be unanimous before there could be a resignation, or anyone new admitted. If a partner escaped by dying, then the others had to find his share of the money to pay his heirs, and raising a lump sum at a difficult time might bring ruin.

Finally the law did not view a partnership as an entity but as a group of individuals. That could be an advantage, for anyone bringing an action had to sue them all separately, but, on the other hand, if they wanted to go to court, each one had to present his own case. Similarly they all had to sign every legal agreement that was made.

JOINT STOCK COMPANIES

In spite of these problems, though, most eighteenth-century businesses were small enough to be run perfectly well by sole traders or little groups of partners. There were some projects, however, like canals, that needed a lot of capital, and the only way to raise it was to offer shares for sale to the general public. An organisation which did this was called a joint stock company.

One of the first in England was the Muscovy Company, formed in the reign of Elizabeth I. Frobisher's journey to Russia had shown the possibility of a rich trade in furs, but as it was beyond the resources of any one merchant, a group of them worked together. Other trading ventures followed, like the East India Company. By the eighteenth century there were joint stock companies for all sorts of purposes and to run them they had a well-developed organisation.

In the first place there was the General Court, which was open to everyone who had shares in the company. This body decided policy, for example whether extra stock should be issued or whether they should amalgamate with another company. Issues like this were not often raised, so usually General Courts were badly attended and met infrequently to transact dry-as-dust business in a desultory fashion. What could liven them was a report that the Directors were sitting on the profits instead of paying dividends; then the shareholders came in force, and spectators as well. Dubois says: 'Attendance at the frequently heated debates of the East India Company appears to have been regarded as a piquant and costless treat for the country cousin.' (op. cit., pp. 288–9)

As well as the General Court to decide policy, there was a much smaller Court of Directors whose duty it was to carry out that policy. The directors were elected by the General Court, and they in turn appointed salaried officials to do the humdrum day-to-day work, while they supervised.

From what has already been said, it can be seen that a joint stock company had two advantages over a partnership. It could accept money from the general public, so building up a large capital, and it could delegate its work to a select group who were, hopefully, the most zealous and efficient of its members. There were other advantages as well. In the first place there was limited liability. If the company went bankrupt, a shareholder could well lose all the money he had invested, but not a penny more. He knew exactly how much he was risking. Also, if at any time he wanted to withdraw from the company, he needed no one's consent, but simply sold his shares on the open market. Since a joint stock company was a corporation, it was one body in the eyes of the law, so any legal document just needed its common seal, and if there was a court case the company fought it as an individual would. In practice, the Court of Directors made their officials handle such problems, and the shareholders had nothing to do.

However, in spite of all these advantages, there was no rush by groups of partners to turn themselves into joint stock companies. Apart from the fact that few firms were large enough to merit the change, it was a very difficult thing to do. There had been trouble with the South Sea Company in the early years of the century. Speculation in its shares had pushed their price to a ridiculous height, and when their value collapsed, many people were ruined. This was 'the bursting of the South Sea Bubble'. Parliament determined nothing like it should happen again and, in 1720, passed 'An Act to Restrain the Extravagant and Unwarrantable Practice of Raising Money by Voluntary Subscriptions for Carrying on Projects Dangerous to the Trade and Subjects of this Kingdom'. It was called the 'Bubble Act' for short. The Act made it illegal to form a joint stock company, offering shares to the public, unless it had a charter either from the Crown or from Parliament. The men of state, it was felt, would be able to identify dubious organisations and also to lay down the right conditions for those who did pass their scrutiny. Applications to the Crown went before the Attorney-General and the Solicitor-General, but they had long noses and all too often refused. It was usually easier to obtain an Act, but, even so, that was no formality. As we have seen with the canals and railways, the whole procedure was tedious and costly.

Many firms preferred to form unincorporated companies, and then obtain as many of the advantages of incorporation as they could. They usually found that there were partial solutions to their problems, or at least that their very existence brought some compensation.

Joint stock companies

In place of a General Court and a Court of Directors they had an Assembly of Subscribers and a Committee of Management, and in place of a Charter they had Articles of Association. The Articles had no standing at law, but they could be changed at will, while only Parliament could alter the Charter of a corporate body. To avoid involving everyone in every single transaction the shareholders made the Committee of Management their trustees. They could then conduct the ordinary business of the company, like buying and selling goods, but not, however, litigation. Sometimes the officers tried their luck in court, even though they were likely to be challenged. Fortunately, most eighteenth-century disputes never went to court. Legal procedure was so tedious, and costs were so high, that most people were willing to put their case to an arbitrator and make a gentleman's agreement to accept his decision. Shareholders found ways of buying and selling shares freely. Sometimes the Committee of Management bought the shares and resold them, which was legal. Sometimes the Articles of Association allowed the sale of shares on the open market, which was directly against the Bubble Act, and was done in the hope that no one would be bothered enough to take action. Matthew Boulton had such a clause in the Articles of the Cornish Metal Company which he founded in 1785, and it was just the sort of thing a man with his optimistic temperament would do. There was no way to secure limited liability, but even this had one compensation, since its absence made people more willing to lend money to an Association. Theoretically, unincorporated bodies had no legal protection, but the Court of Chancery especially could not bring itself to turn away good business, and would bend the law rather than do so.

There were even a few clear advantages in not being incorporated. Chartered companies lived under the constant threat of investigation by parliamentary committees, but the unincorporated were beneath such attentions. Should a chartered company step out of line anyone could frighten it with a writ of *quo warranto* (by what authority) or *scire facias* (tell me what you are up to). Proceeding against an unincorporated body meant suing a host of subscribers in the Court of Chancery, a prospect that made the strongest men blench.

However, seeing they were somewhat insecure, unincorporated associations took care not to give offence, so that neither the Government nor other business people had any motive to take action against them. As Dubois says: 'It was not until the early nineteenth century that there arose a recrudescence of the old spirit of swindle.' (*The English Businesses Company after the Bubble Act 1720–1800*, p. 236) Then there were some court cases. The result, however, was that the old Bubble Act had the dust blown off it, was examined, and was found unsuitable for the nineteenth century. Parliament repealed it in 1825. One of the old rules did remain, which was that no company could enjoy limited liability without an Act authorising it. Even that was ended in 1856 when the Joint Stock Company Act made limited liability available to any organisation, as long as it registered itself and submitted its books for public audit.

31 Capital and the economy

The financial institutions we have been describing were valuable in a number of ways. Even in prehistoric times currency did away with the need to barter, while in our period banks went one stage further and solved the problems of handling large quantities of coin by issuing notes and making credit transfers. However, the most important question we have to consider is the complex one of how institutions helped the accumulation of capital.

It will help us to understand the role of capital if we have a look at a Robinson Crusoe economy. Here the shipwrecked sailor may spend all his time satisfying his immediate needs by hunting goats, climbing trees for coconuts, or collecting shellfish. In such ways he may keep alive, but he will certainly not improve his standard of living. If he is wise he will give a certain amount of time each day to his future good, adding to his store of capital. He may clear a piece of ground to grow crops, or make a fishing-net, and these will be his fixed capital, or the things he will use to produce more wealth. He may prepare a stock of seed, or cure goatskins, and these will be his working capital, or the raw materials of his trade. He may build himself a hut or clear a path to the beach, and these will be his social overhead capital. This last does not produce more wealth in itself, but it allows the other economic activities to take place. A man will not be an efficient farmer or fisherman if he has no home, or if he has to fight his way everywhere through the undergrowth.

Clearly, while our sailor is creating his capital he will have to forgo the occasional meal of shellfish and coconuts, but if he will do so, the chances are that he will ensure a more secure and pleasant existence for himself. Moreover, once he has developed the habit of working regularly for the future, he will probably go on setting aside a regular amount of time and goods to keep his capital in order and add to it.

An industrial economy is the same. It has its fixed capital such as the cultivated land with its farm equipment, and the factories with their machines; it has its working capital, such as fertilisers, coal, raw cotton and customers' debts; and it has its social overhead capital, such as houses, schools, hospitals, roads, canals, railways and docks. Moreover, if the economy is to grow, people must be willing to give up a proportion of the things they would like to have immediately, and accumulate the capital which will increase their wealth in the future.

To grow in this way, though, a society needs to be reasonably wealthy. If people are very poor, then they have no surplus they can save. If, however, they do not save, they remain poor. Here is a vicious circle that it is difficult to break.

Even more important, a society must have the correct attitudes and ideas. Not all shipwrecked sailors are Robinson Crusoes. Others, placed as he was, have been too idle or disorganised to improve their lot, while some perhaps have had a different scale of values and scorned material improvement. Nor need we think only in terms of individuals and desert islands. From being almost uninhabited, North America became the most prosperous continent in the modern world in less than four hundred years, a striking contrast with India and China. There are many complex reasons for this, but the radical differences between the philosophies of the inhabitants of these places must certainly be one of them.

Even where a society is willing to accumulate capital it is still important that it should be willing to invest it productively. In medieval times, men's concern for the next life led them to build churches, cathedrals and monasteries. These, though aesthetically and spiritually valuable in themselves, hardly compare with cotton factories or ironworks as means of increasing wealth. In modern times governments have squandered capital for political reasons and it is rare for the results to have the redeeming features of being aesthetically pleasing. An exception is the Humber Bridge. This unwanted structure was built at the cost of some £60 million in order to help Labour win the North Hull by-election in 1965, but it is at least elegant. Finally, if society is to accumulate any quality of capital, it must have the right institutions. In the eighteenth century many small business men were able to find the money they needed by borrowing from relations, friends and acquaintances. Alternatively a man could mortgage his house or his factory to someone with whom he had no social contact but who lived in his area, and knew about him and his business. However, as firms grew in size, they had to go further afield to seek 'blind' capital. This is where the institutions helped.

First we will look at the banks. They were wary of providing social overhead capital, because it was too permanent. If money went into the building of a canal, for example, there it remained, and a banker would think anxiously of the day when there might be a queue of depositors at his door demanding gold, while all he had in his vaults was the canal shares. None the less, banks could help. They handled the accounts of turnpike trusts and canal companies and from time to time they gave them short-term loans. A bank might also lend money to its local corporation for perhaps a bridge, a prison or a new town hall. Then, as now, local authorities were free with their ratepayers' money when they wanted prestige buildings. None of this, though, amounted to much.

Similarly banks were not interested in providing fixed capital. It was a long-term investment and they had to remain liquid. The few that did put a lot of money into factories or mines usually regretted it. However, the crying need was for working capital, and here the banks gave invaluable help. Almost every man in business discounted his bills, but usually the one who gave credit needed his money at once for another transaction. He took his bills to his bank manager and, provided they were 'good paper', he was well received, for here was just the sort of business a bank wanted. It could ask a reasonable rate of interest but, more important, it was 'lending short', since bills of exchange fell due for payment within three months. However, even though the credit was short, few merchants or manufacturers could have stayed in business without it. Pressnell says, 'the country banker's investment in inland bills of exchange was by far the most significant for the country as a whole' (op. cit., p. 434).

We have seen, too, that the country banks were linked to the London banks and, through them, to the rest of the country. This was important for the economy as a whole because then, even more than now, growth was faster in some areas than others. In certain counties trade was stagnant and surplus money lay idle; other regions needed every penny they could find. No one could have expected a Somersetshire widow or clergyman to lend to some unknown and probably uncouth North Country industrialist, but they would willingly make deposits in the nice bank which the respectable Mr Cross kept at Wells. They then collected their interest and bothered no more, but their money could quite well find its way through the London bill market to a Manchester cotton factory, a Nottingham lace mill, a South Wales ironworks or a Bristol firm of sugar importers. The country banks drew cash from odd, unlikely corners, and the London banks channelled it where it would do most good. The country's capital was mobilised to help its trade and industry, and the banks as much as the railways played their part in dissolving the little local economies to make a national one.

Next we come to the joint stock companies. They were to the business world what steam-engines were to industry and transport, which is to say they had tremendous potential, but were only beginning to bulk large by 1850. None the less, the joint stock companies were playing a vital part in the economy, since it was they who provided the most important part of the country's social overhead capital, its transport system. In other countries governments helped to do this and, admittedly, the British Government contributed a little towards the construction of roads and docks. For the most part, though, it was a positive hindrance since, as we have seen, every scheme required an Act and that required an outlay of tens or even hundreds of thousands of pounds to pay for the dubious services of Members of Parliament and lawyers. Further, most projects were too ambitious for any individual, or group of partners, while the banks, as we have seen, were not interested, for the best of business reasons. It was left, therefore, to the joint stock companies to provide these essential public works.

The accumulation of fixed capital was not such a problem as might appear, for the amount needed was not enormous. One may imagine that a business man would have had far more money in his buildings and machinery than in his raw materials and unsold goods. In fact, during the Industrial Revolution, it was often the other way round. S. D. Chapman gives these figures for the firm of Coltman & Gardiner, who were stocking manufacturers:

	1783	1792	1800
Fixed capital:			
Warehouse	580	580	580
Frames	186	896	823
Working capital:			
Raw materials, work in progress, stock		1319 2305 2967	
Customers' debts:		3125 3844 5874	

The following shows the fixed and working capital as percentages:

	1783	1792	1800
Fixed	14.7	19.4	13.6
Working	85.3	80.6	86.4
	100.0	100.0	100.0

The more highly developed industries used the factory system, so they had more fixed capital, but it was not excessive. By 1800 only £10 million had been spent in the cotton industry, which amounted to only two weeks of the nation's income. Admittedly it was possible to spend nearly £100 000 on a new, fully equipped, fully integrated cotton factory in the 1830s, but that was exceptional. A water-frame mill cost £5000 at the most, while in the woollen industry even less was needed. An old barn could be converted and the most expensive piece of equipment, the steam-engine, need cost no more than £150. If the textile factory was a modest one, the fixed capital might be a third of the total, rising to a half if the factory were more elaborate. All this meant that a man or a group of partners with moderate wealth could start a business easily enough, and then build it up, provided only they had the self-discipline to plough back their profits.

Sidney Pollard has shown how this was done in a yarn-spinning and cloth-finishing concern near Huddersfield ('Fixed Capital in the Industrial Revolution in Britain', in Crouzet, op. cit.). The mill was already well established in 1825 when old William Brooke handed it to two of his sons. They took heavy commitments as well, because the father wanted £2000 a year rent, and 5 per cent interest on his investment of £65 000 in machinery and stock. There was also a third brother, a sleeping partner, who was due for £1000 a year for six years, and for interest at 5 per cent on £9000 he had in the firm. All this came to £6700 a year. On top of that the two partners agreed to take 5 per cent on their own capital, which was £27 000, and then divide the profits equally.

In spite of their expenses the brothers modernised their mill and expanded their business. Within a few years they had spent £48 000 on new buildings and equipment, had paid off an overdraft of £10 000, and had credits of £40 000, money owed to them by other people. This was done not just by good management but by taking only a fraction of what was due to them under their partnership agreement. Between 1830 and 1836 they could have drawn £140 000; as it was, they had £55 000, or less than 40 per cent. One year, indeed, they took only 12 per cent.

Generally industry generated its own fixed capital in this way with little outside help. How efficient was the supply of capital? W. W. Rostow says that a traditional society invests less than 5 per cent of its income, whereas one that has 'taken off into self-sustained growth' invests at least 10 per cent. There was such a change in Britain some time during the Industrial Revolution. Gregory King's survey of 1698 shows that in his day investment was less than 5 per cent of national income, while, by the middle of the nineteenth century, it was 10 per cent in any normal year and sometimes more. Rostow says that the 'take off' is compressed into twenty years, which he gives very precisely for Britain as being between 1783 and 1802. It is highly unlikely, though, that the change came in so brief a time. During the middle of the eighteenth century the pace of investment quickened with more enclosures and the building of roads and canals. However, national income was growing too, and it is not certain that investment took an increased share. That does indeed seem to have happened in the period Rostow gives, since cotton, iron, canals and docks all needed large slices of capital. It is unlikely, though, that they took more than an additional 1½ per cent of the national income. After the Napoleonic Wars there were even heavier investments in cotton while, towards the middle of the century, others followed in wool and iron. Then came the railway boom, and it was that which pushed the level of investment to more than 10 per cent of national income. Indeed, for a while, the railways took that amount for themselves alone.

The switch from a traditional to a modern level of investment, then, may well have taken a hundred years, rather than the twenty which Rostow suggests. This slow development could have been due to a shortage of capital, coupled with inefficiency in institutions channelling it, or it could have been because of a shortage of investment opportunities. It is impossible to be sure, but we do have two pointers. In the first place there were, on occasions, sudden demands for capital, from the rebuilding of London after the Great Fire in 1688 to the railway boom of the late 1840s. These demands were met without apparent difficulty. Secondly capital was cheap. though risk capital offered somewhat higher returns, government securities paid only 3 per cent for much of the eighteenth century. If any article is cheap, it usually means that there is more than enough of it to meet current needs. It would seem, then, that the slow growth in the volume of investment was the result more of a lack of openings than of a shortage of capital. It is reasonable, moreover, to assume that this was so, since it was the modern sector which needed capital, and before the middle of the nineteenth century that was but a small proportion of the whole.

As for the institutions, it would appear that when there was a need for capital they either channelled it or, if they could not, they grew and multiplied in order to meet the demand. We have seen, for example, how country banks increased in number towards the end of the eighteenth century and how, later on, joint stock companies appeared. This is not to say that the country's financial institutions were perfect. One obvious cause of instability was the country banks. Limited as they were to six partners, few were strong, and every trade depression brought with it a crop of bank failures. Nor was the Bank of England as solid as Sir John Soane's building suggested, and some remarkable things happened. A small party of French soldiers landing in Wales led to the suspension of payments in gold for over twenty years. In 1825 one of its own clerks saved it from collapse. There was a run on it and, just as they thought their reserves were exhausted, the clerk found a parcel of a million £1 notes that had been forgotten. In 1866, during another panic, the Rothschilds saved it by a massive draft of credit from Paris.

Nor were the banks able to regulate properly the money supply or maintain confidence, but instead they joined in the game of swings and roundabouts along with everyone else. When times were good, the most staid of men lived in a euphoria and sometimes parted with money quite rashly. As Bagehot said of the fall of Overend and Gurney, 'One would think a child who had lent money in the City of London would have lent it better.' On the other hand, when times were bad, bankers hugged their reserves to themselves, and the best of customers approached them in vain.

The banks could not have prevented the swing of the trade cycle, but they might have checked it had they acted against their own inclinations. That would have meant tightening credit when the boom approached its peak, and being free with it during a depression. The banks, however, felt that their duty was to make money for themselves and their depositors. It was not their task to look after the economy as a whole.

However, we cannot blame bankers of the eighteenth and early nineteenth centuries for failing to solve problems that are intractable today. On the whole the financial institutions were remarkable. Money is the one raw material that all businesses need, and the men who supplied it played as vital a part in the Industrial Revolution as those who manufactured goods or traded with foreign countries.

How important was the accumulation of capital to the progress of the Industrial Revolution? It appears that it was absolutely essential. T.S. Ashton has pointed out the importance of low rates of interest:

If we seek – it would be wrong to do so – for a single reason why the pace of economic development quickened about the middle of the eighteenth century, it is to this we must look. The deep mines, solidly built factories, well constructed canals and substantial houses of the Industrial Revolution were the products of relatively cheap capital. (op. cit., p. 9)

Ashton also shows that while the new inventions were essential for rapid progress, they were not enough on their own: 'It was the growth of savings, and of a readiness to put these at the disposal of industry that made it possible for Britain to reap the harvest of her ingenuity.' (ibid., p. 76)

As we have seen, W.W. Rostow says that a cardinal difference between a traditional and a modern economy is their different rates of investment. W.J. Ashley said that in the Industrial Revolution 'the primary force that was at work was Capital' (op. cit., p. 93).

However, putting capital into an economy is not like putting a coin into a slot-machine. The slot-machine will deliver a precise volume of goods for a precise input, but an investment is not nearly as sure. We have seen in Britain during the 1970s that there are industries which demand massive injections of capital, yet fail dismally to give adequate returns. Equally, it is possible to secure a handsome yield for a very small outlay, or indeed no outlay at all. The factory owners of the early nineteenth century increased output simply by increasing hours of work. Reorganisation of existing resources can have the same result, a good example being a farmer who adopts a better crop rotation. He needs no more land, perhaps even no more machinery, but his output increases none the less. Looking at the country as a whole, we have seen that during the crucial years at the end of the eighteenth century investment probably increased by no more than $1\frac{1}{2}$ per cent of national income. Certainly there were dramatic changes in the economy before there was one in the level of investment.

However, this is a long way from denying the importance of investment. It may not have been the prime mover, the force that drove all the rest, but it was an indispensable part of the machinery of growth.

32 Case history: Robert Tasker and the Waterloo Ironworks

Tasker was born in 1785 at Stanton St Bernard in the Vale of Pewsey. He was apprenticed to his father, who was a blacksmith, and when he was out of his indentures he decided he would go to London to seek his fortune. He needed money to get married. However, when he reached Andover, he heard that a local blacksmith needed an assistant, so he went to work for him. He was Thomas Maslen who lived in Abbots Ann, a remote village in the north-west of Hampshire. Tasker was able to marry, and it was not long before he was able to take over the forge, on Maslen's retirement. There followed a difficult time, for Tasker was a nonconformist and the villagers persecuted him. One of them even tried to kill him. He could find no customers near home, but had to go far afield for them. Then, in a moment of inspiration, he designed a plough which was

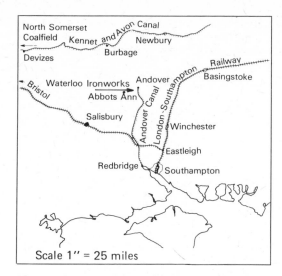

North Somerset
Coalfield
Kennet and Avon Canal
Newbury
Burbage
Devizes
Bristol
Waterloo Ironworks
Abbots Ann
Andover
Railway
Basingstoke
Andover Canal
London-Southampton
Salisbury
Winchester
Eastleigh
Redbridge
Southampton

Scale 1" = 25 miles

Map to show position of Waterloo Ironworks

particularly suitable for the chalky soils of that area and the local people, finding him useful, forgot about his religion.

The next step came when Tasker heard of an idea of Robert Ransome's. Ploughshares were of wrought iron which blunted quickly, but Ransome found that, if he cast them in a mould which was sand at the top and iron at the bottom, the under-side was 'chilled' and a good deal harder. Passing through the ground, the top of the share wore away more quickly than the bottom, so he had achieved the miracle of making a self-sharpening plough-share. Tasker wanted to manufacture these himself, but in a blacksmith's shop it was impossible. He had to have a foundry.

By now his brother William had joined him, which meant he had help. However, the two men had little capital, so they had to substitute hard work. They bought a plot beside the Pillhill Brook that the owner almost gave away because it was marshland. They then took chalk from the common, which they were allowed free of charge, and tipped it into their marsh until it was solid ground. Next they dug a leat from the brook, which, though it only gave a modest fall of 2 feet, allowed them to drive an undershot wheel powerful enough for their needs. They built the water-wheel house, a forge, a foundry and a workshop in brick. They made some less important buildings from chalk, pounding it, mixing it with water, and then pouring it between wooden shuttering, as if it were concrete. Their equipment was a lathe, a drilling machine, a cupola furnace for melting the iron and two forges. By 1814 they were in business.

They prospered and expanded their works.

Partly this was because they were joined by John Fowler, half-brother to Robert's wife, who had been a yeoman and had sold his farm, presumably to put money into the firm. They also ploughed back their profits. At the foundry they added more workshops and equipment, and for their workers they built terraces of houses, an Independent chapel and a school.

In 1830 there was a set-back because their works were damaged during the Swing Riots. Why the farm workers attacked the foundry is not clear, for Tasker did not make the threshing-machines which they hated. Possibly they saw the remote and unprotected little foundry as an easy victim on which to vent their spite. At their trial, Robert made light of the damage, but twelve were sentenced to death and two were actually hanged.

As the firm grew, its partners began to feel the disadvantages of being so isolated. To sell their goods they opened depots in Winchester, Salisbury and Basingstoke, and fortunately improvements in transport helped them with the carriage of their coal and iron. The foundry was only a mile from the Andover Canal, which led down the valley of the Test to Redbridge and Southampton Water. Most of their iron came that way, having made the long sea voyage round Cornwall, from South Wales. To the north was the Kennet and Avon Canal, with a wharf at Burbage, 19 miles away. It carried a little of their iron from the Forest of Dean, and all of their coal from North Somerset. Then came the railway from London to Southampton. In 1839 it had reached Basingstoke, and in 1840 Winchester. There was a branch line from Eastleigh to Salisbury in 1847, and by 1856 the G.W.R. had linked Salisbury to Bristol. Then the foundry was using 200 tons of coal a year, and 500 tons of iron, the railway having cut the price of iron by half.

However, apart from the Andover Canal, no main line of communication came really close, so that Tasker's depended on their wagons. They had so many horses that it was worth their while to buy a farm to keep them. As in so many other places, the railways brought an increase in horse traffic, not a decline.

The foundry produced many articles that would once have been made of timber or stone. Iron replaced wood in ploughs, railings, gates, garden seats, signposts, window-frames, pumps, and the huge gear wheels for water-mills and horse gins. It replaced stone in rollers, bridges, milestones, rick saddles and the columns of Andover Guildhall.

Above all, though, the firm made farm machinery, especially during the 'golden age' of agriculture between 1850 and 1870. There were chaff cutters, reapers, a Tasker speciality which was a combined fertiliser distributor and seed drill, and some of those giant traction-engines that frightened Parliament into passing the Red Flag Act. With the coming of motor transport, they concentrated on trailers, producing the 'Queen Mary' type that played such a useful part in the Second World War.

The history of the Waterloo Ironworks is the history of the Industrial Revolution in miniature. On the technical side there was the original inspiration of the new plough, followed by the copying and adaptation of the ideas of others. There were mechanical power and machinery with their attendant Luddism; there was the union of coal and iron; there was the spread of iron, as it ousted traditional materials; finally there was the progress from the manufacture of fairly simple pieces of engineering, like ploughs, to highly complicated equipment, like traction-engines.

On the transport side there was the contribution of canals, turnpike roads, coastal shipping and, later, railways. They brought materials from as far away as South Wales and widened the market from the immediate neighbourhood to Salisbury, Winchester and Basingstoke.

On the social side there were the houses, chapel and school, all provided by the employer and catering for the physical and moral needs of the workers, though not for their relaxation and amusement. One of the secrets of Tasker's success was that he was a stern nonconformist who had no time for frivolities.

However, from the point of view of this chapter, what is interesting is the commercial side. It is remarkable that the organisation was so basic. Here was a successful firm started by one man on his own, and, in our period, it grew to no more than a partnership of three. John Fowler, possibly, gave some capital from the sale of his land, but not even that is certain. For the most part, progress came from some ingenuity, a lot of hard work, and ploughing back the profits methodically

year after year. In all this, the Waterloo Ironworks was more typical of its age than any of the great joint stock companies.

PROBLEMS

1 How did the South Sea Bubble affect the development of business organisation?

2 What problems hindered the general acceptance of the principle of limited liability? How far did this check the growth of the economy?

3 How far did the development of financial institutions match the progress of the economy?

4 What was the role of the country banks? Explain the increase in their numbers during the period around 1800.

5 Did the banking system contribute in any way to economic instability?

6 What were the aims of the Bank Charter Act of 1844? How successful was the Act in meeting them?

7 How far was eighteenth-century business able to function without the aid of institutions?

8 In what ways did business men raise capital during the Industrial Revolution? What problems did they meet, and how were they overcome?

9 Contrast the ways in which capital was raised for agriculture, transport and industry.

10 What effects did low rates of interest have on economic development?

11 Who made the more important contributions to the Industrial Revolution, the inventor or the innovator?

12 Assess the role of capital formation in advancing the Industrial Revolution.

FURTHER READING

Bagehot, Walter. *Lombard Street*. 1st ed. 1873; Kegan Paul, 1896.
Crouzet, Francois (ed.). *Capital Formation in the Industrial Revolution*. Methuen, 1972.
Dubois, A.B. *The English Business Company after the Bubble Act 1720–1800*. O.U.P., 1938.
Morgan, E. Victor. *A History of Money*. Penguin, 1965.
Perry, F.E. *The Elements of Banking*. Methuen, 1975.
Pressnell, L.S. *Country Banking in the Industrial Revolution*. O.U.P., 1956.
Rolt, L.T.C. *Waterloo Ironworks*. David & Charles, 1969.

Population

33 Population growth

The first official census was in 1801 and, since many people were suspicious of the Government's motives, it is none too reliable. Further, there was no civil registration of births and deaths until 1837. For our period most statistics must come from parish records, either directly, when their collection is a tedious business, or from the Parish Register Abstracts printed in the 1801 census. The Abstracts were compiled by John Rickman from returns sent to him by keepers of records, for every tenth year in the eighteenth century. Parish records, however, are not of births and deaths, but of baptisms and burials conducted by the Church of England. Their weaknesses are that nonconformists shunned the Church of England, that not all incumbents were as meticulous in making their entries as they should have been, and that books of records were sometimes lost. The statistics in this chapter are from *British Economic Growth 1688–1959* by Phyllis Deane and W. A. Cole, and, as the authors themselves admit, they can be no more reliable than their sources. However, it is better to reach some tentative conclusions rather than no conclusions at all.

If we draw a graph to show population changes in England and Wales, we have a curve showing an increasing rate of growth (Fig. A). This means that the progress of the economy was matched by a growth in population. It is possible to analyse this for the country as a whole, but before doing so it is worth considering regional differences. These curves (Fig. B) show the differences between two extreme examples, Sussex and Lancashire. The whole question of population is

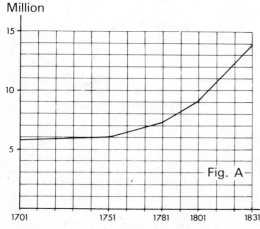

Population of England and Wales

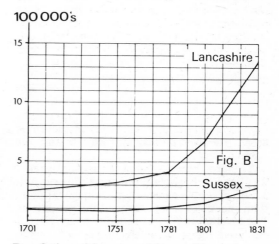

Population of Sussex and Lancashire

173

not only highly conjectural but far more complex than the smooth curve of the national figures would suggest.

The uneven growth we have just glimpsed produced changes in the distribution of population. In the first place we find there was a marked increase north of a line running from the Severn to the Wash. In 1700 the northern section had about 43 per cent of the population, while by 1800 it had increased its share to 50 per cent. Moreover, the North included, as it still does, a great many wide, sparsely populated tracts of country.

However, a more useful division is a threefold one into industrial and commercial, agricultural, and mixed counties. The table shows the different rates of growth in these areas:

	Industrial and Commercial	Agricultural	Mixed
1701	2.0	1.9	1.9
1751	2.3	2.0	1.9
1781	2.8	2.4	2.3
1801	3.8	2.6	2.8
1831	6.3	3.7	4.0

(all figures in millions)

Some agricultural counties actually lost population down to 1750, Cumberland, Derbyshire and Lincolnshire, for example, all declining by some 10 per cent. There was an increase almost everywhere after 1750, but it was the industrial and commercial counties that grew by far the most rapidly. Even here, though, there were important differences. Where the woollen manufacture had been long established, as in Norfolk and Wiltshire, the population grew slowly. Deane and Cole dub these counties 'agricultural', which indeed they became as their industry declined. On the other hand Monmouth, Cheshire and the mining counties of the North-East doubled their population during the eighteenth century, while in Lancashire, the West Riding, Warwickshire and Staffordshire the increase was threefold.

The next question is whether the regions that grew did so by reason of natural increase or immigration. Here it is useful to divide the country in yet another way, and contrast three areas, the North-West, the South and the London area.

The area that attracted the most migrants was London. Between 1700 and 1750 over half a million people moved there, which was more than enough to offset the appalling death rate. The level of migration remained high, but it did lose some of its relative importance as the century wore on: even London began to show a

Migration and Natural Increase by Regions (000s) *

	North-west	South	London
Percentage of population			
1701	20.3	38.7	17.8
1751	21.5	37.8	17.5
1781	24.2	35.6	17.4
1801	26.1	33.4	18.3
1831	28.3	31.4	19.0
Population increase(000's)			
1701–1750	138	66	35
1751–1780	500	356	234
1781–1800	569	381	366
1801–1850	1589	1307	998
Natural increase(000's)			
1701–1750	350	250	−568
1751–1780	604	570	−171
1781–1800	535	640	81
1801–1850	1476	1821	525
Net migration (000's)			
1701–1750	−212	−184	602
1751–1780	−104	−214	405
1781–1800	33	−258	285
1801–1830	113	−515	473

SOURCE: Deane and Cole, p. 118.

*Deane and Cole have a fourth area which they call the North, but as this includes Wales and much of the Midlands, as well as Northumberland and Durham, it is hard to see the value of studying it as if it were an entity. The other three regions, though, do have meaning, geographically and economically.

natural increase, for its death rate fell below its birth rate. Comparing the North-West with the South, we can see that the South lost increasingly from migration, as time went on, while the North-West gained. It is clear, however, that natural increase was far more important to the North-West than migration, so it owed its greater share in the population to the greater fecundity of its people.

We will now look at two counties within the North-West—Lancashire and the West Riding of Yorkshire (see following table). Both had a high rate of natural increase, but that of the West Riding was overall the higher. The migration figures show even more striking differences, for the West Riding lost people down to 1800, while Lancashire gained heavily. There were important economic differences between the counties, for in the West Riding industry was scattered over the countryside, while in Lancashire it was concentrated in urban areas. To say, then, that industrial growth stimulated population is too broad a generalisation. At least down to 1780 it was more likely to do so if the industry took place in cottages and in villages.

174

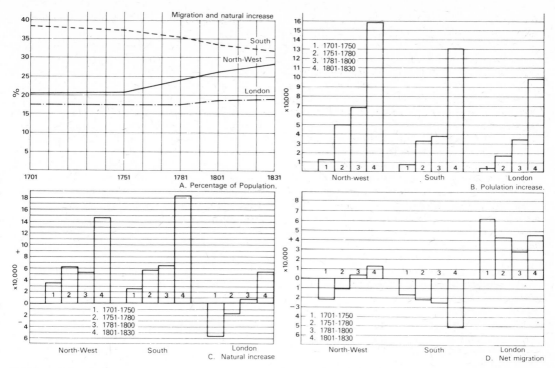

A. Percentage of Population.

B. Polulation increase.

C. Natural increase

D. Net migration

Birth and death rates

However, the counties surrounding Lancashire show high rates of natural increase and heavy losses by migration. It looks as if industrial South Lancashire stimulated population growth over a wide catchment area, and then took the surplus. It is a pity that the figures are all for entire counties. If we could look at South Lancashire and North Cheshire as a unit, and compare it with the rural areas around, the contrast might well be more striking.

To summarise so far, we have seen there were changes in the distribution of population. In the London area this was due, in great measure, to migration, whereas in the newer industrial regions, natural increase was more important. We will now see how movements in the birth and death rates contributed to these changes.

Diagram (d) above shows what happened in the country as a whole. The birth rate increased in the first half of the eighteenth century, then remained fairly steady. The death rate fell and with increasing rapidity, though the bar diagrams do conceal two temporary increases. The first, and more serious, was down to 1740, and it is possible that the death rate was higher than the birth rate in the 1730s. The second increase, in the 1770s, was less important. It is, of course, the widening gap between the birth and death rates that explains the growth in population. Moreover, apart from the initial rise in the birth rate before 1780, the gap grows because of the falling death rate.

Regional differences were important. In London the birth rate showed no substantial rise, and then fell somewhat. The death rate was abominably high before 1750, being 48.8 per 1000. London was killing her own young and many of the hopeful thousands who migrated there. There was the same increase in

Average Annual Rate of Migration and Natural Increase 1701–1830

	Rates of Natural Increase				Rates of Migration			
	1701–50	1751–80	1781–1800	1801–30	1701–50	1751–80	1781–1800	1801–30
West Riding	8.1	14.6	12.6	15.9	−3.4	−0.8	−0.6	1.6
Lancashire	2.7	10.6	13.6	16.0	3.0	−1.2	11.6	6.2
Cumberland	7.8	13.4	10.8	16.3	−10.0	−4.5	−4.2	−4.6
Westmorland	5.4	15.0	12.4	17.1	−7.6	−12.7	−7.0	−8.5

SOURCE: Deane and Cole, p. 115.

175

death rate until 1740, and another rise in the 1770's, but overall it fell rapidly.

The South conforms fairly well to the national average. The birth rate was fractionally lower during the eighteenth century, and a little higher from 1801 to 1830, while the death rate was lower throughout. It is not surprising to find a lower death rate in the countryside.

The North-West shows a totally different picture. The death rate fell, but it began at a much lower level, and finished at roughly the national average. What is remarkable here, is the increase in birth rate down to 1780, and the high level at which this was maintained. In the growing industrial areas, then, the increase in population was due more to a high birth rate than to a declining death rate.

Once again it is instructive to compare Lancashire and the West Riding.

As the cotton industry grew, Lancashire's birth rate soared until it passed the West Riding's. It then maintained its high level, while the West Riding's dropped away. The death rate also grew in Lancashire, to become substantially higher than in the West Riding. That high level was not maintained after 1800, but in both counties the fall was about the same, so they kept their relative positions, more or less.

It seems, then, that industrialisation and high birth rates went together. However, where the industry was concentrated, as in Lancashire, the birth rate was even higher than where it was more diffused, as in Yorkshire. On the other hand the death rate was higher in the industrial towns than in the industrial villages, and that at least is exactly what one would expect.

MIGRATION FROM IRELAND AND THE HIGHLANDS OF SCOTLAND

These two regions have to be treated separately, for their story is quite different from that of the remainder of the British Isles.

The Irish proved more mobile than the British. They had to be. The population of Ireland grew, but there was too little industry to absorb the surplus, so farms were divided and subdivided, particularly in the west. A man with 3 acres grew potatoes on one of them, fed his cow on the second, and grew a cash crop, like oats, on the third, so that he could pay his rent. A man with 1 acre grew potatoes, and his family could go without milk, but he still had his rent to pay. By the time large numbers were in this predicament, however, steamers were giving a regular service on the Irish Sea, so the journey to England was not too difficult. A man could plant his potatoes in the spring, and leave them for his family to tend, while he went to England to help with the haymaking and the corn harvest. With care he could save enough money to pay his rent. He then came home to dig his potatoes and take a holiday through the winter.

The Irish peasant loved his land dearly, but two forces turned his seasonal migration into permanent emigration. The first was the demand for unskilled labour in Britain. Much of the work was irregular and badly paid: working in industry meant living in towns. None the less, uncertainties in Ireland were such that many made the change. Then, on top of the dubious attractions of Britain, came a

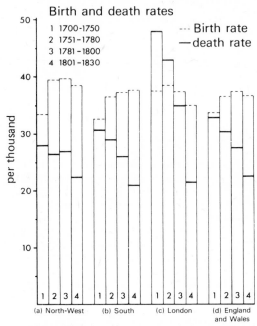

Birth and death rates

1 1700-1750
2 1751-1780
3 1781-1800
4 1801-1830

--- Birth rate
— death rate

per thousand

(a) North-West   (b) South   (c) London   (d) England and Wales

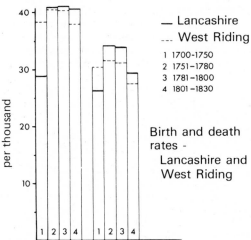

— Lancashire
--- West Riding

1 1700-1750
2 1751-1780
3 1781-1800
4 1801-1830

Birth and death rates -
Lancashire and West Riding

per thousand

force that drove the Irish from home as never before – the potato famine. The crops failed in 1845, 1847 and 1848. Possibly 1½ million people perished, while Britain swarmed with beggars, dying from hunger and typhus. In 1848, 230000 fled to Britain and North America. Emigration did not stop with the famine, the peak year being 1851 when 250000 left. The numbers of emigrants fell after that, but a steady flow continued. The Irish had learnt the bitter lesson that the land must not be expected to feed too many people. So that the eldest child might inherit a viable farm, the remainder had to go.

The other mass exodus was from the Scottish Highlands. During the Napoleonic Wars the price of mutton rose so much that the impoverished chiefs saw a chance of restoring their lost fortunes. All they had to do was to lease their land to sheep graziers from the Lowlands or Northumbria. First of all, though, they had to evict the native inhabitants and their black cattle. For the most part these men were tenants at will, so that there was no legal problem, and during the sixty years following 1790 the chiefs ruthlessly cleared their fellow-clansmen from the Highlands.

The majority of the Irish and Scottish who left their homes went overseas, but large numbers remained in Britain's industrial towns. Their effect on the economy was equivocal. When there was a sudden demand for unskilled labour, as during the railway boom, they were there to meet it. On the other hand there was no shortage of unskilled labour during normal times, so in the long term the immigrants probably checked the growth of the economy. They certainly added to the social problems they found in the industrial towns when they arrived.

34 Population and the economy

The population and the economy of Britain grew together. What were the links between them?

It is tempting to look to agriculture rather than industry, since it would seem that a greater supply of food is more likely to increase population than a greater supply of, say, cotton or iron. More food will result in more people, more people will need more food, so that agriculture and population will spiral upwards together. We cannot demonstrate that this actually happened in Britain, but we do have positive proof that there can be a large increase in population without any help from industry. In 1701 the population of Ireland was perhaps 2.5 million; in 1801 in was 5.2 million, and in 1841 8.2 million. During this time Irish industry was if anything in decline, because of British Government policy and competition from British manufacturers. There were no improvements in public health, medical care or any of the factors traditionally given as reasons for population growth in Britain: there was simply an increase in the number of potatoes.

Much the same thing might have happened in Britain, but if so, how was the cycle set in motion? Did the demands from a growing population encourage progress in agriculture, or did more food give the population the chance to grow?

As we have seen, agricultural improvements had a long history, stretching back to the sixteenth century. Moreover, there was in the 1730s and 1740s a run of good harvests, so that Britain was able to export substantial quantities of grain. Something reversed the rise in the death rate after the 1740s, and something encouraged a rise in the birth rate. It may well have been this abundance of food.

Have we now unearthed the causes of the Industrial Revolution? In the long term there were the agricultural improvements like 'up and down' husbandry and the floating of water-meadows, while in the short term there was the happy accident of twenty years of good weather. Between them they produced an abundance of food, which triggered off the growth in population, and that in turn kindled the Industrial Revolution. Is it safe to assume, though, that the growing population stimulated industry to such an extent? There are authorities who think that it did. J.R. Hicks says: 'The whole Industrial Revolution of the past 200 years has been nothing else but a vast secular boom, largely induced by the unparalleled rise in population.' (*Value and Capital*, p. 302)

Certainly growing population can help industry. Miss Deane argues that because of the growth in population labour was cheap, and that this encouraged investment. If anyone starts a new process or opens a new factory, then he has to attract workers. If there is a shortage of labour he can only do so by offering high wages. On the other hand, if there is unemployment, he can have workers without paying them more than the going rate. Since this will keep his costs low, he can expect good profits, which gives him an incentive to invest. Moreover, he will make his goods cheaply, so demand for them will rise. His profits will grow still more and he will plough them back into his business, the new investment creating an even bigger demand for labour. (Deane, *The First Industrial Revolution*, Chap. 9)

There is a further argument based on the proposal that a growing population means a growing market for goods. Much has been made of foreign trade, but it was erratic, a lot of it was in re-exports, while domestic exports were only in a limited range of goods. Home demand was greater than foreign: as we have seen, the coastal trade alone was more important than overseas trade until the twentieth century. The growing population, then, meant an increasing market, along with an increase in the division of labour, which in turn meant more efficiency in industry. Not only must gross output have increased, but also output per capita.

On the other hand it could be argued that it was industry which stimulated population. We have seen that it encouraged migration into Lancashire and even more into London. Redford in his *Labour Migration in Britain* has shown what happened. Wages were by no means the same everywhere, being highest in the towns, and nearly as high in the villages close by. As the distance from a town increased, though, wages fell, so that they were lowest in the remote areas. A town acted like a magnet. Drawn by the higher wages people would come in from the nearest villages to be replaced by others from beyond, and so on. Clearly industry was calling the tune, attracting workers with its high wages.

Also, growing industries can encourage a high birth rate, as happened in Lancashire and Yorkshire. One is tempted to ask what there was about a cotton mill that encouraged people to have babies. There are a number of possibilities. In the first place quite young children could work in the textile industries, whether they were organised on the factory system or on the domestic. To the workers here a child was an investment that would mature reasonably soon. Secondly the higher wages in the industrial counties may have encouraged people to marry young. Thirdly moral restraints were weaker in the towns, so possibly there were more illegitimate children there than in the country.

We have seen, then, that industry could stimulate population growth by encouraging migration and a higher birth rate. It also saved the country from the 'Malthusian Trap'. Thomas Robert Malthus had prophesied that population would outgrow food supplies: 'Population, when unchecked, increases in a geometrical ratio. Subsistence only increases in an arithmetical ratio. A slight acquaintance with numbers will show the immensity of the first power in comparison with the second.' (*Essay on the Principles of Population*, 1798) As time went on, more and more land would have to come into cultivation, but it would be marginal land and remote from cities. It would need a lot of capital to develop it, a lot of labour to work it, while the transport costs would be high. In other words, agriculture would show diminishing returns. Malthus thought the only civilised way to solve the problem would be for people to delay their marriages, but as this was unlikely he said there would be the savage natural checks of famine and disease. The history of Ireland showed he was not far wrong, and even Britain might have had problems. After 1750 farmers were well able to feed the growing population in normal years, but from time to time a bad harvest brought a shortage. When that happened the country was able to import grain, because it could export manufactured goods to make payment.

We have seen that population and industry can stimulate each other. However, it is not easy to see which was the prime mover. Population may have grown before industry, industry may have grown before population, or both may have grown together. Until we can be precise about timing, we cannot decide between these possibilities. There are these further points to consider: that growing industry can check population, and growing population can check industry.

The concentration of industry in large towns had unfortunate results. We have seen how high the death rate was in London, a city which lured many to high wages and early graves. Also, more people died in Lancashire than in Yorkshire. Moreover, even if they did not die, people who lived in slums were not efficient workers. Lord Shaftesbury described what happened to them:

A young artisan in the prime of life, capable of making his 40/- or 50/- a week, comes up to

London; he must have lodgings near his work; he is obliged to take, he and his wife, the first house that he can find. In a very short time his health is broken down; he himself succumbs, and he either dies or becomes perfectly useless. The wife falls into despair; in vain she tries to keep her house clean; her children increase upon her and at last they become reckless, and with recklessness comes drinking, immorality, and all the consequences of utter despair. (First Report of H.M. Commissioners for Inquiring into the Housing of the Working Classes, 1885, p. 5)

Equally, a growing population can hamper industry. We have seen how the extra people absorbed all the produce of agriculture, which ended exports in corn. Moreover, in order to grow food, farmers gave up industrial crops, so that substitutes had to be imported. Both these developments cost the country foreign exchange.

When a population is increasing it has a high proportion of children and, as any father knows, the surest way to poverty is to have children. Admittedly in the old days parents were ruthless. Mothers would leave their infants on their own for hours so that they could go to the factories, and children started work at any age from three upwards. None the less, a woman cannot work for some time after having a baby, and children and dependants demand food. The average working man had to spend too much money nourishing his young and providing business for farmers. With less children he could have bought more manufactured goods and encouraged industry.

We have seen that a large population can mean a good supply of labour and low wages. However, low wages are a mixed blessing to industry. In the first place people may be so poor that, though the needs are present, there is no effective demand. It would appear that the upsurge in production which came towards the end of the eighteenth century was due more to higher incomes among the middle classes rather than to an increase in the numbers of the labouring poor.

Secondly low wages meant low morale. Adam Smith said, 'When wages are high, we shall always find the workmen more active, diligent and expeditious than when they are low.' At one time it was the tradition that a man stopped work when he had enough money for the week, but that was when there was little to buy but leisure. It was a tradition that died hard, and still lingers in some industries like mining, but by the time Adam Smith made his comment it was on the decline.

Thirdly low wages can discourage innovation. They may encourage investment, but that is not necessarily the same thing. An employer who wishes to increase output may employ more people to work in the same old way, and that is what he is likely to do if labour is plentiful and cheap. He will give work to the unemployed, and he will produce more goods, but he will not increase per capita output, so progress is limited. For example, powerlooms were adopted slowly because there were many handloom weavers. On the other hand if any employer wishes to expand and finds wages are high, he will look for some promising invention that will cut his costs. Innovation will then lead to higher output per capita, and progress is more striking.

A growing population may stimulate the economy in the ways we saw earlier, but it is important that population should not outstrip industry. This happened, so it would seem, in the early nineteenth century. Certainly rapid growth continued, but the economy was progressing like a car that accelerates with its brakes on, and those brakes were the excess population. By reproducing too many of his own kind the British labourer did much to discourage the development of the industries which gave him his livelihood.

35 Case history: an industry in stagnation – hosiery 1800–1850

The stocking-frame was invented by the Reverend William Lee in the reign of Elizabeth I. By the early eighteenth century framework knitting was well established in the 'stocking counties' of Leicestershire, Derbyshire and Nottinghamshire. It was a domestic industry with knitters working in their own homes and 'gentlemen hosiers', who were primarily merchants, in charge. During the course of the eighteenth century business boomed and there were many improvements to the stocking-frame. One of the new inventions was made soon after the turn of the century. It was the notorious 'wide frame' which was to be the target of the Luddites. On it an unskilled man could knit seven or eight times as fast as a skilled man on the traditional narrow frame. The goods were poor quality, but they were cheap, and well suited to the mass market.

There were two unfortunate developments. One was the charging of frame rents in ways which were often unfair to the knitters. The other was the intrusion of middlemen called 'bag-hosiers' between the knitters and the gentlemen hosiers. The bag-hosiers were ruthless and unsympathetic, while the gentlemen hosiers lost contact with manufacturing.

However, at the beginning of the nineteenth century the future of the hosiery industry looked bright enough. Inventors had worked so well on the stocking-frame that it could produce an astonishing variety of fancy goods for the rich, and, moreover, large quantities of the cheap kind for the poor. Spinning had been mechanised, so there was no shortage of raw materials. Admittedly hosiery was still a domestic industry, with the problems of frame rent and middle men, but the gentleman hosiers were still ultimately in control. Also, they had capital, so it only remained for them to imitate the cotton manufacturers and introduce the factory system. This, however, they delayed for fifty years, and their industry suffered.

It was not that the hosiery industry stood still during the first half of the nineteenth century, yet progress came not from new techniques but, as an economist would say, by multiplying the existing units of production, that is by buying more and more frames. Their numbers grew from 30 000 in 1818 to 48 000 in 1844: and as most were wide frames, it is likely that output more than doubled. That apart, though, there was unrelieved gloom.

The framework knitters were soon in as miserable a state as the handloom weavers. In 1810 they were earning up to 15 shillings for a four-day week, but by 1820 they were lucky to make 7 shillings in six days of hard toil. William Felkin described a family he visited at Nottingham in 1844:

I found a female at work between nine and ten at night, her husband and two journeymen at work above her head up the step-ladder over the kitchen place she was occupying. Her age she stated to be 53; she had the appearance of being 70; there were bones, sinews and skin, but no appearance of flesh. She had been the mother of fifteen children, ten of whom her husband and herself had bred up to be stockingers. From sickness in the morning she could not work before her breakfast tea, but laboured at night till ten o'clock, and her clear earnings were about 2/6 weekly. The rent of her frame was 1/6 a week. The house rent was 2/6 a week. It was ill-drained, damp and unhealthy, as were all around it. She was, however, cheerful, uncomplaining, thankful. (op. cit., p. 459)

There were many who were not 'cheerful, uncomplaining, thankful' and who showed their feelings in no uncertain way. The most famous of these were the Luddites who began frame smashing in 1811 and went on, sporadically, until the military and the yeomanry gained the upper hand in 1816. There was a strike in 1819 when the knitters loaded their frames on handcarts and deposited them outside the hosiers' warehouses. There was another strike in 1826 when, as Felkin said, 'scarcely a dozen of hose were made in the three counties for two months', another in 1824, and a final one in 1827. Thereafter the knitters lacked the spirit to fight.

One reason given for the framework knitters' misery was, quite simply, trousers. With the outbreak of war a military style of dress became fashionable, so men wore trousers, which meant they no longer needed fancy stockings. However, changes in fashion were not new; the clothing industry had been buffeted by them before, as it has been many times since. Certainly the stocking-frame could produce all manner of goods, and it was easy enough to adapt to the market. The problems were much deeper.

Another possible reason for the depression was over-production, as the Nottingham hosiers told their workpeople when they demanded higher wages in 1819. It does seem, indeed, that frame rent had encouraged hosiers to invest in too many machines, including the highly productive wide frames. However, when prices fall, the right thing to do is increase production. The cotton manufacturers had countered falling profits on individual items by making more of them, and selling in an ever-widening market. This strategy will not work, though, if it is impossible to increase sales, and here the hosiers met trouble, because of foreign competition.

The hosiery industry had grown so much that half its products went abroad, the two main markets in the eighteenth century being Germany and America. After the Napoleonic Wars, the Saxons, sheltered by tariffs, developed their own industry and captured the German market. Not content with that, they took the American one as well, so that in 1844 they sent 1½ million pairs of stockings across the Atlantic, to Britain's ½ million.

The loss of the export markets explains why the English hosiers could not combat falling prices with higher output, but why did they not mechanise their industry to fight the competition? The answer is that they did, but not until after 1850. The reason for the delay may perhaps be found in the attitudes of the workers and their employers.

If the ordinary man sees his livelihood is in danger because of some new technique, he will be against it. For him, next week's wages are more important than any nebulous future good of his country, or even of the industry he serves. The stocking weavers were typical. They had been earning good wages by making quality goods, and then came the wide frame, which dragged down standards of workmanship, prices and, apparently, wages as well. Their answer was to join the Luddites, seek out the wide frames, and smash them. They were attacking their own industry's most promising invention, but they could hardly be expected to realise that future prosperity depended on mass production for the mass market. The Luddites did have some success, but by 1816 the yeomanry and the hangman had frightened them into good behaviour. They were not, then, responsible for the depression that lasted until after 1850.

If anyone is to be blamed, it was the hosiers. They controlled the industry, they had capital, and they had the authorities on their side to discipline the workers. It was not that they lacked enterprise. Men like Strutt and Morris protected inventors, and they created the highly successful machine-made lace industry. It was not that they were ignorant of the way forward, for as early as 1816 Marc Isambard Brunel had invented a knitting machine he called a 'tricoteur'. It was worked simply by turning a handle, and since its needles were in a circle, it knitted a seamless tube. There was a problem in that it could not vary the number of stitches, so that when it made a stocking it was the same width all the way down, and had to be tortured into shape by steam and hot irons. However, much greater difficulties than that had been overcome in the past, while the rotary motion made it obvious that a steam-engine would drive the machine. The hosiers turned away, shrugging their shoulders, and it was over thirty years before they tried anything like Brunel's tricoteur.

We have already seen how the clothiers caused the death of the woollen industry in East Anglia and the West of England, and here was the same story. The hosiers had become merchant princes, who left the care of the manufacturing to the despised middle men while they concentrated on marketing the finished goods. Many, too, were the heads of old-established firms, and men who inherit wealth are not always as energetic as those who are making their fortunes for themselves. It is hard to believe, though, that all hosiers were the same. Eventually a small progressive group did shoot ahead, dragging the rest after them, so we must ask yet again why it did not happen sooner.

There may be a clue in Felkin's remarks about the family he visited in 1844. His description of the wife is on p. 180. He went on:

Here was the female frame-work knitter, the mother of other female stocking makers, and of sons too – ten in all – added to the numbers of a trade grievously over-loaded with labourers ever since they had belonged to it, and without prospect of relief. Her husband was a man of some character and standing. He was one who made charges on his journeymen, as well as paid them to the hosier; yet neither his labour, and the sum he received as a percentage of theirs, nor his poor wife's long hours, nor, it seems, any other available means or motives operated to send his children one after another into better paid and more promising occupations. (op. cit., p. 459)

Nor was this couple alone, for the population of Nottingham increased from 29 000 in 1801 to 53 000 in 1841.

This helps us understand the hosiers. They had the wide frame together with unlimited cheap labour. When they wanted more stockings all they did was to buy more wide frames and employ more knitters. There seemed no point at all in spending thousands of pounds on machinery when the other way was so much cheaper, in the short term. It was foreign competition, 'the steam driven circulars of Chemnitz', which drove them to action, eventually. In 1851 Hine and Mundella built a mill at Nottingham containing rotary frames, each of which made thirty dozen pairs of hose a week, as against the wide frame's six dozen. At first the factory goods were coarse, but the machines were improved until in the 1860s they were making the highest quality patterned, fully fashioned and seamless hose. The change came late, but, fortunately, not too late to save the industry.

PROBLEMS

1 What, broadly, were the theories of Thomas Robert Malthus? Why did the disaster which he foresaw fail to materialise?

2 What were the factors which led to migration in Britain? How did migration affect economic development?

3 Describe and account for the changes in the geographical distribution of population in Great Britain between 1700 and 1850.

4 Why were there such striking differences in the demographic history of London and industrial Lancashire?

5 Assess the relative importance of agriculture and industry in stimulating population growth.

6 How far was population growth a cause, and how far was it a result of industrial growth?

7 How did population changes (a) assist, and (b) hinder the growth of the economy?

8 Discuss the view that there could have been no Industrial Revolution without an increase in population.

FURTHER READING

Coontz, S.H. *Population Theories and the Economic Interpretation.* 1957.
Flinn, M.W. *British Population Growth 1700–1850.* Economic History Society.
Redford, A. *Labour Migration in England.* Manchester U.P., 1926.

Economic Policy

36 Economic theory and government policy

We can summarise the changes in economic thought by saying that mercantilism gave way to *laissez-faire*.

MERCANTILISM

Mercantilism is not easy to describe because it never existed as a coherent body of ideas. It was, rather, a miscellaneous collection of theories, most of them related, even if rather loosely, but some of them contradictory. Here we can only touch on a few.

Governments in the seventeenth and eighteenth centuries wanted power for themselves and the states which they ruled, so that their aims were no different from those of governments in other periods. Their methods, however, were.

In the first place they wished to keep as much gold and silver as possible in their own countries. No statesmen were so simple that they thought bullion was wealth, but they did know that, if their subjects had plenty, it was easier to raise taxes to pay for an army or a navy in the event of a war. At times there were crude attempts to prohibit the export of bullion, but they failed, so governments tried to regulate trade instead. The aim was to have a favourable balance of payments. If a country exported goods to a greater value than it imported them, foreigners had to pay the balance in gold and silver. To bring this about there were bounties on exports, and heavy duties on foreign manufactured goods, or even outright prohibitions. On the other hand imports of raw materials might be encouraged. The ideal situation was to import raw materials from a neighbour, manufacture them, and then return the finished goods, taking payment in gold coin. For a long time Britain imported wool from Spain and sold cloth to her, a trade which our government thoroughly approved. On the other hand the East India Company could not persuade orientals to buy our goods, so that when their ships came back with calicoes that had not only been bought with gold, but which also competed with English woollens, Parliament prohibited their import.

For Britain, sailors were as essential as gold. During peace-time most ships of the Royal Navy were laid up, to save money. As soon as war came, though, trained sailors were needed in a hurry, so there had to be a large merchant navy to supply them. The press-gang was a vivid example of mercantilism in action. In the seventeenth century the Dutch seemed to threaten Britain more with their large fleet of efficient merchantmen than they did with their warships. They carried English goods, taking gold for their services, and they put English shipowners out of business, driving their men to look for work ashore. To end their competition, Parliament passed a series of Navigation Acts. Briefly, they said that goods carried between England, her colonies and all places outside Europe, had to be taken in English, or English colonial ships. Goods produced in Europe could be imported only in English ships, or those of their country of origin. The coastal trade was for English ships only. As the Dutch felt the same about their merchant navy as Britain did about hers, the Navigation Acts caused wars.

To be powerful a country needs to be self-sufficient. Here again, restrictions on imports helped because they encouraged native industries. There were complications, though, because with the discovery of new lands people had developed a liking for goods such as sugar, tobacco, rum and mahogany. The answer was to have colonies that produced these things, but as other countries had the same idea there were a number of wars, especially with France and Spain. Colonies, once they had been taken, were not allowed to trade with foreigners, or set up industries of their own. It was not altogether unfair, since Britain gave the settlers protection and a market, but it was frustrating for colonial merchants not to be able to buy and sell where they wanted. Britain's mercantilist policy was one reason for the American War of Independence.

Mercantilism and monopoly tended to go together. There was little economic growth in those days, so there was a limited amount of wealth, and governments were logical in preventing people competing with each other to have it. One man's gain was another man's loss, and the state was no richer than before. There were, for example, the Charters granted to the great trading companies, like the Levant Company. These companies had to equip large, heavily armed ships to fight pirates, there were storms and there were foreign rivals. They had enough problems without competitors from England itself, who would only have weakened them and given the Dutch or the French more opportunities. Similarly we have seen how, in the early sixteenth century, Parliament gave a monopoly to the rope-makers of Bridport, in their immediate area. There were only a certain number of ropes to be made, so rivals would weaken Bridport, and it was better for the Navy to buy from one reliable source than to search among several that were destroying each other with competition.

Much in mercantilism had been inherited from the medieval guilds. There was, for example, the Statute of Artificers of 1562, which, among other things, limited the number of apprentices a man might engage, so that no one could ever have enough employees to put others out of business. There were also many regulations saying precisely how goods should be made, what standards they should meet, and at what prices they should be sold. These rules, too, made competition all but impossible, as well as giving the customer a guarantee of quality. Here the aim was to have a harmonious, stable society, with peace between one manufacturer and another, between master and man, and between trader and customer. All the controls checked growth, but that did not matter to them, because growth was not something they expected.

Some mention must be made of the Corn Laws, because they were an essential part of government policy until 1846. Indeed they were strengthened after 1815, when many other restrictions were being removed. Their aim was to encourage exports of corn by bounties and to discourage imports by duties. This was good mercantilism, but it is doubtful whether the governments of the day thought of it as such. The landed interest kept them in office, so they gave them favours.

In mercantilism, then, we see not one policy, but several. However, they did all tend to one course of action, and that was close government control of trade and industry. Those who believed in *laissez-faire* wished that control to end.

LAISSEZ-FAIRE

It was a group of economists, later known as the 'Classical School', who developed the ideas of *laissez-faire*. The term 'classical' implies that, like Homer in the field of literature, they were originators and that they reached the acme of perfection, so that all others had to be judged by their standards. Certainly they were the first to think systematically about economics, and on the other point they seem to be gaining rather than losing respect in the present day. The first and the most famous of the school was Adam Smith, other leaders being Thomas Malthus, David Ricardo and John Stuart Mill. Between them they spanned three-quarters of a century, for Adam Smith's *Inquiry into the Nature and Causes of the Wealth of Nations* appeared in 1776, and Mill's *Principles of Political Economy* in 1848. Toynbee summarised their contributions. Smith analysed the origins of wealth, and Malthus the origins of poverty; Ricardo showed how wealth was distributed, and Mill, how it ought to be. Here it will be enough to consider Adam Smith's work. The others had definite ideas of their own, so they contradicted much that was in the *Wealth of Nations* and elaborated a good deal more. Mill, particularly, had grave doubts about many aspects of *laissez-faire*, suggesting all sorts of ways the state should intervene, especially to solve social problems like poverty and bad housing. None of the writers, though, not even Mill, moved far from Adam Smith's basic idea that the best thing a government could do to increase wealth was to leave business men to pursue their own interests in their own ways.

Adam Smith was born in 1723 and was brought up by his widowed mother. He became Professor of Moral Philosophy at Glasgow University, but in 1762 he gave up his Chair to become tutor to the son of the Duke of Buccleuch. He now had plenty of spare time, which he used to write the *Wealth of Nations*. From 1777 until his death he had an undemanding job as His Majesty's Commissioner of Customs for Scotland, an extraordinary position for someone who was so enthusiastic about free trade.

For Smith, wealth consists of tangible goods. People who make them create wealth, and the remainder are unproductive. He says:

In the same class must be ranked, some both of the gravest and most important, and some of the most frivolous professions; churchmen, lawyers, physicians, men of letters of all kinds; players, buffoons, musicians, opera singers, opera dancers etc. The labour of the meanest of these has a certain value, regulated by the very same principles which regulate that of every other sort of labour; and that of the noblest and most useful, produces nothing which could afterwards purchase or procure an equal quantity of labour. Like the declamation of the actor, the harangue of the orator, or the tune of the musician, the work of all of them perishes in the very instant of its production. (Bk II, Chap. 3)

On this theory, then, manufacturers of plastic gnomes are productive, but members of the Royal Shakespeare Company are not.

How is wealth created? Very important is the division of labour, which Adam Smith explained with his description of pin making:

One man draws out the wire, another straights it, a third cuts it, a fourth points it, a fifth grinds it at the top for receiving the head; to make the head requires two or three distinct operations; to put it on is a peculiar business, to whiten the pins is another; it is even a trade by itself to put them into the paper; and the important business of making a pin is, in this manner, divided into about eighteen distinct operations, which, in some manufactories, are all performed by distinct hands, though in others the same man will sometimes perform two or three of them. I have seen a small manufactory of this kind where ten men only were employed, and where some of them, consequently, performed two or three distinct operations. But though they were very poor, and therefore but indifferently accommodated with the necessary machinery, they could, when they exerted themselves, make among them about

twelve pounds of pins in a day. There are in a pound upwards of four thousand pins of a middling size. Those ten persons, therefore, could make among them upwards of forty-eight thousand pins in a day. Each person, therefore, making a tenth part of the forty-eight thousand pins, might be considered as making four thousand eight hundred pins a day. But if they had all wrought separately and independently, and without any of them having been educated to this peculiar business, they certainly could not each of them have made twenty, perhaps not one pin in a day. (Bk I, Chap. 1)

Another important source of wealth is capital. To produce goods, a man must have a place of work, tools and a stock of raw materials. All these come from people who have a surplus of money, and the will to save and invest it. Who are these people? Smith divides society into three groups: wage-earners, landowners and capitalists. Wage-earners have no surplus, so it is useless to look to them. Landowners have a large surplus, but they squander it on high living, employing for example numbers of 'menial servants' who are quite unproductive. That leaves capitalists. Adam Smith has no illusions about the motives of such men: 'People of the same trade seldom meet together, even for merriment and diversion, but the conversation ends in a conspiracy against the public, or in some contrivance to raise prices.' (Bk I, Chap. 10) However, if a capitalist is allowed to follow his own selfish

Business men. 'People of the same trade seldom meet together . . . but the conversation ends in a conspiracy against the public, or in some contrivance to raise prices.' (*Adam Smith*)

ends, he is almost bound to do good to the rest of society. For example, he will usually invest his money in his own country, where he can keep an eye on it and where he understands the people, their laws and their customs. Further, he will choose those trades and industries which will give the best profits, which means the ones that produce most wealth.

He generally, indeed, neither intends to promote the public interest, nor knows how much he is promoting it. By preferring the support of domestic to that of foreign industry, he intends only his own security; and by directing that industry in such a manner as its produce may be of the greatest value, he intends only his own gain, and he is in this, as in many other cases, led by an invisible hand to promote an end which was no part of his intention. (Bk IV, Chap. 2)

Obviously Adam Smith disliked mercantilism. How could the market expand and the division of labour increase, and how could the 'invisible hand' guide the men of business when there were all the guild regulations, monopolies and government restrictions that had accumulated over the years? The message was clear: trade and industry had to be set free.

Such then were the theories. We must now see how they were put into practice in industry and in trade, and look at the new role adopted by the government as a result.

Many of the old guild regulations died a natural death. If by the eighteenth century everyone in a particular trade agreed that the rules were a nuisance, then they could forget about them, for it was nearly certain that no one in authority would enforce them. Probably that was what happened at Bridport, where the regulation of the hemp and flax industries seems to have ended without any fuss or bother. It was different, though, if there was disagreement. A group of masters might like the old rules or, more probably, the journeymen realised they gave them protection. For example, the law put a limit on the number of apprentices a man could have, so he was compelled to employ adults as soon as his business grew to a certain size.

Towards the end of the eighteenth century workers and others sometimes asked the courts or Parliament to enforce archaic laws, but they met little sympathy. What they did do was to force Parliament to take note, and go to the trouble of repealing the laws. In 1814 the Statute of Artificers was repealed, and then, one by one, individual industries were liberated from their restrictions. In 1825 Huskisson said of the woollen industry:

Within my memory, more than a hundred statutes for the protection of this branch have been repealed. All who dealt in this manufacture were obliged to attend to the most minute legislative regulations. Some statutes regulated the clipping of sheep, some the packing of wool, some the mode of transferring it from one place to another. All the regulations were most precise, and the violations of them were subject to penalties, some amounting to felony. This was most injurious to the manufacture. Most of these laws are now swept away. (Speech in the House of Commons, 26 March 1825)

Introducing free trade was difficult, because powerful interests were against it. None the less, there were some moves, even in the eighteenth century. William Pitt brought a sort of order to the Customs duties, and made the Eden Treaty with France. Pitt's plans were ruined by the war, and after it duties were higher than ever. In the 1790s they had been on average 30 per cent of net imports, while in the 1820s they were around 50 per cent, 1822 being the peak year with 64 per cent. It was not that the rates had been increased but that Britain was importing a larger proportion of goods that paid high duties. However, the Government was not altogether displeased. It had abolished income tax as soon as the war had ended, and badly needed the Customs and Excise money to meet its expenses.

However, as we have seen, there were politicians who wanted free trade. One of these was William Huskisson, who in 1823 became President of the Board of Trade. That same year Parliament passed the Reciprocity of Duties Act. Foreign ships were paying higher port charges than British ships, and the goods they carried paid higher duties as well. The new Act allowed the Government to give foreign ships the same treatment as British ships in our ports, provided they reciprocated. Next, in 1824 and 1825, Huskisson introduced new duties. There was an end to prohibitions and to bounties on exports. Duties on manufactured goods were lowered, and those on raw materials were virtually abolished. As we have seen, the duty on wool came down from sixpence a pound to one penny. Finally the colonies were allowed to trade directly with foreigners, provided they gave preference to Britain.

After 1825, and all through the 1830s, nothing was done save the signing of numerous Treaties of Reciprocity. In the early 1840s the average duty on net imports was still 30 per cent, which was as high as it had been before the war. There were 1146 articles liable for duty, and seventeen of them produced

95 per cent of the revenue; 531 produced only £80000 a year together, showing that the duties on them were virtually prohibitive. Then in 1841 Peel became Prime Minister and he set about completing Huskisson's work. In the first place he reintroduced income tax, so that the Government had an alternative revenue. Next he fixed a maximum duty of 5 per cent on raw materials, and 20 per cent on manufactured goods. In 1845 he went a step further, abolishing duties entirely on some 450 articles, and lowering those on the remainder to 10 per cent.

Peel's greatest achievement was the repeal of the Corn Laws. Agriculture had prospered during the war, with wheat prices reaching as high as 126 shillings a quarter. After the war, though, they fell, being as low as 39 shillings a quarter in 1835. As the landed interest controlled Parliament, there was an Act in 1815 prohibiting the import of wheat unless the home price was 80 shillings a quarter. In 1828 this was changed to a sliding scale, with the duty rising or falling according to price. It was a less rigid system, but it still gave agriculture a good deal of protection.

The Corn Laws caused annoyance to many foreigners, who would gladly have exchanged their wheat for British industrial goods. Traders and manufacturers realised this, and they also felt that the Corn Laws were inflating the price of food and making them pay high wages. Consequently the prices of the goods they manufactured were high as well, which made it difficult to compete with foreigners. They blamed the landed aristocracy for losing them valuable export markets, and in 1838, under the leadership of Cobden and Bright, formed the Anti-Corn Law League. The League mounted an effective campaign, Peel sympathising with them in secret. However, he was leader of the Tory party, which represented the landed interest, and he would never have become Prime Minister if he had not promised to maintain the Corn Laws. Then came the Irish potato famine. People were dying in their thousands, so it was essential to find cheap food, and it seemed as though the Corn Laws stood in the way. In 1846, after months of argument, Peel persuaded Parliament to repeal them. The Tory Party agreed with bad grace, and immediately afterwards many of them joined with the Whigs to drive Peel from office.

The end of the Corn Laws made no difference to the famine, and little difference to agriculture, but it did persuade many foreigners that Britain was sincere when she said she wanted free trade.

Finally, in 1849, the Navigation Acts were repealed. Even Adam Smith had approved of them, because they guaranteed the safety of the country which, he said, was more important than its prosperity. However, as the Royal Navy began to employ more and more professional sailors, the Navigation Acts lost their value. Moreover, the shipping industry became so prosperous that it no longer needed protective laws.

THE NEW ROLE OF GOVERNMENT

Laissez-faire, then, meant an end to the old guild and mercantile restrictions in industry, and free trade. It did not mean, though, that the Government gave up its interest in the economic life of the country but, on the contrary, it intervened more effectively than it had ever done before. All the mercantilist controls looked formidable, but they were not enforced with vigour. The guild restrictions had been largely ignored, while those pioneers of free trade, the smugglers, had pursued their calling largely undisturbed, and quite often with the connivance of the authorities. However, the politicians and civil servants of the nineteenth century were a different breed from those of the eighteenth. As children they had been deprived of mother love, to be brought up in public schools under a regime of Greek and Latin grammar, religious education in which hell-fire figured prominently, cold baths and frequent floggings. Lord Shaftesbury was typical of the new race – a dour, dedicated man, resolved to do people good, however painful they might find the experience. However, although the Government still intervened, and with more force than ever, its aims were different. Above, all, it tried to create the right environment in which trade and industry could flourish.

The nation had to be protected from enemies abroad, and criminals at home, while its laws had to be administered with firmness, tempered by moderation and justice. We see these things happening in, for example, the maintenance of a strong navy, the Metropolitan Police Acts, and the reform of the criminal law.

There was valuable social legislation. *Laissez-faire* did not mean encouraging bullies, so there were measures like the Mines Act and the Factory Acts to regulate working conditions, the Railways Act to ensure that travellers had a fair deal, and in the Public Health Act.

Anomalies, waste and inefficiency in central and local government were attacked. The Reform Act of 1832 produced a more rational electoral system, the Municipal Reform Act tidied local government, while the Poor Law

Amendment Act attempted to clear away a tangled undergrowth that had appeared over the centuries, especially in the forty years of the Speenhamland System. The founder of the new Poor Law System, Edwin Chadwick, was as typical of the reforming civil servants as Shaftesbury was of the politicians. He regularly worked a sixteen-hour day, he was completely dedicated and, as a good disciple of Jeremy Bentham, he had a horror of untidiness and inefficiency. He was, of course, completely incorruptible.

Finally there was an intensification of something which the Government had always done, which was to carry on commercial diplomacy. In her excellent book *British Commercial Policy and Trade Expansion* Judith Blow Williams shows how hard the Government and its diplomats worked to wring concessions from foreigners for the benefit of British traders.

All this is like the change which took place in gardening, when the formal style gave way to the informal. The gardener no longer tortured plants into predetermined shapes by pruning and training, but instead left them alone to grow naturally to their full size, and with full vigour. That did not mean, however, that he gave up working, for the result would have been a jungle. Instead he concentrated not on the plants themselves but on creating the right conditions for them. Whether the result was more pleasing is a matter of taste, but there was certainly more growth.

It has sometimes been asked how far Adam Smith and others of his school influenced economic policy. The question can never of course be answered fully, but it would be naïve to suppose it was simply a matter of politicians' reading the *Wealth of Nations*, being convinced by its arguments, and then changing government policies. It is far more likely that the economists, the business men and the politicians all responded in their different ways to the same stimulus. The static economy which had produced mercantilism gave way to a dynamic economy which produced *laissez-faire*. The economists wrote their books, the business men demanded those freedoms which suited them, and the Government adopted complete free trade as its policy. The business men probably started it all, because they saw they needed certain freedoms if they were to seize new opportunities, but they were not convinced free traders, for they still wanted the restrictions that favoured them. Politicians were bombarded with conflicting claims, but those who could be dispassionate saw that free trade all round was the best policy. They then drove the business community to it blow by blow, insisting with each group that if it were to have those freedoms of which it approved, then it must accept those which it did not. The fact that an economist of Adam Smith's stature gave the politicians theoretical justification for their actions must have comforted them, even though, one suspects, they only knew of his ideas second-hand from the occasional society lecture, and the writings of Harriet Martineau.

37 Case history: Free trade in wool

Free trade in wool was largely the result of conflict between the wool growers and the woollen manufacturers.

During the eighteenth century the Government took great care of the country's leading industry, and in the early nineteenth century was still pampering it. In the first place imported manufactures were subject to a duty of 50 per cent which virtually kept them out; secondly, imported raw wool was subject to a nominal duty of one penny a pound only; and thirdly, English growers were forbidden to export any of their own clip.

However, at the end of the Napoleonic Wars, the growers claimed that they had problems. Some farmers, they said, had no choice but to keep sheep, even if it was just to manure their upland pastures where the dung cart could not go. Often their wool was an embarrassment to them, since it did not sell, and they had to keep it in store for a year or more. They proposed that in time of glut they should be allowed to export their wool and that imports should pay an increased duty.

Lord Erskine put the growers' point of view in a book called *Armata*, a fictional name for Great Britain:

We have a creature called the bletur, which is not only the perfection of animal food, but whose covering, given it by nature, becomes, when manufactured, our own also, and for many ages has been the pride and wealth of our country. Would you then believe, that though other nations produce the same animals at an inferior price, from their climate and untaxed condition, so as to render all competition ridiculous, yet this raw material is suffered to be imported, and worked up here, whilst the breeders of Armata can scarcely pay their shepherds for the care of their flocks, and are everywhere breaking up their farms, even in those parts of the island proverbially famous for their production? (Quoted in Bischoff, op. cit., Vol. 1, p. 428)

He went on to complain that Parliament had not considered the alarming increase there had been in imports, the possibility of improving breeds – probably a reference to the merino – or the damage to the balance of payments caused by importing a raw material that could be produced at home.

For their part, the manufacturers were worried that a rise in the price of raw wool would make their finished goods too dear to compete in the export markets, especially Europe. They argued also that English wool was of such poor quality that they needed to import to keep their goods to standard. Addressing his colleagues, James Bischoff, the Chairman of the London Committee of the Woollen Trade, said:

You, as manufacturers, are as good judges of the quality of wool as the growers; you see it in all its stages, and have the best means of obtaining a perfect knowledge of its properties. I would, therefore, ask if you have ever seen any produced in England equal to the finest qualities of wool imported from Spain and Germany? I admit that it is very possible that a very wealthy agriculturist, by the greatest care and attention, might produce a small quantity of beautiful wool, but I think you will agree with me, that you could not collect in England sufficient to supply a single loom, for one year, equal to the finest Saxon and Spanish wools you are in the habit of working up. My argument then holds good, that foreign wool is necessary for our manufactures of superfine cloth, and that wool for that purpose cannot be grown in England of sufficient quality or quantity. It consequently becomes a question of serious moment, whether it be prudent and politic to tax a raw material absolutely necessary to a most important branch of our manufactures. (ibid., p. 447)

Such was the argument for free imports. Against free exports it was said that British wool was so excellent that it would be fatal to allow foreigners to have any! They would mix it with their own to produce woollens the equal of any made in Britain. Bischoff wrote to Lord Milton: 'The length of the staple of foreign wool is about two inches; the length of Lincolnshire wool from four to five inches; foreign wool is brittle; it will not bear the process of combing; English wool is more tough, and is not only finer and better in appearance, but in reality.' He admitted farmers sometimes had four or five years' growth in their barns, but claimed: 'I should think it more for the interest of the country and its future prosperity, that the raw material should rot in their chambers, or even be burnt, than that it should be allowed to be exported.' (ibid., pp. 414–15)

A fair point which Bischoff made was that, since foreign industries were heavily protected, the British one needed to be as well. France, Holland and Belgium all put prohibitive duties on exported raw wool, while Spain charged anything up to a shilling a pound, which was expensive enough.

Inevitably manufacturers complained about the Corn Laws. They drove up the cost of food, which in turn drove up wages, and hence the price of their finished goods. They were already fighting foreign competitors under the disadvantage of a tax on food and, if they had to pay one on their raw material as well, it would bring ruin.

Neither growers nor manufacturers, then, believed in *laissez-faire*, since both groups wanted the restrictions that suited them. On the other hand growers wanted free exports, and manufacturers free imports, so that between them they were advocating complete free trade in raw wool. An unbiased outsider was bound to see this. One such was Lord Milton, M.P. for York, who took the view that it was unfair to forbid a grower to sell his wool abroad when the British manufacturer would not buy it. Equally, though, Lord Milton was against import duties: 'First, because I believed them calculated to injure our manufactures; secondly, because they appeared to me founded upon the unjust principle of affording relief to one description of persons at the expense of another; and finally, because they militated against those maxims of free trade which commercial nations are, above all others, interested in advocating, even in cases where a departure from them appears to promise some immediate advantage.' Duties and controls, he said, would not bring prosperity to the industry. 'It depends, I conceive, together with all other branches of our commerce, upon the security of our persons, the free enjoyment of our property, and the impartial administration of justice.' (ibid., pp. 410–11)

Lord Milton wanted the role of the State to be reduced to the absolute minimum.

Unfortunately for the manufacturers, the Government was having problems. It needed revenue, so in 1819 it placed a duty of sixpence a pound on imported wool. One result of the duty was that it gave the Government a lever. When it could afford to, it offered to reduce the duty to a nomimal penny a pound, if the manufacturers agreed to the free export of wool. In 1823 they were asked their opinion, and we can see the agony of their dilemma from a reply sent by a group in Leeds:

Resolved unanimously, that it is the opinion of this meeting that the prosperity, and almost the existence of our foreign trade in woollen cloth, to any other countries than our own colonies, depends upon the repeal of the tax on the importation of foreign wool.

That as manufacturers and exporters of woollen cloths, we are persuaded that the exportation of the wool of the growth of this country will be a smaller evil to us than that we are now suffering from the tax on import.

That in this painful alternative, we are reduced to the necessity of consenting to the export of our native wools, only as the less evil, although not without the deep-felt conviction that such export must be a serious injury to the worsted manufactures of this country, which, under the present system, have flourished, are increasing, and give employment to a very extensive population. (ibid., Vol. II, p. 40)

The proposals became law in 1824, but clearly there was no willing acceptance of free trade. The manufacturers agreed to a hard bargain, but they were still thinking longingly of the privileges they had once enjoyed.

There remained the duties on manufactured goods. Huskisson wished to reduce them and, luckily for him, he had yet another lever he could use against the manufacturers. There were import duties on the olive oil they needed, and on dyestuffs such as indigo and logwood. In 1825 Huskisson approached Bischoff, and asked him about a reduction of duties. Bischoff in his reply said a lot about the low costs of manufacture in European countries, especially wages: 'So long as the price of bread in Prussia is threepence or fourpence, and in England elevenpence and one shilling, a heavy protecting duty must be required on all woollen articles, sufficient to cover the taxes falling peculiarly on the trade and the increased cost of labour.' (ibid., Vol. II, p. 71) Not only must the duties on raw materials go, so must the Corn Laws. It was a good try, but James Bischoff could hardly achieve what Peel only managed with difficulty, and with the Irish potato famine for a reason. What Huskisson offered was to end the duties on raw materials, and to keep enough duty on foreign manufactures to compensate for the extra costs inflicted by the Corn Laws. They agreed to 15 per cent. This was later reduced in stages to a nominal amount, first by Peel and then by Gladstone.

PROBLEMS

1 What were the aims of the Corn Laws? How far were they achieved?

2 What were the aims of the Navigation Acts? How far were they achieved?

3 What was mercantilism? Does the fact that it was considered the wrong policy by 1850 mean that it was also wrong in 1700?

4 How far did the policy of protection help, and how far did it hinder (a) agriculture, (b) industry, and (c) trade?

5 How much did the writings of the Political Economists contribute to the demise of mercantilism?

6 Why did it take so long to introduce free trade? Why was it somewhat easier to end restrictions in industry?

7 Which institutions and activities suffered as a result of free trade, and which ones benefited?

8 How did the role of government change during our period?

9 Discuss the view that government intervention in the economic life of the country was more effective by 1850 than at any time before.

FURTHER READING

Barber, William J. *A History of Economic Thought*. Penguin, 1967.
Barnes, D. G. *A History of the English Corn Laws*. Kelly, 1930.
Taylor, A. J. *Laissez-faire and State Intervention in Nineteenth-century Britain*. Macmillan, 1972.

Conclusion

Interpreting the Industrial Revolution

Interpretations of the Industrial Revolution are as numerous as its historians. There have, however, been two main controversies – one about results, and the other about causes. The first of these excited most interest down to the 1930s, and the other since the Second World War.

The first important group of writers were the novelists of Dickens's generation. They exposed the social evils of their times vividly, and with great force, though they were not consciously commenting on the Industrial Revolution. Carlyle did so, however, when in his *Past and Present* he looked back with nostalgia to the golden age of pre-industrial England. Carlyle, though, made no systematic study of the Industrial Revolution, the first historian of note to do so being Arnold Toynbee. It was he who gave currency to the phrase 'Industrial Revolution', though he was not the first to use it.

Toynbee taught political economy at Oxford, so his work led him to think about the social problems that came in the wake of industrialisation. He was a practical man, as well as being an academic, for he became a Poor Law Guardian, took an active part in politics, and worked hard for trade unions and co-operative societies. He also spent many of his holidays living in the slums of the East End of London. Unfortunately he was physically weak, dying at the age of thirty. His *Industrial Revolution* has a strange distinction in that it was, in a sense, written after the author's death. Two of his students compiled it from their lecture notes.

Toynbee had only a passing interest in causes. When he emerged from the London slums he was burning to discuss them, and he also wished to describe the Industrial Revolution that had created them. Why that revolution had come about hardly concerned him, so he was content to ascribe it to Adam Smith and the steam-engine.

Toynbee's view of life in pre-industrial Britain was balanced, in that he did not see it as a golden age, and he recognised that there had been improvements since, especially in the wages of artisans. However, he firmly believed that the old semi-rural society had been tightly knit, stable and relatively contented until the Political Economists unleashed the hell-hound of free competition. *Laissez-faire* destroyed all harmony, and put in its place the clash of warring interests:

These antagonisms were to come out more strongly than ever after Adam Smith's time. There were dark patches even in his age, but we now approach a darker period – a period as disastrous and as terrible as any through which a nation ever passed: disastrous and terrible, because, side by side with a great increase in wealth, was seen a great increase in pauperism: and production on a vast scale, the result of free competition, led to a rapid alienation of classes and to the degradation of a large body of producers. (op. cit., p. 84)

In Toynbee's view, students of the Industrial Revolution should concentrate on its social problems, since these were its most important facet.

The Fabian Socialists took up the cause. In the early years of the twentieth century two husband and wife teams, the Hammonds and the Webbs, produced monumental works cataloguing the sufferings of the working classes

191

at the hands of the capitalists. They attempted to show that the advance of the Industrial Revolution had meant an increase in degradation, poverty and strife. 'The history of England at this time,' said the Hammonds, 'reads like the history of civil war.' (Skilled Labourer)

The Fabians were supported, of course, by the Marxists, whose whole view of history depended on a belief in the increasingly unequal distribution of wealth under capitalism. They held that more and more wealth would become concentrated in fewer and fewer hands, so that the rich would become richer, and the poor poorer, until revolution established the dictatorship of the proletariat, and fair shares for the survivors.

There were voices on the other side. Macaulay wrote a measured defence of industrialisation (Edinburgh Review, January 1830). Trollope in The Warden dismissed Dickens as 'Mr Popular Sentiment'. Towards the end of the century A.L. Bowley and G.H. Wood both produced statistics of wages which showed that the Industrial Revolution had brought an improvement in the living standards of the working classes. The articles by Bowley and Wood appeared before the Hammonds and the Webbs wrote their books, but they were either unaware of the research or chose to ignore it.

However, as the enemies of the Industrial Revolution wrote with more force and feeling than the members of the other school, they held the field until 1926. That year J.H. Clapham published the first volume of his Economic History of Modern Britain. In his introduction he had something to say about legends in history, while in the main body of the work he systematically demolished the fancy that living standards in general declined during the years from 1800 to 1850.

After the Second World War there came a shift in interest. Western governments were giving underdeveloped countries massive economic aid, and they wanted it spent wisely. They turned to economists to instruct them in the tricks of economic growth, and the economists looked, among other places, to the first Industrial Revolution. They felt that if its causes could be discerned they would provide valuable lessons that could be applied in the twentieth century. However, the economists looked in vain. The historians had a deplorable lack of system, appearing to be groping around in candlelight. The economists determined to penetrate the blackness with the twin searchlight beams of measurement and economic theory. All would have been splendid had they discovered enough data to measure

and had they agreed over their theory. As it was, they fuelled the controversies they found, and started a good many more.

The most lively contribution to the debate has come from W.W. Rostow, so it is worth spending some time considering his Stages of Economic Growth. Rostow defines five stages of growth: the traditional society, the preconditions for take-off, the take-off, the drive to maturity, and the age of mass consumption.

The traditional society is almost static. There may be changes caused, for example, by peasants grabbing land from each other, but they do not increase total wealth. There may be some growth in trade and production, but it has definite limits because people know so little of science and technology. Also, if there is any surplus wealth, land-owners and clerics take it and squander it on high living or on such non-productive institutions as baronial halls, monasteries and cathedrals. English society was traditional in the Middle Ages, and for some time afterwards.

Under the pre-conditions for take-off some growth appears, particularly in mining and agriculture, which are the easiest to develop. Farmers supply food to the towns and, if there is a surplus, it can be exported to earn foreign currency, or, if not, then at least there will be no need to import. Farmers prosper and buy manufactured goods, while, along with the mine-owners, they may supply much of the capital needed to develop industry. Social overhead capital will accumulate, particularly transport. Rostow points out that roads, canals and railways are so expensive that government help is usually needed to pay for them. There are new political attitudes, 'reactive nationalism' being particularly likely to stimulate change. Germany modernised her economy after her conquest by Napoleon, and so did Russia after losing wars throughout the nineteenth century, and China, following a hundred years of humiliation. There was reactive nationalism in Britain, a small island close then to a hostile continent and which suffered at the hands of the Spaniards, the Dutch and the French. Britain met the preconditions for take-off in the early and middle years of the eighteenth century.

The third stage, and the most crucial, is the 'take-off into self-sustained growth'. Rostow says:

The take-off is the interval when the old blocks and resistances to steady growth are finally overcome. The forces making for economic progress, which yielded limited bursts and enclaves of modern activity, expand and come to dominate the Society. Growth becomes its normal condition. Compound interest becomes built, as it were, into its habits and institutional structure. (op. cit., p. 7)

The take-off is powered by 'leading sectors'. They develop rapidly and have 'forward, backward and lateral effects'. The forward effects of the cotton industry, for example, were on the manufacture of clothing, the backward effects were on coal and engineering, and the lateral effects were on transport and housing for workers. Rostow says that textiles are rarely a leading sector, but the British cotton industry was an important exception.

For leading sectors to appear, productive investment must increase from about 5 per cent of national income to about 10 per cent. It sounds easy, but it is like asking someone who has just run half a mile in two minutes to carry on and complete the mile in four. In the first place there have to be institutions that encourage and handle savings, such as joint stock companies and banks. Secondly there must be 'income shifts' from people like landowners, to productive men who will plough their profits back into their businesses. This, in turn, supposes that a class of 'productive men' exists. It depends on the traditional society. The upper classes must form a tight magic circle which ambitious outsiders cannot easily enter, so making them frustrated, but, on the other hand, the society must be free enough to allow them to make their way in business. Here, it is usual to say something about the 'protestant ethic'. In Britain, nonconformists who had no hope of high office in Church or State compensated themselves by making fortunes in business and, consequently, some writers have given them the main credit for the Industrial Revolution. However, Rostow warns:

In a world where Samurai, Parsees, Jews, North Italians, Turkish, Russian and Chinese civil servants (as well as Huguenots, Scotsmen and British north-countrymen) have played the role of a leading élite in economic growth, John Calvin should not be made to bear quite this weight. (ibid., p. 51)

The take-off is compressed into twenty years, which Rostow dates precisely in Britain as coming between 1783 and 1803.

Following take-off comes the drive to maturity. Of societies at this stage, Rostow says: 'They were all run by men who knew where they were going. They were all caught up in the power of compound interest and in the possibility of transforming one sector after another, by extending the tricks of modern technology.' (ibid., p. 70) At the same time the old leading sectors lose their momentum, but others appear, like the railway industry in Britain. The drive to maturity normally takes forty years, and in Britain was complete by 1840.

Finally we enter the age of mass consumption. Here, as indeed at every stage, a society has several choices. It can, if it wishes, burn up its wealth in an armaments race, ending in total war with its neighbours. More hopefully, it will follow the American example of pleasant suburban houses containing every gadget known to man, very large motor cars and lots of babies. To build a welfare state is another possibility. Indeed, there is no reason why a modern society should not have all these things and many others, provided of course it avoids the total war.

There is now a very awkward gap in the British development, for the United Kingdom did not enter the age of mass consumption until the 1930s at the earliest or, more likely, the 1950s. Frankly, Rostow's explanations are lame. His main point is that in 1850, and for a long time afterwards, many people lived in poverty. We were a mature society but a poor one, and it took us a long time to become rich. However, it is clear from the rest of the book that a mature society is, by definition, a wealthy one. Rostow comes close to saying that by 1850 Britain was wealthy but not rich.

Rostow's views have not passed unchallenged. He was bound to agitate communist economists, but others who keep their political views out of sight have also had their misgivings. As far as British history is concerned, the facts do not fit the theories any too well. We have already seen that there is a gap of eighty or a hundred years between supposedly reaching maturity and entering the age of mass consumption, and there are problems earlier than that. H. J. Habbakuk and Phyllis Deane cannot believe that the British take-off was compressed into the twenty years between 1783 and 1803. There are no figures to prove or disprove that in that time investment increased from 5 per cent of national income to 10 per cent, but they say it could not possibly have happened. They admit that there were striking changes in iron and cotton, but they were not strong enough to have 'ignited' the Industrial Revolution. If anything did act as a leading sector at the end of the eighteenth century, then most likely it was foreign trade, but precisely how it influenced the rest of the economy we do not know. On the face of it, it looks as if it had more to do with the success of the Royal Navy than with the growth of British industry.

Not only is it difficult to find anything decisive in the twenty years singled out by Rostow, but plenty happened both before and after. Growth began as early as 1740, but the first major outburst of industrial activity did not come until the railway boom a hundred years later. Then capital investment did indeed take 10 per cent of national income. Habbakuk and Deane summarise their arguments as follows:

In the end it seems that the most striking characteristic of the first take-off was its gradualness. Professor Nef has traced the process of industrialisation back to the sixteenth century. The sustained rise in the rate of growth in total output probably dates back to the 1740's. If the 1780s be taken as the starting point for the revolutionary changes in industrial technique and organisation, then it took about a century for the long term rate of growth in real incomes to rise from about 1% per annum to just over 2% per annum. It took as long for the share of agriculture in the national product to drop to near 10% and another half century for it to fall below 5%. The evidence suggests a long, steady climb, inspired by periodic bursts of energy or of enterprise and lagging seriously only in the twentieth century inter-war period. ('The Take-off in Britain' in Rostow, *The Economics of Take-off into Sustained Growth*.)

Apart from attacks on individual points in Rostow's theories, there is a rival school of thought that discounts them entirely. The fundamental question is whether economic growth is balanced or unbalanced. Suppose the government of an underdeveloped country wishes to stimulate its economy, how should it proceed?

Economists who believe in balanced growth stress the importance of interrelations. Industries and services must grow together, because they have to create markets for each other. Demand is all-important, as it is demand that creates growth. Investment, therefore, should be over a wide range of activities, which will give each other support. The weakness of this argument is that it assumes that there will be enough talented managers and skilled workers, together with raw materials in sufficient variety and quantity to meet so many needs. Balanced growth, then, looks after demand, and leaves supply to look after itself.

Those who favour unbalanced growth point out that in a primitive society there is likely to be a shortage of human talent and materials. They stress, too, that for industry to be successful, there must be economies of scale. Per capita output will be higher in a few large concerns than in a large number of small ones, because there can be more division of labour, a greater degree of mechanisation, and so forth. Investment, therefore, should be concentrated in a few sectors which can be readily supplied with materials and labour, and in which economies of scale are possible. Care should be taken, of course, to select those that have strong linkages with the rest of the economy. As the favoured industries develop, there will be what J.A. Schumpeter, in his *Theory of Economic Development*, calls 'creative disturbance'. Other sectors will be faced with sudden and heavy demands which they can only meet if they stir themselves. Growth, therefore, will be rapid instead of leisurely. The weakness of the theory of unbalanced growth is that it assumes it will be possible to sell a large volume of goods which are limited in variety. Unbalanced growth, therefore, looks after supply, but leaves demand to look after itself.

Which type of growth took place during the British Industrial Revolution? Clearly Rostow thinks it was unbalanced growth, but there are others who disagree, as for example E.M. Hartwell. In one way the present book supports Hartwell. We have looked at the most important sectors of the economy in turn – agriculture, industry, transport, trade, capital and population. We have seen that they all made such vital contributions, that there could not have been an Industrial Revolution without any one of them. Equally, though, it does seem that progress in each individual sector was as much the result of the more general growth as its cause. The impression is of a highly complex machine, far more complex than, say, a motor car where the various parts only react on the ones near to them. In the economic machine every part reacts on every other, and the web of their relationships is so complex that it defies analysis. Surely, then, the British Industrial Revolution was an example of balanced growth.

On the other hand we cannot dismiss the cotton industry at all lightly. Within forty years it overtook wool, formerly the largest industry in Britain: it adopted a new technology: it left its workers' cottages to move into highly organised factories: it dominated the export trade. More than that it stimulated other activities, like chemicals, building, engineering, coal, iron, banking and transport. It even encouraged a rapid increase in population. Surely we see here a leading sector working just as Rostow describes.

Such, then, are the two rival opinions. Unfortunately it is impossible to decide between them, because no one understands the secrets of economic growth.

GENERAL BIBLIOGRAPHY

Ashton, T.S. *The Industrial Revolution.* Home University Library, 1948.
——. *Economic Fluctuations in England 1700–1800.* Manchester U.P., 1959.
Clapham, J.H. *An Economic History of Modern Britain.* C.U.P., 1939.
Deane, Phyllis. *The First Industrial Revolution.* C.U.P., 1965.
Deane, Phyllis and Cole, W.A. *British Economic Growth 1688–1959.* C.U.P., 1969.
Flinn, M.W. *The Origins of the Industrial Revolution.* Longmans, 1966.
Gayer, A.D., Rostow, W.W. and Schwartz, A.J. *The Growth and Fluctuations of the British Economy 1790–1850.* O.U.P., 1953.
Hartwell, R.M. *The Industrial Revolution and Economic Growth.* Methuen, 1971.
Mantoux, P. *The Industrial Revolution in the Eighteenth Century.* Cape, 1928.
Rostow, W.W. *The Stages of Economic Growth.* O.U.P., 1960.
——. *The Economics of Take-off into Sustained Growth.* Macmillan, 1963.
Toynbee, Arnold. *The Industrial Revolution.* 1884; David & Charles, 1969.

Other works consulted
Ackland, John, E. 'Dorset Buttony', *Proceedings of the Dorset Natural History and Antiquarian Field Club,* Vol. XXXV, 1914.
Addington, Stephen. *An Inquiry into the Reasons for and against Inclosing Open Fields.* J.W. Piercy, Coventry, 1772.
Ashley, W.J. *British Industries.* Longmans, 1903.
Baines, Edward. *History of the Cotton Manufacture of Great Britain.* Fisher & Jackson, 1837.
Banks, John. *Treatise on Mills.* W. Richardson, London, 1795.
Bischoff, James. *A Comprehensive History of the Woollen and Worsted Manufactures.* Smith Elder, 1842.
Bond Head, Sir Francis. *Stokers and Pokers, or the London and North Western Railway 1849.* Cass, 1968.
Booth, Henry. *An Account of the Liverpool and Manchester Railway.* Wales & Baines, 1831.
Bover, M.C. *The City of London.* Museum Press, 1962.
Bright, Mervyn. *Buttony: The Old Button Shop, Lytchett Minster.* 1971.
Britten, J. and Brayley, E.W. *The Beauties of England and Wales,* Vol III. London, 1802.
Brown, Robert (Brown of Markle). *Treatise on Rural affairs.* Longmans, 1811.
J.C. *The Compleat Collier.* G. Conyers, 1708.
Chambers, J.D. *Nottinghamshire in the Eighteenth Century.* Cass, 1960.
Church, R.A. *Victorian Nottingham 1815–1900.* Cass, 1966.
Claridge, A. *General View of the Agriculture in the County of Dorset.* Board of Agriculture, 1793.
Clew, Kenneth. *The Dorset and Somerset Canal.* David & Charles, 1971.
Cooke Taylor, W. *Notes of a Tour in the Manufacturing Districts of Lancashire.* Duncan & Malcolm, 1842.
A Country Gentleman. *The Advantages and Disadvantages of Inclosing Waste Lands and Open Fields.* London, 1772.
Cross, Thomas. *The Autobiography of a Stage-Coachman.* Hurst & Blackett, 1861.
Davies, David. *The Case of the Labourers in Husbandry.* Robinson, 1799.
Dunn, Mathias. *Treatise on the Winning and Working of Collieries.* Newcastle upon Tyne, 1848.
Economic History Review.
Farey, John. *A Treatise on the Steam Engine.* Longmans, 1827; David & Charles, 1971.
Felkin, William. *History of the Machine-wrought Hosiery and Lace Manufacture.* 1867; David & Charles, 1967.
Forbes, Francis. *Dissertation on Great and Small Farms.* London, 1778.
Francis, J. *A History of the English Railway 1820–1845.* 1845.

Fynes, Richard. *The Miners of Northumberland and Durham*. John Robinson, 1873.

Galloway, Robert L. *A History of Coal Mining in Great Britain*. Macmillan, 1882.

Griffith, G. T. *Population Problems of the Age of Malthus*. Cass, 1967.

Guest, Lady Charlotte. *Extracts from Her Journal*, ed. Earl of Bessborough. John Murray, 1850; 2 vols, 1952.

Hammond, J. L. and Barbara. *The Skilled Labourer*. Longmans, 1919.

Helps, Arthur. *The Life and Labours of Mr Brassey*. 1872; Evelyn, Adams & MacKay, 1969.

Henson, Gravenor. *History of the Framework Knitters*. 1831; David & Charles, 1970.

Howitt, William. *The Rural Life of England*. Longmans, 1838.

Hutton, W. *History of Derby*. J. & J. Robinson, London 1817.

Jackson, J.A. *The Irish in Britain*. Routledge & Kegan Paul, 1963.

James, John. *History of the Worsted Manufacture in England*. Longmans, 1857.

Jeans, J.S. *A History of the Stockton and Darlington Railway*. Longmans, 1875.

Jenkins, Alan. *Stock Exchange Story*. Heinemann, 1973.

Johnson, Cuthbert W. *The Advantages of Railways to Agriculture*. n.d. c.1836.

King, Gregory. *National and Political Observations and Conclusions upon the State and Condition of England*. London, 1696.

Lawson, A. *The Farmer's Practical Instructor*. Mackenzie & Dent, 1827.

Leifchild, J.R. *Our Coal Fields and Our Coal Pits*. Longmans, 1853.

Loudon, J.C. *Designs for Laying Out Farms and Farm Buildings*. J. Harding & Longman, 1811.

Low, David. *Elements of Practical Agriculture*. Longmans, 1847.

Lyell, K.M. (ed.) *Memoir of Leonard Horner*. Women's Printing Society, 1890.

Mathias, Peter. *The First Industrial Nation*. Methuen, 1969.

Mushet, David. *Papers on Iron and Steel*. John Weale, 1840.

Nimrod. *The Chase, the Road and the Turf*. Edward Arnold, 1898.

Orwin, C.S. and Sellick, R.J. *The Reclamation of Exmoor Forest*. David & Charles, 1970.

Pahl, Janice. *The Rope and Net Industry of Bridport*. Unpublished thesis, 1959 (in Poole Library).

Parliamentary Papers 1839, Vol. XLII, *1840* Vol. XXIII. Reports from the Assistant Hand-Loom Weavers' Commissioners.

Parliamentary Papers 1842, Vol. XV. Children's Employment Commission (Mines).

Priestley, Joseph. *Historical Account of the Navigable Rivers, Canals and Railways throughout Great Britain*. 1831; Cass, 1967.

Radcliffe, William. *Origin of the New System of Manufacture Commonly Called 'Power Loom Weaving'*. 1828.

Raistrick, A. *Dynasty of Iron Founders – The Darbys of Coalbrookdale*. Longmans, 1853.

Roll, Sir Eric. *History of the Firm of Boulton and Watt 1775–1805*. Cass, 1968.

Russell, C.A. *Mineral Resources and the Growth of Technology*. Open University, 1970.

Schumpeter, E.B. *English Overseas Trade Statistics 1697–1808*. C.U.P., 1960.

Schumpeter, J.A. *Theory of Economic Development*. Cambridge, Mass., 1934.

Searle, Mark. *Turnpikes and Toll Bars*. Hutchinson, 1930.

Sharp, Dr William. *A Treatise upon Coal Mines*. 1769.

Sinclair, Sir John. *General Report on Enclosures*. Board of Agriculture, 1808.

Smith, Adam. *The Wealth of Nations*. 1776; Everyman ed., 1910.

Stevenson, William. *General View of the Agriculture of Dorset*. Board of Agriculture, 1812.

Thomas, R.H.G. *London's First Railway – The London and Greenwich*. Batsford, 1972.

Tull, Jethro. *The New Horse Hoeing Husbandry*. 1731; Corbett edn, 1829.

Ure, Andrew. *The Philosophy of Manufactures*. 1835; Cass, 1967.

———. *The Cotton Manufacture of Great Britain*. 1836; Cass, 1967.

Victoria County History of Dorset.

Watson, J.S. *Reign of George III*. O.U.P., 1960.

Whishaw, F. *The Railways of Great Britain and Ireland*. London 1840.

Williams, Judith Blow. *British Commercial Policy and Trade Expansion 1750–1850*. O.U.P., 1972.

Young, Arthur. *General View of the Agriculture of the County of Norfolk*, Board of Agriculture, 1813.

INDEX

silk 75, 83; *see also* Far Eastern
    trade
Singapore 150
slaves 77
slave-trade 145, 149, 152
sleepers 110–11, 137
slubbing 82
Small, James 18
Smeaton, Sir John 34, 35, 41,
    105, 111, 123
Smith, Adam 81, 152, 179, 184–
    8, 191
smuggling 150
social legislation 187
social savings and railways 131
sole traders 164
South American trade 149
Southampton and Salisbury
    Canal 109
South Durham coalfield 136, 138
South Durham and Lancashire
    Union Railway 138
South Sea Bubble 165–6
South Sea Company 165
South Wales coalfield 64, 112,
    124
Spain 94, 146, 148, 149, 183
Spedding, Carlisle 56
spinners, wool 79
spinning
    cotton 60–70
    jenny 68
    wool 79, 82
Staffordshire and
    Worcestershire Canal 103,
    123, 132, 133
Staffordshire coalfield
stages of growth – *see* also
    Rostow, W.W.
stations 119–20
Statute Labour 97, 98, 99
steam-carriages 102
steam-engines 39–46, 48–50,
    62, 75
    and agriculture 17, 18
steamships 141–2, 151
steel 64–5
    manufacture 58, 64–5
Stephenson, George 111, 114,
    118, 120, 136–7
Stephenson, Robert 92, 119
Stock Exchange 162
stocking-frame – *see* hosiery
Stockton and Darlington
    Railway 114, 115, 120, 121,
    130, 135–8
Stourport 123

Stroudwater Navigation 132–4
Strutt, Jediah 50, 70, 76, 91
Surrey Iron Railway 112
surveyors, road 99, 100
Sussex, population of 173
Sweden 58, 62, 65, 145
Swedes 5
Swindon 126
Swing Riots 171

Tasker, Robert 171–2
taxation 25
teasing 78
Tees, River 136, 138
Teign, River 50
Telford, Thomas 91, 100, 105,
    107, 142
Tennant, Charles 73, 155
terms of trade 153
Thames, River 104, 132–5, 141
Thames and Severn Canal 104,
    107, 132–5
threshing 16–17
Tithe Redemption Act 24
tobacco trade 145, 153–6
tolls, collection of 99
Tonbridge 20
Toynbee, Arnold 191
trade 143–50
    coastal 143–4
    cycle 160, 170
transport costs, road 122
travelling times, road 122
Tredegar 64
Trent and Mersey Canal 103
Trevithick, Richard 43, 44, 113
tricoteur 181
Trollope, Anthony 191
Tull, Jethro 14–16
tunnels
    canal 107
    railway 119
turnips 5
turnpike roads 97–102, 118,
    122–3, 131
turnpike trusts, organisation
    98–100, 161
Tyne, River 141, 143, 144

'up and down' husbandry 3, 4, 6,
    7
U.S.A. – *see* North America

ventilation of mines 55
Vermuyden, Cornelius 21
Vinci, Leonardo da 39
Virginia 153–6

wagons 101, 122
wagon ways 54
Wallingford 26
Wantage 26
water
    frame 69
    meadows 6
    mills 34–6
    power 49–51, 59, 75
    supplies (canals) 106, 107
Waterloo Ironworks 171–2
waterways 102–10
Watt, James, and engine 39–46,
    54, 113
Weald 9, 20, 64
weavers, handloom 67, 74–5
weaving
    cotton 67
    wool 79, 82
Webbs, B. and S. – *see* Fabian
    Socialists
Wedgwood, Josiah 104
Wellington, Duke of 116, 128
West Country woollens 79–81
West Indies 144, 145, 152, 155
Weston, Sir Richard 104
West Riding, population of 175–
    8
West Riding woollens 79–81,
    94–5
Wey, River 104
wheat – *see* grain
Whitney, Eli 77
wide frame 180
Wilkinson, John 42, 63, 64, 92,
    163
Wilts and Berks Canal 104, 133,
    135
Winchcombe, John (Jack of
    Newbury) 80, 87
windmills 33–4, 48
Wood, G.H. 191
wool 78–83, 94–5, 146, 150, 186,
    188–90
wool combers 78, 79
woollen
    imports 82–3, 94, 189
    industry 78–83
    products 83
Worseley 103

Yorkshire woollens – *see* West
    Riding woollens
Young, Arthur 7, 122

Zollverein 147–8